Communications
in Computer and Information Science 1955

Rationale

The CCIS series is devoted to the publication of proceedings of computer science conferences. Its aim is to efficiently disseminate original research results in informatics in printed and electronic form. While the focus is on publication of peer-reviewed full papers presenting mature work, inclusion of reviewed short papers reporting on work in progress is welcome, too. Besides globally relevant meetings with internationally representative program committees guaranteeing a strict peer-reviewing and paper selection process, conferences run by societies or of high regional or national relevance are also considered for publication.

Topics

The topical scope of CCIS spans the entire spectrum of informatics ranging from foundational topics in the theory of computing to information and communications science and technology and a broad variety of interdisciplinary application fields.

Information for Volume Editors and Authors

Publication in CCIS is free of charge. No royalties are paid, however, we offer registered conference participants temporary free access to the online version of the conference proceedings on SpringerLink (http://link.springer.com) by means of an http referrer from the conference website and/or a number of complimentary printed copies, as specified in the official acceptance email of the event.

CCIS proceedings can be published in time for distribution at conferences or as post-proceedings, and delivered in the form of printed books and/or electronically as USBs and/or e-content licenses for accessing proceedings at SpringerLink. Furthermore, CCIS proceedings are included in the CCIS electronic book series hosted in the SpringerLink digital library at http://link.springer.com/bookseries/7899. Conferences publishing in CCIS are allowed to use Online Conference Service (OCS) for managing the whole proceedings lifecycle (from submission and reviewing to preparing for publication) free of charge.

Publication process

The language of publication is exclusively English. Authors publishing in CCIS have to sign the Springer CCIS copyright transfer form, however, they are free to use their material published in CCIS for substantially changed, more elaborate subsequent publications elsewhere. For the preparation of the camera-ready papers/files, authors have to strictly adhere to the Springer CCIS Authors' Instructions and are strongly encouraged to use the CCIS LaTeX style files or templates.

Abstracting/Indexing

CCIS is abstracted/indexed in DBLP, Google Scholar, EI-Compendex, Mathematical Reviews, SCImago, Scopus. CCIS volumes are also submitted for the inclusion in ISI Proceedings.

How to start

To start the evaluation of your proposal for inclusion in the CCIS series, please send an e-mail to ccis@springer.com.

Kousik Dasgupta · Somnath Mukhopadhyay ·
Jyotsna K. Mandal · Paramartha Dutta
Editors

Computational Intelligence in Communications and Business Analytics

5th International Conference, CICBA 2023
Kalyani, India, January 27–28, 2023
Revised Selected Papers, Part I

Springer

Editors
Kousik Dasgupta 🆔
Kalyani Government Engineering College
Kalyani, India

Somnath Mukhopadhyay 🆔
Assam University
Silchar, India

Jyotsna K. Mandal 🆔
University of Kalyani
Kalyani, West Bengal, India

Paramartha Dutta 🆔
Visvabharati University
Santiniketan, West Bengal, India

ISSN 1865-0929   ISSN 1865-0937 (electronic)
Communications in Computer and Information Science
ISBN 978-3-031-48875-7   ISBN 978-3-031-48876-4 (eBook)
https://doi.org/10.1007/978-3-031-48876-4

This Springer imprint is published by the registered company Springer Nature Switzerland AG
The registered company address is: Gewerbestrasse 11, 6330 Cham, Switzerland

Paper in this product is recyclable.

Preface

It is with immense pleasure that we present the proceedings of the Fifth International Conference on Computational Intelligence in Communications and Business Analytics (CICBA 2023), organized by the Department of Computer Science & Engineering at Kalyani Government Engineering College, Kalyani, during January 27–28, 2023. CICBA has evolved into a flagship event at the intersection of computational intelligence, communications, and business analytics, fostering international collaboration and the dissemination of cutting-edge research.

CICBA 2023 welcomed distinguished keynote speakers, each a luminary in their field. We were honoured to have with us Bhabatosh Chanda from the Indian Statistical Institute, Kolkata, Amit Konar from Jadavpur University, Kalyanmoy Deb from Michigan State University, Hisao Ishibuchi from the Southern University of Science and Technology, China, Jayant Haritsa from IISc Bangalore, Narayan C. Debnath from Eastern International University, Vietnam, Celia Shahnaz from Bangladesh University of Engineering and Technology, Hiroyuki Sato from The University of Electro-Communications, Japan, Debashis De from Maulana Abul Kalam Azad University of Technology, West Bengal, India, and Mohd Helmy Bin Abd Wahab from University Tun Hussein Onn Malaysia, Malaysia.

In technical collaboration with IEEE CIS Kolkata, IEEE Kolkata Section, and IETE Kolkata, CICBA 2023 garnered substantial interest from the global research community. Springer CCIS Series was our esteemed publication partner, ensuring the high quality and widespread dissemination of the conference proceedings.

We are pleased to present the submission statistics for CICBA 2023. We received 187 initial submissions, which is evidence of our conference's growing significance. 52 papers were approved and registered, representing an impressive acceptance rate of 27%.

The conference proceedings are organized into two volumes, each featuring distinct tracks. In Volume 1, you will find 26 insightful papers in the "Computational Intelligence" track. Volume 2 is divided into two tracks: "Theories and Applications to Data Communications" with 17 papers, and "Theories and Applications to Data Analytics" with 9 papers. These contributions represent the cutting edge of research in computational intelligence and business analytics and cover a wide range of topics.

As we reflect on the history of CICBA since its inception in 2017, we are pleased with its growth and impact. This conference series has consistently attracted high-quality research from around the world. We are grateful for the contributions of our esteemed keynote speakers, organizing committees, and evaluators, who have made CICBA a remarkable venue for the exchange of knowledge.

We sincerely thank all the authors who submitted their work, the reviewers who diligently evaluated the submissions, and the participants who contributed to vibrant discussions during the conference. Your collective efforts have enriched the academic discourse in computational intelligence, communications, and business analytics.

We hope you find these proceedings enlightening and inspiring, and that they serve as a valuable resource for researchers and practitioners in the field. We look forward to future editions of CICBA, which we are committed to making even more intellectually stimulating and professionally rewarding.

Sincerely,

Kousik Dasgupta
Somnath Mukhopadhyay
Jyotsna K. Mandal
Paramartha Dutta

Organization

Chief Patron

Anindita Ganguly   D.T.E, Govt. of West Bengal, India

Patron

Sourabh Kumar Das   Kalyani Government Engineering College, India

General Chair

Nikhil R. Pal   Indian Statistical Institute Kolkata, India

Organizing Chairs

Swapan Kumar Mondal   Kalyani Government Engineering College, India
Sourav Banerjee   Kalyani Government Engineering College, India

Program Committee Chairs

Kousik Dasgupta   Kalyani Government Engineering College, India
Somnath Mukhopadhyay   Assam University, India
Jyotsna K. Mandal   University of Kalyani, India
Paramartha Dutta   Visva Bharati University, India

International Advisory Board

A. Damodaram   JNTU, India
Amit Konar   Jadavpur University, India
Atal Chowdhury   Jadavpur University, India
Aynur Unal   Stanford University, USA
Banshidhar Majhi   VSSUT, India
Carlos. A. Coello Coello   CINVESTAV-IPN, Mexico

Edward Tsang   University of Essex, UK
Hisao Ishibuchi   SUSTech, China
Kalyanmoy Deb   MSU, USA
L. M. Patnaik   IISc Bangalore, India
P. N. Suganthan   Qatar University, Qatar
Pabitra Mitra   IIT Kharagpur, India
S. N. Srirama   University of Tartu, Estonia
Subir Sarkar   Jadavpur University, India
Sushmita Mitra   ISI Kolkata, India
Umapada Pal   ISI Kolkata, India

Organizing Committee

Angsuman Sarkar   Kalyani Government Engineering College, India
Malay Kumar Pakhira   Kalyani Government Engineering College, India
Manju Biswas   Kalyani Government Engineering College, India
Anup Kumar Biswas   Kalyani Government Engineering College, India
Sandip Nandi   Kalyani Government Engineering College, India
Anup Mallick   Kalyani Government Engineering College, India
Surya Sarathi Das   Kalyani Government Engineering College, India
P. S. Banerjee   Kalyani Government Engineering College, India
Tapan Kumar Santra   Kalyani Government Engineering College, India
Kuntal Bhowmick   Kalyani Government Engineering College, India
D. K. Jha   Kalyani Government Engineering College, India

Technical Program Committee

Alok Chakraborty   National Institute of Technology Meghalaya, India
Anamitra Roy Chaudhury   IBM Research, India
Angsuman Sarkar   Kalyani Government Engineering College, India
Animesh Biswas   Kalyani University, India
Anirban Chakraborty   IISc Bangalore, India
Anirban Mukhopadhyay   University of Kalyani, India
Arindam Sarkar   Belur Vidyamandir, India
Arnab Majhi   NEHU, India
Arundhati Bagchi Misra   Saginaw Valley State University, USA
Asif Ekbal   Indian Institute of Technology Patna, India
B. B. Pal   University of Kalyani, India
B. K. Panigrahi   Indian Institute of Technology Delhi, India
Basabi Chakraborty   Iwate Prefectural University, Japan

Biswapati Jana	Vidyasagar University, India
Chandreyee Chowdhury	Jadavpur University, India
Debaprasad Das	Assam University, India
Debarka Mukhopadhyay	Christ University, India
Debashis De	Maulana Abul Kalam Azad University of Technology, India
Debasish Chakraborty	ISRO Kolkata, India
Debotosh Bhattacharjee	ISRO Kolkata, India
Deepsubhra Guha Roy	University of Tartu, Estonia
Dhananjay Bhattacharyya	Saha Institute of Nuclear Physics, India
Dilip Kumar Pratihar	Indian Institute of Technology Kharagpur, India
Farukh Hashmi	National Institute of Technology Warangal, India
Gopa Mandal	Jalpaiguri Govt. Engg. College, India
Girijasankar Mallik	University of Western Sydney, Australia
Hasanujjaman	Govt. College of Engg. & Textile Tech, India
Himadri Dutta	Kalyani Govt. Engg College, India
Hrishav Bakul Barua	TCS Innovations Kolkata, India
Indrajit Saha	National Inst. of Tech. Teachers' Training & Research Kolkata, India
Indranil Ghosh	Institute of Management Technology Hyderabad, India
J. K. Singh	Jadavpur University, India
Jabar H. Yousif	Sohar University, Saudi Arabia
Jaydeb Bhaumik	Jadavpur University, India
Jayeeta Mondal	TCS Innovations Kolkata, India
Jeet Dutta	TCS Innovations Kolkata, India
Joshua Thomas	Penang University, Malaysia
Jyoti Prakash Singh	National Institute of Technology Patna, India
Kakali Dutta	Visva Bharati University, India
Kamal Sarkar	Jadavpur University, India
Kartick Chandra Mondal	Jadavpur University, India
Kaushik Dassharma	Calcutta University, India
Khalid Yahya	Istanbul Gelisim University, Turkey
Kouichi Sakurai	Kyushu University, Japan
Koushik Majumder	Maulana Abul Kalam Azad University of Technology, India
Koushik Mondal	Indian Institute of Technology (ISM) Dhanbad, India
Kousik Roy	WB State University, India
Krishnendu Chakraborty	Govt. College of Engg. and Ceramic Technology, India
M. S. Sutaone	College of Engineering Pune, India

Manju Biswas	Kalyani Govt. Engg. College, India
Megha Quamara	IRIT, France
Mili Ghosh	North Bengal University, India
Mita Nasipuri	Jadavpur University, India
Mohammed Hasanuzzaman	Munster Technological University, Ireland
Mohsin Kamal	National University of Computer and Emerging Sciences, Pakistan
Moirangthem Marjit Singh	NERIST, India
Moumita Ghosh	Narula Institute of Technology, India
Mrinal Kanti Bhowmik	Tripura University, India
Muhammad Naveed Aman	National University of Singapore, Singapore
Nabendu Chaki	University of Calcutta, India
Nguyen Ha Huy Cuong	University of Danang, Vietnam
Nibaran Das	Jadavpur University, India
Nilanjana Dutta Roy	Institute of Engineering and Management, India
Partha Pakray	National Institute of Technology, Silchar, India
Partha Pratim Sahu	Tezpur University, India
Parthajit Roy	University of Burdwan, India
Pawan K. Singh	Jadavpur University, India
Prasanta K. Jana	Indian School of Mines Dhanbad, India
Prashant R. Nair	Amrita Vishwa Vidyapeetham, India
Prodipto Das	Assam University Silchar, India
Rajdeep Chakraborty	Netaji Subhas Institute of Technology, India
Ram Sarkar	Jadavpur University, India
Ranjita Das	National Institute of Technology Mizoram, India
Ravi Subban	Pondicherry University, India
S. B. Goyal	City University of Malaysia, Malaysia
Samarjit Kar	National Institute of Technology Durgapur, India
Samir Roy	NITTTR, Kolkata, India
Samiran Chattopadhyay	Jadavpur University, India
Sandeep Kautish	Lord Buddha Education Foundation, Nepal
Sankhayan Choudhury	University of Calcutta, India
Santi P. Maity	Indian Institute of Engg, Science and Technology Shibpur, India
Sharmistha Neogy	Jadavpur University, India
Shashank Mouli Satapathy	VIT University, India
Shrish Verma	National Institute of Technology Raipur India
Sk. Obaidullah	Aliah University, India
Somenath Chakraborty	West Virginia University Institute of Technology, USA
Soumya Pandit	Sheffield Hallam University, UK
Soumya Shankar Basu	Sheffield Hallam University, UK

Sriparna Saha	Indian Institute of Technology Patna, India
Subarna Shakya	Tribhuvan University, Nepal
Subhadip Basu	Jadavpur University, India
Subrata Banerjee	National Institute of Technology Durgapur, India
Sudarsun Santhiappan	BUDDI AI, India
Sudhakar Sahoo	Institute of Mathematics & Applications, India
Sudhakar Tripathi	National Institute of Technology Patna, India
Sudipta Roy	Assam University Silchar, India
Sujoy Chatterjee	UPES Dehradun, India
Sukumar Nandi	Indian Institute of Technology Guwahati, India
Suman Lata Tripathi	Lovely Professional University, India
Sunil Mane	College of Engineering Pune, India
Sunita Sarkar	Assam University Silchar, India
Tamal Datta Chaudhury	Calcutta Business School, India
Tandra Pal	National Institute of Technology Durgapur, India
Tanmoy Chakraborty	IIIT Delhi, India
Tanushyam Chattopadyay	TCS Innovations Kolkata, India
Tapodhir Acharjee	Assam University Silchar, India
Tien Anh Tran	Vietnam Maritime University, Vietnam
Utpal Sarkar	Assam University Silchar, India
Varun Kumar Ojha	University of Reading, UK

Contents – Part I

Contents – Part II

Theories and Applications to Data Analytics

A Review on Machine Learning and Deep Learning Based Approaches in Detection and Grading of Alzheimer's Disease

Sampa Rani Bhadra[1](✉) and Souvik Sengupta[2]

[1] Kalyani Mahavidyalaya, Kalyani, West Bengal 741235, India
sampa.rani.bhadra@gmail.com
[2] Aliah University, Kolkata, West Bengal 700156, India

Abstract. Alzheimer's disease (AD) is an incurable neurodegenerative disease which is one of the leading causes of death in elderly people. Early and accurate detection of AD is vital for appropriate treatment. AI-based automated techniques are widely used to help early diagnosis of AD. In recent years, machine learning and deep learning has become the preferred method of analyzing medical images, and it has also attracted a high degree of attention in AD detection. Researchers have proposed many novel approaches for automated detection and gradation of the disease. The success of any such approach depends on the appropriate selection of pre-processing, biomarkers, feature extraction, and model architecture. This paper presents a review of the efficacy of different methods used by the researchers for these components with the aim to understand the state-of-the-art architecture. A comparative analysis of their advantages, disadvantages, and performance accuracy is reported.

Keywords: Alzheimer's disease · MRI images · Biomarker · Feature extraction · Machine learning · Deep learning · Transfer learning

1 Introduction

Alzheimer's disease (AD) is a chronic degenerative disease of the brain caused by the death and malfunctioning of the neurons. It primarily affects adults above 65 years by interrupting the neurogenesis functions and resulting in dementia. The symptoms include forgetfulness, confusion, depression, hallucinations, and inability to speak and do daily routine tasks [1]. Although there is no cure for AD, early detection of the disease can help to slow down the progress. A proper diagnosis is required to identify and differentiate between Alzheimer's disease and mild cognitive impairment (MCI) [2]. While MCI is not that severe, AD can even lead to death if not treated properly. Therefore, a proper diagnosis is required to identify and detect AD stages in order to start the medication and treatment as early as possible. Machine learning (ML) and deep learning (DL) based approaches have been used frequently in the last decade to aid doctors and health professionals in detecting and grading AD more accurately than only human interpretation.

K. Dasgupta et al. (Eds.): CICBA 2023, CCIS 1955, pp. 1–13, 2024.
https://doi.org/10.1007/978-3-031-48876-4_1

Machine learning and deep learning are both branches of AI that try to mimic the human learning process for making decisions. Supervised ML algorithms like Logistic Regression (LR), Naïve Bayes (NB), Decision Tree (DT), Support Vector Machine (SVM), K-Nearest Neighbor (KNN), and Artificial Neural Networks (ANN) are commonly used for the classification of medical images. DL is a subset of machine learning that combines multiple layers of convolutional neural network (CNN) with ANN for the classification task.

The pipeline for AD detection has three essential components, preprocessing, feature extraction, and classification. ML and DL-based approaches differ primarily on the feature extraction part. DL models use CNN-based deep features for classification, whereas ML models primarily rely on classical rule-based feature extractions. In addition, there is a third approach where researchers use deep features with ML classifiers. In this work, we cover all three types of paradigms. Figure 1 depicts the overall framework for automated AD detection.

This paper presents a review of the efficacy of different methods used by the researchers, with the aim to understand the state-of-the-art architecture and the role of its components in the automatic detection and gradation of Alzheimer's disease. The rest of the paper goes as follows. Section 2 describes different image modalities. Next, Sect. 3 narrates different preprocessing methods. Section 4 illustrates biomarkers and feature extraction methods. Then, Sect. 5 reviews the performances of different ML/DL-based approaches grouped by common dataset repositories. Finally, Sect. 6 concludes the work.

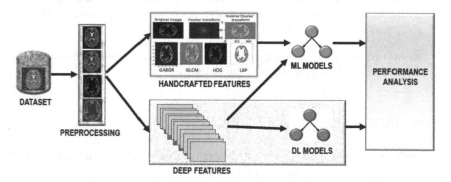

Fig. 1. Framework of Automated AD Detection.

2   Image Modalities

Different image modalities are used in AD detection and gradation; the most common are Positron Emission Tomography (PET), Computer Tomography scan (CT scan), and Magnetic Resonance Imaging (MRI) [3]. PET imaging uses radiotracers (radioactive substances) to capture the metabolic changes and physiological activities in the region of interest to detect the disease. It reveals the metabolic or biochemical functions of the target tissues and organs. A public repository of PET images of the brain can be found at [4]. CT scan uses X-rays to create cross-sectional images of bones, tissues, and blood vessels to provide more detailed information towards the detection of the disease. It combines a series of X-ray images taken from different angles around the region of interest and uses computer processing to create cross-sectional slices of the target. An open-access dataset for brain CT scans is available at [5].

On the other hand, MRI uses magnetic field response to produce three-dimensional detailed anatomical images. It is considered the preferred neuroimaging modality for AD over the other alternatives because it allows more precise measurement of the volume of several brain regions in 3-dimensional (3D), particularly the size of the hippocampus and associated areas. MRI can further be classified into structural MRI (sMRI) and functional MRI (fMRI) based on whether the modality captures the structure of the brain (size, shape, volume) or the function of the brain (brain metabolism, blood flow, oxygen level, etc.) [6].

Many researchers have advocated that a multimodal approach by combining PET and CT/MRI provides complementary information and is thus more useful in AD detection than using any single modality [7–9]. However, in this work, we have confined our review to works performed on the single modality for the most common MRI datasets available at the public repositories namely, OASIS, ADNI, and Kaggle.

3 Image Pre-processing

All MRI images require preprocessing for the removal of possible noises and for the correction of intensity non-uniformity before they are used for feature extraction and classification. Standard brain MRI preprocessing steps includes image registration, bias field correction, and removal of non-brain tissue. Bias field noise is a low-frequency signal that corrupts MRI images. It hampers the efficiency of other image processing algorithms used in segmentation and texture analysis that uses the gray-level values of the image. Intensity homogeneity ensures bias field correction. Gaussian and Median filters are commonly used for noise removal and intensity correction. The Gaussian filter makes the image more sensitive and homogeneous, while the median filter is used to remove noise artifacts and sharpen the edges of the image.

Various software tools and packages have been exhaustively used by the researchers for preprocessing tasks. Some of the popular names are- Forensic Science Laboratory Division (FSL) [10], Statistical Parametric Mapping (SPM) [11], and Freesurfer [12]. FSL toolbox supports many features for structural as well as functional MRI. Many researchers [1, 13] have used two popular features, namely Voxel Based Morphology (FSL-VBM) and Brain Extraction Tool (FSL-BET), for brain measurement and brain extraction, respectively. FSL-VBM is an excellent utility for identifying and extracting local grey matter volume based on voxel-wise differences. Besides, nonlinear registration, correction of local expansion/contraction (modulation), spatial transformation, and smoothing with isotropic Gaussian kernel are also supported. The advantage of FLS-VBM is that it requires no prior knowledge of the location of the grey matter and is not operator-dependent. On the other hand, FSL-BET deletes non-brain tissue from the brain images, for example skull removal, also known as skull stripping.

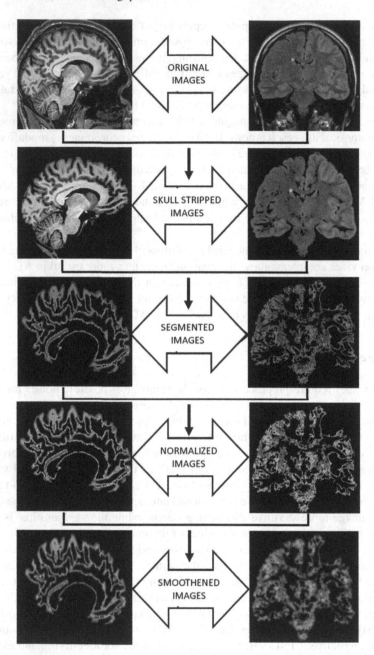

Fig. 2. Preprocessed Images.

SPM uses statistical processes to test hypotheses about functional imaging data. It can perform tasks like bias correction, co-registrations, smoothing, tissue segmentation, etc. Automated anatomical labeling (AAL) is a unique feature available in SPM. Researchers

[14–16] have used different versions of SPM, from SPM2 to SPM12, for various preprocessing tasks like bias correction, co-registrations, smoothing, tissue segmentation, etc. On the other hand, FreeSurfer is an open-source, free image preprocessing software for brain images. Unlike SPM, which works on fMRI, FreeSurfer supports both structural and functional analysis. Researchers [16, 17] have used FreeSurfer for a wide range of preprocessing tasks like - skull stripping, bias field correction, registration, anatomical segmentation, cortical surface reconstruction, registration, and parcellation. Figure 2 shows the different preprocessing methods applied on a sagittal view (left) and a coronal view (right) of the T1w MRI brain images.

4 Biomarkers and Feature Extractions

A biomarker is a biological trait that is objectively examined and evaluated as a sign of a positive or negative sample. Imaging biomarkers represent biological characteristics that are detectable on an image and can be used to classify the image. These identifiable features on MRI images can be explicitly marked for the training of ML models or could be implicitly learned by DL models. Four biomarkers of an MRI image are found to be helpful in AD detection, namely, white matter (WM), grey matter (GM), cerebrospinal fluid (CSF), and hippocampus [18, 19]. Figure 3 shows an axial view of the T2w MRI brain image where the bones are shown in black, GM in grey, WM in dark grey, and CSF and adipose in white. Identification and comparison with the normal control of these components are essential for AD detection because the accuracy of a model greatly depends on the sensitivity of the biomarker. For example, WM, GM, and hippocampal volume decrease while CSF increases in Alzheimer's patients [18]. These markings could be done by human expertise or automated segmentation methods.

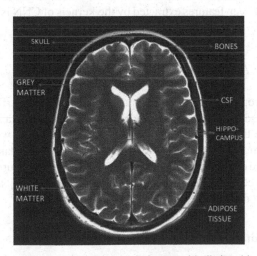

Fig. 3. Axial view of T2w MRI brain image with distinct biomarkers.

Feature extraction is the process of extracting relevant features (information) from the data which are suitable for machine learning and deep learning. In case of machine learning, the feature extraction is done manually, whereas for deep learning, the feature extraction is done automatically by the CNN layers. In handcrafted features, researchers have commonly used methods like Gray-Level Co-Occurrence Matrix (GLCM), Local Binary Pattern (LBP), Histogram of Oriented Gradients (HOG), Scale Invariant and Feature Transform (SIFT), Gabor filter, etc. In image processing, the spatial changes in the pixel's brightness intensity are considered the image's texture. GLCM and LBP are two effective texture descriptor methods for enhancing the information available from medical images. GLCM extracts features by calculating the spatial relationship among the pixels, whereas LBP uses a threshold among each pixel's neighboring based on the current pixel's value. HOG and SIFT are two similar feature descriptors. Both are based on first-order image gradients in the localized portion of an image. SIFT additionally uses a 16x16 window divided into 4 patches and applies HOG in each of them. Gabor filter is another texture descriptor that checks for any specific frequency content in any specific direction in a localized region of the image. It is also a popular texture segmentation method, best known for its localization properties in both the spatial and frequency domains.

The DL-based models are widely used in the medical classification task mainly because of their automatic feature extraction ability, and the success of a CNN-based deep neural system depends heavily on the efficiency of CNN as the feature extractor. These deep features are not only good for accurate image classification but also avoid complicated and expensive handcrafted feature engineering. The introduction of deep features in medical image classification tasks has seen significant growth in the last ten years for its exceptional performance, particularly with smaller dataset [20]. The feature maps of a DL model capture the result of applying the learned filters to an input image. The intermediate feature maps of a deep CNN represent features detected at different abstraction levels. The deeper the level of CNN is, the more abstract the features are. This large number of deep features extracted by the kernels of CNN is key to the accurate classification of AD.

5   Performance Analysis

Researchers have proposed many novel approaches based on ML/DL architecture for AD detection and grading. However, as they have used different datasets for their works, in order to compare the performance efficiency of their method, we group the works based on using common datasets. In this review, three large public dataset repositories of brain MRI images are considered, namely, Alzheimer's Disease Neuroimaging Initiative (ADNI) [4], Open Access Series of Imaging Studies (OASIS) [21], and Kaggle 4-class [22] and 5-class [23] datasets.

5.1   Dataset Repository: OASIS

Jha and Kwon [24] performed a binary classification task of detecting healthy and AD affected. They tested two models, namely, K-Nearest Neighbour (KNN) and Artificial Neural Network (ANN), on structural Magnetic Resonance Imaging (sMRI) images. All the images are first intensity normalized and then passed to curvelet transformation for feature extraction. The high dimensionality of the extracted features is reduced using PCA before finally passing it to the classifiers. KNN and ANN recorded a testing accuracy of 89.47% and 88.4% on the reduced number of features. Hon and Khan [25] used transfer learning of the models VGG16 and Inception-V4 on the dataset without any preprocessing and handcrafted feature extraction. However, as the CNN of these deep learning models is designed to extract deep features, they are suitable for classification. An entropy-based estimation is applied to the extracted features for feature selection and then fed to the last fully connected layers of VGG16 and Inception V4 for classification and prediction. The models obtained testing accuracy of 92.3% and 96.25%, respectively. In a similar work, Lu et al. [26] adopted transfer learning of MobileNET and VGG-16 models for AD detection. This work used the deep features directly to the classification task without preprocessing, feature extraction, and feature selection. The models achieved testing accuracy of 98% and 93%, respectively. In another work, Fulton et al. [27] used Gradient Boosted Machine (GBM) and Residual Network with 50 layers (ResNet-50). The input images are preprocessed with gain-field correction, atlas registration, and spatial Normalization. PCA is used for feature selection from the CNN-extracted deep features. The classification models reported testing accuracy of 91.3% and 98.99%, respectively.

5.2 Dataset Repository: ADNI

Herrera et al. [28] used the SVM model for AD detection from MRI images. The authors used Discrete Wavelet Transform (DWT) for feature extraction and Principal Component Analysis (PCA) for dimensionality reduction. No preprocessing is done in this work. This work reported a testing accuracy of 83.63% with radial bias function kernel in SVM. Sarraf and Tofighi [1] used two benchmark models, namely LeNet and GoogleNet, to predict Alzheimer's disease from sMRI images. The image preprocessing is done using two tools, FSL-BET for brain extraction and FSL-VBM for grey matter template. No handcrafted feature extraction and feature selection are done; it relies entirely on the deep features extracted by the CNNs. The authors reported that GoogleNet showed a better accuracy with 98.84% than LeNet with 97.81% accuracy. Wang et. al. [14] proposed the use of ElasticNet (EN) classifier for predicting AD from MRI images. This work tested their model on both Original Digital Imaging and Communications in Medicine (DICOM) and MRI images. SPM8 was used for the standard preprocessing of the images. ROI parts are extracted manually before passing them to the DL model. This work reported an accuracy of 95% in AD detection. Wu et al. [29] used CaffeNet, a variation of AlexNet, and GoogleNet AD detection from the MRI images. Both the models are transfer learned from training on ImageNet. No image preprocessing, feature extraction, or feature selection is performed before passing the images to the CNN models. The models are tested for a three-class classification problem where the classes are NC is Normal Control, sMCI is stable Mild Cognitive Impairment, and cMCI is converted to Mild Cognitive Impairment. The authors reported testing accuracy of 98.71%, 72.04%, 92.35%, and 97.58%, 67.33%, and 84.71% by CaffeNet, and GoogleNet, respectively. They claimed that CaffeNet outperformed GoogleNet. Duraisamy et al. [15] proposed a novel Fuzzy C-means (FCM) based Weighted Probabilistic Neural Network classification model named FWPNN. This work used some of the sMRI images from Bordeaux-3city along with ADNI. Image preprocessing steps include normalization and extraction of ROI, performed using the Automated Anatomical Labeling (AAL) method. This work fuses atlas-based and handcrafted features and uses conventional wrapper and filter methods for feature selection. The proposed classification model reported an accuracy of 98.63%. In another work, Nanni et al. [30] proposed a multi-domain set of features extracted by different feature extractors and texture analysis tools and fused them. They used an SVM classifier and obtained the highest classification accuracy of 78.8%. All the image preprocessing, like reorientation, cropping, skull stripping, normalization, and segmentation, is done with SPM8 and VBM8 software tools. VOXEL-level feature extraction and texture analysis are done using GABOR, WAVE, and Gaussian of Local Descriptors (GOLD). In order to identify the most relevant features and reduce the high dimension of extracted features from VOXEL, three feature selection methods, namely, Fisher score (Fi), Kernel Partial Least Squares (KPS), and Aggregate selection (AS), are applied. In some recent works, Xiao and Cui [16] used the Sparse Logistic Regression (SLR) model for AD detection from MRI images, where the preprocessing of the raw images was done by the SPM8 and VBM8 toolbox. DWT is used as a feature extractor, and PCA is used for dimensionality reduction. This work reported a testing accuracy of 93.33%. Song et al. (2021) [17] performed preprocessing using the FreeSurfer tool and Gini Index for feature selection. This work used Random Forest (RF) to identify different biomarkers like the hippocampus, amygdala, and inferior lateral ventricle and reported a classification accuracy of 90.2%.

5.3   Dataset Repository: Kaggle

Fu'adah et al. [31] used AlexNet for the AD gradation task on the four-class dataset from Kaggle. No preprocessing and handmade feature extraction is done. The DL model is hyper-tuned by selecting an 'adam' optimizer and reduces the learning rate to 0.0001. It is observed that prediction accuracy improved significantly with this setup. This work reported a testing accuracy of 95%. Tougaccar et al. [32] used VGG-16-based feature extraction and an SVM model to classify the four-class Alzheimer's dataset from Kaggle. This approach of deep features with SVM obtained an accuracy of 96.31%. In another approach, the authors used handcrafted features with fuzzy color image enhancement (FCIE) and hypercolumn techniques, and with the same SVM classifier yielded 98.94% accuracy. In another work, Murugan et al. [33] proposed a customized CNN model called DEMNET and trained it on the four-class dataset from Kaggle. It obtained a training accuracy of 99%, validation accuracy of 94%, testing accuracy of 95.23%, Area Under Curve (AUC) of 97%, and Cohen's Kappa value of 0.93%. Then in order to validate the robustness of the model, they tested the trained model on the five-class dataset from Kaggle and obtained 84.83% testing accuracy. To counter the class imbalance problem on both datasets, they applied the over-sampling technique called Synthetic Minority Over-sampling Technique (SMOTE). Only image resizing and normalization was done in image preprocessing, and no handcrafted feature extraction was made. Nagarathna and Kusuma [34] used CNN layers of VGG-19 for deep feature extraction to achieve 95.52%

testing accuracy. Some preprocessing steps like rescaling, data augmentation, and resampling are applied on the raw data before passing them for deep feature extraction without any handcrafted feature extraction or feature selection.

Table 1. Comparative study of different approaches.

Author(s)	Model	Preprocessing	Feature extraction	Feature selection	Dataset	Accuracy
Jha and Kwon (2016) [24]	[1]KNN [2]ANN	ONIS	Curvelet Transformation	PCA	OASIS	[1]89.47% [2]88.4%
Hon and Khan (2017) [25]	[1]VGG16 [2]Inception V4	None	CNN	entropy estimator	OASIS	[1]92.3% [2]96.25%
Lu et. al (2019) [26]	[1]MobileNet [2]VGG16	None	CNN	None	OASIS	[1]98% [2]93%
Fulton et. al. (2019) [27]	[1]GBM [2]ResNet-50	gain-field correction, Atlas registration, Spatial Normalization	Same model	PCA	OASIS	[1]91.3% [2]98.99%
Herrera et. al. (2013) [28]	SVM	None	DWT	PCA, NMIFS	ADNI	83.63%
Sarraf and Tofighi (2016) [1]	[1]LeNet [2]GoogleNet	FSL-BET FSL-VBM	CNN	None	ADNI	[1]97.81% [2]98.84%
Wang et. al (2017) [14]	ElasticNet	SPM8	Manual	None	ADNI	95%
Wu et. al (2018) [29]	[1]CaffeNet [2]GoogleNet	None	None	None	ADNI	[1]97.81% [2]98.84%
Duraisamy et. al. (2019) [15]	FWPNN	AAL method	Atlas	Wrapper & Filter method	ADNI	98.63%
Nanni et. al (2019) [30]	SVM	SPM8 VBM8	VOXEL + GABOR, WAVE, GOLD	Fi, KPS, AS	ADNI	78.8%
Xiao and Cui (2021) [16]	SLR	SPM8 VBM8	DWT	PCA	ADNI	93.33%
Song et. al. (2021) [17]	RF	FreeSurfer	None	Gini Index	ADNI	90.2%

(continued)

Table 1. (*continued*)

Author(s)	Model	Preprocessing	Feature extraction	Feature selection	Dataset	Accuracy
Fu'adah et. al. (2021) [31]	AlexNet	None	None	None	Kaggle	95%
Tougaccar et. al. (2021) [32]	SVM	None	CNN + [1]DeepDream [2]FCIE [3]Hypercolumn	LR	Kaggle	[1]82.0% [2]98.94% [3]95.38%
Murugan et. al. (2021) [33]	DEMNET	Normalization	CNN	None	[1]Kaggle [2]Kaggle	[1]95.23% [2]84.83%
Nagarathna and Kusuma (2022) [34]	VGG19	Rescaling, data augmentation, resampling	CNN	None	Kaggle	95.52%

5.4 Discussion

Table 1 shows a comparative study of the reviewed works. It can be observed from the above-reviewed works that three approaches are commonly used in AD detection and gradation tasks. First, handcrafted features with ML models, second, CNN-based deep features with DL models, and third, deep features with ML models. Most researchers have used tool-based preprocessing for tasks like gain field correction, Atlas registration, and spatial normalization [1, 14, 16, 17, 28]. Some of the researchers skipped preprocessing for DL models [29, 31]. However, it is observed in general that preprocessing helped in the prediction of accuracy, particularly in datasets used from ADNI and Kaggle repositories. It is also found that handcrafted features and deep features are equally efficient for the binary classification task, i.e., AD detection, whereas, in multi-class AD gradation tasks, deep features have shown better performances [29, 31].

Principal Component Analysis (PCA) is widely used for feature selection [16, 24, 27, 28]. The main role of PCA is dimensionality reduction and eliminating redundant features from the extracted features. It passes only the high-variance features to the classifier. Besides PCA, two decision tree-based feature selection methods are also used by the researchers, the entropy elimination method [25] and the Gini index [17]. Broadly classifying, there are three types of selection methods, namely, wrapper method (e.g., forward, backward, and stepwise selection), filter method (e.g., ANOVA, Pearson correlation, variance thresholding), and embedded method (e.g., Lasso, Ridge, Decision Tree). The main difference between the wrapper-based and the filter-based method is that the wrapper method measures the usefulness of a feature by actually training a model on it, whereas in the filter method, the importance of the features is measured by their relevant correlations. On the other hand, the embedded method combines the wrapper and filter methods for feature selection. In [15], Duraisamy et al. used a wrapper and filter method for feature selection, whereas in [32], Tougaccar et al. used a linear regression-based feature selection method to select features from a merged set of deep features and handcrafted features.

In DL models, VGG-16 and AlexNet are the preferred baseline model among the researchers [25, 26, 31]. They are popular for their simpler architecture which consists of repeated convolutions, each followed by ReLU and max-pooling and stride for down-sampling. In most of the current research, fine-tuning a pre-trained Google's Inception V3 network on MRI data is becoming popular for attaining performance accuracy close to human experts [1, 25, 29]. Most of the transfer learning models are pre-trained on the ImageNet dataset. In addition, other state-of-the-art DL models like MobileNet, CaffeNet, ElasticNet, and ResNet-50 are also effectively used by researchers for AD detection and grading. The convolutional layers in DL are capable of detecting minute characteristics from the images at different abstraction levels. Moreover, different kernels capture different feature artifacts like edges, lines, shapes, patterns, etc., which is the possible reason for the success of deep features in AD detection and grading. However, it is also observed that although automated detection of AD by ML/DL algorithms from MRI imaging is the fastest-growing research area, it has some challenges and lacunas. Some major challenges include the limited availability of datasets due to privacy and legal issues, non-standardization and class imbalance in datasets, and infrastructural and computational cost of running ML/DL models on large datasets.

6 Conclusions

In this paper, we present a review of different machine learning and deep learning-based approaches in detecting and grading Alzheimer's disease from MRI images. We explored multiple preprocessing methods, feature extraction techniques, and feature selection procedures used in the previously done works. A comparative study on the performance of the different approaches grouped by common datasets is presented. Three paradigms of classification models are compared. It is observed that there is no significant change in accuracy while using handcrafted and deep features in the Alzheimer's disease detection task. However, deep features outperformed handcrafted features in the Alzheimer's disease gradation task. It is also observed that combining different biomarkers with extracted features generates a better result. Finally, some common challenges of automatic detection and gradation of Alzheimer's disease with machine learning and deep learning models are discussed. This review work would be helpful for future researchers to understand the state-of-the-art architecture and the role of its components in the automatic detection and gradation of Alzheimer's disease.

References

1. Sarraf, S., Tofighi, G.: Classification of Alzheimer's Disease Using FMRI Data and Deep Learning Convolutional Neural Networks. arXiv preprint arXiv:1603.08631 (2016)
2. Lyketsos, C.G., et al.: Neuropsychiatric symptoms in Alzheimer's disease. Alzheimers Dement. 7(5), 532–539 (2011)
3. Richerson, S., Christe. B.: Healthcare Technology Basics (1), 21–50 (2020)

4. https://adni.loni.usc.edu/
5. http://headctstudy.qure.ai/#dataset
6. Baskar, D., Jayanthi, V.S., Jayanthi, A.N.: An efficient classification approach for detection of alzheimer's disease from biomedical imaging modalities. Multimedia Tools and Appl. **78**(10), 12883–12915 (2019)
7. Kaltoft, N.S., Marner, L., Larsen, V.A., Hasselbalch, S.G., Law, I., Henriksen, O.M.: Hybrid FDG PET/MRI vs. FDG PET and CT in patients with suspected dementia–a comparison of diagnostic yield and propagated influence on clinical diagnosis and patient management. Plos One **14**(5), e0216409 (2019)
8. Teipel, S., et al.: Multimodal imaging in Alzheimer's disease: validity and usefulness for early detection. The Lancet Neurology **14**(10), 1037–1053 (2015)
9. Catana, C., Drzezga, A., Heiss, W.D., Rosen, B.R.: PET/MRI for neurologic applications. J. Nucl. Med. **53**(12), 1916–1925 (2012)
10. https://fsl.fmrib.ox.ac.uk/fsl/fslwiki/FslInstallation/Windows
11. https://www.fil.ion.ucl.ac.uk/spm/
12. https://surfer.nmr.mgh.harvard.edu/
13. Despotović, I., Goossens, B., Philips, W.: MRI segmentation of the human brain: challenges, methods, and applications. Computational and Mathematical Methods in Medicine (2015)
14. Wang, L., Liu, Y., Cheng, H., Zeng, X., Wang, Z.: Elastic net based sparse feature learning and classification for alzheimer's disease identification. In: Proceedings of 39th Annual International Conference of the IEEE Engineering in Medicine and Biology Society (EMBC), pp. 2288–2291. IEEE (2017)
15. Duraisamy, B., Shanmugam, J.V., Annamalai, J.: Alzheimer disease detection from structural mr images using fcm based weighted probabilistic neural network. Brain Imaging Behav. **13**(1), 87–110 (2019)
16. Xiao, R., Cui, X., Qiao, H., Zheng, X., Zhang, Y.: Early diagnosis model of alzheimer's disease based on sparse logistic regression. Multimedia Tools and Appl. **80**(3), 3969–3980 (2021)
17. Song, M., Jung, H., Lee, S., Kim, D., Ahn. M.: Diagnostic classification and biomarker identification of alzheimer's disease with random forest algorithm. Brain Sciences **11**(4), 453 (2021)
18. Mirzaei, G., Adeli, A., Adeli. H.: Imaging and machine learning techniques for diagnosis of alzheimer's disease. Reviews in the Neurosciences **27**(8), 857–870 (2016)
19. Wehling. M.: Chapter 12 - biomarkers. In Martin Wehling, editor, Principles of Translational Science in Medicine (Third Edition), pp. 135–165. Academic Press, Boston (2021)
20. Yadav, S.S., Jadhav, S.M.: Deep convolutional neural network based medical image classification for disease diagnosis. J. Big Data **6**(1), 1–18 (2019)
21. https://www.oasis-brains.org/
22. www.kaggle.com/datasets/tourist55/alzheimers-dataset-4-class-of-images
23. www.kaggle.com/datasets/madhucharan/alzheimersdisease5classdatasetadni
24. Jha, D., Kwon, G.: Alzheimer disease detection in mri using curvelet transform with knn. J. Korean Institute of Information Technol. **14**(8), 21–129 (2016)
25. Hon, M., Khan, N. M.: Towards alzheimer's disease classification through transfer learning. In: Proceedings of IEEE International Conference on Bioinformatics and Biomedicine (BIBM), pp. 1166–1169. IEEE (2017)
26. Lu, X., Wu, H., Zeng, Y.: Classification of alzheimer's disease in mobilenet. In proceedings of Conference Series of Journal of Physics, IOP Publishing **1345**, 042012 (2019)
27. Fulton, L.V., Dolezel, D., Harrop, J., Yan, Y., Fulton, C.P.: Classification of alzheimer's disease with and without imagery using gradient boosted machines and resnet-50. Brain Sci. **9**(9), 212 (2019)

28. Herrera, L.J., Rojas, I., Pomares, H., Guillén, A., Valenzuela, O., Baños, O.: Classification of mri images for alzheimer's disease detection. In Proceedings of International Conference on Social Computing, pp. 846–851, IEEE (2013)

29. Wu, C., Guo, S., Hong, Y., Xiao, B., Wu, Y., Zhang, Q.: ADNI: Discrimination and conversion prediction of mild cognitive impairment using convolutional neural networks. Quant. Imaging Med. Surg. **8**(10), 992 (2018)

30. Nanni, L., Brahnam, S., Salvatore, C., Castiglioni, I.: ADNI: texture descriptors and voxels for the early diagnosis of alzheimer's disease. Artif. Intell. Med. **97**, 19–26 (2019)

31. Fu'adah, Y.N., Wijayanto, I., Pratiwi, N.K.C., Taliningsih, F.F., Rizal, S., Pramudito, M.A.: Automated classification of alzheimer's disease based on mri image processing using convolutional neural network (cnn) with alexnet architecture. In Proceedings of Conference Series of Journal of Physics, IOP Publishing, 1844, 012020 (2021)

32. Toğacar, M., C¨omert, Z., Ergen, B.: Enhancing of dataset using deepdream, fuzzy color image enhancement and hypercolumn techniques to detection of the alzheimer's disease stages by deep learning model. Neural Computing and Applications **33**(16), 9877–9889 (2021)

33. Murugan, S., et al.: Demnet: a deep learning model for early diagnosis of alzheimer diseases and dementia from mr images. IEEE Access **9**, 90319–90329 (2021)

34. Nagarathna, C.R., Kusuma, M.I.: Automatic diagnosis of alzheimerâ s disease using hybrid model and CNN. International J. Innovative Res. Science, Engineering and Technol. **3**(1), 1–4 (2022)

Assessment of Slope Instability in a Hilly Terrain: A Logistic Regression and Random Forest Based Approach

Sumon Dey$^{(\boxtimes)}$ (iD) and Swarup Das

Department of Computer Science and Technology,
University of North Bengal, Darjeeling, West Bengal, India
sumon.csa.nbu@gmail.com

Abstract. Landslides are one such spontaneous natural disaster which has the potential to effect human lives as well as economic property in any region. The continuous exploration of qualitative and quantitative approaches augmented with RS-GIS methodologies for assessing landslides have given new dimensions to the area of research. The main obstacle of these methodologies remains in the fact that the hypothesis needs to be taken as true even before the analysis. To overcome the same, with the development of machine learning methodologies, the exhibits are found to be more objective in terms of quantification as well as the quality of research. The current assessment was aimed to evaluate the execution of two machine learning approaches namely; logistic regression and random forest for the assessment of slope instability in Darjeeling Himalayas. Eight geo-environmental factors were taken into consideration for the said assessment. The susceptibility models prepared with the said approaches were substantiated using receiver operating characteristics curves. The assessed accuracies were 76.8% and 79.7% for logistic regression and random forest respectively with the dataset(training and validation), the accuracies measured were 76.8% and 77.7% respectively.

Keywords: Slope Instability · Darjeeling Himalaya · Machine Learning · Logistic Regression · Random Forest · Receiver Operating Characteristic

1 Introduction

Natural disasters are unforeseen natural occurrences including landslides, earthquakes, tsunamis, and more that have a large negative impact on both the environment and people on the surface of the Earth. Landslides, also referred to as mudslides or landslips and capable of producing a wide range of ground movements, are among the deadliest and most expensive natural disasters on Earth. Landslides occur due to the earth's gravitational pull [1]. Darjeeling Himalayan region, which is a part of the Eastern Himalayan range, unexceptionally, is susceptible to slope instabilities due to the top of rug cliff topographical structure, destructive rainfall throughout the year [2]. According to the International Disaster Analysis Study, there were a total of 266 landslides between the

K. Dasgupta et al. (Eds.): CICBA 2023, CCIS 1955, pp. 14–27, 2024.
https://doi.org/10.1007/978-3-031-48876-4_2

years 2000 and 2022, with 13,000 individuals losing their lives and over 44,33,518 people being affected. For the Asian countries, the economic damage was roughly 29,23,863 USD in addition to the loss of human lives. Use of cutting-edge, rational mitigation strategies become essential to reduce landslide damage in order to examine how stability is impacted by different components and sub-factors and establish how susceptible a place is to landslides [3]. It may be possible to learn important details regarding the incidence of landslides by carefully examining the various slope failure-causing influencing factors. It is believed that the application of landslide susceptibility mapping is necessary for a professional technique to evaluate slope instabilities, disaster mitigation and management. Only the susceptibility maps show how the possibility of landslides taking place in a particular research area varies geographically based on the local climatic and geo-environmental factors [4]. Compared to other prediction techniques or models, mapping landslide susceptibility provides the best model for managing the region dynamically and making quick adjustments to it because it is a scientifically established approach. Some of the procedures in a landslide susceptibility study include the establishment of an inventory of landslides, pointing out the landslide causative features (LCFs), the spatial connection of these influencers with a modelling approach, and validating the model. The models' ability to predict outcomes is correlated with precision and caliber of the landslide inventory and the optimal LCF option [5, 6]. The accurate mapping of landslides and identifying plausible and logical influencing factors are requirements for determining the susceptibility of a given area to landslides. For susceptibility mapping of slides in various locations, various researches have previously used a range of approaches. Both qualitative and quantitative methodologies can be used to categorize these distinct techniques. Qualitative approaches weigh each factor that contributes to landslides based on the expertise of the specialists [7]. These methods, which are viewed to be subjective in nature, have been employed frequently to find out areas that are prone to landslides. One of the quantitative methods that has recently been created and utilized extensively is known as multi criteria decision making (MCDM) and involves evaluating the linkages between the causes of landslides based on probabilistic models [8, 9]. They are regarded as having an impartial nature. Researchers have utilized methodologies from factor analysis, multicollinearity evaluation, linear correlation, certainty factor technique, and multifactor set for choosing the optimal LCF due to the advancement of machine learning techniques [10–12]. Usually, these techniques were found to be inefficient or to be very time-taking. As a result, there are no established guidelines for selecting the ideal LCF. A suitable method for selecting optimally the landslide causal factors (LCFs) must be devised to quickly accomplish high prediction capacity from the applicable models. The current study was aimed to delineate the susceptible areas for landslides in the Darjeeling Himalayan region with the exploitation of logistic regression (LR) and random forest (RF) models.

2 Study Area

The 2034 square kilometer Darjeeling district, situated in India's eastern Himalayas, is mostly comprised of stony, arid hilly terrain. Latitudes $26^0 27'$ to $27^0 13'$ N and longitudes $87^0 59'$ to $88^0 30'$ E define the boundaries of Darjeeling. Between 61 and 3616 m ASL is the research area. The regional climate gets impacted to a good extent by south-west and north-east monsoon seasons. Winter and summer seasons are incredibly chilly and soggy. Very often, the regional temperature goes below zero. The Indian Meteorological Department reported that, in the year 2020–2021 the approximate rainfall in the area was between 340 cm and 473 cm. Four geological epochs can be distinguished in the research area: Precambrian (Kanchenjunga Gneiss, Lingtse Gneiss, Chungthang Fm.), Permian (Bhareli, Daling-Reyang, Gorubathan, and Buxa Fm., and Damuda-Lower Gondwana Group), Pleistocene (Undifferentiated Fluvial), and Miocene (Siwalik Group-Upper Siwalik) [13]. The Gorubathan and Rangamati surfaces provide evidence of the lithological positions of these terrains. Most of the rocks in the study region were created during the Triassic era. The research region has an active flood plain, a piedmont plain, an alluvial plain, a folded ridge, a profoundly broken hilly terrain, all according to its geomorphology [14]. The area under consideration in delineated by Fig. 1.

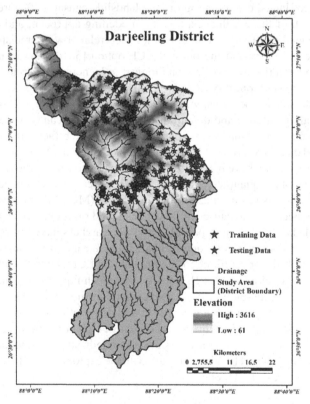

Fig. 1. Study Area Map

3 Materials and Methodology

For assessing slope instability in proposed area, the following steps were followed. Figure 2 represents the flowchart of the followed methodology in detail.

Step 1:- Preparation or construction of landslide directory for landslide inventory map preparation.

Step 2:- Determination of the landslide causative factors through multi-collinearity assessment.

Step 3:- Implementation of logistic regression and random forest models for suscepti-bility map preparation for landslides in the study area.

Step 4:- Performance assessment of the constructed maps for landslide susceptibility through area under curve (receiver operating characteristics curve).

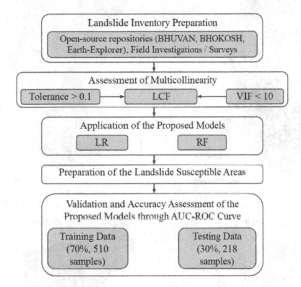

Fig. 2. Flowchart for the Assessment

3.1 Data Collection and Acquisition for landslide Inventory Creation

It's important to look at how landslides are distributed and the elements that influence them in order to determine the area that is most susceptible to landslides. The landslide inventory map (LIM) is a crucial part in determining how likely a landslide is to occur. In order to obtain these details, Google Earth imagery was examined, the repositories of GSI, India (BHUKOSH), repositories of NRSC, India (BHUVAN), USGS Earth Explorer, were examined, and the locations of the landslides were later verified through a series of field examinations and surveys [14, 15]. The creation of landslide inventory map was accomplished using ArcGIS 10.8 IDE.

3.2 Causal Factors for Slope Instability

Since the accuracy and precision of a geo-environmental study heavily depend upon the choice of the causative factors, the purpose of slope instability assessment in an area demands adequate selection of elements stimulating the stabilization disruption of the terrain. To accomplish the current study, eight geo-environmental factors were taken into consideration namely; slope, elevation, rainfall, geology, proximity to toads, proximity to streams, lineament density, land use-landcover. Delineated maps for landslide influencing factors, created using ArcGIS 10.8 IDE are represented by Fig. 3.

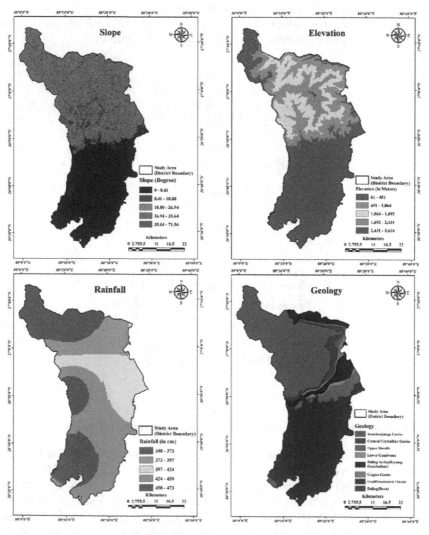

Fig. 3. Landslide Influencing Factors

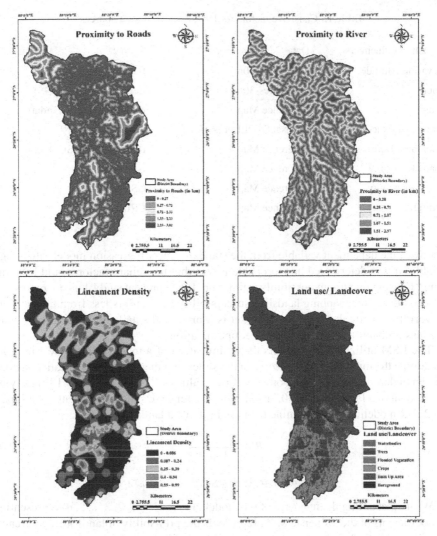

Fig. 3. (*continued*)

Table 1 represents the influencing factors for slope instability with their sources of collection.

3.3 Susceptibility Mapping Models

Logistic Regression. It is an effective multivariate statistical method, which stipulates the correlations between one dependent variable (landslide) and a variety of independent variables (predictive factors). The variety of slide predictive features can be of any combination among discrete, continuous and/or nominal and it is one feature that distinguishes the LR from other approaches [16-18]. In a conventional LR modelling, the dependent factor simply has the values "1" and "0". A link function was used in the LR

Table 1. Causative factors for landslides with their sources

Landslide Influencers	Data	Source
Elevation/Altitude	DEM (Res-30m)	Earth Explorer (USGS)
Slope	DEM (Res-30m)	Earth Explorer (USGS)
Geology	Reference Map	BHUKOSH (GSI, India)
Land use/Landcover	Landsat 8 (OLI, Res-10m)	ESRI
Lineament Density	Reference Map	BHUVAN (NRSC, India)
Roads Proximity	Reference Map	GSI, India
Rivers Proximity	Reference Map	GSI, India
Rainfall	Reference Map	CRU Dataset

to convert the dependent variable from the standard linear regression model into a logit variable. It was determined how probable it was that the reliant factor would have the value "1" using maximum possibility estimation. In the present study, logistic regression was considered for mapping landslide susceptibility as it suffers less from the problem of overfitting while the size of the dataset is limited and small and hence there comes very less probability for hyperparameter optimization.

The LSM utilizing LR attempts the optimization of a model that fits best in order to examine the interdependence between the slides and their expected causative factors. The dependent feature can take on one of two values—"1" or "0," with "1" signifying the incident of a landslide and "0," for its non-existence. Using below-mentioned Eqs. 1 and 2, LR modeling can determine the possibility of a landslide.

$$P_{ls} = \frac{1}{1 + e^{-z}} \tag{1}$$

$$z = \alpha_0 + \alpha_1 x_1 + \alpha_2 x_2 + \cdots + \alpha_n x_n \tag{2}$$

With α_0 denoting the intercept of the model, and $\alpha_j (j = 1, 2, 3, \ldots, n)$ representing the coefficients of the influencers, P_{ls} represents the probability of landslide occurrence, whereas $x_j (j = 1, 2, 3, \ldots, n)$ represents the causal factors for slope instabilities.

Random Forest. Using random sampling, the random forest method creates numerous independent decision trees and combines them for classification and prediction. Breiman was the first to recommend this strategy [19]. The random forest algorithm's working concept is summarized as follows: (i) build n decision trees using n new sample sets from the original training sample set with replacement using the bootstrap method; (ii) randomly choose n features for each re-sampling; and (iii) assemble the constructed trees into a random forest before using the random forest for classification of the new data. Decision tree voting produces the classification results. The RF model is quite good at handling noise issues and default values, and it is not prone to overfitting. RF model performs with robustness and precision when processing complex data [20, 21]. Depending on the aforementioned benefits, the RF model was used in this study to assess the susceptibility to landslides for the study region.

The RF Model constitutes spontaneous generation of random vector i_v (representing the causal factors for landslides in the current study), and the same gets distributed to all the trees. The training data and the input vector get coupled and each tree in the model is extended with the same. The exhibits of the said approach result in group of tree-structured classifiers. With the RF model, the slide and non-slide trees were individually constructed by taking into consideration the said geo-environmental factors.

The generalization error in RF model is represented as follows:

$$Gen_{err} = P_{x,y}(margin_{fn}(x, y) < 0) \tag{3}$$

With x, y representing the likelihood over x, y space, $margin_{fn}$ represent the margin function which is mathematically represented as:

$$margin_{fn}(x, y) = average_i I(h_i(x) = y) - max_{k \neq y} avg_i I(h_i(x) = k) \tag{4}$$

Here $I(*)$ denotes the indicator function which was represented by [19].

3.4 Assessment of Multicollinearity

In a qualitative, quantitative or machine learning approach for any study, it becomes an important necessity to figure out whether or not there is any existence of multicollinearity in order to determine the degree of interdependence among the independent factors [22]. If there happens to be any case of multicollinearity issues, then the issue must be resolved to ensure that the analysis is not biased. In the present study, the assessment of multicollinearity was accomplished with PyCharm IDE (version 2021.3) and the parameters for the assessment were tolerance and variable inflation factor (VIF). The permitted bound for tolerance value and VIF value are > 0.1 and < 10 respectively. It was found that the values of the said parameters were under the permitted bound and hence there was no issue of multicollinearity for the parameters under consideration for the slope instability assessment. Table 2 represents the finding of multicollinearity assessment for the study under consideration. However, Random Forest classification does not get effected by any occurrence of multicollinearity issues, but the performance of Logistic Regression gets effected by the same issue. Since the present study was aimed at the comparative assessment of two widely used models (i.e., Logistic Regression and Random Forest) for assessing landslide susceptibility, hence the multicollinearity assessment was thought to be essential.

Table 2. Multicollinearity Diagnostics

Landslide Influencing Factors	Tolerance	VIF
Elevation	0.394	2.539
Slope	0.389	2.569
Geology	0.623	1.605
LULC	0.87	1.149
Lineament Density	0.531	1.882
Proximity to Roads	0.36	2.779
Proximity to Rivers	0.583	1.715
Rainfall	0.748	1.338

4   Results and Exhibits

For the current assessment under consideration, a total of 728 landslide locations were identified through several field investigations, Google Earth imagery, BHUKOSH (an open-source data depository maintained by Government of India). The identified landslide sites were then partitioned randomly with a ratio of 70:30 as train-test split.

4.1   Results of Logistic Regression Model

Exploiting the logistic regression model, roughly 306 sq. km. And 124 sq. km. of the entire study region were covered under high and very highly susceptible to slides. Table 3 represents the intercept and coefficient values for the independent factors. Figure 4(a) delineates the susceptibility map produced with logistic regression model.

Table 3. Intercept and co-efficient values for logistic regression

Landslide Influencing Factors	Coefficients
Intercept (α_0)	-4.812
Elevation (α_1)	-5.639
Slope (α_2)	22.336
Geology (α_3)	0.212
LULC (α_4)	0.424
Lineament Density (α_5)	1.343
Proximity to Roads (α_6)	3.482
Proximity to Rivers (α_7)	0.333
Rainfall (α_8)	3.041

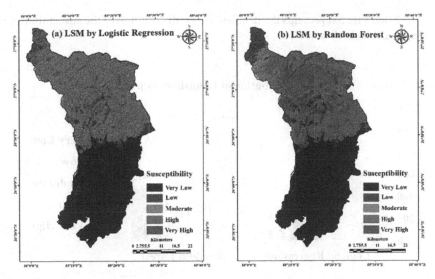

Fig. 4. Susceptibility Maps produced by (a) Logistic Regression, (b) Random Forest

4.2   Results of Random Forest Model

Roughly, 208 sq. km. And 475 sq. km. Area of the entire study region were covered under high and very highly susceptible to slides with exploitation of the random forest model. The relative implication of all the unconstrained features were calculated with respect to node purity increment, which is Gini-based importance and is computed depending on the reduction in aggregation of squared errors whenever a variable is chosen to split. A calculation of the Gini impurity is used to determine which feature should be divided at each node when a tree is constructed. Table 4 represents the increase in node purity for the random forest model utilized for construction of susceptibility maps for slope instability in Darjeeling Himalayan region. Figure 4(b) delineates the susceptible map prepared by the said model.

Table 4. Importance of the predictive factors

Landslide Influencing Factors	Increase in Node Purity
Elevation	58.53
Slope	553.36
Geology	48.13
LULC	15.78
Lineament Density	5.75
Proximity to Roads	21.92
Proximity to Rivers	14.23
Rainfall	2.69

Table 5 and Fig. 5 represents the detailed spatial distribution of the susceptible areas using both, LR and RF model.

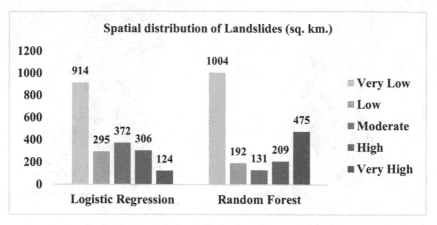

Fig. 5. Spatial distribution of landslides (graphical representation)

Table 5. Spatial distribution of landslides

Classification	Area in Square Kilometers	
	Logistic Regression	Random Forest
Very Low	914 sq. km	1004 sq. km
Low	295 sq. km	192 sq. km
Moderate	372 sq. km	131 sq. km
High	306 sq. km	209 sq. km
Very High	124 sq. km	475 sq. km

4.3   Performance Assessment for the Susceptible Maps

To establish the scientific importance of susceptible maps produced by the proposed models, it becomes very crucial to substantiate them. In the current study, the receiver operating characteristics curves were utilized to assess the performance of the susceptibility models [23]. With X-axis showing the specificity (false positive rate), Y-axis representing the sensitivity (true positive rate), the logistic regression model exhibited 76.8% accuracy with both, training and validation samples, whereas the random forest model attained 79.7% and 77.7% accuracy with the training and testing samples which were obtained by randomly splitting the total set of 728 landslide location samples in a 70:30 ratio. The training samples were 510 in number whereas validation samples were 218 in total. Figure 6(a) and 6(b) represents the area under curve (AUC) scores for the proposed models under consideration for both, training and testing dataset respectively.

The classification metrics for the landslide susceptibility models under consideration are represented in detail by Table 6.

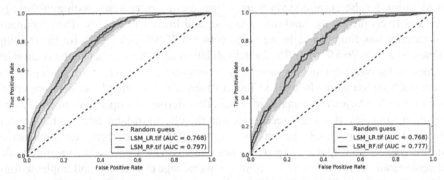

Fig. 6. AUC Curve for (a) training dataset (on the left), (b) validation dataset (on the right)

Table 6. Classification Metrics for the Proposed Models

Classification Metrics	Proposed ML Models	
	Logistic Regression	Random Forest
Mean Absolute Error (MAE)	0.0019	0.0021
Root Mean Square Error (RMSE)	0.0385	0.0421
Kappa Coefficient	0.4748	0.4709
Precision	0.3592	0.3494
Recall value	0.7037	0.7269
F1 Score	0.4757	0.4720

5 Conclusion and Future Directives

The maps for landslide susceptibility are essential for directing decision-makers in landslide-prone areas to take the appropriate actions. In addition to being fatal, landslides frequently destroy homes, roadways, and agricultural land. A crucial tool for lowering landslide incidences and hazards, protecting the eco-system, and assisting communities in potentially dangerous landslide susceptibility zones is this study's evaluation of landslide risks utilizing LSMs. The present study constituted logistic regression and random forest models for the simulation of landslide susceptibility maps. The objectivity remains in the fact that there was no use of any qualitative methods or methodologies in the determination of the factor's weight while preparing the susceptibility maps for the intended study region, furthermore, there existed no hypothesis on the selection of the causal factors through expert opinion or heuristic methods. With the historical data of landslides and field investigation along with the support of Google Earth imagery, the proposed methodologies were utilized for the preparation of the susceptibility maps. The primary obstacle of the susceptibility study was the scarcity of high-resolution digital elevation model for the study area. The driving influencers of slope instabilities taken under consideration for the current study were, slope, elevation, rainfall, geology/lithology, roads and rivers proximity, land use-landcover and lineament density. The attainment of accuracies was found to be in the range between 76.8% and 79.7% for the training samples, and from 76.8% to 77.7% for the validation datasets, and hence the accuracies obtained by the proposed models were found to be good. The main area of susceptibility for the study region were close to the Teesta River, which is one of the most important tributaries in the Darjeeling Himalayan region. By offering appropriate steps and hazard mitigation strategies, this study seeks to lessen the effects of landslides on the general public and the government. In the sensitive sections of the region, certain essential tactics and strategies must be applied. The risk of landslides can be decreased by locating faults and geologically sensitive locations, controlling drainage effectively, and implementing afforestation projects. The findings of this inquiry might give individuals in charge of creating policy and practitioners in disaster-prone areas relevant and important data and figures.

References

1. Gerrard, J.: The landslide hazard in the Himalayas: geological control and human action. Geomorphology **10**, 221–230 (1994). https://doi.org/10.1016/0169-555x(94)90018-3
2. Solaimani, K., Mousavi, S.Z., Kavian, A.: Landslide susceptibility mapping based on frequency ratio and logistic regression models. Arab. J. Geosci. **6**, 2557–2569 (2012). https://doi.org/10.1007/s12517-012-0526-5
3. Tien Bui, D., Tuan, T.A., Klempe, H., Pradhan, B., Revhaug, I.: Spatial prediction models for shallow landslide hazards: a comparative assessment of the efficacy of support vector machines, artificial neural networks, kernel logistic regression, and logistic model tree. Landslides **13**, 361–378 (2015). https://doi.org/10.1007/s10346-015-0557-6
4. Fan, X., et al.: Two multi-temporal datasets that track the enhanced landsliding after the 2008 Wenchuan earthquake. Earth System Science Data. **11**, 35–55 (2019). https://doi.org/10.5194/essd-11-35-2019
5. Chen, W., Pourghasemi, H.R., Naghibi, S.A.: A comparative study of landslide susceptibility maps produced using support vector machine with different kernel functions and entropy data mining models in China. Bull. Eng. Geol. Env. **77**, 647–664 (2017). https://doi.org/10.1007/s10064-017-1010-y
6. Pradhan, S.P., Siddique, T.: Stability assessment of landslide-prone road cut rock slopes in Himalayan terrain: a finite element method based approach. J. Rock Mechanics and Geotechnical Engineering. **12**, 59–73 (2020). https://doi.org/10.1016/j.jrmge.2018.12.018
7. Kanwal, S., Atif, S., Shafiq, M.: GIS based landslide susceptibility mapping of northern areas of Pakistan, a case study of Shigar and Shyok Basins. Geomat. Nat. Haz. Risk **8**, 348–366 (2016). https://doi.org/10.1080/19475705.2016.1220023
8. Chen, W., Ding, X., Zhao, R., Shi, S.: Application of frequency ratio and weights of evidence models in landslide susceptibility mapping for the Shangzhou District of Shangluo City. China. Environmental Earth Sciences **75**, (2015). https://doi.org/10.1007/s12665-015-4829-1
9. Juliev, M., Mergili, M., Mondal, I., Nurtaev, B., Pulatov, A., Hübl, J.: Comparative analysis of statistical methods for landslide susceptibility mapping in the Bostanlik District. Uzbekistan. Science of The Total Environment. **653**, 801–814 (2019). https://doi.org/10.1016/j.scitotenv.2018.10.431

10. Chen, W., et al.: Applying population-based evolutionary algorithms and a neuro-fuzzy system for modeling landslide susceptibility. CATENA **172**, 212–231 (2019). https://doi.org/10.1016/j.catena.2018.08.025
11. Youssef, A.M., Pourghasemi, H.R.: Landslide susceptibility mapping using machine learning algorithms and comparison of their performance at Abha Basin, Asir Region. Saudi Arabia. Geoscience Frontiers **12**, 639–655 (2021). https://doi.org/10.1016/j.gsf.2020.05.010
12. Ado, M., et al.: Landslide susceptibility mapping using machine learning: a literature survey. Remote Sensing **14**, 3029 (2022). https://doi.org/10.3390/rs14133029
13. Mondal, S., Mandal, S.: Geomorphic diversity and landslide susceptibility in the Balason River Basin. Darjeeling Himalaya. HKIE Transactions **27**, 13–24 (2020). https://doi.org/10.33430/v27n1thie2017-0054
14. Chawla, A., Pasupuleti, S., Chawla, S., Rao, A.C.S., Sarkar, K., Dwivedi, R.: Landslide susceptibility zonation mapping: a case study from Darjeeling District, Eastern Himalayas, India. J. Indian Society of Remote Sensing **47**, 497–511 (2019). https://doi.org/10.1007/s12524-018-0916-6
15. Roy, J., Saha, S.: Landslide susceptibility mapping using knowledge driven statistical models in Darjeeling District, West Bengal, India. Geoenvironmental Disasters **6** (2019). https://doi.org/10.1186/s40677-019-0126-8
16. Hemasinghe, H., Rangali, R.S.S., Deshapriya, N.L., Samarakoon, L.: Landslide susceptibility mapping using logistic regression model (a case study in Badulla District, Sri Lanka). Procedia Engineering **212**, 1046–1053 (2018). https://doi.org/10.1016/j.proeng.2018.01.135
17. Rasyid, A.R., Bhandary, N.P., Yatabe, R.: Performance of frequency ratio and logistic regression model in creating GIS based landslides susceptibility map at Lompobattang Mountain, Indonesia. Geoenvironmental Disasters **3** (2016). https://doi.org/10.1186/s40677-016-0053-x
18. Gayen, A., Saha, S.: Deforestation probable area predicted by logistic regression in Pathro river basin: a tributary of Ajay river. Spat. Inf. Res. **26**, 1–9 (2017). https://doi.org/10.1007/s41324-017-0151-1
19. Breiman: Random Forests. Machine Learning **45**, 5–32. https://doi.org/10.1023/A:1010933404324
20. Stumpf, A., Kerle, N.: Object-oriented mapping of landslides using random forests. Remote Sens. Environ. **115**, 2564–2577 (2011). https://doi.org/10.1016/j.rse.2011.05.013
21. Taalab, K., Cheng, T., Zhang, Y.: Mapping landslide susceptibility and types using Random Forest. Big Earth Data. **2**, 159–178 (2018). https://doi.org/10.1080/20964471.2018.1472392
22. Oh, H.-J., Lee, S., Hong, S.-M.: Landslide susceptibility assessment using frequency ratio technique with iterative random sampling. J. Sensors **2017**, 1–21 (2017). https://doi.org/10.1155/2017/3730913
23. Samui, P.: Slope stability analysis: a support vector machine approach. Environ. Geol. **56**, 255–267 (2008). https://doi.org/10.1007/s00254-007-1161-4

A Comparative Study on the Evaluation of k-mer Indexing in Genome Sequence Compression

Subhankar Roy[1]([✉])[iD] and Anirban Mukhopadhyay[2][iD]

[1] Academy of Technology, Adisaptagram, Hooghly 712121, West Bengal, India
subhankar.roy07@gmail.com
[2] University of Kalyani, Kalyani, Nadia 741235, West Bengal, India
anirban@klyuniv.ac.in

Abstract. Low-cost and faster next-generation sequencing (NGS) technology generates huge sequence data for living organisms in the terabyte range. Storing, transferring, and analyzing these data is a real challenge for researchers. An efficient compression algorithm is the ultimate solution to this challenge. Three benchmark methods are tested on the Amazon Web Services (AWS) virtual cloud platform in this article: High-performance referential genome compression (HiRGC), High-efficiency referential genome compression (SCCG), and Hybrid referential compression method (HRCM). Eight benchmark human genomes, coronavirus genome, and a few additional species in FAST-ALL (FASTA) and Raw formats are used to test these algorithms. The widely-used FASTA format, which is utilized in GenBank, makes data analysis and reading easier for researchers. A very fast k-mer hashing method is used for indexing, which is efficient for pairwise and batch-wise compression. HiRGC offers a good trade-off between compression ratio and time, according to experimental data. The SCCG technique takes longer to compress data but significantly reduces the amount of available space. HRCM does not perform as well for pairwise compression, but it makes significant strides for batch processing. These facts motivate us to propose an improved and efficient compression algorithm in the future.

Keywords: Sequencing · Compression · Lossless · Reference · Metrics · k-mer · Indexing · Hashing

1 Introduction

The production of genomic sequences has increased as a result of the highly efficient NGS [18] technology's quick development. In 2010, the cost of whole-genome sequencing was \$30,000, but by 2021 it has dropped significantly to \$562, surpassing Moore's Law [22]. Modern sequencing technology, along with its decreasing cost, is helping public health by preventing diseases, treating them when they occur, and enabling the development of personalized medicine at a faster rate. According to current projections, by 2025, the growth of genome sequences will be one zettabyte per year [20]. However, this high-throughput sequencing technology also makes data storage and processing costs increasingly challenging, as they are growing at a higher rate than the cost of sequencing [20]. Therefore, when compared to sequencing costs, data storage costs could become a bottleneck. In this regard, genome sequence compression can be considered a very efficient solution.

There are two main types of genome compression: reference-free and reference-based. This article focuses on reference-based compression due to the following reasons: Pairwise or multiple reference-based compression from the genome chromosome of the same species is the foundation step for compressing collections of genomes. Although reference-free compression is faster, it lacks the good compression ratio that reference-based compression has. Reference-based compression requires access to a proper reference genome file. For example, human genomes have over 99% similarity.

The most crucial step in vertical or reference-based compression is mapping the genome sequence that needs to be compressed to a reference genome sequence. An efficient mapping depends on an efficient indexing procedure. Some state-of-the-art data structures for indexing are hash tables, suffix trees, suffix arrays, Full-text index that occupies a minute amount of space (FM indexing), Burrows-Wheeler Transform, Wavelet Tree, etc. [7]. In this paper, we have done a comparative study of three recent hash-based excellent benchmark sequence compression HiRGC [10], SCCG [19], and HRCM [24].

Compression ratio, compression gain, compression duration, decompression time, and peak memory consumption are the performance measurement parameters taken into consideration for comparison. By dividing the original size by the compressed size, the compression ratio is determined. The relative compression advantage is calculated as follows: 1 - size of post compression/size of post compression by another algorithm, multiplied by 100. The time it takes to generate a final compressed file is the compression time. The maximum primary memory consumption is the highest memory usage.

This article is divided into the following sections: Sect. 2, which analyzes relevant literature; Sect. 3, which defines techniques; Sect. 4, which discusses system requirements and benchmark data sets; Sect. 5, which discusses results; and Sect. 6, which serves as the article's conclusion.

2   Literature Survey

Some benchmark predecessors of HiRGC, SCCG and HRCM are GDC [5], CoGI [23], GDC-2 [4], ERGC [16], and NRGC [17].

Genome differential compressor (GDC) is similar to the algorithm Relative Lempel-Ziv Optimized (RLZ Opt) [8]. It segmentizes genome sequences into blocks containing 8192 characters. Then, it uses Lempel-Ziv 1977 (LZ77) parsing using hashing. The reference sequence is selected by a heuristic method that provides fast random access. A local no-collision hash table is used for indexing while compressing genomes as an image (CoGI). The main distinction from

GDC is that it also supports reference-free compression. GDC and Genome Differential Compressor 2 (GDC-2) vary primarily in that GDC-2 uses two levels of LZ77 processing to compress a large number of genomes. The positions and lengths of the two-level matches are encoded using various contextual encoding methodologies.

Efficient referential genome compression (ERGC), like GDC, segments genome sequences into equal blocks except for the last block. Each reference sequence's i^{th} segment matched the corresponding target sequence's i^{th} segment using a greedy algorithm with k-mer hashing, where $k = \{21, 9\}$. A high compression ratio is obtained only when two sequences are highly similar locally. The author's next algorithm, novel referential genome compression (NRGC), provides a better result for dissimilar reference and target sequences by optimizing the placement of segments. The same k-mer hashing is used but with a different k-mer set, as $\{11, 12, 13\}$.

The shortcoming of GDC, ERGC, and NRGC is that dividing may break the sequence of long matches into short matches. This main drawback was first identified and eliminated by HiRGC's global hash table, followed by SCCG and HRCM, respectively. A very fast k-mer hashing for indexing is used with different k-mer lengths.

The bfMEM [13] algorithm employs the bloom filter to remove pointless k-mer before adding the passed k-mer to the hash table for indexing. Thus, bfMEM is 1.8 times faster than the benchmark algorithms currently in use. Mem-RGC [11] uses a coprime double-window k-mer sampling search methodology to find the maximal matches between two genomes. The approach then extends these matches to include mismatches and the neighboring maximal matches to create lengthy and mutation-containing matches. The MapReduce programming model from Hadoop is used to create the FastDRC [6] method. The minicom [12] approach subgroups reads with the same minimizer and uses huge k-minimizers to index the reads before compressing them.

Hashing is faster than the suffix array at the cost of more memory consumption. The longest exact match (LEM) between the sequences is generated by a separate hash chaining, which improves greatly over its predecessor. For example, there is a huge improvement in compression performance on eight benchmark human genomes by HiRGC over its last predecessor, NRGC, from 15137.04 MB to 1020.2 MB, i.e., a gain of 93.26%. Using local and/or global hash tables and the combined ERGC and HiRGC concept, SCCG was able to further improve this compression ratio to 898.55 MB at the expense of more compression time. HiRGC and SCCG give excellent pairwise compression results due to single-level matching. HRCM's performance for a collection of sequences is excellent as it employs 2-level matching. The compressed total size that HRCM obtained for the same data sets as mentioned above is 694.7 MB. Motivated by the above facts, a detailed comparative study of three efficient existing reference-based genome compression algorithms is conducted, which might inspire researchers to propose more efficient compression algorithms in the future.

3   Methodologies

HiRGC [10], SCCG [19], and HRCM [24], three recently developed lossless state-of-the-art genome sequence compression algorithms, are compared using large-scale FASTA format chromosomal files as a benchmark. For indexing, these methods have used k-mer hashing [7].

3.1   HiRGC

The HiRGC [10] algorithm's performance improvement over its predecessors on eight benchmarks human genome (YH, hg17, hg18, hg19, hg38, HuRef, KO131, KO224) FASTA files is phenomenal. The average relative compression gain is more than 90% higher than its predecessors, such as GDC-2 [4], ERGC [16], and NRGC [17], and 75% more than iDoComp [14]. The compression time fluctuation is very low, approximately in the range of 34 min for hg19 to 47 min for HuRef, and the same is very close for hg17, hg18, hg19, and hg38. Preprocessing, advanced greedy matching in the global hash table, and post-processing are the three stages of the HiRGC algorithm.

3.1.1   Preprocessing The reference sequence and target sequences are pre-processed independently. The specifics of the reference sequence's preprocessing are as follows:

Step 1: Remove the identifier (first line).
Step 2: Convert lowercase characters Σ = {a, c, g, t, n, k, m, r, s, w, y, b, d, h, v} to uppercase Ω= {A, C, G, T, N, K, M, R, S, W, Y, B, D, H, V}.
Step 3: Remove other characters except Φ= {A, C, G, T}.
Step 4: Use the 2-bit coding rule T - 3, G - 2, C- 1, and A - 0 to convert and store the sequence.

The details of the preprocessing of the target sequence are as follows:

Step 1: Stores the identifier.
Step 2: Stores lowercase characters Σ begin positions and lengths in two different arrays.
Step 3: Convert lowercase characters Σ to uppercase Ω.
Step 4: Store N characters beginning positions and lengths in two arrays, respectively.
Step 5: Stores other characters Ψ= {K, M, R, S, W, Y, B, D, H, V} (positions - preceding N character numbers) and (other characters - 'A') into two arrays, respectively.
Step 6: Store line lengths in an array.
Step 7: Remove other characters except for Φ.
Step 8: Store Φ characters sequence by the same coding rule.

The positions in Step 2, Step 4, and Step 5 are encoded by delta coding, which needs to record the relative increment of position p_{n+1} over p_n, not the exact value of p_{n+1}. Example 1 shows the output obtained in the preprocessing stage on a pair of sample references and a target sequence.

Example 1. Let us consider a sample reference sequence, FASTA chromosome
file name Ref.fa:

>chr1.fa

NNNNACGTcgtgnnnATGCgtcYYY

TCGTcgtgnnnATGCATGTGTGCTG

GTCGA

The result of the above sequence

0123123203212313123123203210323213223120

For a sample FASTA chromosome target file, Tar.fa:

>chr1.fa

NNNCACGTCgtgnnnATGCgtaYYY

TCGTcgtgnnnCATGCATGTGTGGC

GTCGAV

The output is given by the above steps 1, 2, 4, 5, 6, and 8, respectively, in the
following lines:

>chr1.fa

{[10, 6], [20, 3], [30, 7]}

{[1, 3], [13, 3], [34, 3]}

{[17, 24], [18, 24], [19, 24], [47, 21]}

{[25, 25, 6]}

1012312320321230312312321032103232322123120

3.1.2   Advance Greedy Matching
The following two steps are used in
advanced greedy matching with a static k-mer global hash table size of $k =$
20:

Step 1: Preprocessing the reference sequence
Step 2: Searching for matching

The actual HiRGC implementation's optimal k-mer size is $k = 20$. However,
in the following discussions, we have taken a small $k = 4$ on a short sample
sequence for the readers' convenience. The reference sequence obtained from
the preprocessing step depicted in Fig. 1 is used to build a hash table in the
preprocess reference stage. Two arrays carry out the hash table concept. The
second array is used to hold all identical k-mer places using a hash chaining
approach. This facilitates the LEM (longest exact match) search. By moving
one base character, the sliding window technique is used to find all k-mer. When
l is the length of the sequence, then there are (l - k - 1) of these k-mers. Searching
the LEM between reference and target sequence is demonstrated by Fig. 2. LEM
of target k-mer {0123} starting at reference sequence positions {0, 6, 11, 17,
25} is 17 and previous position = 0 as this is the first matching. The length is
(length - k-mer length) = (8 - 4) = 4. Therefore, encoded as {17, 4} followed
by mismatch 33, the referential match entry (RME) is {17, 4, 33}. The LEM of
k-mer {3320} start at position 3, and the previous position = (17 + 8) = 25,
so the current position encoded by delta coding is (3 - 25) = -22. The length is
(length - k-mer length) = (13 - 4) = 9. Therefore encoded as {-22, 9} followed

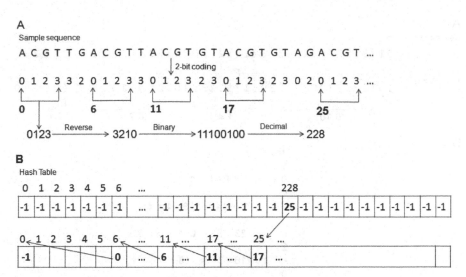

Fig. 1. Reference sequence preprocessing (A) A sample sequence encoded by 2-bit coding and calculating a hash value of k-mer = 4 (B) Storing all identical k-mer in a hash table by hash chaining

Reference Sequence

```
      0 1 2 3 3 2 0 1 2 3 3 0 1 2 3 2 3 0 1 2 3 2 3 0 2 0 1 2 3 ...
                      (3, 13)                  (17, 8)
Target Sequence
      0 1 2 3 2 3 0 2 3 3 3 3 2 0 1 2 3 3 0 1 2 3 2 0 2 1 1 2 3 ...
```

Fig. 2. LEM match finding between reference and target genome sequences

by mismatch, i.e. {021123} and RME = {-22, 9, 021123}. These two RMEs are obtained in the post-processing step.

3.1.3   Post-processing RLE is able to encode line length. In this stage, most data is encoded by delta encoding, including the begin position of matches, the begin position of lowercase characters, the begin position of the N character, and the position of other characters as shown by Fig. 3. The other characters Ψ are mapped to digits starting from 0 to 9 respectively. The above target sequence mapping will be Y $\rightarrow$ 0, and V $\rightarrow$ 1 respectively.

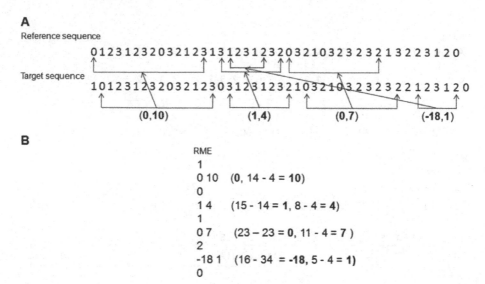

Fig. 3. (A) Reference and target sample genome sequence by 2-bit coding (B) RME obtained in the post-processing step with delta encoding on positions and static encoding (LEM - k) on length

The 7-zip [1] tool, which is an implementation of the PPMD algorithm, an optimized version of the PPM (Prediction by Partial Matching) algorithm, compresses the finished file after post-processing.

3.2   SCCG

In the actual SCCG implementation, the optimal k-mer size is 21 or shorter. Here we demonstrate it by k-mer size 4 on a short sample reference and to-be-compressed genome sequence. Like HiRGC, it also has three stages: preprocessing, matching (local or global), and post-processing.

3.2.1   Preprocessing In global matching, the lowercase changes to the uppercase, and then N is removed. Then stores the identifier, first-line length, lowercase characters start position and length-1, and N characters start position and length of T recorded in an intermediate file. The preprocessing of local matching is the same as global matching, except that local matching does not delete and store N. Figures 4 and 5(A), respectively, depict the implementation process used in Example 1.

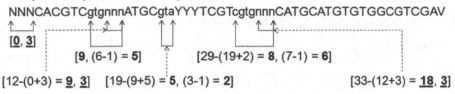

Fig. 4. The process of calculating the position and length of lowercase characters and N

3.2.2 Matching There are two phases of matching: local greedy matching on genome sequence segments and global greedy matching on a limited range or whole genome sequence.

Local Matching: Local matching is performed on the same segments length ($l = 30000$) of the reference and target genome sequences. Segments have equal size except for the last one, whose length is less than or equal to l. If two sequences are highly similar, local matching gives a better result. It finds the LEM in the same way that HiRGC does. In the case of no-matching between segments T_i and R_i, the k-mer length is shortened (E.g. $k = 11$). Still, if no matching is found, then the segment T_i is stored directly.

Global Matching: Global matching is performed on the whole reference sequence. If the target sequence length is less than five times the segmentation length (=30000), i.e., small size, then it goes for global matching directly. In the global hash table (H_G) all ($l - k + 1$) reference genome sequence k-mer positions are stored using the same hash chaining concept as HiRGC or HRCM algorithms. But unlike HiRGC and HRCM, the hash value of a k-mer is obtained directly by the hashCode() method. The poorly matched segment is determined by a threshold $T_1 = $ (number of directly stored characters/segment length) * 100%. If $T_1 > 50\%$ then it is considered a poorly matched segment. When the number of consecutive poorly matched segments reaches some threshold value T_2 ($= 4$) then the two sequences are considered to have a lower similarity. But only the N characters segment is not counted for T_2. If the target sequence length is less than 1333*segmentation length, then $T_1 = 10\%$ and $T_2 = 0$ respectively. Upon failing this T_2 the result will be poor, so it goes for global matching. Global matching improves the compression efficiency for significantly dissimilar sequences. The k-mer matching process of local and global schemes is the same. The main difference between local and global searching is that in global matching there is a search limit (-100 to 100) in the reference sequence. The limit is withdrawn in the absence of matching in the H_G. Due to the greedy matching strategy, the far-away LEM from the previous matching is unstudied. The matching process is shown in Fig. 5(B) and (C).

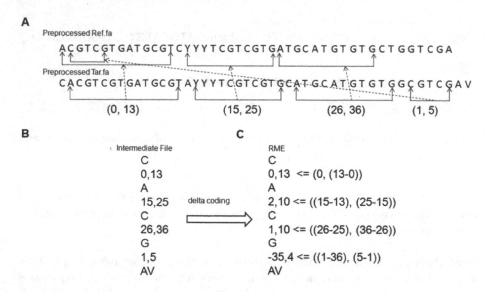

Fig. 5. (A) Preprocessed reference and target sequence for global matching; (B) RME before applying delta coding (C) RME after applying delta coding

3.2.3 Post-processing

In the tuple (position, length, mismatch characters) after matching, the position is encoded by delta coding. Positions for local matching across the border of segments are merged first then delta coding is used. The final file is encoded by the 7-zip compression tool. Decompression is the opposite of compression and is faster because no hashing is required. The compression time taken by SCCG is longer than that of HiRGC and HRCM. The reason is that two types of matching are also used in global matching. Searching is first done in a limited range, and if no match is found, then the whole sequence is searched.

3.3 HRCM

Like HiRGC and SCCG, HRCM also consists of three stages. The stages are preprocessing, matching, and encoding, respectively. The actual HRCM implementation's optimal k-mer size is $k = 14$, but we demonstrate the process by taking a small $k = 4$ on a short sample sequence for better understanding.

3.3.1 Preprocessing

This stage is almost similar to HiRGC, except HRCM also stores small character information about reference sequences to match and encode them with the target. One more difference is that in this stage it does not encode the characters by the 2-bit coding rule, which is done at the matching stage. Unlike HiRGC, delta encoding is applied at this stage, and it stores only first-line width. The process has been explained in Example 2.

Example 2. Let us consider a sample FASTA reference file Ref.fa
>chr1.fa
NNNNACGTcgtgnnnATGCgtcYYY
TCGTcgtgnnnATGCATGTGTGCTG
GTCGA
Let us take two sample FASTA to-be-compressed sequence files, Tar1.fa and
Tar2.fa respectively:
>chr1.fa
NNNCACGTCgtgnnnATGCgtaYYY
TCGTcgtgnnnCATGCATGTGTGGC
GTCGAV
>chr1.fa
NNNNACGTCgtgnnnATGCgtcZZZ
TCGTCgtgnnnCATGCATGTGTGGC
GTCGAX

The preprocessed output of Ref.fa file is
Reference chromosome: ACGTCGTGATGCGTCTCGTCGTGATGCATGT-
GTGCTGGTCGA
Lowercase information: {[8, 7], [4, 3], [7, 7]}

The preprocessed output of the Tar1.fa file is
Target chromosome: CACGTCGTGATGCGTATCGTCGTGCATGCATGT-
GTGGCGTCGA
Lowercase information: {[9, 6], [4, 3], [7, 7]}
N character information: {[0, 3], [9, 3], [18, 3]}
Identifier: >chr1.fa
First line length: 25
Other character information: {[16, 24], [0, 24], [0, 24], [27, 21]}

The preprocessed output of the Tar2.fa file is
Target chromosome: ACGTCGTGATGCGTCTCGTCGTGCATGCATGTG-
TGGCGTCGA
Lowercase information: {[9, 6], [4, 3], [8, 6]}
N character information: {[0, 4], [8, 3], [18, 3]}
Identifier: >chr1.fa
First line length: 25
Other character information: {[15, 25], [0, 25], [0, 25], [27, 23]}

3.3.2 Matching HiRGC has only one type and one level of matching. HRCM
has two types of matching one is preprocessed reference and the target sequence
consists of only Φ characters and the second is lowercase character matching. If
more than one target sequence is needed to compress, then second-level matching
is used among target sequences. Like HiRGC, the same matching strategy is used,
i.e., finding LEM using a separate chaining array.

First-Level Matching : In HiRGC before matching i.e. at the preprocessing stage
all characters of Φ are encoded by 2-bit encoding rule T - 3, G - 2, C - 1,

A - 0. However, HRCM uses the same formula as HiRGC to calculate the hash value on the integer sequence during matching and encrypts each k-mer with a 2-bit encoding. All identical k-mer positions are stored in a second array used to find LEM. Figure 6(A) demonstrates the sample sequence in which k-mer hash matching takes place. Figure 6(B) determines the process of finding the RME. Delta encoding on positions and static encoding on length is shown in Fig. 6(B). But in the actual implementation of HRCM, it is applied at the encoding stage.

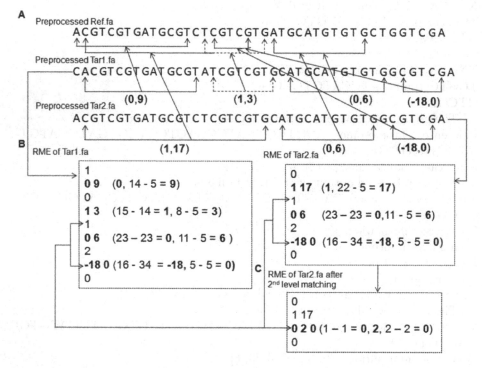

Fig. 6. (A) Preprocessed reference and two target genome files of Ref.fa, Tar1.fa, and Tar2.fa (B) RME of Tar1.fa and Tar2.fa obtained by 1st level matching with delta encoding on positions and static encoding (LEM - k - 1) on length (C) RME of Tar2.fa obtained by 2nd level matching

Second-Level Matching: A very complicated second-level matching is used when two or more to-be-compressed genome sequences are available. Second-level matching is different from first-level matching. The second level matching hash value is generated not only from Φ but also from the RME triplet, i.e., (position, length, mismatch). To generate a unique hash value for each triplet three large prime numbers are used to multiply with position, length, and each mismatch character respectively. Here more than one reference sequence is possible. To manage memory consumption $p\%$ (= 10%) of the target sequence is used as a reference sequence. The same separate chaining concept is used to avoid conflict. Second-level matching is represented by a triplet (sequence-id, position, length). The Id and position are starts from 0, and for length a minimum of two consecutive matches are taken i.e. encode as (length - 2) as shown in Fig. 6(C).

Lowercase Matching: A modified RLE is used for matching. Ref.fa lowercase characters tuples are {[8, 7], [4, 3], [7, 7]}, Tar1.fa lowercase characters tuples are {[9, 6], [4, 3], [7, 7]} and Tar2.fa lowercase characters tuples are {[9, 6], [4, 3], [8, 6]}. Matching information (Flag, match encode by improved RLE, number of mismatch, mismatch-tuples) gives the following result 1 4 0 1 2 2 1 9 6 and 0 3 9 6 4 3 8 6.

3.3.3   Post-processing RME, special characters, and the N character's position are encoded by delta coding. RME's LEM is encoded by (LEM - k - 1), in HiRGC it was (LEM - k). In the encoded hrcm file the first line indicates the lowercase character's information, N-character position and length, other character's positions, and (characters - 'A') respectively. The second value in the first line counts the number of tuples (position, length) of N-characters and (position, characters - 'A') for special characters. The rest lines are for RME in the hrcm file. In the encoded desc file first line bold value is the code length followed by the sequence first line length encoded by RLE. The next lines are identifiers. Finally, all the encoded information of the hrcm and desc file is compressed by the PPMD encoder's implementation 7-zip compressor.

4   System Requirements and Benchmark Data Sets

The algorithms' performance was evaluated using a standard AWS cloud virtual machine running Ubuntu 18.04.1 LTS (64 bit) and equipped with two Intel Xeon E5-2650 v4 processors clocked at 2.20 GHz and 32 GB of RAM. Utilizing the most recent JDK Java version, compilation and execution were completed.

The algorithms are tested on eight benchmark human genomes, such as the UCSC genomes hg17, hg18, hg19, and hg38; K131, K224 [3]; HuRef [9]; YH [21]. These data sets are 23.09 GB in size and include chromosomes 1 through 22 as well as the X and Y sex chromosomes. Additionally, tests were conducted on three Caenorhabditis elegans (ce6, ce10, ce11), two Saccharomyces cerevisiae (sacCer2, sacCer3), two Arabidopsis thaliana (TAIR9, TAIR10), three Oryza sativa (TIGR5.0, TIGR6.0, TIGR7.0), and a raw sequence corpus [15]. These benchmark data sets are widely used [10, 11, 14, 16, 17, 19, 24]. A very important data set in the current scenario is Novel Severe acute respiratory syndrome coronavirus 2 (denoted as SARS-CoV-2) that is obtained from the National Center for Biotechnology Information (NCBI) [2].

5   Results and Discussion

Three superb, cutting-edge genome sequence compression algorithms-HiRGC, SCCG, and HRCM-that have just been published are used and tested. Performance parameters used by most benchmark compression sequence algorithms are compression ratio, compression and decompression time, and memory usage. The data sets taken for testing is the human genome, other species, and SARS-CoV-2. The experimental value is obtained by averaging over three executions.

Table 1. Compressed file sizes (MB) of human genome data sets via cutting-edge methods

Reference Genome	Initial Target Size	Size of a compressed file by		
		HiRGC	SCCG	HRCM-B
hg17	20654.08	102.81	88.47	**81.21**
hg18	20654.08	96.92	81.87	**78.69**
hg19	20633.60	95.71	81.64	**78.18**
hg38	20643.84	95.71	81.43	**76.27**
HuRef	20930.56	251.20	233.10	**98.25**
K131	20664.32	124.25	109.18	**92.45**
K224	20664.32	124.90	109.97	**95.16**
YH	20664.32	128.72	112.89	**94.48**
Total Size	165509.12	1020.2	898.55	**694.7**

* Best values are indicated by bold

Table 1 lists the original and compressed file size on eight human genomes by HiRGC, SCCG, and HRCM-B. HRCM-B is the HRCM with batch processing mode. The last row of Table 1 is the total compressed size obtained of the individual algorithm by the sum over the individual value. HRCM-B performs better for the given data sets. The total compressed size for other species obtained by HRCM-B is 1484 KB, HiRGC is 2114 KB and SCCG is 2243 KB respectively. For SARS-CoV-2 data sets, the reference sequences are chosen from the same geographic region to have more similarity as shown by the researcher. From Asia's geographic region source oronasopharynx uncompressed size is 32839.2 KB, the compressed size by HiRGC is 303.2 KB, by SCCG is 303.2 KB, and HRCM-B is 32.95 KB respectively.

For eight human genomes, HiRGC and SCCG are slower than HRCM-B. The compression time of SCCG is greater than the sum of the compression times of HiRGC and HRCM-B because of two-level and two-type matching. For reference genome, YH compression time by HRCM-B is 19 min, by HiRGC and SCCCG 39 min and 70 min respectively. The total compression time for HRCM-B is 210 min, HiRGC is 301 min and SCCG is 654 min respectively. The sum of decompression time in other species obtained by HiRGC, SCCG, and HRCM-B is 109.9 S, 148.16 S, and 451.46 S respectively.

The peak compression memory usage on eight benchmark genomes is 5.09 GB, 8.5 GB, and 2.95 GB. The decompression memory usage is 0.88 GB, 6.75 GB, and 0.93 GB. SCCG takes more memory as it might build both local and global hash tables.

6 Conclusion

Genome sequence compression is crucial in bioinformatics, as more genome sequencing is required with the emergence of new virus variants. Compression techniques are useful for storing, transferring, and analyzing this data efficiently. Reference-based compression is generally more efficient than reference-free compression for compressing sequences of the same species. The three benchmark reference-based DNA sequence compression algorithms HiRGC, SCCG, and HRCM are examined and tested on FASTA-formatted data in this article using their default settings. To the best of our knowledge, a detailed comparative analysis of these algorithms using a sample sequence has not been examined in previous research. We provide a step-by-step analysis of the output on a small FASTA sample sequence. The performance of these algorithms is tested on Amazon AWS virtual cloud using JDK 16. We measure common parameters such as compressed size, compression time, decompression time, peak compression memory, and peak decompression memory usage. The HiRGC algorithm provides a good balance between space and time for pair-wise compression. SCCG offers higher compression gains at the cost of longer compression time in most cases. The overall performance of HRCM-B is excellent in a collection of benchmark data sets genome. This detailed explanation should encourage other researchers to explore reference-based compression on collections of FASTA/Multi-FASTA formatted genome sequences.

References

1. 7 zip. https://www.7-zip.org/. Accessed 11 March 2022
2. Ncbi virus. National Center for Biotechnology Information (2022). https://www.ncbi.nlm.nih.gov/labs/virus/vssi. Accessed 10 Mar 2022
3. Ahn, S.M., et al.: The first Korean genome sequence and analysis: full genome sequencing for a socio-ethnic group. Genome Res. **19**(9), 1622–1629 (2009)
4. Deorowicz, S., Danek, A., Niemiec, M.: Gdc 2: compression of large collections of genomes. Sci. Rep. **5**(1), 1–12 (2015)
5. Deorowicz, S., Grabowski, S.: Robust relative compression of genomes with random access. Bioinformatics **27**(21), 2979–2986 (2011)
6. Ji, Y., et al.: Fastdrc: Fast and scalable genome compression based on distributed and parallel processing. In: Algorithms and Architectures for Parallel Processing: 19th International Conference, ICA3PP 2019, Melbourne, VIC, Australia, December 9–11, 2019, Proceedings, Part II 19, pp. 313–319. Springer (2020)
7. Kumar, S., Agarwal, S.: Ranvijay: fast and memory efficient approach for mapping ngs reads to a reference genome. J. Bioinform. Comput. Biol. **17**(02), 1950008 (2019)

8. Kuruppu, S., Puglisi, S.J., Zobel, J.: Optimized relative lempel-ziv compression of genomes. In: Proceedings of the Thirty-Fourth Australasian Computer Science Conference-Volume 113, pp. 91–98 (2011)

9. Levy, S., Sutton, G., Ng, P.C., Feuk, L., Halpern, A.L., Walenz, B.P., Axelrod, N., Huang, J., Kirkness, E.F., Denisov, G., et al.: The diploid genome sequence of an individual human. PLoS Biol. **5**(10), e254 (2007)

10. Liu, Y., Peng, H., Wong, L., Li, J.: High-speed and high-ratio referential genome compression. Bioinformatics **33**(21), 3364–3372 (2017)

11. Liu, Y., Wong, L., Li, J.: Allowing mutations in maximal matches boosts genome compression performance. Bioinformatics **36**(18), 4675–4681 (2020)

12. Liu, Y., Yu, Z., Dinger, M.E., Li, J.: Index suffix-prefix overlaps by (w, k)-minimizer to generate long contigs for reads compression. Bioinformatics **35**(12), 2066–2074 (2019)

13. Liu, Y., Zhang, L.Y., Li, J.: Fast detection of maximal exact matches via fixed sampling of query k-mers and bloom filtering of index k-mers. Bioinformatics **35**(22), 4560–4567 (2019)

14. Ochoa, I., Hernaez, M., Weissman, T.: idocomp: a compression scheme for assembled genomes. Bioinformatics **31**(5), 626–633 (2015)

15. Pratas, D., Pinho, A.J.: A DNA sequence corpus for compression benchmark. In: Fdez-Riverola, F., Mohamad, M.S., Rocha, M., De Paz, J.F., González, P. (eds.) PACBB2018 2018. AISC, vol. 803, pp. 208–215. Springer, Cham (2019). https://doi.org/10.1007/978-3-319-98702-6_25

16. Saha, S., Rajasekaran, S.: Ergc: an efficient referential genome compression algorithm. Bioinformatics **31**(21), 3468–3475 (2015)

17. Saha, S., Rajasekaran, S.: Nrgc: a novel referential genome compression algorithm. Bioinformatics **32**(22), 3405–3412 (2016)

18. Shendure, J., Ji, H.: Next-generation dna sequencing. Nat. Biotechnol. **26**(10), 1135–1145 (2008)

19. Shi, W., Chen, J., Luo, M., Chen, M.: High efficiency referential genome compression algorithm. Bioinformatics **35**(12), 2058–2065 (2019)

20. Stephens, Z.D., et al.: Big data: astronomical or genomical? PLoS Biol. **13**(7), e1002195 (2015)

21. Wang, J., et al.: The diploid genome sequence of an Asian individual. Nature **456**(7218), 60–65 (2008)

22. Wetterstrand, K.A.: Dna sequencing costs: Data. Genome.gov (2022). https://www.genome.gov/sequencingcostsdata

23. Xie, X., Zhou, S., Guan, J.: Cogi: towards compressing genomes as an image. IEEE/ACM Trans. Comput. Biol. Bioinf. **12**(6), 1275–1285 (2015)

24. Yao, H., Ji, Y., Li, K., Liu, S., He, J., Wang, R.: Hrcm: an efficient hybrid referential compression method for genomic big data. BioMed research international 2019 (2019)

Classification of Text and Non-text Components Present in Offline Unconstrained Handwritten Documents Using Convolutional Neural Network

Bhaskar Sarkar, Saikh Risat, Asha Laha, Sanchari Pattanayak,
and Showmik Bhowmik$^{(\boxtimes)}$ (iD)

Ghani Khan Choudhury Institute of Engineering and Technology, Malda 732141,
India
showmik@gkciet.ac.in
https://www.gkciet.ac.in/

Abstract. Identification of text parts and non-text parts present in offline unconstrained handwritten manuscripts is an essential step toward the construction of an effective optical character recognition (OCR) system. To address the said issue researchers mostly extracted handcrafted features which capture the texture information in order to recognize text or non-text components separately. In presence of noise, these types of feature descriptors badly suffer. Therefore, in this paper, a Convolutional Neural Network (CNN) is designed to separate these extracted components. To evaluate the developed model, an in-house dataset of 150 pages is created. In this dataset, the present model has achieved 85.07% accuracy. The performance of the present model is compared with three recent works where it has outperformed these existing works.

Keywords: Convolution Neural Network · Handwriting · Text · Non-text · Classification

1 Introduction

Documents play a vital role in our society. It is one of the important mediums of information sharing and storage. However, preserving documents with vital information in their physical form is difficult. These may be lost due to various reasons like natural calamity, casual handling, aging etc. Only digitization of these documents is not enough. For effective handling and interpretation of digitized documents, OCR is required. The major obstacle in the path of developing an efficient OCR system is OCR can only deal with text parts. The presence of non-text can misguide the outcome of an OCR engine. Therefore, the separation of non-text is necessary at the early stage [1].

To isolate the non-text part from the text part in a document image, many challenges need to be overcome which are posed due to the variation in document

K. Dasgupta et al. (Eds.): CICBA 2023, CCIS 1955, pp. 43–50, 2024.
https://doi.org/10.1007/978-3-031-48876-4_4

background color, height, width, and orientation of the components. It becomes more difficult when we deal with unconstrained handwritten documents. Components in unconstrained handwritten documents have huge variations in shape size and orientation compared to printed documents. The major reason behind that is the wide diversity in the writing style of the writers, paper quality, ink quality etc. Moreover, in handwritten documents often text gets attached with non-text which can further misdirect the recognition process. For that reason, in the present scope of the work, a CNN is developed to isolate the text part from the non-text part present in a handwritten manuscript image.

The remaining part of this paper is arranged as; in Sect. 2, related literature is presented, in Sect. 3, the present method is described, in Sect. 4, experimental outcomes are discussed and at the end, in Sect. 5, the conclusion is given.

2 Related Literature

Despite the importance of this problem, very few works are available in the literature, which has addressed the isolation of text and non-text in unconstrained handwritten manuscripts. However, for printed documents a significant number of methods can be found [2,3]. Most of the early works on text non-text isolation, introduced for printed ones, consider hand crafted features like GLCM [4], HOG [5], etc. Later researchers started using deep learning based methods as well. For example, 1D and 2D CNN are used in [6] for document region classification in printed documents. Similarly, a CNN model inspired by the Lnet5 architecture is used in [7] for the said purpose. Although the mentioned methods achieved good results, their performance for the unconstrained handwritten documents is not estimated.

In contrast to the printed ones, very few attempts are made for text non-text isolation in offline unconstrained handwritten manuscripts. Moreover, most of these methods followed feature engineering based approach. For example, In [8], rotational invariant local binary pattern (RILBP) based feature is extracted from the connected components and then using multi-layer perceptron (MLP) these are identified as text or non-text. In [9], authors empirically show the performance of various local binary pattern based features in separating text and non-text components present in an unconstrained handwritten manuscripts. For that cause, authors consider five well known classifiers. Authors in [10], consider collision game based feature selection method to localize the informative regions of the images to classify these as text or non-text. In [11], a two-stage shape based method is used to classify the extracted component present in scientific handwritten documents.

The existing methods developed for text non-text isolation in unconstrained handwritten manuscripts have mostly extracted handcrafted features to perform the classification at the component level. For that purpose, LBP based feature descriptors are commonly used. LBP descriptors extract local texture patterns within a 3X3 window and thereby capture the texture information of an input image. Although, LBP has obtained good results, it is very sensitive to noise.

Therefore, in this work, a CNN is developed to classify the extracted components present in an unconstrained handwritten document. A CNN consists of a set of convolution layers. Every convolution layer extracts the local connectivity of the pixels in order to capture some primary features like edges, oriented edges, corner points etc. The use of local receptive fields facilitates dealing with distortion present in the input image. This is the reason CNN based classification model is considered in the present work.

3   Present Work

In this work, the isolation of text and non-text is performed at the connected component (CC) level. To do that initially the input images are binarized and then the region boundaries of the CCs are identified so that from the corresponding color image the gray version of the components can be extracted. Each extracted CC is then considered as a single input image. To recognize these CCs as text or non-text a convolutional neural network is developed (see Fig. 1). Therefore, in this section first, the component extraction process is explained then the architecture of the developed CNN is explained.

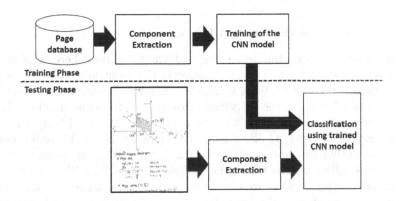

Fig. 1. Presents the diagram of the entire workflow

3.1   Connected Component Extraction

Let I be the input gray image. First, the input image I is binarized using the method present in [12] to generate the corresponding binary image B such that $\forall_{(x,y)} B(x,y) \in 0, 1$. Then every pixel in the binary image is labeled with an integer so that each adjacent pixel gets the same label. This generates the label image L. Using L the gray version of the CCs are extracted from I as follows,

Suppose the bounding box of the ith component CC_i in L is represented using the coordinate of the upper left corner i.e. (X_u^i, Y_u^i) and the lower right corner i.e. (X_R^i, Y_R^i) then the corresponding gray version of the component CC_i can be represented as

$$CC_i^{gray}(x,y) = \{I(x,y)|CC_i(x,y) = i \& X_u^i \le x \le X_R^i \& Y_u^i \le y \le Y_R^i\} \quad (1)$$

A pictorial representation of a sample extracted non-text and text component is given in Fig. 2.

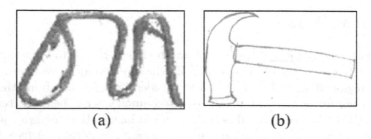

Fig. 2. Illustrates (a) image of a text component (b) image of a non-text component.

3.2 Architecture of the Present CNN

This subsection describes the architecture of the CNN used here. The present CNN model possesses 8 layers. The 1st layer is the input layer which considers an input image of size $64 \times 64 \times 1$. The 2nd layer is a convolution layer with 32 filters of size 5×5. As the activation function, ReLU is used. The 3rd, and 5th layers are max pooling layers with kernel size 2×2. The 4th layer is again a convolutional layer with 32 filters respectively of size 5×5. These layers have ReLU as an activation function. The output of the 5th layer is flattened and inputted to a fully connected layer with 128 neurons. The 7th layer is also a fully connected layer of 80 neurons. In this architecture, a dropout layer of 0.3 is used to avoid overfitting. The final layer possesses 2 neurons with softmax as the activation function as follows,

$$\sigma(X_i) = \frac{e^{X_i}}{\sum_{j=1}^{M} e^{X_j}} \quad for \ i = 1, 2, \ldots, K \quad (2)$$

here, X_i is the input vector and M is the number of classes here M = 2. A diagrammatic view of the present CNN model is provided in Fig. 3.

4 Experimental Outcomes

For the evaluation of the proposed method, an in-house dataset of 150 pages is prepared. For that purpose, handwritten class notes are collected which are

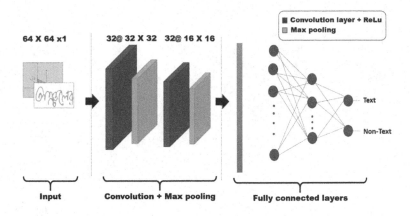

Fig. 3. Presents the architecture of the present CNN model

mostly written by the school level students. Initially, all the pages are converted to .bmp images by scanning these in 300 dpi using a flat board scanner. The sample-wise ground truth images are generated manually. Figure 4 presents a sample input image and the corresponding ground truth from the present dataset. From 150 pages total 31482 CCs are extracted. Out of these 31482 CCs, 23,608 are text, and 7,874 are non-text CCs.70% of the total CCs is used for training and 30% for testing. In training set, 16000 text and 5338 non-text components are considered whereas in test set 7,608 are text and 2,536 are non-text components. As the performance metric, in the present experiment Precision, Recall, F-Measure, and accuracy are used.

To train the present network, SGD optimizer is used. The learning rate is experimentally fixed to .001. As the loss function, the binary cross entropy B_L is used as

$$B_L = -\frac{1}{x}\Sigma_{i=1}^{x}p_i \log(p_i + (1 - p_i).\log(1 - p_i) \qquad (3)$$

During the training, 20% of the training data is randomly selected for validation. The detailed model loss and accuracy optimization history of the model during training with different epochs is depicted in Fig. 5.

The present model has obtained 85.07% accuracy on the test set. The performance of the present model is compared with some existing work in Table 1.

Table 1 says that the present CNN model has achieved significantly better results compared to these two existing methods. However, there are multiple occasions where the model has failed to correctly classify the components. Two such samples are given in Fig. 6.

Text misclassifications mostly occur in case of components like 'Ekar', 'akar', 'Hossoikar' etc. in Bangla and 'I', 'f' etc. in English. Non-text misclassifications mostly occur for the strikethrough or partially scribbled words which are considered here as non-text (see Fig. 6(b)). The probable reason could be the shape similarity.

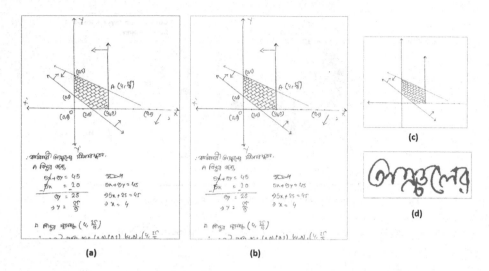

Fig. 4. Shows (a) sample input page from the current dataset (b) corresponding labeled image where blue colored CCs are non-text and red colored CCs are text. (c) non-text CC, and (d) text CC. (Color figure online)

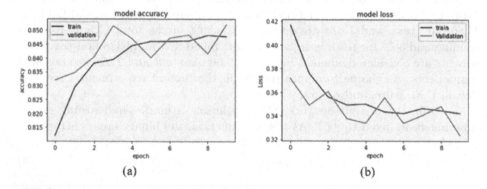

Fig. 5. Illustrates the performance history in the form of (a) accuracy vs epoch chart (b) Loss vs epoch chart.

Table 1. Performance assessment of the present model along with some existing methods in the current dataset.

Method	Text			Non-text			
	PR	RE	FM	PR	RE	FM	ACC
Bhowmik et al. [8],	0.849	0.939	0.892	0.68	0.489	0.569	71.4
Ghosh et al. [9],	0.855	0.912	0.883	0.625	0.531	0.574	72.5
Bhowmik et al. [2],	0.863	0.924	0.888	0.685	0.601	0.643	79.8
Present	0.877	0.942	0.901	0.713	0.512	0.591	85.07
PR: Precision, RE: Recall, FM: F-Measure, ACC: Accuracy(in %)							

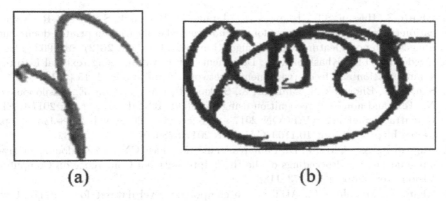

Fig. 6. Illustrates cases of misclassification (a) text component written in Bangla misclassified as non-text (b) Non-text component misclassified as text.

5 Conclusion

Isolation of Text and non-text separation in offline unconstrained handwritten manuscripts is a very crucial task to perform in order to build an effective OCR system. This is because OCR systems mostly emphasize on text portion. Therefore, presence of non-text can degrade their performance. Despite its importance, only a few methods are introduced in the literature. In the developed methods, researchers mainly followed feature engineering based methods. To do that LBP based features are commonly used. LBP features can effectively capture texture information from the input image but suffer badly in presence of noise. To cope with this issue in this paper, a CNN is developed to classify extracted components from unconstrained handwritten manuscripts as text or non-text. CNNs can effectively capture local connectivity and therefore estimate the texture information efficiently. Even in presence of noise, these models often perform well compare to the traditional handcrafted features. To evaluate the developed model, an in-house dataset of 150 pages is generated. The present dataset contains 23,608 text and 7,874 non-text components. In the present dataset, the developed model has outperformed two recent methods.

In future, the authors plan to prepare a larger database with more real world handwritten pages and to develop a more sophisticated model to minimize the misclassifications of the components due to shape similarity.

References

1. Bhowmik, S., Sarkar, R., Nasipuri, M., Doermann, D.: Text and non-text separation in offline document images: a survey. Int. J. Doc. Anal. Recognit. **21**(1–2), 1–20 (2018)
2. Bhowmik, S., Kundu, S., Sarkar, R.: BINYAS: a complex document layout analysis system. Multimed. Tools Appl., 8471–8504 (2020). https://doi.org/10.1007/s11042-020-09832-3

3. Ghosh, S., Hassan, S.K., Khan, A.H., Manna, A., Bhowmik, S., Sarkar, R.: Application of texture-based features for text non-text classification in printed document images with novel feature selection algorithm. Soft. Comput. **26**(2), 891–909 (2022)
4. Oyedotun, O.K., Khashman, A.: Document segmentation using textural features summarization and feedforward neural network. Appl. Intell., 1–15 (2016)
5. Sah, A.K., Bhowmik, S., Malakar, S., Sarkar, R., Kavallieratou, E., Vasilopoulos, N.: Text and non-Text recognition using modified HOG descriptor. In: 2017 IEEE Calcutta Conference, CALCON 2017 - Proceedings, 2018, vol. 2018-Janua, pp. 64–68. https://doi.org/10.1109/CALCON.2017.8280697
6. Augusto Borges Oliveira, D., Palhares Viana, M.: Fast CNN-based document layout analysis. In: Proceedings of the IEEE International Conference on Computer Vision Workshops, pp. 1173–1180 (2017)
7. Khan, T., Mollah, A.F.: AUTNT - a component level dataset for text non-text classification and benchmarking with novel script invariant feature descriptors and D-CNN. Multimed. Tools Appl. **78**(22), 32159–32186 (2019). https://doi.org/10.1007/s11042-019-08028-8
8. Bhowmik, S., Sarkar, R., Nasipuri, M.: Text and non-text separation in handwritten document images using local binary pattern operator, vol. 458 (2017)
9. Ghosh, S., Lahiri, D., Bhowmik, S., Kavallieratou, E., Sarkar, R.: Text/non-text separation from handwritten document images using LBP based features: an empirical study. J. Imaging **4**(4), 57 (2018)
10. Ghosh, M., Ghosh, K.K., Bhowmik, S., Sarkar, R.: Coalition game based feature selection for text non-text separation in handwritten documents using LBP based features. Multimed. Tools Appl., 1–21 (2020)
11. Bhowmik, S., Kundu, S., De, B.K., Sarkar, R., Nasipuri, M.: A two-stage approach for text and non-text separation from handwritten scientific document images. In: Advances in Intelligent Systems and Computing, 2019, vol. 699. https://doi.org/10.1007/978-981-10-7590-23
12. Bhowmik, S., Sarkar, R., Das, B., Doermann, D.: GiB: a game theory inspired binarization technique for degraded document images. IEEE Trans. Image Process. **28**(3) (2019). https://doi.org/10.1109/TIP.2018.2878959

Motion Detection Using Three Frame Differencing and CNN

Tamal Biswas[✉], Diptendu Bhattacharya, Gouranga Mandal, and Teerthankar Das[✉]

Department of Computer Science and Engineering, NIT Agartala, Tripura, India
tamal.cse01@gmail.com, teerthankardas86@gmail.com

Abstract. The three-frame difference is a renowned tactic for detecting moving items. According to the idea, the existence of a moving object can be inferred by removing three subsequent image frames that display the moving object's edges. However, information is lost as a result of the method because these edges do not convey all of the information about the moving item. To obtain all of the information about a moving object, post-processing techniques like morphological operations, optical flow, and combining these techniques must be used. In this study, we introduce a novel method to detect moving objects in video sequences without any post-processing steps, dubbed Selected Three Frame Difference (STFD). We first provide an algorithm that selects three images while accounting for the local maximum value of frame disparities rather than employing successive. The logical operator is applied to three frames of three different picture variations that contain non-overlapping object frames. We mathematically show that the entire moving object is always discernible in the second image that was selected. We investigated the proposed strategy on a dataset collected in our lab and a public benchmark dataset. We compared the effectiveness of our approach to the three-frame difference method and background subtraction-based traditional moving object recognition methods on a few sample videos selected from different datasets.

Keywords: Convoluted Neural Network · Frame Difference · Three Frame Difference · Detection of Moving Objects

1 Introduction

Understanding human activity from a video is a significant area of computer vision research that has become increasingly important in recent years. The availability of inexpensive hardware like video cameras, recent advancements in computer vision, and a wide range of innovative and exciting applications like visual surveillance and personal identification are the main drivers of the growing interest in human motion analysis. Finding moving objects in the two provided images is the goal of motion detection. Finding an object's motion can also help with object recognition. The primary goal of the research is to identify pixels that belong to the same object. However, the current study is predicated on the following notions.

(1) If you wish to isolate motion, a well-fixed camera is essential.

K. Dasgupta et al. (Eds.): CICBA 2023, CCIS 1955, pp. 51–63, 2024.
https://doi.org/10.1007/978-3-031-48876-4_5

(2) Consistent, flicker-free lighting.
(3) A background with contrast.
(4) High frame rate and resolution [3].

The majority of the aforementioned issues have been the focus of several research projects conducted globally. Here are some of the issues that were raised. Using non-hardhat use (NHU) and the deep learning approach, a video surveillance system may be able to detect live objects in a remote field. In order to regulate traffic, a multi-sensor video monitoring system is employed to access the road capacity. A cutting-edge Smart IS technology is used to track MAC ids and log position information in portable Smartphone Units. (PSUs). The most recent whereabouts of the suspected persons are then ascertained using the Latest Location Retrieval method. A distributed, cloud-edge smart video surveillance system is provided for the protection of important structures. To address the problems with motion detection, researchers have tried various approaches. This study suggests a dynamic acquisition method for frames with various resolutions depending on the presence of suspicious item movement. For real-time video surveillance, this technique can be utilized to intelligently optimize memory space. The frames that contain any ongoing suspicious item movement are highlighted in high-quality recordings.

The following is a summary of this paper's main contributions:

- To give the suspected pixels and locations more weight, the dynamic-patch idea is applied. Pixels that are suspicious are given a smaller patch size.
- When using real-time video surveillance, a patch-based frame differencing technique is used to quickly and effectively identify suspicious items in a series of frames.
- The "Contrast Limited Adaptive histogram Equalization (CLAHE) based on Color Channel" is applied to all frames as a post-processing step for improved contrast adjustment in order to more precisely identify suspicious things.
- The frames that appear to move suspiciously in comparison to earlier frames are saved in high resolution. These frames are given a lot of attention.
- To conserve memory, low-resolution frames that have no suspicious movement but had a suspicious movement in the previous 100 frames are recorded. These frames are given less weight.
- To conserve memory, the last 100 frames that haven't shown any suspicious movement for several preceding frames are skipped. These frames are assigned no weight.
- The suggested approach has more cleverly addressed the issue of real-time long-duration video surveillance's storage capacity scarcity without degrading the video quality of suspicious moments.

2   Literature Review

Selected Three Frame Differencing (STFD) is used to detect an object is proposed. First, select three images with local maxima value of frame difference and finally, this frame difference is applied for logical operation for moving object detection [5]. It represents to introduces a novel frame-based technique for distinguishing moving items from a static background scene [3]. The numerous techniques for object identification and tracking in real-time video surveillance to identify objects like faces or to identify persons or vehicles in a security camera [6]. In order To recover lost detail through a super-resolution process, patch-based super-resolution looks for identical patches between an upscale non-key-frame and the accompanying, high-resolution key-frame [8]. Patches are only formed at the boundary in the proposed work since occlusion first happens there. The occluded patches can be recognized and their related patches' colors can be changed by using the patch-based framework [10]. Frame differencing is utilized to track an object's movement, and a contour tracking technique is employed to detect it [12]. In Approaches to patch-based DE noising, patches are made from the input noisy image. After that, the blocks are handled separately to get an estimation of the actual pixel values. This section presents different patch-based image-DE noising methods and analyses how effective they are at picture-DE noising [13]. It is based on a brand-new patch-based energy-minimization formulation that unifies alignment and reconstruction through an equation we refer to as the HDR picture synthesis equation [16]. Using this method, the image is filled patch by patch. It looks for replacement parts from the intact parts of the image that are well-matching. These patches may alternatively be referred to as candidate patches. The hole was patched using the dynamic patch selection method. Small target patches are applied in the high-frequency region. The patches are chosen using an angle-aware patch-matching technique from a context-aware source region. For the best match from a patch, the picture is searched from other areas of the image [17]. All current basic and non-trivial extensions of patch-based DE noising techniques for multi-frame images are outperformed by the extension [18]. For the groups of patches, various models have been put forth. Generally speaking, more sophisticated models take longer to run but produce better results. However, there are also differences between the methods suggested in the literature and the modeling of the groups of patches. The type of patches, the search techniques used to identify clusters of related patches, and the weights used in the aggregation might all change. Because of this, it is challenging to gauge the patch model's true influence on the outcomes [19]. It offers a brand-new frame difference-based technique to isolate moving objects from a scene in the background. The static camera first records the first frame, and then a series of frames are recorded at regular intervals after that. After determining the absolute difference between the successive frames, the system then records the difference image. The difference image is converted into a binary image in the fourth and final step. Morphological filtering is then used to reduce noise [3]. The difference between the image of the current frame and the backdrop frame is referred to as background subtraction. A differential operation is carried out in the two adjacent video frames in a sequence using the frame difference method. Due to its low computational complexity and ease of implementation, it is the simplest and fastest way to identify moving objects. When the object's speed is too low, though, it will lead to the worst issue, which is inaccurate target recognition. The most popular approach for detecting moving objects. After creating the backdrop model, the background model is then subtracted to create the current frame image. The pixel area of these coordinates in the current image is identified as the foreground motion area if the pixel threshold is larger than or equal to a specific threshold, otherwise, it is identified as the background area [4]. By subtracting the current frame from the background frame—which required background modeling before removing the object to obtain the background frame—moving object identification is accomplished. Global resolving is used to acquire the moving object's foreground image. A supervised machine learning approach is used to categorize the detected item using a Support Vector Machine (SVM), which is utilized to classify the identified object [20]. During the initialization stage, the backdrop representation is produced by averaging a number of photos over time. If the difference between the input image and the background model is greater than a learned threshold, which is calculated according to the particular approach, pixels are then identified as foreground. The background model is then updated over time with fresh photos using a variety of techniques to accommodate dynamic scene changes [21]. It offers a brand-new background subtraction technique for locating foreground objects in dynamic situations with moving foliage and flags. The majority of approaches that have been put out so far modify the range of background image alterations that are permitted in accordance with training background image samples. As a result, the detection sensitivity drops at pixels with large allowed ranges. The detection sensitivity can be increased if we can reduce the ranges by examining the input photos [22]. A probability density function for each individual pixel is present in the scene model in the case of common pixel-level background subtraction. If a pixel's new value is accurately predicted by its density function, it is regarded as a background pixel. The simplest model for a static scene might simply be a snapshot of the scene without the obtruding items [23]. The inter-frame difference method extracts a moving target using a differential operation on a continuous video frame picture. It is easily adaptable to environmental changes. However, using this method to detect moving targets results in a cavity effect, which reduces target detection accuracy. The fundamental goal of background subtraction is to create a backdrop model, from which the moving target is extracted by subtracting the current frame image. To detect a whole moving object, background subtraction primarily relies on establishing a stable background model in order to acquire a complete foreground feature [24]. The suggested moving object detection technique uses high-speed background subtraction. Convolution filtering is used to smooth out the images once the video has been converted to streams, which eliminates high-frequency noise components. The background removal technique with adaptive threshold is then applied to the smoothed pictures to find objects that are present in the background image [25]. Since it may be utilized in numerous applications, including intelligent and autonomous video surveillance, motion analysis, human-machine interaction applications, and many more, detecting abandoned objects from video frames is a developing study area. Nowadays, it's fairly usual for people to have security systems installed in their homes, apartments, workplaces, and other locations so they can independently assess security hazards. Having surveillance systems in place at both public and private locations to maintain constant security checks has become one of the fundamental requirements for public safety purposes. The identification of abandoned objects has recently been successfully accomplished using the Background Subtraction technique. The system's capabilities go beyond simple object detection, which is why it is referred to as an advanced and intelligent abandoned object-detecting system [26]. The background removal techniques take into account more than just the single visible optical channel (such as the audio and the infrared channels). The opportunities that these approaches offer up are quite intriguing in addition to the description of fresh types of background; in particular, the multi-sensor route appears to be well-suited to resolve or simplify a number of venerable background removal issues [27]. An effective and extremely accurate update mechanism is used after the estimated pixel density, allowing our system to automatically adjust to operational conditions that are constantly changing. We suggest a reference implementation of our approach in hardware that is reconfigurable, delivering both sufficient performance and reasonable power usage. Demanding floating point arithmetic operations are mapped in reconfigurable hardware using a High-Level Synthesis design, showcasing quick prototyping and real-time customization [28]. It is a technology that detects the motion region by comparing the differences between the current image and the background image, and it may typically offer data that includes object information [29]. Using a model of how each pixel appears when it is a part of video frame classes, we may categorize each pixel based on the moving item in the foreground and backdrop conditional environment [30]. In order to give smaller patches for darker pixels and larger patches for brighter pixels, a dynamic patch is implemented to achieve frame inversion [39]. To prevent excessive augmentation for the darker part of frames, the dynamic-patch concept is applied. Darker pixels receive a smaller patch size, and vice versa [40].

3 Proposed Methodology

Object detection and tracking are the two phases of the proposed CNN-based moving object detection system. Figure 1 displays the generalized block diagram of the proposed system.

Fig. 1. Block Diagram Of The Proposed System.

The video is fed into the system in this system as an input. Extracting frames allows for additional processing. Deep learning techniques are used to process the two primary algorithms, object detection, and object tracking. The flow below provides a detailed explanation of object detection. The system has trouble detecting many objects when utilizing a computer vision algorithm because of factors including light fluctuation, lighting, and occlusion [2].

3.1 Input Video

Image processing is a technique for applying various procedures to an image in order to improve it or extract some relevant information from it. It is a kind of signal processing where the input is an image and the output can either be another image or features or characteristics related to that image.

3.2 Frame Extraction

Key frame extraction is a potent method that uses a set of summary key-frames to represent video sequences in order to implement video content. The majority of key frame extraction techniques now in use do not comply with the criteria for video copyright protection. The key-frame for video copyright protection has a few distinctive characteristics. So, before video pre-processing and key frame extraction, the key frame for video copyright protection is defined.

The following three requirements should be fulfilled by the key-frames.

(1) A critical frame's grey value falls within a specific range to allow viewers to form their own opinions about the video's subject matter.
(2) To satisfy temporal features and distinguish them from the brief promotional trailer, the final key-frame sequence must be organized chronologically in accordance with the original video sequence.
(3) Key frame redundancy is permitted when necessary to guarantee the times or intervals during the processing of video content.

3.3   Motion Detection of 3 Frame Differencing

By removing successive images, the moving regions are found. It is expected that a stationary camera is used to record image sequences. Let's assume that ilk (x, y) represents the Kath frame's intensity. The following formula is used to calculate the difference image Id (x, y) utilized to detect moving regions.

$$(x, y) = |Ik + 1(x, y) - (x, y)| \tag{1}$$

where the coordinates are x and y. The difference image is subjected to the median filter in order to eliminate noise. Then, to convert grayscale photos to binary images, the global threshold value Td is utilized.

$$(x, y) = \{0 : (x, y) <= Td \ 1 : \ otherwise \tag{2}$$

where the binary image at the coordinates (x, y) exists. The TFD method was first created using frame difference, followed by the application of a logical operator from a series of images. With this technique, three successive photos are combined to produce two outputs for frame differences. Applying the logical "AND" (&) operator to these output frames calculated as follows allows the moving regions to be spotted.

$$Ib = If1 \& If2 \tag{3}$$

where If is the three-frame difference binary output of images, If1 is the difference between kit and (k + 1) the images and If2 is the difference between (k + 1) the and (k + 2) the images. [5].

3.4   Get Object Location

A reference point known as the origin must be mentioned in order to describe the location of an object. A reference point is a constant location in space that is used to measure one object's distance or position in relation to another. The goal of this system is to locate the path of a moving obstacle, hence determining the object's coordinates in the real world is not necessary and does not fall under the same heading.

The suggested approach's goals are:

- To create a new technique of target identification and position specification by analysing images of objects falling from the sky to the ground, then determining the location of the item to determine how far it is from the target point in relation to the centre.
- To create a methodology that can accurately detect and locate a position using just one digital camera.
- To create an approach that can be used on areas that are both flat and rise/tilt.
- To provide an automated system for identifying and pinpointing the location of an object that is falling to the ground from the air [37].

3.5   Tracking Object Using Cnn

The crucial phases of a computer vision algorithm are object detection and tracking. Due to the variances in the scenes, robust object detection is a challenge. The ability to track an item under occlusion conditions is another difficult task. The object tracking method is also given the location of the object that was spotted. For reliable object detection, a brand-new CNN-based object tracking method is employed. The suggested method can find the item in various lighting and occlusion conditions. The suggested method had a 90.88% accuracy rate on self-generated image sequences. Their locations are crucial for beginning the tracking procedure after the object has been detected. In this method, a tracking algorithm based on convolutional neural networks (CNNs) is employed in place of a traditional computer vision-based technique [2] (Figs. 2 and 3).

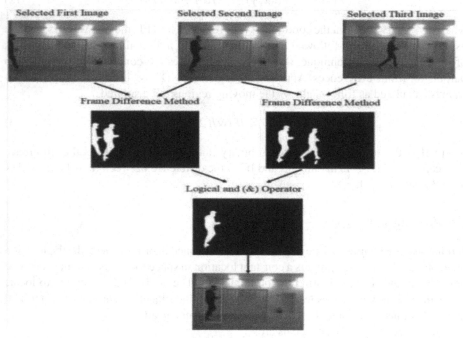

Fig. 2. The output images produced from the output frames of our proposed STFD approach using the logical u "AND" (&) operator.

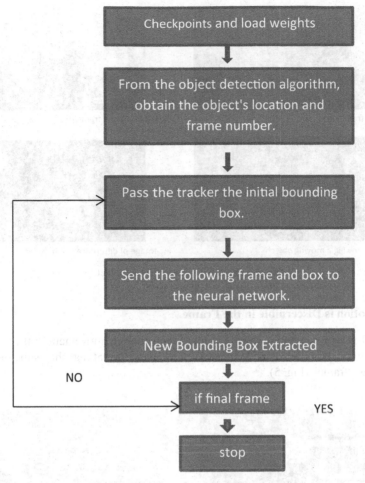

Fig. 3. Flowchart for object Detection.

4   Experimental Results

The results of image sequences created using this technique are displayed in the following figures.

4.1   When the Frames Are not Moving

The binary output picture is black when there is no movement in the image sequences, indicating that there is not even a single pixel of difference between the two images (Fig. 4).

Initial input frame (a).

Second input frame (b).

Two frame showing a moving object.

Image of difference in binary form.

Fig. 4. There is no frame in the object.

4.2 If Motion is Discernible in the Frame

Movement is represented by a white colour when there is movement in the scene and a black colour when there is no movement in a binary format that shows the difference between two frames (Fig. 5).

Initial input frame (a).

Second input frame (b).

Two frame showing a moving object.

Image of difference in binary form.

Fig. 5. There is no movement in the object.

4.3 Limitation

The recommended method also detects motion resulting from air movement. Even when no objects are moving, the camera induces motion and creates gaps in the binary output image since it doesn't remain stationary while the air moves (Fig. 6).

Initial input frame (a).   Input second frame (b).

Fig. 6. Frame differencing between two consecutive frames.

5 Conclusion and Future Work

The whole information of moving objects is more precisely acquired than with the TFD approach, which is a noteworthy outcome that we found. We noticed from the testing findings that the suggested algorithm's accuracy is rather high when there is only one moving detected item accessible, regardless of whether the setting is indoors or outside. When more than one moving item is recognised in the same scene, accuracy suffers and noisy results are produced. Despite these unfavourable findings, STFD method accuracy is still much greater than TFD method. Studying the frame difference method's underlying principles and finding solutions to the many issues is the work's clear cornerstone. The experiment demonstrates that the strategy performs well and is effective. Future improvements might warn the user by email, SMS with multimedia, or video recording and web streaming. In this paper The proposed work will be enhanced by including more capabilities to prevent motion-based household items like curtains, ceiling fans, table fans, wall clocks, etc. Moving household items shouldn't be labelled as suspicious. Real-time surveillance video improvement will also be done in dimly lit or gloomy environments utilising sophisticated techniques.

Acknowledgement. The National Institute of Technology Agartala, Tripura, India, provided a top-notch research environment, including the research laboratory, which the authors would like to recognize.

References

1. Singla, N.: Motion detection based on frame difference method. International Journal of Information & Computation Technology. ISSN 0974–2239 **4**(15), 1559–1565 (2014)
2. Simsek, E., Ozyer, B.: Selected three frame difference method for moving object detection. International Journal of Intelligent Systems and Applications in Engineering ISSN:2147–67992147–6799
3. Patel, S., Kumar, K.S.: Different techniques of object detection and tracking. In: Video Monitoring System (2020)
4. Glaister, J., Chan, C., Frankovich, M., Tang, A., Wong, A.: Hybrid video compression using selective keyframe identification and patch-based super-resolution. 2011 IEEE International Symposium on Multimedia
5. Suresh, S., Chitra, K., Deepak, P.: Patch based frame work for occlusion detection in multi human tracking. 2013 International Conference on Circuits, Power and Computing Technologies [ICCPCT-2013]
6. Ghode, N., Bhagat, P.H.: Motion detection using continuous frame difference and contour based tracking. Proceedings of the Third International Conference on Trends in Electronics and Informatics (ICOEI 2019) IEEE xplore Part Number: CFP19J32-ART; ISBN: 978–1–5386–9439–8
7. Alkinani, M.H., El-Sakka, M.R.: Patch-based models and algorithms for image denoising: a comparative review between patch-based images demonising methods for additive noise reduction. Alkinani and El-Sakka EURASIP Journal on Image and Video Processing, 58 (2017). https://doi.org/10.1186/s13640-017-0203-4
8. Sen, P., Kalantari, N.K., Yaesoubi, M., Darabi, S., Goldman, D.B., Shechtman, E.: Robust Patch-Based HDR Reconstruction of Dynamic Scenes. https://dl.acm.org/toc/tog/2012/31/6
9. Sonawane, R.P., Yawalkar, P.M.: A review on image in painting techniques. International Journal of Engineering Research & Technology (IJERT) **9**(6) (2020). ISSN: 2278–0181
10. Bodduna, K., Weickert, J.: Enhancing patch-based methods with inter- frame connectivity for denoising multi-frame images. 2019 IEEE International Conference on Image Processing (ICIP)
11. Arias, P., Facciolo, G., Morel, J.-M.: A Comparison of Patch-Based Models in Video Denoising. https://doi.org/10.1109/IVMSPW.2018.8448824
12. Xu, Z., Zhang, D., Du, L.: Moving object detection based on improved three frame difference and background subtraction. 2017 International Conference on Industrial Informatics - Computing Technology, Intelligent Technology, Industrial Information Integration
13. Kumar, M.: Moving object detection and classification for visual surveillance system. Malaviya National Institute of Technology Jaipur (2017)
14. Huerta, I., Amato, A., Roca, X., González, J.: Exploiting Multiple Cues in Motion Segmentation based on Background Subtraction. https://doi.org/10.1016/j.neucom.2011.10.036
15. Seki, M., Wada, T., Fujiwara, H., Sumi, K.: Background Subtraction based on Cooccurrence of Image Variations. https://doi.org/10.1109/CVPR.2003.1211453
16. Zoran Zivkovic , Ferdinand van der Heijden.: Efficient adaptive density estimation per image pixel for the task of background subtraction , doi:https://doi.org/10.1016/j.patrec.2005.11.005

17. Zuo, J., Jia, Z., Yang, J., Kasabov, N.: Moving Target Detection Based on Improved Gaussian Mixture Background Subtraction in Video Images. https://doi.org/10.1109/ACCESS.2019.2946230

18. Hanchinamani, S.R., Sarkar, S., Bhairannawar, S.S.: Design and implementation of high speed background subtraction algorithm for moving object detection. 6th International Conference On Advances In Computing & Communications, ICACC 2016 (2016)

19. Hargude, S., Idate, S.R.: Intelligent Surveillance System Using Background Subtraction Technique. https://doi.org/10.1109/ICCUBEA.2016.7860046

20. Cristani, M., Farenzena, M., Bloisi, D., Murino, V.: Background Subtraction for Automated Multisensor Surveillance: EURASIP Journal on Advances in Signal Processing Volume 2010, Article ID 343057. https://doi.org/10.1155/2010/343057

21. Makantasis, K., Nikitakis, A., Doulamis, A., Doulamis, N., Papaefstathiou, Y.: Data-Driven Background Subtraction Algorithm for in-Camera Acceleration in Thermal Imagery (2017). arXiv:1608.00229v2 [cs.CV]

22. Rakibe, R.S., Patil, B.D.: Background subtraction algorithm based human motion detection. International Journal of Scientific and Research Publications 3(5) (2013). ISSN 2250–3153

23. Chinchkhede, D.W., Uke, N.J.: Image segmentation in video sequences using modified background substraction. International Journal of Computer Science & Information Technology (IJCSIT) 4(1) (2012)

24. Mandal, G., De, P., Bhattacharya, D.: Real-time fast fog removal approach for assisting drivers during dense fog on hilly roads. J Ambient Intell Human Comput 12, 9877–9889 (2021). https://doi.org/10.1007/s12652-020-02734-0

25. Mandal, G., Bhattacharya, D., De, P.: Real-time fast low-light vision enhancement for driver during driving at night. J Ambient Intell Human Comput 13, 789–798 (2022). https://doi.org/10.1007/s12652-021-02930-6

26. Mane, S., Mangale, S.: Moving object detection and tracking using convolutional neural networks. Proceedings of the Second International Conference on Intelligent Computing and Control Systems (ICICCS 2018) IEEE Xplore Compliant Part Number: CFP18K74-ART; ISBN:978–1–5386–2842–3

27. Kesrarat, W., Sortrakul, T.: An object location specifying methodology using one camera. International Journal of Uncertainty, Fuzziness and Knowledge-Based Systems 9(6), 685–702 (2001)

Advance Detection of Diabetic Retinopathy: Deep Learning Approach

Ankur Biswas[1]([✉]) [iD] and Rita Banik[2] [iD]

[1] Tripura Institute of Technology, Narsingarh, West Tripura, India
abiswas.tit@gmail.com
[2] ICFAI University, Tripura, West Tripura, India
ritabanik@iutripura.edu.in

Abstract. Diabetic retinopathy (DR) is an ophthalmological ailment wherein the diabetic individuals suffer from the formation of blockages, lesions, or hemorrhages predominantly in light-sensitive portion of said retina. Because of the increase in blood sugar, vascular blockage drives new vessel creation, giving rise to mesh-like patterns. As lack of timely treatment of DR results in vision loss, early diagnosis and professional assistance plays a crucial role. This can be achieved with a computer-aided diagnostic (CAD) system based on retinal fundus images. Various steps are involved in a CAD system, including as the detection, segmentation, and categorization of abnormalities in fundus images. This study is an effort to expedite the first screening of DR so as to meet the need of the increasing population of diabetic patients in the future. On publicly accessible datasets, we have trained and validated reliable classification algorithms enabling timely detection of DR. Convolutional neural networks (CNN)-based advanced deep learning models are used to fully use data-driven machine learning techniques for this purpose. We also defined the issue as the detection of DR of any grade (Grades 1–4) vs. No-DR in a binary classification (Grade 0). For training the models, we used 56,839 fundus pictures from the EyePACS dataset. On a test set from EyePACS, the models were put to the test (14,210 images). As compared to the established methods, experimental findings demonstrate superior outcomes through DenseNet with pre-trained weights. In the model's evaluation on the EyePACS datasets, it achieved good results with an of 97.55% in binary and 78% in multiclass-classification.

Keywords: Diabetic retinopathy · Machine learning · CNN · fundus images · EyePACS

1 Introduction

A severe public health issue, diabetes mellitus now distresses 463 million of individuals globally and is predicted to exceed 700 million [1]. Diabetes is a condition that worsens when insulin levels are low, increasing blood glucose levels which in turn effects the retinal nerves, heart, and kidneys. About 33% of diabetics also develop eye disorders, the most prominent of them being diabetic retinopathy (DR), which is associated to diabetes

K. Dasgupta et al. (Eds.): CICBA 2023, CCIS 1955, pp. 64–77, 2024.
https://doi.org/10.1007/978-3-031-48876-4_6

[2]. Any person suffering from diabetes, irrespective of severity can advance to DR, characterized by growing vascular disruptions that causes the capillaries of retina to enlarge and leaking of fluid and blood caused by chronic hyperglycemia [3]. If DR reaches a severe level, visual loss could occur. Hence, patients with diabetes who have suffered from the illness for a prolonged period of time are more likely to have DR. Frequent eye scanning is crucial for diabetics' individuals to detect and medicate DR initially in order to limit the risk of blindness [4]. Several forms of lesions detected on a retinal scan might be employed to determine DR. Microaneurysms (MA), haemorrhages (HM), and soft and hard exudates (EX) are the lesions [5, 6]. Even if the initial stages of DR are often symptomless, neural retinal impairment and clinically undetected microvascular changes could occur. Therefore, diabetics should get periodic eye exams since early diagnosis and treatment of the condition are vital. Given that treating hyperglycemia, hyperlipidemia, and hypertension is the major preventive strategy, early detection of DR is even more important. Timely detection and identification [7] can prevent visual loss or slow the progression of DR. The numerous signs of DR include blood vessel leakage, aberrant blood vessel growth, and injury to nerve tissue, retinal enlargement, and aneurysms [8]. Moreover, utilizing the present accessible treatments like laser photocoagulation, the risk of loss of sight is reduced by 98% if proliferative retinopathy and diabetic maculopathy are treated early in the course of the illness.

The stages in DR are also classified as: proliferate, severe, moderate, and mild which are graded as grades 4, 3, 2 and 1 respectively [9]. Miscommunication, delayed findings, therapy, and other factors make DR identification difficult. The abnormalities induced in the retina are recognized in the early stages by screening the retina. Because DR is asymptomatic at first, many individuals are uninformed about the illness. Grading manually in DR detection needs more knowledge and experience. An expert can also diagnose DR based on the aberrant alterations associated with the disease's vascular anomalies. As a result, screening a diabetic individual is recommended [10]. The progression of lesions in the fundus scans aids in the early detection of the DR. To give computerized scanning systems with color generated visuals, several initiatives are made nowadays. However, it is still thought that DR detection is a challenge, and additional advancements are needed to create a different approach. A computer vision-based system and fundus images are also taken into consideration, in addition to the development of an intelligent diagnosis system [11]. Presently, automatic computer-aided diagnosis (CAD) is being used extensively due to its precision and dependability of quick diagnoses. These automated approaches for DR detection are more effective than a manual diagnostic in terms of cost and time savings. The quality and accuracy of the fundus image extraction methodology in combination with effective image processing approaches for recognizing the abnormalities strongly influence the screening approach's performance. On the other hand, a manual diagnostic system is more labor-intensive and prone to error than automatic ones. Methods built on machine learning (ML) and deep learning (DL) are more frequently employed to maximize results and reduce effort. In recent years, DR detection and classification have made extensive use of DL. Even with the integration of several heterogeneous sources, it may still learn the characteristics of the supplied data. Numerous DL-based techniques exist, including convolutional neural networks (CNNs), auto encoders, restricted Boltzmann machines (RBMs), and sparse coding [12]. In contrast to ML methods, the efficiency of these techniques enhances as the quantity of training sample grows since the number of learnt features increases [13]. Additionally, DL techniques eliminated the need for manual feature extraction.

In medical image analysis, CNNs are more often employed than the other techniques, and they are also much more efficient [14]. On the ImageNet dataset [15], many pre-trained CNN architectures are accessible, like AlexNet, Inception-v3 [16], and ResNet [17]. In order to expedite the training, some researchers used transfer learning from these pre-trained networks, whilst other studies create their own CNNs from start for classification [18]. However, there is still opportunity to build low-cost DL techniques which offer high classification results with no intricate and costly architectures, given that deep-learning-based classification approaches for retinal blood vessels have shown to be more effective and reliable (low number of trainable parameters). Therefore, in this study we present the neural network architecture with three pre-trained networks: DenseNet, MobileNet and Inception for classification of DR. We present two modes of classification for DR: Binary (to initially check the presence of DR in an individual) and multi-class (four classes viz. Mild, Moderate DR, Severe DR and Proliferate DR). Publicly available fundus image dataset— EyePACs (Eye Picture Archive Communication System) [19] were employed to assess the performance of our suggested task. Investigational data demonstrate that our neural network architecture pre-trained with DenseNet is better in comparison to the standard approaches for retinal image classification in binary and also multiclass modes. The remainder of the paper is organized as follows: Section II presents the prior researches relating DL based DR grading. In Section III, we presented the methodologies of the approach shown in the study. Section IV presents the results obtained through the advanced models on EyePACs dataset. Section V presents the concluding remarks.

2 Related Work

A subset of machine learning known as "deep learning" deal with developing models that can be learnt to solve problems by examining enormous amounts of data. Long-term use in the medical industry has demonstrated the efficacy of deep learning in anticipating the onset of diabetic retinopathy. Deep learning has been used by researchers to detect diabetic retinopathy from fundus images with high accuracy and low false positive rate (FPR). Several techniques for detecting DR were developed as the DR rate increased. One of the earliest types of research using a CNN-based architecture for the quinary categorization of DR (5-class - comparable to the medical leveling process) was reported. To account for the dataset's class imbalance as well as lessen over-fitting, the authors updated the parameters during backpropagation using a class-weighted method for each batch. In order to achieve the categorization, Torre et al. [20] used a CNN architecture that examined the inputs of both eyes and successfully integrated the representations. Additionally, they suggested making changes to the network's architecture and employing tiny convolutions to get a final receptive field that was as close as feasible to the size of the actual images. For the identification and classification of DR images, Shankar et al. [21] presented a deep neural network with moth search optimization (DNN-MOS) technique. It uses a variety of techniques, including feature extraction, segmentation, and classification. First, the contrast of the picture was enhanced by means of a contrast limited adaptive histogram equalization approach. Following pre-processing, the histogram model was used to segment the DR picture. The retrieved features were then categorized with the help of DNN-MDO classifier procedure once the feature vectors had been extracted. For the purpose of classifying DR and extracting characteristics from the segmented fundus images, suggested an interesting DL method. The fundus image was first pre-processed, and after that, it was segmented. The branching blood arteries were removed using the maximal primary curvature model, which use the highest Eigenvalues. To improve and disregard the erroneous area, morphologic openings and an adaptive histogram equalization approach were used. Diabetics have been reported to have a greater proliferation of the optic nerve, CNN was used to classify using DR. The input layer, convolution layer, and pooling layer are all parts of the CNN. In experimental context, 97.2% precision and 98.7% accuracy were attained. The patients' length of suffering, however, could not be determined. DL based architectures are used for segmentation of fundus images for DR classification [22]. Several other studies are also available on detection of DR, macular oedema and inadequate glucose regulation using deep learning [23]. Recently, the impact of AI in detection and screening of DR has been extensively studied [24] and several advancements in the detection of DR using CAD and ML are presented [25].

3 Methods

This section outlines our approach for a thorough comparative examination of a number of cutting-edge pre-trained deep learning networks for image classification, segmentation, and object recognition on difficult diabetic retinopathy datasets with diverse sample sizes. We have tried to use DL to automatically detect and classify DR lesions through binary as well as multi-level classification. It is an attempt to have an automated diagnosis method for diabetic retinopathy that classifies, identifies objects, and segments pictures of the diabetic retinopathy fundus. The various modules in the framework are then described. In either of the classification methods, each image has passed through the pre-processing stage.

3.1 Dataset

The dataset that is chosen must have a wide variety of images, thus this is a significant consideration. In this study, publicly accessible dataset from Kaggle containing a sizable quantity of images from each of the five DR phases are taken into account. These files are from the EyePACs, which includes fundus image from each of the five phases of DR. This data collection contains pictures of human eyeballs. It was developed to assist in the research and creation of algorithms for the segmentation and categorization of data used in the medical industry. It is a well-known multi-class unbalanced diabetes datasets with varied sample sizes that has been taken into consideration when performing the tests. These datasets may be divided depending on their sizes into small, medium, and big dataset categories. This dataset includes 35,126 retinal pictures of a size of 3888 by

2951 pixels for each left and right eye, with 25,810 photos classified as 0 DR (no DR), 2,443 as mild DR, 5,292 as moderate DR, 873 as severe DR, and 708 as extreme DR. Another dataset obtained from Asia Pacific Tele-Ophthalmology Society (APTOS 2019) [26] is also used for validation of the model. The APTOS dataset has also undergone similar pre-processing stages before applying into the model.

3.2 Pre-processing

Pre-processing is a technique used to cut down on the amount of input data. The supplied data can be transformed, resized, or filtered to achieve this. Typical images available in the dataset can indeed be processed for DR image detection. For the purpose of producing an effective categorized result, image alterations like resizing, conversion and augmentation are required. Before being utilized for any subsequent phase, each image goes through pre-processing. To guarantee that the dataset is consistent and only shows features that are pertinent, preprocessing is necessary. The images are downsized to a standard size and converted into grayscale format as part of pre-processing. Usually, the R, G, and B values are employed for estimating the grayscale picture using the relation [27].

$$G = [0.587R + 0.299G + 0.114B] \tag{1}$$

Here the red hue is given more weight than the other two colors in order to retrieve the blood vessels and red clots. Contrast Enhancement through Contrast limited adaptive histogram equalization (CLAHE) filter is used to further enhance the image's attributes. By using this filter, the problem of noise amplification is reduced and the contrast of the picture is improved. CLAHE performs contrast-limiting histogram equalization in tiny patches or tiles with great precision. The images after gray-scale conversion and contrast enhancement are shown in Fig. 1.

3.3 Binary Classification

The classification of diabetic retinopathy is crucial for locating people who require immediate care and are at a high risk of complications. A series of characteristics, including the degree of vascularization, the thickness of the arterioles, the presence of microaneurysms, haemorrhages, and exudates, are derived from fundus pictures collected by an ophthalmologist during an eye examination by the classifier. Binary classification is often preferred due to the misclassification issues, of multiclass classification. The formulation of binary classification is to initially check the presence of DR in an individual. Classifying grades "0,1 versus 2,3,4" or "0 versus 1,2,3,4" is a popular formulation in binary classification. This will categorize the DR dataset into two groups alone viz., 'normal' or 'affected' using a CNN. The procedure adopted for this task includes the initial pre-processing as discussed in earlier sections. The main objective is to determine whether or not a person has diabetic retinopathy. However, when diabetic retinopathy is present, it cannot accurately forecast how severe it will be. Perhaps, due to the fact that a doctor's assessment of the intensity level is subjective and various doctors do not utilize the same criteria to evaluate patients. Perhaps there are more considerations for assessing the intensity that are separate from the images. Without more information regarding the data, we can only make assumptions. Since determining whether or not someone has diabetic retinopathy is the most crucial element of this research, we reduced the label to a two-class model initially. The class 'No_DR' remained unchanged while all the classes are considered as 'Affected'.

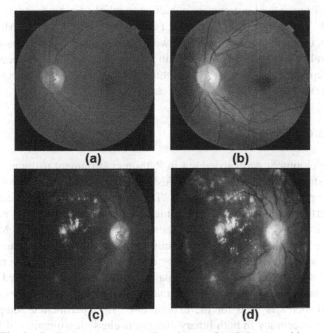

Fig. 1. EyePACs dataset (a) (c)Raw image. (b) (d) Processed image

3.4 Multi-Class Classification

Here the dataset will be classified into five classes (viz. No_DR, Normal, Moderate DR, Proliferate DR and Severe DR). Moderate DR misclassification was more frequent than the other classes verify the difficulty in detecting mild DR and the difficulty in identifying the disease's fine characteristics due to their small size and low prevalence (around 1% of image). Importantly, in order to detect small lesions, the model should be trained with extremely high-quality fundus images. Also, this is prohibited by deep CNNs' vanishing/exploding gradient issue and computational cost. However, immediately downsampling the images causes a significant loss of information.

3.5 Model Development

The CNN algorithm is the most commonly used well-known architecture in the field of DL. The fundamental benefit of CNN over its forerunners is that it does it inevitably and without human intervention, identifying the essential characteristics. Similar to a traditional neural network, the development of CNNs has been enthused by neurons available in human's brain. Three main advantages of the CNN: similar representations, sparse interactions, and parameter sharing. In contrast to typical fully connected (FC) networks, the CNN employs weight sharing and localized interconnections to completely utilize 2-dimensional input-data structures, such as visual signal. This procedure uses a very minimal number of parameters, which streamlines training and accelerates the neural network. The weight sharing feature of CNN is the primary factor to be considered since it lowers the amount of trainable network parameters, which helps the network, improve generalization and prevent overfitting. Also, the model output becomes highly ordered and dependent on the extracted features as a result of simultaneously learning the feature extraction layers and the classification layer.

4   Results and Discussion

The model development was carried out in Python environment using an Intel i7 2.30 GigaHz workstation having 16 GB of RAM, and a GeForce RTX 3060 GPU were used to run the program on the workstation. The Python sklearn.metrics class was used to compute performance measures. These measures are recall, f1-score, accuracy, and precision. With the help of the EyePACs dataset and the DenseNet201, MobileNetV2 and InceptionV3 architecture, we carried out severity grading using transfer learning to mimic real-world scenarios. After blurry and overlapping images were eliminated from the 3662 scans in the training set,remaining images were processed. A different set of feature values for images of the normal retinal fundus and images of the retina damaged by diabetes is used for the experiments. In experimental setup, DenseNet obtained highest accuracy in both binary and multi-class classification of DR grading. To further validate the performance of DenseNet, the model is also evaluated on Asia Pacific Tele-Ophthalmology Society (APTOS 2019) Blindness dataset.

4.1   DenseNet Architecture

Each layer in the DenseNet design is linked to all adjacent levels, resulting in a densely connected convolution network. All preceding layers' features mappings are applied as inputs for each layer, and each successive layer's features mappings are likewise taken as input. Unlike standard L-layer convolutional networks, which have N interconnections across each layer, the DenseNet network has $N(N + 1)/2$ explicit interconnections. DenseNet overcomes the gradient diminishing issue, increases feature propagation, stimulates feature reuse, and decreases the number of parameters greatly. The DenseNet121 model from DenseNet is employed in our proposed method. The actual grading prediction result obtained from the model along with its original grading for three images is shown in Fig. 2.

Here, we have presented three cases of correct prediction by the model. The actual is the true class of DR in the image and the predicted is the class predicted by the model during evaluation. The accuracy and loss per epoch diagram during binary classification of the model is revealed in Fig. 3.

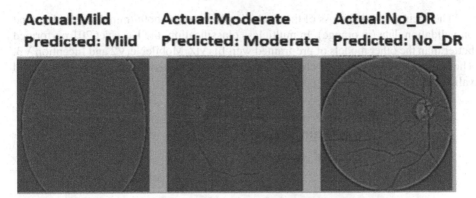

Actual:Mild   **Actual:Moderate**   **Actual:No_DR**
Predicted: Mild   **Predicted: Moderate**   **Predicted: No_DR**

Fig. 2. Comparison of Actual and Predicted grading of DR

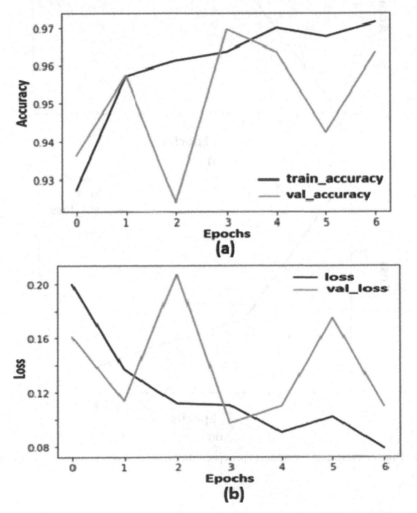

Fig. 3. Graph representing (a) Accuracyper epoch (b) Loss per epoch in binary grading of DR

The accuracy and the loss of the model is presented on both train data (in blue) and on validation data (in orange). In multiclass classification, the DeseNet 201 performed better than the other models of pre-trained weights viz. MobileNetV2 and Inception V3. The accuracy and loss per epoch diagram in multi-class classification on both train and validation data is shown in Fig. 4.

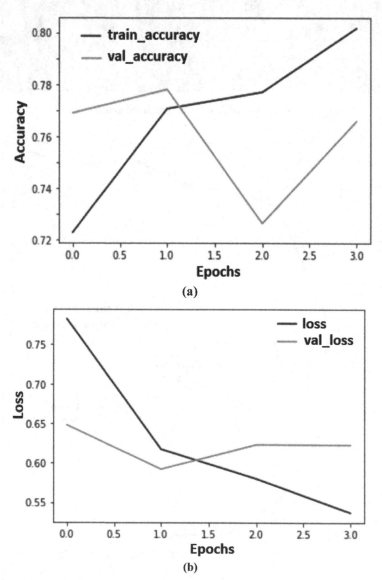

(a)

(b)

Fig. 4. Graph representing (a) Accuracyper epoch (b) Loss per epoch in multi-class grading of DR

4.2 Evaluation Metrices

By comparing multiple state-of-the-art pre-trained networks utilizing various performance assessment measures, we have conducted comparative study in this research. Several performance assessment metrics are taken into account for the classification job, including accuracy, precision, f1-score, and support. The confusion matrix may be used to illustrate how well a binary classification model is performing. Considering the forecasts and the ground truth, the metrices in the confusion matrix is computed as revealed in Fig. 5.

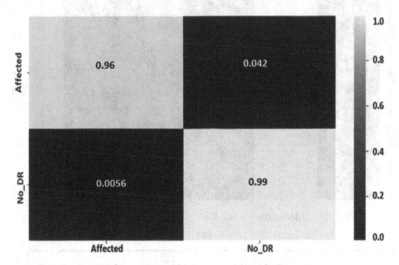

Fig. 5. The Confusion matrix of Binary classification

The accuracy in detecting the normal eyes is 99% while the accuracy in detecting the severity is 96%. The overall classification report under initial binary classification for detection of DR presence into two classes viz. 'No_DR' and 'Affected' is shown in Table 1.

Table 1. Binary Classification descriptions

	precision	recall	f1-score	support
Affected	0.99	0.96	0.98	190
No_DR	0.96	0.99	0.98	177
accuracy			0.98	367
macro avg	0.98	0.98	0.98	367
weighted avg	0.98	0.98	0.98	367

Again, in multi-class classification, the model could compute the No_DR class with a higher accuracy of 98%. The class Moderate DR and Mild DR classification obtained accuracy of 92% and 64% respectively, which reduced the overall accuracy of the model. However, the model could not classify the proliferate and severe stages of DR. The overall statistics of multiclass classification of DR as depicted in Fig. 6.

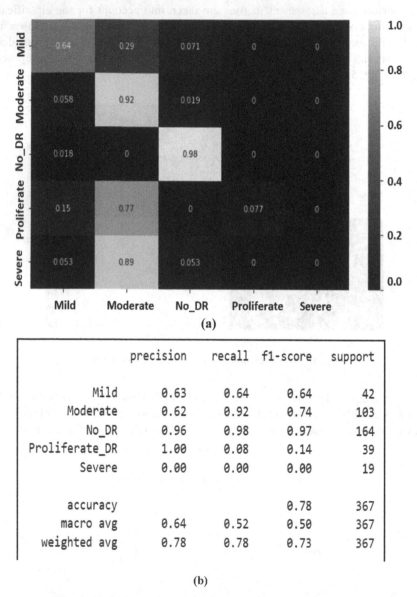

(a)

	precision	recall	f1-score	support
Mild	0.63	0.64	0.64	42
Moderate	0.62	0.92	0.74	103
No_DR	0.96	0.98	0.97	164
Proliferate_DR	1.00	0.08	0.14	39
Severe	0.00	0.00	0.00	19
accuracy			0.78	367
macro avg	0.64	0.52	0.50	367
weighted avg	0.78	0.78	0.73	367

(b)

Fig. 6. Multiclass (a) Confusion matrix (b) Evaluation metrices

The comparison of three pre-trained network in multi-class classification of DR on EyePACs is presented in Table 2. On the training set, MobileNet attained best accuracy with 73% followed by DenseNet with 71% and InceptionV3 with 70%. However, while computing the accuracy on validation data, DenseNet201 attained highest accuracy with 78%. The accuracy on validation data by Inception and MobileNet is 77%. For further validation, the networks are applied on APTOS dataset whose results are shown in Table 3.

Table 2. Multi-class classification on EyePACs

Sl	Model_name	train_accuracy	val_accuracy
1	DenseNet201	0.7127	0.7812
2	MobileNetV2	0.7303	0.778
3	InceptionV3	0.7084	0.775

Table 3. Multi-class classification on APTOS

Sl	Model_name	train_accuracy	val_accuracy
1	DenseNet201	0.832	0.818
2	MobileNetV2	0.856	0.760
3	InceptionV3	0.848	0.724

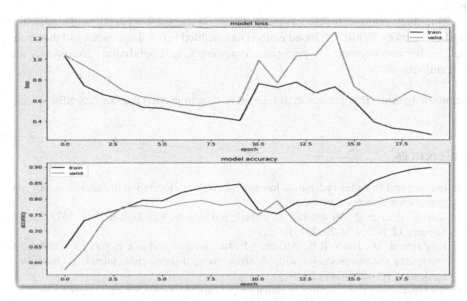

Fig. 7. Accuracy and Loss graph of DenseNet

On APTOS dataset, MobileNet performed best on training set attaining accuracy of 85% followed by InceptionV3 with 84% and DenseNet with 83%. However, while computing the accuracy on validation data, DenseNet201 attained highest accuracy with 81%. The accuracy on validation data by Inception is 72% and MobileNet is 76%. The final accuracy and loss graph of DenseNet architecture with higher number of epochs are presented in Fig. 7.

5 Conclusion and Future Work

Diabetic retinopathy is a critical repercussion of diabetes causing slow deterioration of retina and can result in loss in vision. It is critical to detect and treat it early to prevent it from worsening and causing retinal damage. The level of interest has grown more intense in employing DL systems to detect DR since several DL methods have established and been adopted into medical practice. This will allow doctors to care for the victims in more efficient and effective manner. In this study, machine learning approaches based on CNNs are used to pre-process and extract features from the diabetic retinal fundus picture in order to diagnose diabetic retinopathy. Using pre-trained architectures models were trained. The images were split into two separate datasets: one contained images of retinas damaged by diabetes, and the other had images of a normal stimuli. From normal and diabetic retinal fundus imaging data sets, relevant characteristics are retrieved. Most important characteristics out of all the retrieved data are utilized for comparison; rating these features is relatively straightforward and essential for distinguishing between a normal and diabetic fundus picture. From the outcomes, it can be seen that DenseNet outperformed MobileNetV2 and InceptionV3 architecture both in binary and multi-class grading.

This study summarizes the advanced studies on using DL systems to diagnose diabetic retinopathy. While DL based method has enabled better diagnostics and therapeutics, further improvements in performance, accuracy, and ophthalmic consistency are still anticipated.

Acknowledgment. This research study received funding from AICTE under RPS-NER scheme.

References

1. International Diabetes Federation. International diabetes federation diabetes atlas, 9th edn. https://www.diabetesatlas.org/en/
2. Jenkins, A.J., et al.: Biomarkers in diabetic retinopathy. Rev Diabet Stud. 2015 Spring-Summer 12(1–2), 159–95 (2015)
3. Janghorbani, M., Jones, R.B., Allison, S.P.: Incidence of and risk factors for proliferative retinopathy and its association with blindness among diabetes clinic attenders. Ophthalmic Epidemiol. 7(4), 225–241 (2000)
4. Bourne, R.R.A., et al.: Causes of vision loss worldwide, 1990–2010: a systematic analysis. Lancet Global Health 1(6), 339–349 (2013)
5. ETDRS report no 10. Grading diabetic retinopathy from stereoscopic color fundus photographs- an extension of the modified Airlie House classification. Ophthalmology 98(5), 786–806 (1991)

6. Scanlon, P.H., Wilkinson, C.P., Aldington, S.J., Matthews, D.R.: A Practical Manual of Diabetic Retinopathy Management. 1st edn. Wiley-Blackwell (2009)
7. Safi, H., Safi, S., Hafezi-Moghadam, A., Ahmadieh, H.: Early detection of diabetic retinopathy. Surv. Ophthalmol. **63**(5), 601–608 (2018)
8. Karim, T., Riad, M.S., Kabir, R., Symptom Analysis of Diabetic Retinopathy by MicroAneurysm Detection Using NPRTOOL. In 2019 (ICREST) IEEE, pp. 606–610 (2019)
9. Nakayama, L.F., Ribeiro, L.Z., Gonçalves, M.B., et al.: Diabetic retinopathy classification for supervised machine learning algorithms. International J. Retina and Vitreous **8**, 1 (2022)
10. Vujosevic, S., et al.: Screening for diabetic retinopathy: new perspectives and challenges. The Lancet Diabetes, Endocrinology **8**(4), 337–347 (2020)
11. Esteva, A., Chou, K., Yeung, S., Naik, N., Madani, A., Mottaghi, A.et al.: Deep learning-enabled medical computer vision. NPI Digital Med. **4** (2021)
12. Chen, X.W.: Lin,X.: Big data deep learning: challenges and perspectives. IEEE Access 20142, 514–25 (2014)
13. Guo, Y., et al.: Deep learning for visual understanding: a review. Neurocomputing, 18727–48 (2016)
14. Bakator, M., Radosav, D.: Deep learning and medical diagnosis: a review of literature. Multimodal Technol Interact **2**(3), 47 (2018)
15. Krizhevsky, A., Sutskever, I., Hinton, G.E.: ImageNet classification with deep convolutional neural networks. Commun ACM60(6) (2017)
16. Faizal, S., Rajput, C.A., Tripathi, R., et al.: Automated cataract disease detection on anterior segment eye images using adaptive thresholding and fine tuned inception-v3 model. Biomed. Signal Process. Control **82**, 104550 (2023)
17. Sunnetci, K.M., Kaba, E., Çeliker, F.B., Alkan, A.: Comparative parotid gland segmentation by using ResNet-18 and MobileNetV2 based DeepLab v3+ architectures from magnetic resonance images. Concurrency and Computation: Practice and Experience **35**(1), e74053 (2023)
18. Alzubaidi, L., et al.: Review of deep learning: concepts, CNN architectures, challenges, applications, future directions. Journal of Big Data **8**, 53 (2021)
19. EyePACS Dataset, "Kaggle." http://www.eyepacs.com
20. Torre, J.L., Valls, A., Puig, D.: A deep learning interpretable classifier for diabetic retinopathy disease grading. Neurocomputing **396**, 465–476 (2020)
21. Shankar, K., Perumal, E., Vidhyavathi, R.: Deep neural network with moth search optimization algorithm-based detection and classification of diabetic retinopathy images. SN Applied Sciences **2** (2020)
22. Venkaiahppalaswamy, B., Reddy, P.P., Batha, S.: Hybrid deep learning approaches for the detection of diabetic retinopathy using optimized wavelet based model. Biomed. Signal Process. Control **79**(2), 104146 (2023)
23. Babenko, B., Mitani, A., Traynis, I., et al.: Detection of signs of disease in external photographs of the eyes via deep learning. Nature Biomedical Engineering **6**, 1370–1383 (2022)
24. Huang, X., Wang, H., She, C., Feng, J., et al.: Artificial intelligence promotes the diagnosis and screening of diabetic retinopathy. Front. Endocrinol. **13**, 946915 (2022)
25. Selvachandran, G., Quek, S.G., Paramesran, R., et al.: Developments in the detection of diabetic retinopathy: a state-of-the-art review of computer-aided diagnosis and machine learning methods. Artificial Intelligence Review (2022). https://doi.org/10.1007/s10462-022-10185-6
26. Karthik, M., Dane, S.: APTOS 2019 Blindness Detection, Kaggle (2019). https://kaggle.com/competitions/aptos2019-blindness-detection
27. Das, S., Kharbanda, K., Raman, S.M.R., Dhas, E.: Deep learning architecture based on segmented fundus image features for classification of diabetic retinopathy. Biomed. Signal Process. Control **68**, 102600 (2021)

Load Flow Solution for Radial Distribution Networks Using Chaotic Opposition Based Whale Optimization Algorithm

Suvabrata Mukherjee$^{(\boxtimes)}$ and Provas Kumar Roy◉

Kalyani Government Engineering College, Kalyani, West Bengal, India
elec.engg07@gmail.com

Abstract. A radial network is one that traverses a network without connecting to another source of supply. It is utilised for remote loads, such as in rural areas. For the load flow analysis of radial distribution systems, various forward-backward sweep techniques exist. This study explains a novel approach to load flow analysis for radial distribution systems. Encouraged by whales' use of bubble-net hunting, WOA imitates humpback. The suggested technique is applied on IEEE 33-bus and IEEE 69-bus balanced radial distribution test networks to validate performance in tackling the described problem. The results show that the suggested approach produces workable and efficient solutions and may be successfully substituted for in real-world power systems for radial network load flow analysis. Additionally, to the best of the authors' knowledge, this is the first report on the use of WOA in resolving the optimal DG.

Keywords: Load flow analysis · Power flow · Whale Optimization Algorithm · Chaos · Chaotic whale optimization algorithm

1 Introduction

To provide steady, dependable, and economical electric energy transmission to consumers from generators, load flow analysis is a crucial prerequisite for power network analysis. Data availed from the load flow analysis can be practiced for dispatching, stability, contingency analysis, outage security evaluation, and normal operating mode analysis. For the operation, control, and planning of power systems, competent, economical, and trustworthy load flow solutions, Gauss-Seidel, Fast Decoupled load flow, and Newton-Raphson approaches have been developed. For the radial networks (distribution) that aren't in great shape, there are two different types of approaches that have been developed. [3][5] The first is to apply the forward-backward sweep method, while the second is to modify currently used techniques [1,2]. A backward method that uses a backward operation to update equivalent impedance at the transmitting end, was introduced by Berg et al. in 1967 [3]. Additionally, because to the high X/R ratio, using a compensation strategy Luo et al. presented the citation for weakly meshed networks [4]. It begins by analyzing the network topology to identify the interconnection connections. These interconnection points are then broken using the compensated approach, allowing the meshed structure to produce a straightforward tree-type radial system. During the feeder's forward sweep, a voltage drop calculation is used or lateral from the transmitting end to the distant end. During the backward sweep, the current is added which updates the transmitting end voltage. Voltage drop is then determined using KVL and KCL. Due to the differing load behavior, the distribution system no longer benefits from the strategies implied to transmission systems. In that case, load current injection is a wise decision [5–7]. This model is also nodal. When the system's load model is voltage vulnerable, the computations are difficult and expensive. The transmitting end voltage was determined using the backward sweep approach since the substantial load at the feeder's far end causes additional iterations. Thus, a specific value must be determined in order for the voltage profile to converge during iterations, and this special value's exact calculation is not explained. For networks with multiple feeding nodes, Haque offered a novel strategy [8]. According to Shrimohammadi, the ladder network method [9] may be used in both ways. The computation of the forward voltage is followed by a backward sweep method for summing the current. The convergence might be sped up by contrasting this iteration process to the forward ladder network approach. These techniques make use of the radial network's inherent property that every bus has a distinct route to the source. While a power system is in use, many loads, including commercial, industrial, and residential is existent and naturally depend on the system's voltage and frequency [10]. Another extremely straightforward and effective technique is the power loss method [11]. There is a sizable difference between the predicted and actual values for invariable impedance loads and current. Because of this, the power loss values will also deviate. Additionally, a sharp rise in electrical power demand has been seen in recent years. Due to costs and environmental risks, there is constantly a push to utilize the advantages of the current power system fully. The regulation of load flow and raising the current power transmission system's loading limit create new challenges. Therefore, ineffective conditions prevented conventional methods from handling power flow issues. In order to overcome this issue and have a better load flow solution, many meta-heuristic optimization approaches have been investigated. For systems using FACTS devices, evolutionary programming techniques are being used to address the load flow problem [12]. Owing to its consistency, brevity, and reliable confluence, particle swarm optimization (PSO) has recently acquired appeal for usage in a variety of applications [13,14]. While modified PSO methods can handle problems with continuous non-linear optimization, conventional PSO relies heavily on parametric parameters. Thus, results often get stuck in nearby optimum. Clonal Selection Algorithm [15] and Actual Coded Genetic Algorithm (RCGA) [16] were subsequently presented for providing practical power flow solutions by the implementation of reducing the difference between the reactive and real power at buses. Reactive power management and economical load dispatch have both been addressed using the hybrid differential evolution algorithm (HDE) [17,18]. Bacterial foraging algorithm (BFA), which is impacted by bacterial foraging patterns depending on their ability for survival, was developed to solve the issue of power system optimization [19]. The use of BFA to execute, in a dynamic power system environment, the ideal power flow (OPF) solution proved successful [20]. [21], inspired by the cuckoo's cunning breeding strategy, developed the cuckoo optimization algorithm (COA) and successfully applied to address the ELD problem. In 2014 [22], the grey wolf optimization (GWO) method was introduced. It is a novel evolutionary optimization technique that takes cues from the grey wolf hawking behavior. The majority of the load flow analysis algorithms that have been suggested so far in the literature have produced better outcomes. Recent study has discovered significant shortcomings in the claimed algorithm, nevertheless. The majority of the population-based methods covered above incur a significantly higher computing cost in large-scale situations. Additionally, the majority of the aforementioned approaches demonstrate an inability to adequately investigate the search space with the rise in system complexity. [1(1)],[2] In addition to the above survey, Particle Swarm Optimization (PSO) is a popular optimization algorithm that is based on simulating the behavior of social groups, such as school of fishes or avian flocks. However, ability of PSO to handle high-dimensional optimization problems, or to find global optima in multimodal landscapes has been observed to be sluggish [23]. GA is another well-known optimization algorithm, which is inspired by natural selection and genetics. However, the performance of GA on constrained optimization problems, or their ability to handle noisy or uncertain fitness landscapes, is not very effective [24]. In this article, Whale optimization algorithm (WOA), a recently developed population-based optimization approach, is implied to adhere to the load flow issue in order to mitigate some of the aforementioned shortcomings. Also, WOA has been utilised successfully to address OPF and ELD issues [25–27]. But a thorough examination of WOA reveals convincing flaws. Firstly, WOA investigation might only be possible for a short time. Second, the application of WOA relies on values chosen arbitrarily. [2] Also, WOA uses a standard. Chaotic population initialization map. In comparison, COWOA uses a new chaotic population initialization map and also introduces a chaos-based mutation operator. Thus, CWOA provides better convergence rates or solution quality compared to WOA. Last but not least, WOA fills the initial populations, like any population-based algorithm, with random positions for each agent in the group. Every agent modifies its present location during the search in accordance with the best outcome thus far or in relation to randomly chosen search agents. In order to overcome the aforementioned issues, the Chaotic-Opposition based Whale Optimization Algorithm (COWOA), a revised form of WOA, has been introduced in this article. Chaos theory has also been applied to solve power flow for linear distribution systems [28] in order to improve solutions.

2   Motivation for the Research Work

The primary inspirations for the paper are: i] According to the "No Free Lunch Theorem" [29], no single optimization strategy can successfully solve every optimization problem, hence there is always room for improvement in any algorithm used to solve real-world problems.
[3][4]So every optimization algorithm has its strengths and weaknesses, and no algorithm can be universally better than all others. Therefore, there is always room for improvement in any algorithm used to solve real-world problems. This inspires researchers to explore and develop new optimization algorithms that can address specific types of problems more effectively.
ii] The use of upgraded mechanism of constraint management to improve the nature of the solutions, the use of chaos theory and opposition based learning initialization for single or multi objective optimization algorithms, and random initialization.
[3][4]Chaos theory can be used to generate random sequences that can help the algorithm explore the search space more efficiently, while opposition-based learning can provide additional training examples to improve the performance of classification algorithms. The paper also suggests the use of random initialization, which can help the algorithm escape local optima and find better solutions.
iii] A more complete set of solutions was collected, and its statistical analysis shows that COWOA is a viable approach for addressing the aforementioned problems.

3   Power Flow Problem

A vital tool for determining factors like voltage magnitude and angle at each bus in a power system under steady-state conditions in a balanced three-phase system is power flow, also known as load flow. Then, all the bus connected components' reactive and active power flows are calculated. As a result, the load flow programme created may calculate:

I each bus's voltage and its phase angle
II sum of all components connected to the buses' reactive and active power. Procedures to follow when doing a load flow analysis have been drawn from [12]. In a setup comprising of R generators and N buses, $2(N-1)-(R-1)$ represents overall number of unknowns.

The real and reactive power balance is provided by the following equations:

$$0 = -P_i + \sum_{k=1}^{N} V_i||V_k| \left(G_{ik}cos\theta_{ik} - B_{ik}sin\theta_{ik}\right) \qquad (1)$$

$$0 = -Q_i + \sum_{k=1}^{N} V_i||V_k| \left(G_{ik}sin\theta_{ik} - B_{ik}cos\theta_{ik}\right) \qquad (2)$$

where G_{ik} and B_{ik} = are the element's real and imaginary parts in Y_{bus}; Pi = bus i's net power injection, and $\theta_{i,k}$ = voltage angle difference enclosed by i^{th} and k^{th} buses

4   Mathematical Problem Formulation

Power flow issue can be viewed to be a minimization-type optimisation issue with the following objective function:

$$OF = \sum_{i=2}^{N_{Bus}} \Delta P_i^2 + \sum_{i=2}^{N_{Bus}} \Delta Q_i^2 \tag{3}$$

where ΔP_i and ΔQ_i are represented as follows:

$$\Delta P_i = P_i^{spec} - P_i^{cal} \tag{4}$$

$$\Delta Q_i = Q_i^{spec} - Q_i^{cal} \tag{5}$$

where ΔP_i, ΔQ_i are the deviated i^{th} bus power; P_i^{spec} is specified i^{th} bus power; P_i^{cal} is the calculated active i^{th} bus power that are derived from (1); Q_i^{cal} is calculated reactive power at i^{th} bus which can be calculated from (2). Initially, for each bus, between a minimum and a high value, random voltage magnitudes and phase angles are collected (0.9 p.u–1.02 p.u and 0 radian - 0.35 radian respectively). The respective active and respective powers are calculated and thereby the deviated power is calculated from (4) and (5). From the deviated active and reactive powers the updated voltage magnitudes and phase angles for each bus are calculated as follows:

$$V_{new}^i = V_{old}^i + \alpha \times (\Delta P_i), \quad i = 1, 2, ... N_{Bus} \tag{6}$$

$$\delta_{new}^i = \delta_{old}^i + \beta \times (\Delta Q_i), \quad i = 1, 2, ... N_{Bus} \tag{7}$$

where α and β are penalty factors and $\alpha = \beta = 0.05$.

4.1   System Constraints

There are two type of constraints.

Equality Constraints. According to the following mathematical formula, the total active and reactive power demand of all units should equal the active and reactive power at the substation:

$$\sum_{i=1}^{N} P_{Di} = P_S \tag{8}$$

$$\sum_{i=1}^{N} Q_{Di} = Q_S \tag{9}$$

where P_S and Q_S are the active and reactive power, respectively, of the substation.

Inequality Constraints. The inequality constraint being considered is:

Voltage Constraint. Each bus' voltage needs to be within an acceptable range.

$$v_i{}^{min} \le v_i \le v_i^{max} \tag{10}$$

5 Whale Optimization Algorithm (WOA)

Whales, considered as one of the largest mammals in the world, are fancy creatures that can expand up to 30 m in length and may weigh up to 180 t. Blue, Right, Minke, Humpback, Sei, Finback, and Killer are the seven variants of this large mammal. Of these variants the algorithm concentrates on humpback whales because of their exclusive hunting technique. This special kind of whales choose to stalk a school of small fishes that are surface proximate.

5.1 Mathematical Model of WOA

Whales are regarded as the most gigantic mammals on Earth and may grow to a maximum length of 30 m and a weight of 180 tonnes. In general, 7 various species of this huge creature, which are namely, Blue, Minke, Killer, Humpback, Sei, Finback and Right, are found. The following equations describe the particular hunting method used by humpback whales, in which they choose to pursue a group of small fish that are present near the water's surface:

$$[\vec{d} = |c.(\vec{x}')(t) - \vec{x}(t)| \tag{11}$$

$$\vec{x}(t+1) = (\vec{x}')(t) - \vec{a}.\vec{d} \tag{12}$$

When x denotes the position vector and x' denotes the ideal position vector for the solution, yields the absolute value. The symbol t denotes the current iteration. The letters a and c stand for the coefficient vectors. It is important to remember that x' must be changed after each cycle to see if a better choice is available. The equations below show the calculation process of vectors a and c:

$$\vec{a} = 2\vec{b}.\vec{r} - \vec{b} \tag{13}$$

$$c = 2.\vec{r} \tag{14}$$

In the exploitation and exploration stages, b decreases linearly across the iterations from 2 to 0. The random vector [0, 1] is called r. The most recent best record position (x', y') is updated to reflect the search agent's initial position at (x, y). By changing the values of the a and c vectors, several positions surrounding the best agent relative to the current position can be achieved. It is noteworthy that by defining r (random vector) any location in the search space can be reached that is located between the key-points. Thus, using Eqs. 12 and 13 every search agent can update its location around the present best solution.

5.2   Method of Bubble-Net Hunting

Regarding mathematical interpretation of bubble-net action of humpback whales, following methods are followed:

Shrinking Encircling Prey. In this approach the value of b in Eq. 13 is decreased thereby also decreasing the range of fluctuation, which is an arbitrary value lying in the interval [−b, b]. Over the course of iterations b is decreased from 2 to 0. Allotting contingent value(s) for a within [−1, 1] the updated location of search agents can lie in any place ranging from current agent position to the current best agent position.

Spiral Position Updating. the separation between the prey's position at (x', y') and the whale's position at (x, y) is initially assessed in this stage. Then, in order to simulate the helix-shaped migration, a spiral equation is created at the positions of the whale and the prey. Following is a representation of this:

$$\vec{x}(t+1) = (\vec{d'}.)e^b l.cos(2\pi l) + (\vec{x'}) \tag{15}$$

Due to the fact that whales swim simultaneously around their target when they are hunting, a 50% chance is used to update whale positions, which can be defined as:

$$\vec{x}(t+1) = (\vec{x'})(t) - \vec{a}.\vec{d}, if p < 0.5 \tag{16}$$

$$\vec{x}(t+1) = (\vec{d'}.)e^b l.cos(2\pi l) + (\vec{x'}), if p \geq 0.5 \tag{17}$$

$$(\vec{d'}) = (\vec{x'})(t) - \vec{x}(t) \tag{18}$$

Equation 18 represents the optimum option in terms of separating whales from their prey. L is between [−1, 1] and b is a constant. The random number p has uniform dissemination and falls between [0, 1].

5.3 Search for Prey

In order to attain the global optimal values rather than the best search agent, the position update is carried out using a randomly selected search agent, as illustrated by the following equations:

$$(\vec{d}) = (\vec{x}')(t) - \vec{x}(t) \tag{19}$$

$$x(t+1) = \overrightarrow{x_{rand}} - \vec{a}.\vec{d} \tag{20}$$

In the above equations $(x_r and)$ is the randomly selected whales in current iteration.

6 Chaotic Process

A chaotic systems improves the optimization algorithms because of some of the following important properties as: 1) ergodicity, 2) stochasticity and 3) sensitivity to the initial conditions [20, 21, 30] and they are converted into chaotic maps [28] exhibiting dynamic and complex performance in non-linear systems. The term "chaos" is the root of the word "chaotic," which refers to a complex system's characteristic of unexpected behaviour. Because of non-repetition and ergodicity properties of chaos, the global search process can be carried out at higher speeds in comparison to stochastic searches, which primarily relies on probability.

Generally, a chaotic system can be considered as a nonlinear random-like deterministic bounded system that is neither periodic nor converging. In addition, there is a sensitive dependence of a chaotic system on its initial conditions and parameters. The random, unpredictable and ergodic essence of chaos makes it a reliable source of randomness. [(2)]Unpredictability and randomness of chaotic systems make them useful for generating random sequences. Unlike a purely arbitrary sequence generated from a uniform dissemination, a chaotic sequence can provide a search method for heuristic optimisation algorithms that is more effective. In optimization, usually, the objective is to identify the ideal response to a certain issue. Within a large search space. Heuristic optimization algorithms use trial and error to explore this space and find the best solution. Also, traditional methods can become trapped in local optima or take a long time to converge to a global optimum. By using chaotic sequences, heuristic optimization algorithms can explore the search space more efficiently and increase the likelihood of finding a global optimum.

7 Opposition-Based Learning Method

According to [28], Opposition-based Learning (OBL) has been shown to be a successful technique for improving optimization algorithms in solving major power network issues.

[(2)]Some highlights of implementing Opposite-based learning are as follows:

Easy to implement: Opposite-based learning can be used with a variety of classification algorithms and is comparatively simple to implement, including decision trees, support vector machines, and neural networks.

Robust to noisy data: Opposite-based learning can be particularly useful in situations where the training data is noisy or contains errors. By providing additional training examples, opposite-based learning can help the classification algorithm to learn more robust decision boundaries that are less affected by noisy data.

Computationally efficient: Opposite-based learning can be computationally efficient because it does not require additional feature engineering or complex preprocessing steps. Instead, it simply uses the existing training data to generate additional examples.

Here, the main idea behind OBL is to calculate an estimate (x') for each possible solution (x) to a given problem. This estimate might be produced at random or using data from an experiment. The equation shown below can be used to get the value Y' that is opposite to the current value x:

$$y' = c + d - y \tag{21}$$

the real value x falls within the range $[a, b]$.

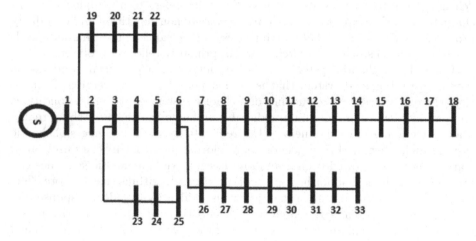

Fig. 1. Single line representation of IEEE-33 bus radial distribution system

8   Simulation Results and Discussion

COWOA have been implemented for solving the load flow issue and the results have been compared with conventional WOA and Network Topology method [32]. The techniques have been used to IEEE-69 and IEEE-33 bus radial distribution test networks with a flat start and a convergence tolerance value of 0.0001. Population size and number have been set by authors for the sake of generality. For larger systems, the fitness value scarcely changes as computation time increases, even when the count is over 50 in the population count and over 100 iterations are performed. The Pentium Dual core, 1800 MHz system uses MATLAB as its computation tool. Additionally, it has been presumed that DG units generate constant power. The performances of the techniques have been monitored for two different test systems, and for each system, the results are listed based on the results of 50 trial observations.

8.1 IEEE 33-Bus System

The necessary information is available from [28]. A single-line representation of the network is provided in Fig. 1. In Table 1 respective values under the base-case situation are shown. Here, the population size has been set at 50, and there have been 100 iterations. The voltage magnitudes (pu) for the 33-bus network are shown in Table 2 above. The first bus voltage is now 1 p.u, and the proposed method's algorithm is then followed going forward. The aforementioned voltages are calculated for composite loads and are displayed in Eqs. 19 and 20. The objective functions and the computational time required for convergence for the various approaches may be seen in Table 3. It can be observed that the computational time taken for COWOA is much lesser that the conventional WOA approach and Network Topology approach.

Table 1. Base-case values for the test network for the IEEE 33-bus radial distribution

IEEE 33-bus network	Values
Power Requirement (Real)	3720 kW
Power Requirement (Reactive)	2300 kVAr
Functioning Voltage	12.66 kV
Bus Count/Max. Voltage	1/1.00
Bus Count /Min. Voltage	18/0.9038
Power Loss (Active)	210.987 kW
Power Loss (Reactive)	143.1284 kVAr
Power Loss (Absolute)	254.9538 kVA

8.2 IEEE 69-Bus System

For the purpose of confirming its applicability in the event of a larger network, the recommended approach is implemented to the IEEE 69-bus radial distribution network. Figure 2 shows a single-line representation of the network. [3][2]The IEEE 69-bus radial distribution system consists of a single substation that supplies power to 69 distribution buses through a series of radial feeders. The buses are interconnected through power lines and transformers and are arranged in a

Table 2. IEEE-33 radial distribution test network voltages at various nodes

Sl. No.	Voltages at different nodes			Sl. No.	Voltages at different nodes		
	WOA	COWOA	Network Topology		WOA	COWOA	Network Topology
1	1	0.9992	1	18	0.8806	0.8792	0.8786
2	0.9972	0.9964	0.9958	19	0.9969	0.9958	0.9951
3	0.9804	0.9763	0.9763	20	0.9921	0.9912	0.9903
4	0.9799	0.9721	0.9659	21	0.9809	0.9798	0.9893
5	0.9641	0.9612	0.9556	22	0.9918	0.9889	0.9884
6	0.9329	0.9314	0.9298	23	0.9876	0.9791	0.9714
7	0.9542	0.9432	0.925	24	0.9807	0.9743	0.9622
8	0.9207	0.9204	0.9182	25	0.9709	0.9659	0.9577
9	0.9342	0.9187	0.9094	26	0.9453	0.9272	0.9272
10	0.9231	0.9113	0.9013	27	0.9397	0.9321	0.9236
11	0.9065	0.9011	0.9001	28	0.9276	0.9164	0.9076
12	0.9154	0.908	0.898	29	0.9112	0.9033	0.8961
13	0.9087	0.8894	0.8894	30	0.9076	0.8988	0.8911
14	0.9062	0.8953	0.8862	31	0.8965	0.8906	0.8852
15	0.8988	0.8887	0.8842	32	0.9038	0.9012	0.8839
16	0.8964	0.8967	0.8823	33	0.9004	0.8942	0.8835
17	0.881	0.8803	0.8795				

Table 3. Computational Time and Objective Function values of IEEE 33 radial bus system

Theorems	COWOA	WOA	Network Topology
Computing Time (sec)	1.16	1.49	1.61
Fitness Function	0.04761	0.8992	0.1543
Iterations taken for convergence	17	23	31

Table 4. Base-case values for the IEEE 69 bus radial distribution test network

IEEE 69 bus network	Values
Real Power Requirement	3800 kW
Reactive Power Requirement	2690 kVAR
Functioning Voltage	12.66 kV
Bus Count /Max. Voltage	1/1.00
Bus Count /Min. Voltage	65/0.9092
Power Loss (Active)	225.461 kW
Power Loss (Reactive)	102.3663 kVAR
Power Loss (Absolute)	247.6116 kVA

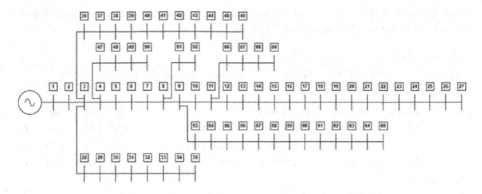

Fig. 2. [3][2] Single line representation of IEEE-69 bus radial distribution system

Table 5. Computational Time and Objective Function values of IEEE 69 radial bus system

Theorems	COWOA	WOA	Network Topology
Computational Time (sec)	1.43	1.89	2.24
Objective Function	0.07782	1.0972	1.1343
Iterations taken for convergence	22	27	36

hierarchical fashion, with the substation at the top and the end-use loads at the bottom. The system includes a variety of components, including transformers, switches, fuses, and capacitors, and is designed to simulate a range of operating conditions, such as different loading levels and fault conditions. The necessary data for the given network can be found in Table 4 and was obtained from [12]. Additionally, the population size has been set at 50 for this system, and 100 iterations have been assumed. The goal functions and the length of time required for convergence for each strategy are displayed in Table 5. It can be observed that the computational time taken for COWOA is much lesser that the conventional WOA approach and Network Topology approach.

9   Statistical Analysis of COWOA

The IEEE CEC benchmark system gathers numerous benchmark functions that are intended to evaluate the functionality and behavioural traits of various algorithms in light of their diverse behaviour, intensification, and convergence. There are various dimensional configurations that can be used to formulate the IEEE CEC benchmark system, including 10D, 30D, 50D, and 100D. The authors took into account the IEEE CEC−2017 benchmark system with 30D including a variety of functions, like unimodal and multimodal. The test procedures for the benchmark system under consideration has been divided into the following groups: F1−F2 are unimodal and F3−F9 are multimodal [31].

Table 6. Statistical comparison of the proposed COWOA with WOA, Network Topology, GA, PSO with 30D considering F1−F10

CEC 2017 (D = 30)						
Function		COWOA	WOA	Network Topology	PSO	GA
Unimodal						
F1	Mean	3.538E+03	4.216E+04	3.869E+05	5.122E+03	5.000E+03
	SD	4.389E+03	4.765E+03	5.918E+05	6.069E+03	6.210E+03
F2	Mean	1.8322E−07	1.221E+02	2.382E+02	1.141E−03	1.277E−03
	SD	4.502E−08	5.0249E−07	2.095E+02	1.781E+02	1.819E+02
Multimodal						
F3	Mean	1.642E+01	1.851E+01	4.406E+01	2.654E+01	2.831E+01
	SD	2.101E+01	2.221E+01	3.809E+02	2.768E+02	2.943E+02
F4	Mean	4.063E+01	4.124E+01	6.848E+01	6.105E+01	6.008E+01
	SD	2.063E+01	2.536E+01	6.329E+01	3.394E+01	3.342E+01
F5	Mean	2.012E−05	2.984E−05	4.122E−02	3.049E−04	3.148E−04
	SD	3.205E−05	3.783E−05	6.354E+01	5.256E−04	5.411E−04
F6	Mean	2.183E+01	2.818E+01	6.207E+02	3.195E+01	3.936E+01
	SD	2.581E+00	2.082E+01	4.428E+02	3.026E+01	3.487E+00
F7	Mean	5.198E+01	1.189E+02	8.152E+01	8.142E+02	1.297E+01
	SD	1.173E+01	1.586E+01	4.493E+01	2.439E+01	2.895E+00
F8	Mean	1.066E+01	1.668E+01	6.023E+04	1.672E+03	1.882E+03
	SD	4.493E+01	4.929E+01	5.993E+04	2.423E+02	2.723E+02
F9	Mean	2.738E+03	3.101E+03	5.724E+05	4.262E+03	4.894E+03
	SD	2.252E+02	2.785E+02	7.949E+02	3.413E+02	3.809E+02

CEC-2017 (30D): For the unimodal and multimodal benchmark functions taking 30D into consideration, Table 6 provides the statistical results showing the best mean error value and standard deviation (SD) obtained by the proposed COWOA, standard WOA, Network Topology method, Particle Swarm Optimisation (PSO), and Genetic Algorithm (GA). The findings clearly show that the suggested COWOA is the most effective at obtaining the ideal objective value for the majority of the test functions when the mean error value is taken into account.

10   Conclusion

In this paper, chaotic and OBL approaches have been used to solve the load flow problem for radial distribution system. A comparative study of the Network Topology approach with the proposed COWOA, WOA has been done and it is noted that the COWOA's computational time is significantly smaller than the Network Topology approach. Also, even though the conventional method, namely WOA, has to able to show good convergence characteristics, the modified COWOA approach have shown further better results. When compared to other algorithms, fitness value along with total iterations needed to reach convergence is significantly decreased. The original and cutting-edge approach used to tune the settings is highly adaptable. There is no published work that we are aware of that addresses the load flow problem by combining chaos and OBL approaches with standard meta-heuristic algorithms. The proposed method converges in all circumstances with a mild change in the number of generations if larger voltage magnitude and phase angle values are used for initiation. When compared to the traditional load flow methods, the algorithm is not sluggish like most population-based approaches, making the method's reliability one of its main advantages. When conventional approaches fail and/or when conventional metaheuristic population-based load flow algorithms exhibit slow performance, the COWOA-based load flow algorithm demonstrates its superiority.

References

1. Salama, M.M.A., Chikhani, A.Y.: A simplified network approach to the VAr control problem for radial distribution systems. IEEE Trans. Power Deliv. **8**(3), 1529–1535 (1993)
2. Srinivas, M.S.: Distribution load flows: a brief review. In: 2000 IEEE Power Engineering Society Winter Meeting. Conference Proceedings (Cat. No. 00CH37077), vol. 2, pp. 942–945. IEEE (2000)
3. Berg, R., Hawkins, E.S., Pleines, W.W.: Mechanized calculation of unbalanced load flow on radial distribution circuits. IEEE Trans. Power Appar. Syst. **1**(4), 415–421 (1967)
4. Luo, G.-X., Semlyen, A.: Efficient load flow for large weakly meshed networks. IEEE Trans. Power Syst. **5**(4), 1309–1316 (1990)
5. Carneiro, S., Pereira, J.L.R., Nepomuceno Garcia, P.A.: Unbalanced distribution system power flow using the current injection method. In: 2000 IEEE Power Engineering Society Winter Meeting. Conference Proceedings (Cat. No. 00CH37077), vol. 2, pp. 946–950. IEEE (2000)
6. Mithulananthan, N., Salama, M.M.A., Canizares, C.A., Reeve, J.: Distribution system voltage regulation and var compensation for different static load models. Int. J. Electr. Eng. Educ. **37**(4), 384–395 (2000)
7. Nanda, J., Sharma Srinivas, M., Sharma, M., Dey, S.S., Lai, L.L.: New findings on radial distribution system load flow algorithms. In: 2000 IEEE Power Engineering Society Winter Meeting. Conference Proceedings (Cat. No. 00CH37077), vol. 2, pp. 1157–1161. IEEE (2000)
8. Haque, M.H.: A general load flow method for distribution systems. Electr. Power Syst. Res. **54**(1), 47–54 (2000)
9. Shirmohammadi, D., Wayne Hong, H., Semlyen, A., Luo, G.X.: A compensation-based power flow method for weakly meshed distribution and transmission networks. IEEE Trans. Power Syst. **3**(2):753–762 (1988)
10. Haque, M.H.: Load flow solution of distribution systems with voltage dependent load models. Electric Power Syst. Res. **36**(3), 151–156 (1996)
11. Amaresh, K., Sivanagaraju, S., Sankar, V.: Minimization of losses in radial distribution system by using HVDS. In:: 2006 International Conference on Power Electronic, Drives and Energy Systems, pp. 1–5. IEEE (2006)

12. Karami, A., Mohammadi, M.S.: Radial basis function neural network for power system load-flow. Int. J. Electr. Power Energy Syst. **30**(1), 60–66 (2008)
13. Liu, B., Wang, L., Jin, Y.-H., Tang, F., Huang, D.-X.: Improved particle swarm optimization combined with chaos. Chaos Solit. Fractals **25**(5), 1261–1271 (2005)
14. Zhang, W., Liu, Y.: Multi-objective reactive power and voltage control based on fuzzy optimization strategy and fuzzy adaptive particle swarm. Int. J. Electr. Power Energy Syst. **30**(9), 525–532 (2008)
15. Rout, U.K., Swain, R.K., Barisal, A.K., Prusty, R.C.: Clonal selection algorithm for dynamic economic dispatch with nonsmooth cost functions. Int. J. Sci. Eng. Res. **2**(12), 1–5 (2011)
16. Udatha, H., Damodar Reddy, M.: Load flow analysis using real coded genetic algorithm. Int. J. Eng. Res. Appl. (IJERA) **4**(2), 522–527 (2014)
17. Bhattacharya, A., Kumar, P.: Chattopadhyay: solving economic emission load dispatch problems using hybrid differential evolution. Appl. Soft Comput. **11**(2), 2526–2537 (2011)
18. Sakr, W.S., El-Sehiemy, R.A., Azmy, A.M.: Adaptive differential evolution algorithm for efficient reactive power management. Appl. Soft Comput. **53**, 336–351 (2017)
19. Passino, K.M.: Biomimicry of bacterial foraging for distributed optimization and control. IEEE Control Syst. Mag. **22**(3), 52–67 (2002)
20. Hooshmand, R.-A., Morshed, M.J., Parastegari, M.: Congestion management by determining optimal location of series facts devices using hybrid bacterial foraging and Nelder-Mead algorithm. Appl. Soft Comput. **28**, 57–68 (2015)
21. Yang, X.S., Deb, S.: Engineering optimisation by cuckoo search. Int. J. Math. Model. Numer. Optim. (IJMMNO) **1**(4), 330–343 (2010)
22. Mirjalili, S., Mirjalili, S.M., Lewis, A.: Grey wolf optimizer. Adv. Eng. Softw. **69**, 46–61 (2014)
23. Li, W., Wang, G.-G., Gandomi, A.H.: A survey of learning-based intelligent optimization algorithms. Arch. Comput. Methods Eng. **28**, 3781–3799 (2021)
24. Huang, M., Zhai, Q., Chen, Y., Feng, S., Shu, F.: Multi-objective whale optimization algorithm for computation offloading optimization in mobile edge computing. Sensors **21**(8), 2628 (2021)
25. Mirjalili, S., Lewis, A.: The whale optimization algorithm. Adv. Eng. Softw. **95**, 51–67 (2016)
26. Bhesdadiya, R.H., Parmar, S.A., Trivedi, I.N., Jangir, P., Bhoye, M., Jangir, N.: Optimal active and reactive power dispatch problem solution using whale optimization algorithm. Indian J. Sci. Technol. **9**(1), 1–6 (2016)
27. Touma, H.J.: Study of the economic dispatch problem on IEEE 30-bus system using whale optimization algorithm. Int. J. Eng. Technol. Sci. **3**(1), 11–18 (2016)
28. Acharjee, P., Goswami, S.K.: Chaotic particle swarm optimization based robust load flow. Int. J. Electr. Power Energy Syst. **32**(2), 141–146 (2010)
29. Wolpert, D.H., Macready, W.G.: No free lunch theorems for optimization. IEEE Trans. Evol. Comput. **1**(1), 67–82 (1997)
30. Nguyen, T.T., Vo, D.N.: The application of one rank cuckoo search algorithm for solving economic load dispatch problems. Appl. Soft Comput. **37**, 763–773 (2015)
31. Awad, N.H., Ali, M.Z., Suganthan, P.N.: Ensemble sinusoidal differential covariance matrix adaptation with euclidean neighborhood for solving CEC2017 benchmark problems. In: 2017 IEEE Congress on Evolutionary Computation (CEC), pp. 372–379. IEEE (2017)

Dimension Reduction in Hyperspectral Image Using Single Layer Perceptron Neural Network

Radha Krishna Bar[1], Somnath Mukhopadhyay[1(✉)], Debasish Chakraborty[2], and Mike Hinchey[3]

[1] Department of Computer Science and Engineering, Assam University, Silchar, India
som.cse@live.com
[2] RRSC-East, Indian Space Research Organization, Kolkata, India
[3] University of Limerick, Limerick, Ireland

Abstract. Hundreds of continuous bands make up a hyperspectral image. All the bands are not equal important. Some of the bands are significant and others are redundant. Band reduction is a typical step before further processing. Instead of attempting to handle the complete information set without losing crucial data, it is essential to select the most valuable bands. Using traditional band selection techniques, the predetermined number of dimensions are selected from the hyperspectral image. In this article, we propose a novel single-layer neural network and a genetic evolutionary approach to reduce a hyperspectral image's high dimension. The process involves selecting the two bands with the lowest correlation in each iteration and eliminating two redundant bands. The suggested framework eliminates the unnecessary bands from a hyperspectral image and then chooses the ideal number of the most crucial bands.

Keywords: Single Layer Neural Network · Dimension Reduction · Band selection

1 Introduction

In remote sensing, a hyperspectral image can be considered as some consecutive spectral images that clearly indicate different types of land covers on the Earth. Hyperspectral imaging (HSI) is extensively and effectively used in a range of areas, including precision agriculture Kanning et al. (2016) and urban planning. Due to the obvious Hughes effect, the high dimensional features Extremely redundant bands and the high dimensional features of Hyperspectral Image form sensible classification of hyperspectral data problematic. The purpose of dimension reduction in an HSI is to maintain important topographical information in lower-dimensional sub-space while maximizing total class scatters and decreasing intra-class variance. Mainly two types of dimension reduction techniques are used in remote sensing, one is Band Extraction, another is Band Selection.

© The Author(s), under exclusive license to Springer Nature Switzerland AG 2024
K. Dasgupta et al. (Eds.): CICBA 2023, CCIS 1955, pp. 93–106, 2024.
https://doi.org/10.1007/978-3-031-48876-4_8

Band extraction is a technique that reduces the dimensions of data by combining various methods. It involves transforming data from a high-dimensional space to a lower-dimensional space, such as principal-component-analysis (PCA) Agarwal et al. (2007), Independent Component Analysis (ICA) Liu Lan (2017), linear-discriminant-analysis Wang et al. (2017), locality-preserving-projection Li et al. (2012), locally linear embedding (LLE) Roweis and Saul (2000), neighboring preserving embedding (NPE) He et al. (2005), kernel principal component analysis (KPCA) Fauvel Mathieu (2009), Stepwise linear discriminant analysis (SWLDA) Ahmad et al. (2016a), Minimum Noise Fraction (MNF) and Factor Analysis (FA) Li et al. (2011). Band reduction (BR) approaches to choose a subset of the original region may be favored when the physical significance of bands must be kept Yuan et al. (2015). Furthermore, the band quantity, the metric and the searching approach for best performance must all be determined to use the existing band reduction approaches. Several methodologies have been developed for identifying the appropriate values for these factors Ahmad et al. (2016b, 2011); Gustavsson and Wadströmer (2016). Two of these strategies are Particle Swarm Optimization (PSO) and Virtual Dimension (VD). The virtual dimension concept determine the number of spectral-signature different which acts as a reference value Chang and Du (2004), and the PSO method can learn the optimum number of bands automatically Su et al. (2014, 2016). Distance measures are used as class separabilities in a number of BR techniques, including Jeffrey's Matusita Ifarraguerri and Prairie (2004a), Bhattacharyya Chang (2003), and divergence-based distance metrics MartÍnez-UsÓMartinez-Uso et al. (2007a). However, a representative spectral signature for each class may be used to derive the least spatial covariance Yang et al. (2011a). Furthermore, the accuracy of a classifier may be used as an objective function in specific cases Nakamura et al. (2014). Band selection, rather than band extraction, can maintain the original band's information or physical meaning, which is important for annotating certain geological properties Brown et al. (2008). In band-selection approaches, an operative band subset is created through selecting particular relevant bands from the actual space of features Feng et al. (2014); Jie Feng (2016); Nahr et al. (2014); Patra et al. (2015). A rough set technique is proposed by Patra et al. Patra et al. (2015) to assess the importance between two spectral bands and created a supervised band selection approach based on a rough set for detecting informative bands in HSI. To quantify classification redundancy, Feng et al. introduced a hyperspectral band selection approach based on search conditions related to trivariate mutual information Feng et al. (2014). Unlike standard mutual information-based principles, the correlations among class labels and two bands are studied simultaneously. Another unsupervised feature selection technique for hyperspectral classification is devised Jie Feng (2016) depending upon the minimal redundancy, maximum information, and the clonal selection algorithm. The authors made an effort to reduce unnecessary information by means of restricting mutual information. In gist, while choosing bands, two major issues must be considered, one is vivid information other redundancy of the chosen bands. Choosing just information-rich bands, in other words, does not assure notable classification results, the method of eliminating duplicated data is crucial. Mainly two types of band selection techniques are there: supervised Yang et al. (2011a) and unsupervised Ahmad et al. (2017); Chang and Wang (2006); Karaca and Güllü (2016); Martĺnez-UsÓMartinez-Uso et al. (2007a); Shuaibu et al. (2018); Shukla and Nanda (2018). In the supervised-selection method a subset of bands are picked that contains the utmost meaningful bands based on historical knowledge or tagged samples. The information and distance parameters are broadly applied in these approaches to give a criterion for the identification of important bands utilizing class label information Estevez et al. (2009); Ifarraguerri and Prairie (2004a); Zhang et al. (2007).

Pooling is used by Paul Arati (2019) but Pooling involves reducing the size of the input data by aggregating information from neighboring pixels. This can lead to information loss, as the pooled values may not fully represent the spectral information of the original pixels. This can result in a loss of accuracy in subsequent analysis.

Self-organized maps (SOM) is used by David Ruiz Hidalgo (2021) but it preserve the topology of the input data, which means that the spatial relationships between the input data are maintained in the output space. However, this can be a limitation when the spatial relationships are not important for the analysis.

The rest of the paper is organized as follows. In Sect. 2, The related works are described. In Sect. 3, The proposed algorithm and the procedure are described in detail. In the next section i.e., Sect. 4, the Experimental result is shown, and compared with other existing methods is described.

2 Related Work

Band ranking Du and Yang (2008); Solorio-Fernández et al. (2010), band subspace decomposition Zhang et al. (1999) and use band clustering Xie et al. (2019); Yang et al. (2017) are the methods that are widely used to choose the most discriminative subset of bands, with the objective of reducing band correlation and maximize the information in the selected bands.

2.1 Band Ranking

Based on the fundamental properties associated with class separability, band-ranking algorithms provide a score to the individual bands or to individual subsets of bands. These methods have a low computing complexity and a great degree of generalization. In ref. Solorio-Fernández et al. (2010), the Laplacian scoring measure is used to arrange bands for reducing the feature space and discover the best set of bands. Similarity comparison was studied based on linear prediction (LP), which could concurrently identify the sameness between a single band and several other bands Du and Yang (2008). Though the indicative bands may be found fast with respect to each band's score, the bands picked are likely to have a strong link.

2.2 Band Clustering

Band clustering approach organizes bands so that variation within each cluster was minimized while variation between clusters was maximized. The clustering approach focuses on the substitution of a set of similar characteristics with a representative in the feature space. The k closest neighbors approach and the maximum information compression index are used to cluster the actual set of bands. The subset of bands having the most compact structure was considered for each cluster. For dimensionality reduction of hyperspectral images, this method grouped all spectral bands into clusters and selected representative bands from these groups. This method computed the distance between two spectral bands using disjoint information, which allowed us to effectively capture the spectral variability and identify the most informative bands. The method utilizes a technique of selecting representative bands from each cluster. This approach reduces computational complexity and enhances efficiency while retaining relevant spectral information. As a result, the method is capable of accurately classifying and segmenting hyperspectral images. In summary, the approach effectively reduces the dimensionality of hyperspectral images and identifies the most informative spectral bands. This process enables the technique to achieve high accuracy and robustness. By effectively selecting representative bands, this able to preserve the essential spectral information while significantly reducing the computational complexity of the method. Based on the band clustering methodology, subsets with the highest similarity are chosen from the whole band space. In general, an actual band can be selected as a class's approximation medoid, resulting in a difference between the chosen band and the actual medoid.

3 Proposed Methodology

We have employed a bisecting K-Means and single-layer perceptron neural-network embedded unsupervised method. It starts having a null subset of chosen bands, $B_s = \emptyset$. Later the selected bands from total feature space (F), will be beaded into B_s. The present technique leverages bisecting K-means to build groups/clusters based on the inherent spectral signature of data set in feature space, solely spectral information into consideration. It separates F into two groups at each iteration. To simplify the task, we assume that all characteristics have the same variance. As a result, all samples fall into equal-size hyperplane clusters. For a two-class scenario, the resultant discriminant function will be linear. So, the Euclidean distance, that is employed using K-Means, is utilized to assign input vectors to a class. Each cluster pair is connected using the single-layer neural network. It can discover one dividing hyperplane among parameters specified and repeats the procedure until the necessary number of bands are obtained. This band selection process is an iterative approach. The function must solve a binary classification issue between K-Means produced partitions at each iteration. Because in each iteration two bands are selected and two bands are eliminated from the feature space, the procedure must be repeated until the required band number K is reached. In this procedure, we have selected K

(here, K is the integer value for the corresponding binary coded chromosome or solution) number of bands from H by using the Algorithm 1.

Figure 1 shows a model structure of a single layer neural network. It allows each band X_i to be attached with one weight w_i. The network is trained from scratch in each iteration for two reasons:

1. To avoid any potential local minimum areas from prior clusters.
2. The feature space F shrinks with each repetition. As an outcome, the sizes of w and b shift. The entire architecture must be retrained.

The bands of a hyperspectral image are continuous, resulting in a strong correlation between adjacent bands. In light of this, we use a strategy that avoids selecting strongly linked bands. We create a vector V_k for each band $a_k \in F$, with the components being the band's indices in descendant order in respect of the band a_k.

The correlation ρ between two bands a_α and a_β is given by using Eq. 1.

$$\rho(a_\alpha, a_\beta) = \frac{cov(a_\alpha, a_\beta)}{a_\alpha . \sigma a_\beta} \tag{1}$$

Here, the standard deviation is denoted by ρ and $cov()$ represents the covariance. The fitness value (Y) for each solution (p) is computed by using average ρ. It is presented in Eq. 2.

Algorithm 1. Proposed Redundant Band Reduction Method

Require: No of bands to be selected (k), Hyperspectral Image (H) of dimension n
Ensure: Reduced number of bands of H

    Start

    Initially set all data as a single cluster B and the set of selected band $B_s = \emptyset$

    Split the total Feature Space(F) into two groups using K-means where $k = 2$.

    for $i \leftarrow 1$ to k **do**

        Single-layer Perceptron Neural Networks is designed for all bands (n). Input nodes are connected to a node in the next layer. A node in the next layer takes a weighted (w) sum of all its inputs as $\sum_{j=1}^{j=n} W_j . X_j$

        Select the bands $B_m, B_l \in B$ whose weight is maximum and minimum respectively.

        Include B_m and B_l to set of selected band. $B_s \leftarrow (B_s \cup (B_m \cup B_l))$

        $F \leftarrow (F - B_s))$

        $\forall F_i \in (F - B_s)$ Find corelation to B_m (ρ_m) $= corr(B_m, X_i)$ and corelation to B_l (ρ_l) $= corr(B_l, F_i)$,

        $\rho(B_m, F_i) = \frac{cov(B_m, F_i)}{\sigma B_m . \sigma F_i}$

        Eliminate most correlated bands to B_m and B_l from F

    end for

    Finally B_s is the set of selected bands.

    End

$$Y_p = \frac{\sum_{\alpha=1}^{K} \left\{ \sum_{\beta=\alpha+1}^{K} \rho\left(a_\alpha, a_\beta\right) \right\}}{\frac{K \times (K-1)}{2}} \tag{2}$$

4   Result and Discussion

4.1   Dataset Description

(1) Indian Pines (AVIRIS): The Indian Pines image was captured using the Airborne Infrared Image Spectrometer (AVIRIS) sensor while it was flying over Indiana's north-western region. The hyperspectral sensor got 200 number of bands that can be used for analysis, and each band contains 145×145 pixels. The spatial resolution of this image is 20 m, providing detailed information about the study area.

The image contains 16 features that can be used to distinguish between 6 different types of vegetation present in the area, mostly consisting of various crops. However, identifying these crops is challenging due to the similarity in their spectral reflectance. The spectral closeness of the different crops makes it difficult to differentiate between them using only spectral data, requiring additional analysis techniques to distinguish between them.

(2) Pavia University (ROSIS): he ROSIS sensor captured an image of Pavia University while flying over the university located in Italy. This hyperspectral image dataset was obtained using a sensor with a spatial resolution of 1.3 m per pixel, which resulted in 610×340 pixels in total. The image has 115 spectral bands that can be used for further analysis and interpretation. The hyperspectral image contains 9 different regions that correspond to various urban areas around Pavia University. These regions can be classified

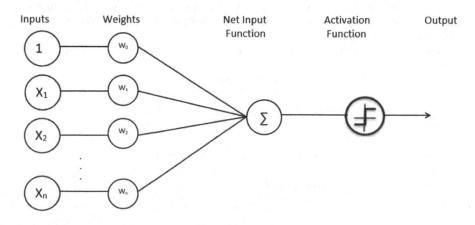

Fig. 1. A Model Structure of Single Layer Perceptron Neural Network

into different classes based on their spectral characteristics, allowing for a more detailed analysis of the urban environment. The high spatial resolution of the ROSIS sensor makes it possible to capture fine details and features within each of the urban areas, providing valuable insights for various applications, including urban planning, environmental monitoring, and disaster management.

4.2 Analysis of Performance

To validate the performance of our proposed technique, a series of experiments were conducted. The first step in this analysis was to reduce the number of bands in the hyperspectral image. Next, the reduced image was segmented using the k-means algorithm to group similar pixels together based on their spectral similarity.

After segmentation, classification algorithms were applied to the segmented image to classify each pixel into its corresponding class. Popular classification techniques were used for this analysis to evaluate the performance of our proposed technique. This process allowed for the comparison of our proposed technique with other existing techniques in the literature. Overall, these experiments provided valuable insights into the effectiveness and accuracy of our proposed technique for hyperspectral image analysis.

The classification outcome are side by side to the classification result of six similar existing band reduction approaches. These are ISD-ABC Xie et al. (2019) and MIMR-CSA Jie Feng (2016). To compare the performance of different techniques, we used three commonly used evaluation metrics: Overall Accuracy (OA),

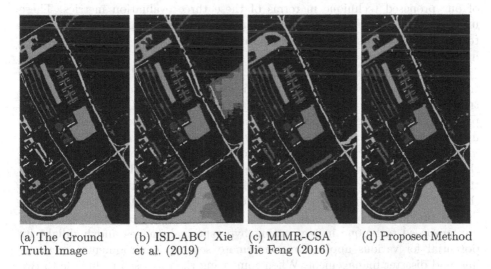

(a) The Ground   (b) ISD-ABC Xie   (c) MIMR-CSA   (d) Proposed Method
Truth Image   et al. (2019)   Jie Feng (2016)

Fig. 2. Pavia dataset obtained by using ROSIS satellite sensor; Spatial resolution: 1.3 m: a) Ground truth; Obtained segmented images by: b) ISD-ABC Xie et al. (2019), c) MIMR-CSA Jie Feng (2016), and d) Proposed Method

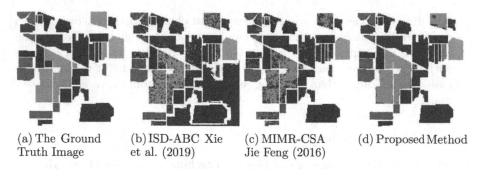

(a) The Ground Truth Image

(b) ISD-ABC Xie et al. (2019)

(c) MIMR-CSA Jie Feng (2016)

(d) Proposed Method

Fig. 3. Indian Pines dataset obtained by using AVIRIS satellite sensor; Spatial resolution: 20 m: a) Ground truth; Obtained segmented images by b) ISD-ABC Xie et al. (2019), c) MIMR-CSA Jie Feng (2016), and d) Proposed Method

Average Accuracy (AA) and Kappa Coefficient (KC). These metrics provide a standardized way of evaluating the performance of different classification and segmentation methods and allow for meaningful comparisons between them.

Average Accuracy (AA) measures the average accuracy of all classes in the classification result. Overall Accuracy (OA) measures the overall accuracy of the classification, which is the percentage of correctly classified pixels. Kappa Coefficient (KC) measures the agreement between the predicted classification and the actual classification, taking into account the possibility of agreement by chance.

By comparing the results of our proposed technique with those obtained from other existing techniques, we were able to evaluate the effectiveness and accuracy of our proposed technique in terms of these three evaluation metrics. These metrics provided a comprehensive evaluation of the performance of our proposed technique, helping us to draw meaningful conclusions about its effectiveness for hyperspectral image analysis.

The segmentation results obtained from our proposed technique for the Indian Pine hyperspectral image are shown in Fig. 2, along with the ground truth and the results obtained from two other competing methods. These images provide a visual representation of the accuracy of our proposed technique in segmenting hyperspectral images. Similarly, Fig. 3 shows the obtained segmented images from the proposed technique, groubd truth and two other methods for the Pavia University hyperspectral image. These images allow us to compare the performance of our proposed technique with other existing techniques in the literature and evaluate its potential for practical applications. Overall, these figures provide valuable visual insights into the effectiveness and accuracy of our proposed technique in segmenting hyperspectral images and highlight its potential for various applications in remote sensing, environmental monitoring, and disaster management. When comparing the proposed technique to two other existing similar techniques, it demonstrates superior accuracy across various metrics such as overall accuracy, average accuracy, and kappa coefficient.

Table 1. Comparison result with other techniques (Indiana Pines Data)

Class	ISD-ABC Xie et al. (2019)	MIMR-CSA Jie Feng (2016)	Proposed Method
1. Alfalfa	86.76 ± 2	65.17 ± 11.5	87.46 ± 2.2
2. Corn-notill	81.08 ± 1	78.87 ± 1.8	83.48 ± 1
3. Cornmintill	71.48 ± 1.3	75.67 ± 2.8	73.98 ± 1.1
4. Corn	72.32 ± 2.4	67.27 ± 4.9	74.82 ± 2.3
5. Grasspasture	94.11 ± 0.5	90.17 ± 2.2	94.31 ± 0.2
6. Grass-trees	96.59 ± 0.5	94.87 ± 0.9	96.99 ± 0.5
7. Grass-pasture mowed	78.70 ± 4.3	68.87 ± 9.9	80.4 ± 4.2
8. Haywindrowed	99.53 ± 0.1	97.67 ± 0.6	99.73 ± −0.3
9. Oats	78.13 ± 4.4	47.17 ± 20.6	79.53 ± 4.3
10. Soybean notill	83.01 ± 0.9	76.87 ± 2.5	85.11 ± 0.7
11. Soybean mintill	88.81 ± 0.5	86.27 ± 0.8	90.01 ± 0.2
12. Soybean clean	84.06 ± 1.3	79.27 ± 3.5	86.96 ± 1.2
13. Wheat	97.56 ± 0.8	96.37 ± 1.8	97.36 ± 0.3
14. Woods	96.51 ± 0.3	93.87 ± 0.8	97.61 ± −0.1
15. Building-grass trees	62.33 ± 2.7	61.17 ± 4.9	65.53 ± 2.6
16. Stone-steel towers	91.33 ± 1.3	82.57 ± 9	93.03 ± 1.3
OA (%)	86.52 ± 0.7	83.27 ± 0.8	87.15 ± 0.4
AA (%)	85.14 ± 1.5	79.97 ± 2	87.01 ± 1.2
KC (%)	84.57 ± 0.8	81.57 ± 1	85.17 ± 0.6

Table 2. Comparison result with other techniques for Pavia University Data

Class	ISD-ABC Xie et al. (2019)	MIMR-CSA Jie Feng (2016)	Proposed Method
1. Asphalt	89.17 ± 0.9	92.91 ± 0.2	93.41 ± 0.1
Meadows	96.57 ± −0.1	97.67 ± 0.3	98.72 ± −0.3
Gravel	60.17 ± 5.5	71.37 ± 1.3	73.81 ± 0.6
Trees	90.07 ± 1.6	93.27 ± 0.7	95.01 ± 0.6
Painted metal sheets	98.87 ± −0.2	99.57 ± 0.5	98.9 ± −0.4
Bare soil	73.97 ± 3.2	89.17 ± 1.0	91.93 ± 0.4
Bitumen	79.27 ± 2	72.50 ± 73.8	81.02 ± 0.4
Self-blocking bricks	87.27 ± 0.6	87.37 ± 0.9	89.04 ± −0.2
Shadows	98.07 ± 0.1	99.97 ± 0.1	99.39 ± −0.3
OA(%)	88.77 ± 0.8	92.57 ± 0.3	94.31 ± −0.4
AA(%)	87.97 ± 0.7	89.17 ± 0.6	92.01 ± −0.2
KC(%)	86.17 ± 0.4	90.17 ± 0.3	93.74 ± 0

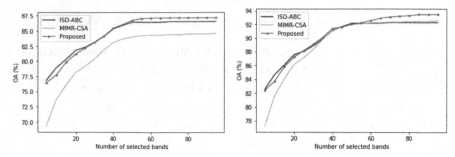

(a) Graphical representation of comparison with others for Indiana Pine
Dataset

(b) Graphical representation of comparison with others for Pavia University Dataset

Fig. 4. Comparing the overall accuracy of our proposed method to other selection techniques

The proposed technique outperforms the alternatives in terms of accurately classifying and segmenting the data, providing more reliable and precise results. It is clear from Fig. 4, that the classification accuracy gradually increases when the no of chosen bands is increased for all the algorithms. Because the selected feature space becomes richer in information when it contains more bands. But after a certain no of selected bands, the accuracy does not change significantly, i.e. it leans towards a stable condition. This indicates the already selected bands are quite sufficient to represent the total hyperspectral image informatively. So the inclusion of more bands will not effectively improve the accuracy further.

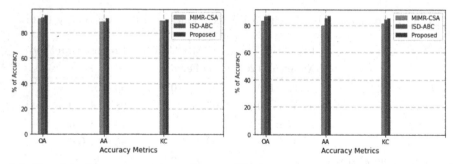

(a) Graphical representation of comparison with others for Indiana Pine
Dataset

(b) Graphical representation of comparison with others Pavia University
Dataset

Fig. 5. Comparison of OA, AA, KC with other band selection techniques to the proposed band selection method

Figure 2 displays the ground truth and segmented images of the Indian Pine hyperspectral image obtained from our proposed method and two other competing techniques. The images provide a visual representation of the accuracy and effectiveness of our proposed method in segmenting hyperspectral images, which is crucial for various applications in remote sensing and environmental monitoring.

On the other hand, Fig. 3 shows segmented images obtained from our proposed method, ground truth and two other methods for the Pavia University hyperspectral image. The images allow us to compare the performance of our proposed method with other existing techniques and assess its potential for practical applications in urban planning, disaster management, and environmental monitoring.

These figures provide valuable insights into the effectiveness of our proposed method in segmenting hyperspectral images and enable us to identify areas for improvement and optimization. The comparison of results with other existing methods is crucial for evaluating the accuracy and robustness of our proposed method, allowing us to determine its potential for practical applications in real-world scenarios. The proposed algorithm outperforms two other existing band selection methods, i.e. ISD-ABC, and MIMR-CSA and it's empirical results reveal that the proposed method gives high classification accuracy for both the hyperspectral dataset. OA, AA, and KC is separately compared with the said six other band selection method and it is shown in Fig. 5. It is clear that in terms of overall accuracy (OA) the proposed band selection technique shows better performance than the other existing works. The methods like ISD-ABC gives 86.52 %, MIMR-CSA gives 83.27% ware as the proposed method gives 88.42% overall accuracy for Indiana Pine dataset.

The above Table 1 describes that the proposed method gives Average Accuracy of 87.14% when other existing works such as ISD-ABC gives 85.14%, MIMR-CSA gives 79.97%. for Indiana Pine dataset.

Again the result shows that the proposed method gives a higher Kappa Coefficient value of 86.67% compared with the existing works such as ISD-ABC gives 84.57%, MIMR-CSA gives 81.57%.

Table 2 show the OA, AA, KC comparison values obtained from Pavia University dataset. For both hyperspectral datasets, the proposed band selection method provides better performance than other band selection techniques mentioned here in terms of AA, OA, and KC.

It is clear from Fig. 4, that the classification accuracy gradually increases when the no of chosen bands is increased for all the algorithms. Because the selected feature space becomes richer in information when it contains more bands. But after a certain no of selected bands, the accuracy does not change significantly, i.e. it leans towards a stable condition. This indicates the already selected bands are quite sufficient to represent the total hyperspectral image informatively. So the inclusion of more bands will not effectively improve the accuracy further.

5 Conclusion

Hyperspectral imaging (HSI) offers comprehensive spectrum information, enabling a detailed description of objects within a scene. Nonetheless, the substantial amount of data associated with HSI presents challenges in terms of processing and storage. Furthermore, feature spaces with huge dimensions suffer from the dimensionality curse. In this study, we introduce a neuroevolutionary approach to address the challenge of high dimensionality in hyperspectral images. Our method involves utilizing a novel single-layer neural network in combination with a genetic evolutionary algorithm. By employing this technique, redundant bands are eliminated, and the significant bands are selected from the original hyperspectral image. The effectiveness of our approach is evaluated using two commonly used hyperspectral datasets, namely Indian Pine and Pavia University. After reducing the dimensionality of the hyperspectral image through band extraction, the resulting image is further processed through segmentation and classification stages. When comparing the proposed technique to two other existing similar techniques, it demonstrates superior accuracy across various metrics such as overall accuracy, average accuracy, and kappa coefficient. The proposed technique outperforms the alternatives in terms of accurately classifying and segmenting the data, providing more reliable and precise results.

References

Agarwal, A., El-Ghazawi, T., El-Askary, H., Le-Moigne, J.: Efficient hierarchical-PCA dimension reduction for hyperspectral imagery. In: 2007 IEEE International Symposium on Signal Processing and Information Technology, pp. 353–356 (2007)

Ahmad, M., Khan, A.M., Brown, J.A., Protasov, S., Khattak, A.M.: Gait fingerprinting-based user identification on smartphones. In: 2016 International Joint Conference on Neural Networks (IJCNN), pp. 3060–3067 (2016a)

Ahmad, M., Khan, A.M., Hussain, R., Protasov, S., Chow, F., Khattak, A.M.: Unsupervised geometrical feature learning from hyperspectral data. In: 2016 IEEE Symposium Series on Computational Intelligence (SSCI), pp. 1–6 (2016b)

Ahmad, M., Protasov, S., Khan, A.: Hyperspectral band selection using unsupervised non-linear deep auto encoder to train external classifiers. Unknown (2017)

Ahmad, M., Ulhaq, D., Mushtaq, Q.: AIK method for band clustering using statistics of correlation and dispersion matrix, pp. 114–118 (2011)

Brown, A., Sutter, B., Dunagan, S.: The MARTE VNIR imaging spectrometer experiment: design and analysis. Astrobiology 8, 1001–11 (2008)

Chang, C.-I.: Techniques for spectral detection and classification. In: Hyperspectral Imaging (2003)

Chang, C.-I., Du, Q.: Estimation of number of spectrally distinct signal sources in hyperspectral imagery. IEEE Trans. Geosci. Remote Sens. 42(3), 608–619 (2004)

Chang, C.-I., Wang, S.: Constrained band selection for hyperspectral imagery. IEEE Trans. Geosci. Remote Sens. 44(6), 1575–1585 (2006)

Hidalgo, D.R., Cortés, B.B., Bravo, E.C.: Dimensionality reduction of hyperspectral images of vegetation and crops based on self-organized maps. Inf. Process. Agric. 8(2), 310–327 (2021)

Du, Q., Yang, H.: Similarity-based unsupervised band selection for hyperspectral image analysis. IEEE Geosci. Remote Sens. Lett. 5(4), 564–568 (2008)

Estevez, P.A., Tesmer, M., Perez, C.A., Zurada, J.M.: Normalized mutual information feature selection. IEEE Trans. Neural Networks 20(2), 189–201 (2009)

Mathieu, F., Jocelyn, C., Benediktsson, J.A.: Kernel principal component analysis for the classification of hyperspectral remote sensing data over urban areas. EURASIP J. Adv. Signal Process. 2009, 783194 (2009)

Feng, J., Jiao, L.C., Zhang, X., Sun, T.: Hyperspectral band selection based on trivariate mutual information and clonal selection. IEEE Trans. Geosci. Remote Sens. 52(7), 4092–4105 (2014)

Gustavsson, D., Wadströmer, N.: Non-linear hyperspectral subspace mapping using stacked auto-encoder (2016)

He, X., Cai, D., Yan, S., Zhang, H.-J.: Neighborhood preserving embedding. In: Tenth IEEE International Conference on Computer Vision (ICCV 2005), vol. 1, 2, pp. 1208–1213 (2005)

Ifarraguerri, A., Prairie, M.: Visual method for spectral band selection. IEEE Geosci. Remote Sens. Lett. 1(2), 101–106 (2004)

Feng, J., Licheng Jiao, F.L.T.S.X.Z.: Unsupervised feature selection based on maximum information and minimum redundancy for hyperspectral images. Pattern Recogn. 51, 295–309 (2016)

Kanning, M., Siegmann, B., Jarmer, T.: Regionalization of uncovered agricultural soils based on organic carbon and soil texture estimations. Remote Sens. 8(11), 927 (2016)

Karaca, A.C., Güllü, M.K.: Comparison of traditional and recent unsupervised band selection approaches in hyperspectral images. In: 2016 24th Signal Processing and Communication Application Conference (SIU), pp. 785–788 (2016)

Li, W., Prasad, S., Fowler, J.E., Bruce, L.M.: Locality-preserving discriminant analysis in kernel-induced feature spaces for hyperspectral image classification. IEEE Geosci. Remote Sens. Lett. 8(5), 894–898 (2011)

Li, W., Prasad, S., Fowler, J.E., Bruce, L.M.: Locality-preserving dimensionality reduction and classification for hyperspectral image analysis. IEEE Trans. Geosci. Remote Sens. 50(4), 1185–1198 (2012)

Liu, L., Li, C.F., Lei, Y.M., et al.: Feature extraction for hyperspectral remote sensing image using weighted PCA-ICA, vol. 10 (2017)

Martínez-UsóMartinez-Uso, A., Pla, F., Sotoca, J.M., García-Sevilla, P.: Clustering-based hyperspectral band selection using information measures. IEEE Trans. Geosci. Remote Sens. 45(12), 4158–4171 (2007)

Nahr, S.T., Pahlavani, P., Hasanlou, M.: Different optimal band selection of hyperspectral images using a continuous genetic algorithm. Int. Arch. Photogramm. Remote Sens. Spat. Inf. Sci. 40(2), 249 (2014)

Nakamura, R.Y.M., Fonseca, L.M.G., dos Santos, J.A., da S. Torres, R., Yang, X.-S., Papa, J.P.: Nature-inspired framework for hyperspectral band selection. IEEE Trans. Geosci. Remote Sens. 52(4), 2126–2137 (2014)

Patra, S., Modi, P., Bruzzone, L.: Hyperspectral band selection based on rough set. IEEE Trans. Geosci. Remote Sens. 53(10), 5495–5503 (2015)

Paul Arati, C.N.: Dimensionality reduction of hyperspectral images using pooling. Pattern Recognit Image Anal. 29, 72–78 (2019)

Roweis, S., Saul, L.: Nonlinear dimensionality reduction by locally linear embedding. Science 290(5500), 2323–6 (2000)

Shuaibu, M., Lee, W.S., Schueller, J., Gader, P., Hong, Y.K., Kim, S.: Unsupervised hyperspectral band selection for apple Marssonina blotch detection. Comput. Electron. Agric. 148, 45–53 (2018)

Shukla, U.P., Nanda, S.J.: A binary social spider optimization algorithm for unsupervised band selection in compressed hyperspectral images. Expert Syst. Appl. **97**, 336–356 (2018)

Solorio-Fernández, S., Carrasco-Ochoa, J.A., Martínez-Trinidad, J.F.: Hybrid feature selection method for supervised classification based on Laplacian score ranking. In: Martínez-Trinidad, J.F., Carrasco-Ochoa, J.A., Kittler, J. (eds.) MCPR 2010. LNCS, vol. 6256, pp. 260–269. Springer, Heidelberg (2010). https://doi.org/10.1007/978-3-642-15992-3_28

Su, H., Du, Q., Chen, G., Du, P.: Optimized hyperspectral band selection using particle swarm optimization. IEEE J. Sel. Topics Appl. Earth Observ. Remote Sens. **7**(6), 2659–2670 (2014)

Su, H., Yong, B., Du, Q.: Hyperspectral band selection using improved firefly algorithm. IEEE Geosci. Remote Sens. Lett. **13**(1), 68–72 (2016)

Wang, Q., Meng, Z., Li, X.: Locality adaptive discriminant analysis for spectral-spatial classification of hyperspectral images. IEEE Geosci. Remote Sens. Lett. **14**(11), 2077–2081 (2017)

Xie, F., Li, F., Lei, C., Yang, J., Zhang, Y.: Unsupervised band selection based on artificial bee colony algorithm for hyperspectral image classification. Appl. Soft Comput. **75**, 428–440 (2019)

Yang, H., Du, Q., Su, H., Sheng, Y.: An efficient method for supervised hyperspectral band selection. IEEE Geosci. Remote Sens. Lett. **8**(1), 138–142 (2011)

Yang, R., Su, L., Zhao, X., Wan, H., Sun, J.: Representative band selection for hyperspectral image classification. J. Vis. Commun. Image Represent. **48**, 396–403 (2017)

Yuan, Y., Zhu, G., Wang, Q.: Hyperspectral band selection by multitask sparsity pursuit. IEEE Trans. Geosci. Remote Sens. **53**(2), 631–644 (2015)

Zhang, L., Zhong, Y., Huang, B., Gong, J., Li, P.: Dimensionality reduction based on clonal selection for hyperspectral imagery. IEEE Trans. Geosci. Remote Sens. **45**(12), 4172–4186 (2007)

Zhang, Y., Desai, M., Zhang, J., Jin, M.: Adaptive subspace decomposition for hyperspectral data dimensionality reduction. In: Proceedings 1999 International Conference on Image Processing (Cat. 99CH36348), vol. 2, pp. 326–329 (1999)

Economic Load Dispatch Problem Using African Vulture Optimization Algorithm (AVOA) in Thermal Power Plant with Wind Energy

Pritam Mandal$^{(\boxtimes)}$, Sk. Sanimul, Barun Mandal, and Provas Kumar Roy[ID]

Kalyani Government Engineering College, Kalyani, India
pritamkgei@gmail.com

Abstract. This article presents an elementary and efficient nature inspired optimization technique namely African vulture optimization algorithm (AVOA) to solve economic load dispatch problems. To make it more cost-effective, wind turbines have been incorporated with the existing thermal generating plants. The stochastic behaviour of wind is considered here. AVOA has been implemented for single objective fuel cost minimization. For demonstrating suitability and scalability of this proposed approach in case of large-scale and real world scenerio, it has been tested against IEEE 6-bus, IEEE 40-bus and IEEE 140-bus network and the outcomes are analyzed against results found by other heuristic approaches that were being used recently. The results clearly shows the potential AVOA has in achieving optimal solution.

Keywords: Economic Load Dispatch (ELD) · African Vultures Optimization Algorithm (AVOA) · Underestimation Of Wind Power · Overestimation of Wind Power · Exploration · Exploitation · Probability distribution function(PDF) · Cumulative distribution function(CDF)

1 Introduction

In thermal power plants, the cost of power generation mostly constitutes of the fuel cost and through economical load dispatch, a reasonable amount of revenue can be saved by minimizing the fuel cost [1]. The economical dispatch of load is a major concern in power system planning and operation. Through optimal load dispatch of generating units, a significant reduction in greenhouse gas emission and also rate of consumption of non renewable resources can be achieved. The primary aim of ELD is to minimize the power generation cost while also satisfying the constraints like valve point effects [2], prohibited zones of operating [3], spinning reserve capacity [4], security constraints [5], etc. ELD uses various formulations to calculate the least cost of power generation to achieve the required power demand and these formulations consider or even neglect power flow constraints [6]. Nowadays, utilization of wind energy in power generation is advancing at a dramatic rate. ELD is traditionally solved using mathematical

© The Author(s), under exclusive license to Springer Nature Switzerland AG 2024
K. Dasgupta et al. (Eds.): CICBA 2023, CCIS 1955, pp. 107–120, 2024.
https://doi.org/10.1007/978-3-031-48876-4_9

based optimization techniques like Newton-Raphson [7], Lambda iteration [8], Dynamic programming [9], the gradient method [10] and so on. Several optimization techniques which includes both stochastic and classical search approaches, have been used to solve ELD problems. The computing speed of these solutions, however, limits their online applications. As these approaches mostly rely on approximation to reduce the complexity of problem, thus result obtained from these approaches tends to get trapped in local optimum. Further, the non-convex fuel cost functions of generation units can not be handled using these approaches. To overcome these restrictions of classical optimization approaches, several heuristic algorithms have been demonstrated in past to solve economic dispatch problem.

Recently, Khan et al. [11] introduced moth flame algorithm for solving eld incorporating wind which considers the stochastic wind. Siddique et al. [12] recently proposed genetic algorithm for solving eld with solar and thermal generating units. Parouha et al. [13] proposed memory based differential evolution algorithm for solving eld which nullifies the inappropriate choice of its mutation and crossover operators. Ameliorated grey wolf optimization introduced by Dhillon et al. [14] potentially solved eld problem with non-linearities. Hybrid BBO proposed by Saha et al. [15] includes renewable sources along with existing sources for solving eld. Sahoo et al. [16] recently proposed harmony search algorithm which solves dynamic economic dispatch problem.

With increasing power demand, the focus is now on improving the performance of these methods. Swarm optimization is a very efficient and widely used optimization approach in recent days because of its ability to tackle complex problems. In recent years, wind power units are being used along with thermal power plants to reduce the cost of power generation [17]. With technology evolving, the power capacity from a large wind farm can be compared to the capacity of a thermal power generation unit. Managing and controlling such a system is one of the most challenging duties of the system operators. Nowadays, the field of nature-inspired metaheuristics is mostly constituted by the evolutionary algorithms. AVOA, a recent nature-inspired metaheuristic algorithm has been identified for solving the ELD problem in this work. Researchers have already worked on AVOA and their works clearly denotes the potential AVOA has in optimizing several problems in power system. Also, AVOA hasn't been implemented for ELD yet.

The paper is arranged as follows: Sect. 2 demonstrates the mathematical model of the ELD problem. Section 3 provides a clear description of AVOA algorithm. Section 4 demonstrates the simulation results with the comparison tables. Finally we wrap up the article with conclusion in Sect. 5.

2   Mathematical Problem Formulation

The idea of ELD is minimization of the cost of electricity generation without sacrificing quality and reliability. Our aim is to obtain the individual generation of different generating units in such a manner that the total cost of generation is minimum and the equality and inequality constraints are contented.

2.1   Quadratic Cost Function

The amount of fuel used to generate electricity depends on the efficiency or heat rate of the generator and the heat content of the fuel being used. Generator curves are generally represented as cubic or quadratic functions and piecewise linear functions. Thermal power plant uses a quadratic fuel cost function such as the fuel cost curve.

Let P_{gj} represents the power generation of jth power unit. Then, Cost of power generation,

$$C = \sum_{j=1}^{N} F_j(P_{gj}) = \sum_{j=1}^{N} [a_j(P_{gj})^2 + b_j(P_{gj}) + c_j] \tag{1}$$

$F_j(P_{gj})$ = Cost of fuel of P_{gj} unit P_{gj} = Production of P_{gj} unit a_j, b_j, c_j = Cost coeficients N = Total no. of generating units of Thermal power plant.

This is the Objective function in Economic Load Dispatch problems.

2.2   System Constraints

There are two type of constraints.

Equality Constraints: The equality constraints being considered are:
Summation of power generation of all units should be equal to the summation of power demand of load (P_D).

$$\sum_{j=1}^{Ng} P_{gj} = P_D \tag{2}$$

where P_{gj} is generation of j_{th} unit, Ng denotes number of generating units.

Inequality Constraints: The inequality constraints being considered are:
Power generated by each unit P_g should be greater than or equal to least amount of power allowed for that unit $P_g{}^{min}$ and must also be less than or equal to maximal amount of power allowed for that unit $P_g{}^{max}$.

$$P_g{}^{min} \leq P_g \leq P_g^{max} \tag{3}$$

2.3   ELD Without Transmission Losses

Let's say there's a station with NG generators and a given demand of power P_D. Then the optimization problem neglecting the transmission loss is approached in the following way-

$$F(Pg_j) = \sum_{j=1}^{NG} (Pg_j)F_j \tag{4}$$

where $F(Pg_j)$ and F_j are the fuel cost and fuel cost coefficients for (j_{th}) unit.

$$\sum_{j=1}^{N}(P_{gj}) = P_D \tag{5}$$

Active power constraint is:

$$Pg^{min} \leq Pg \leq Pg^{max} \tag{6}$$

2.4   Wind Energy

Wind is the fastest-growing and cleanest renewable energy source, and it is being examined as a major non-conventional power source [18]. Due to the variable aspect of wind power, cost of production and the reliability of the generating plant have become a severe concern. Here weibull distribution function is being used to tackle the uncertainity of wind velocity.

$$f(v_w) = \left(\frac{k}{c}\right)\left(\frac{v_w}{c}\right)^{(k-1)} e^{-(\frac{v_w}{c})^k} \text{ for } 0 < v_w < \infty \tag{7}$$

$$F(v_w) = 1 - \exp(-(v_w/c)^k), \ v_w > 0 \tag{8}$$

where Eq. (7) and Eq. (8) potrays the PDF and CDF of weibull distribution respectively. k denotes shape factor and c denotes scale factor.

Now wind turbine's power equation is given by:

$$W = \frac{1}{2}\rho A v^3 c_p \tag{9}$$

where ρ- Air density factor, A - Effective sweep area of blade, v - Wind speed, C_p- Power Coefficient

Underestimation of Available Wind Power: Because of the underestimating of wind power potential, working issues such as transmission line crowding might occur, resulting in wind power restrictions during normal operation. The penalty for refusing to accept available potential of wind for the kth wind plant as follows:

$$Cost_{u,w}^{k} = K_{u,w}^{k} \int_{p_w^l}^{p_{w,r}^k} (p - p_{w,k})f(p)dp \tag{10}$$

where $K_{u,w}^{k}$ denotes underestimated cost coefficient, p denotes available wind power, $p_{w,k}$ denotes estimated wind power and $f(p)$ is the wind power pdf.

Overestimation of Available Wind Power: In order to satisfy the load demand, the authority is compelled to acquire power from the other more costlier reserves due to lack of wind power generation. Following are the mathematical representations for considering the overestimation of wind power the ith wind farm.

$$Cost^k_{o,w} = K^k_{o,w} \int_0^{p,l} (p_{w,k} - p)f(p)dp \tag{11}$$

where $K^k_{o,w}$ denotes overestimated cost coefficient.

2.5 Direct Cost

The projected WE injected in the electrical network is used to calculate the straight expenditure formula for wind power. The Direct cost is calculated as follows:

$$Cost^k_{d,w} = K_{d,w}p_{w,k} \tag{12}$$

where $K^k_{d,w}$ represents direct cost coefficient. Then the total cost is :

$$COST^k_w = Cost^k_{d,w} + Cost^k_{u,w} + Cost^k_{o,w} \tag{13}$$

2.6 Objective Function

The objective function i.e. the total power generation cost is thus the sum of thermal power generation cost, direct cost of wind, penalty cost due to both underestimation and overestimation. It is given by:

$$C_{total} = \sum_{j=1}^{Ng} \left(a_j(P_{gj})^2 + b_j(P_{gj})\right)$$

$$+c_j + K_{d,w}p_{w,k} + K^k_{u,w} \int_{p^t_w}^{p^k_{w,r}} (p - p_{w,k})f(p)dp \tag{14}$$

$$+K^k_{o,w} \int_0^{p,l} (p_{w,k} - p)f(p)dp$$

C_{total} is the total incorporating cost, N_g is total no. of thermal generators and the wind unit costs, which are already explained in previous subsections are added to the cost due to thermal generating units. This overall cost needs to be minimized.

3   African Vulture Optimization Algorithm

AVOA was implemented by Mirjalili et al. [19] as a population-based metaheuristic approach in 2021. This algorithm is based on the hunting behavior and social lifestyle of african vultures. An initial population of vultures is generated.

3.1   Phase 1

This algorithm firstly calculates the fitness function for the initial solution set (initial population). Then these vultures are divided into categories. The fittest (strongest vulture) solution is termed as 'Best vulture' and the second best solution is termed as 'Second best vulture' [20]. As we know, vultures are carcass eaters. They search for food in large groups. So the solutions are divided into groups. The entire population is recalculated after each fitness iteration by the equation as follows:

$$P_j = \frac{F_j}{\sum\limits_{j=1}^{n} F_j} \tag{15}$$

3.2   Phase 2

Vultures are very energetic and can travel miles in search for food if they are satiated. But when hungry, they rely on the stronger vulture for food and becomes violent. This behavior of vulture is mathematically modelled as:

$$t = h \times \left(\sin^w \left(\frac{\pi}{2} \times \frac{Iteration_i}{Maxiterations} \right) + \cos \left(\frac{\pi}{2} \times \frac{Iteration_i}{Maxiterations} \right) - 1 \right) \tag{16}$$

$$F = (2 \times rand_i + 1) \times zi \times \left(1 - \frac{Iteration_i}{Maxiterations} \right) + t \tag{17}$$

where, F denotes the vultures' hunger is fully satisfied, $Iteration_i$ represents the present iteration number, Maxiterations denotes the maximum no. of iterations, zi denotes a random no. between -1 and 1, h denotes random no. within -2 and 2, $rand_i$ represents random no. between 0 and 1, z value denotes vulture is satiated or starved.

3.3   Phase 3

This is the Exploration phase. Generally, vultures are superior in finding food and detecting poor dying animals. But finding food may not be so easy. Vultures need to travel miles to find food. Now vultures explore for food in areas randomly depending on two strategies. A parameter P_1 is taken which occupies random value between 0 and 1 and determines which strategy the vulture will follow. Another random number randP1 is generated that can have values between 0 and 1.

If randP1 $\geq P_1$,

$$P(j+1) = R_i(j) - D_i(j) \times F \tag{18}$$

where,

$$D_i(j) = |X \times R_i(j) - P(j)| \tag{19}$$

If randP1 $< P_1$,

$$P(j+1) = R_i(j) - F + rand_2 \times ((upper - lower) \times rand_3 + lower) \tag{20}$$

where P(j) = Position of vulture in current iteration, P(j+1) = position of vulture in next iteration, $R_i(j)$ = One of the best vultures selected in Phase 1, $D_i(j)$ = Distance of any vulture to one of the best vultures of two different groups, F = Rate of vulture starvation, X = region where the vulture goes to defend their food.

After each iteration,

$$X_{new} = 2 \times X \tag{21}$$

3.4   Phase 4

This the Exploitation Phase. If the rate of starvation of vultures become less than 1, exploitation phase of AVOA starts. There are two internal phases of Exploitation. Each phase has two different strategies. Two random parameters P_2 and P_3 are generated with values between 0 and 1, which decides which strategy the vulture will choose in each phase.

First Phase: $0.5 < F \le 1$, First phase of Exploitation starts. A random number randP2 is generated.

If $randP2 \ge P_2$, Siege fight strategy is followed where strong vultures don't want to share the food whereas weak vultures tend to snatch food from the stronger vultures by roaming over strong vultures, creating small conflicts and tiring them. This behavior is mathematically shown as:

$$P(j+1) = D_i(j) \times (F \times rand_4) - D(t) \tag{22}$$

$$D(t) = R_i(j) - P(j) \tag{23}$$

If $randP2 < P_2$, Rotating flight strategy is followed. Here the vulture does rotational flights which resembles spiral motion. This behavior is mathematically expressed as:

$$S_1 = R_i(j) \times (\frac{Rand_5 \times P(j)}{2\pi}) \times Cos(P(j)) \tag{24}$$

$$S_2 = R_i(j) \times (\frac{Rand_6 \times P(j)}{2\pi}) \times Cos(P(j)) \tag{25}$$

$$P(j+1) = R_i(j) - (S_1 + S_2) \tag{26}$$

where $rand_5$ and $rand_6$ are random numbers between 0 and 1

Second Phase: For $F < 0.5$, Second phase of Exploitation starts. Similar to First phase, a random number randP3 is generated.

If $randP3 \ge P_3$, the idea is that various species of vultures gather over one food source.

$$A_1 = BestVulture_1(j) - \frac{BestVulture_1(j) \times P(j)}{BestVulture_1(j) - P(j)^2} \times F \tag{27}$$

$$A_2 = BestVulture_2(j) - \frac{BestVulture_2(j) \times P(j)}{BestVulture_2(j) - P(j)^2} \times F \qquad (28)$$

$$P(j+1) = \frac{A_1 + A_2}{2} \qquad (29)$$

where, $BestVulture_1(j)$ denotes best vulture of first group in present iteration and $BestVulture_2(j)$ denotes best vulture of second group in present iteration.

If randP3 $< P_3$, the siege-fight strategy is followed. Here, the primary vultures grow weak and hungry, and they lack the energy to cope with the other vultures. The other aggressive vultures, in search for food roam around the primary vultures.

$$P(j+1) = R_i(j) - |D(t)| \times F \times Levy(d) \qquad (30)$$

where levy(d) denotes levy flight pattern.

4   Simulation Results and Discussions

To test the efficacy of AVOA, here 3 types of system which are 6 units, 40 units and 140 units has been considered. This has been implemented in MAT-LAB R2017b. Here in every case, two scenarios are validated. AVOA is implemented to thermal power plant without wind and with wind, and then these results are compared with some other approaches as like Opposition Based Harmony Search Algorithm (OHSA), Ant Colony Optimization (ACO), Seeker Optimization Algorithm (SOA) and Quasi Teaching-Learning-based Optimization (QOTLBO). The input parameters of thermal generation units are taken from [21] and that of wind generation units are taken from [22].

4.1   Case Studies 1

For 6 bus system and a power demand of 1263 MW, we have considered two scenarios- one where all six unit are thermal units and other where two units are of wind plant and rest 4 of thermal plant the simulation results of our algorithm are presented in Table 1, the convergence graph is presented in Fig. 1 and the outcomes are compared with that of some other algorithms previously reported in Table 2 and results of AVOA are comparatively better.

4.2   Case Studies 2

For 40 bus system and a power demand of 10500 MW, we have considered two scenarios- one where all forty unit are thermal units and other where two units are of wind plant and rest thirty eight are thermal units. The simulated results of our algorithm are presented in Table 3 and Table 5, the convergence graph is presented in Fig. 2, for the two scenarios mentioned above and the outcomes are compared to some algorithms previously reported in Table 4 and results of AVOA are comparatively better.

4.3   Case Studies 3

For 140 bus system and a power demand of 49342 MW, we have considered two scenarios- one where all one hundred and forty unit are thermal units and other where two units are of wind plant and rest one hundred and thirty eight are thermal units. The simulation results of our algorithm are presented in Table 6 and Table 8 for the two scenarios and the outcomes are compared to some algorithms previously reported in Table 7 and results of AVOA are comparatively better.

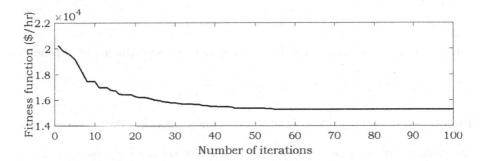

Fig. 1. Convergence graph of AVOA for six unit system excluding wind plant

Table 1. AVOA for single objective of 6 unit system with and without wind and Power Demand 1263 MW

	Without wind		With wind
Generator No.	Generation (MW)	Generator No.	Generator (MW)
P_1	446.7073	P_{w1}	344.9353
P_2	171.2580	P_{w2}	200.0000
P_3	264.1056	P_3	280.9912
P_4	125.2168	P_4	142.1023
P_5	172.1189	P_5	191.1151
P_6	83.5934	P_6	103.8561
Total Cost	15275.9304 ($/hr)	Total Cost	13229.8517($/hr)

Table 2. Comparison Of AVOA with other algorithms for 6 unit system excluding wind

Algorithms	Max Cost ($/hr)	Min Cost ($/hr)	Ave Cost ($/hr)
AVOA	15365.9304	15275.9304	15320.9304
DHS [23]	15449.0000	15449.0000	15449.0000
PSO [23]	15492.0000	15450.0000	15454.0000
GA [23]	15524.0000	15459.0000	15469.0000
DE[23]	15449.0000	15449.0000	15449.0000

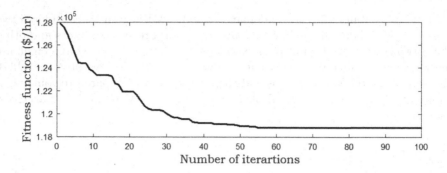

Fig. 2. Convergence graph of AVOA for forty unit system excluding wind plant

Table 3. AVOA for single objective of 40 unit system and Power Demand 10500 MW

Generator No.	Generation (MW)	Generator No.	Generation (MW)	Generator No.	Generation (MW)	Generator No.	Generation (MW)
P_{TH1}	114.0000	P_{TH11}	94.0000	P_{TH21}	550.0000	P_{TH31}	190.0000
P_{TH2}	114.0000	P_{TH12}	94.0000	P_{TH22}	550.0000	P_{TH32}	190.0000
P_{TH3}	120.0000	P_{TH13}	125.0000	P_{TH23}	550.0000	P_{TH33}	190.0000
P_{TH4}	190.0000	P_{TH14}	266.6683	P_{TH24}	550.0000	P_{TH34}	200.0000
P_{TH5}	97.0000	P_{TH15}	267.1454	P_{TH25}	550.0000	P_{TH35}	200.0000
P_{TH6}	140.0000	P_{TH16}	271.1863	P_{TH26}	550.0000	P_{TH36}	200.0000
P_{TH7}	300.0000	P_{TH17}	500.0000	P_{TH27}	10.0000	P_{TH37}	110.0000
P_{TH8}	300.0000	P_{TH18}	500.0000	P_{TH28}	10.0000	P_{TH38}	110.0000
P_{TH9}	300.0000	P_{TH19}	550.0000	P_{TH29}	10.0000	P_{TH39}	110.0000
P_{TH10}	130.0000	P_{TH20}	550.0000	P_{TH30}	97.0000	P_{TH40}	550.0000
Total Cost	118624.3693 ($/hr)						

Table 4. Comparison of AVOA with other algorithms for 40 thermal unit system excluding wind

Algorithms	Max cost ($/hr)	Min cost ($/hr)	Ave cost ($/hr)
AVOA	119246.8965	118624.3693	118975.6329
ABC[24]	NR	121441.7000	121995.82
TS[24]	NR	122288.3800	122424.81
ACO[24]	NR	121811.3700	121,930.58
GWO[24]	NR	121488.4000	NR
[NR: Not Reported]			

Table 5. AVOA for single objective of 40 unit system including wind and Power Demand 10500 MW

Generator No.	Generation (MW)	Generator No.	Generation (MW)	Generator No.	Generation (MW)	Generator No.	Generation (MW)
P_{w1}	120.0001	P_{11}	94.0001	P_{21}	550.0000	P_{31}	190.0000
P_{w2}	194.0783	P_{12}	94.0000	P_{22}	550.0000	P_{32}	190.0000
P_3	120.0001	P_{13}	125.0000	P_{23}	550.0000	P_{33}	190.0000
P_4	190.0001	P_{14}	239.9351	P_{24}	550.0000	P_{34}	200.0000
P_5	97.0001	P_{15}	239.5824	P_{25}	550.0000	P_{35}	200.0000
P_6	140.0001	P_{16}	239.4043	P_{26}	550.0000	P_{36}	200.0000
P_7	300.0001	P_{17}	500.0000	P_{27}	10.0000	P_{37}	110.0000
P_8	300.0001	P_{18}	500.0000	P_{28}	10.0000	P_{38}	110.0000
P_9	300.0001	P_{19}	550.0000	P_{29}	10.0000	P_{39}	110.0000
P_{10}	130.0001	P_{20}	550.0000	P_{30}	97.0000	P_{40}	550.0000
Total Cost	117593.7573 ($/hr)						

Table 6. AVOA for single objective of 140 unit system excluding wind and Power Demand 49342 MW

Unit No.	Gen. (MW)	Unit No.	Gen. (MW)	Unit No.	Gen. (MW)	Unit No.	Gen. (MW)	Unit No.	Gen. (MW)
P_{TH1}	71.0000	P_{TH29}	501.0000	P_{TH57}	103.0000	P_{TH85}	115.0000	P_{TH113}	94.0000
P_{TH2}	189.0000	P_{TH30}	501.0000	P_{TH58}	198.0000	P_{TH86}	207.0000	P_{TH114}	94.0000
P_{TH3}	190.0000	P_{TH31}	506.0000	P_{TH59}	294.9000	P_{TH87}	207.0000	P_{TH115}	244.0000
P_{TH4}	190.0000	P_{TH32}	506.0000	P_{TH60}	282.9000	P_{TH88}	175.0000	P_{TH116}	244.0000
P_{TH5}	152.1000	P_{TH33}	506.0000	P_{TH61}	163.0000	P_{TH89}	175.0000	P_{TH117}	244.0000
P_{TH6}	116.2000	P_{TH34}	506.0000	P_{TH62}	95.0000	P_{TH90}	175.0000	P_{TH118}	95.0000
P_{TH7}	490.0000	P_{TH35}	500.0000	P_{TH63}	238.5000	P_{TH91}	175.0000	P_{TH119}	95.0000
P_{TH8}	490.0000	P_{TH36}	500.0000	P_{TH64}	160.0000	P_{TH92}	580.0000	P_{TH120}	116.0000
P_{TH9}	496.0000	P_{TH37}	241.0000	P_{TH65}	468.3000	P_{TH93}	645.0000	P_{TH121}	175.0000
P_{TH10}	496.0000	P_{TH38}	241.0000	P_{TH66}	240.0000	P_{TH94}	984.0000	P_{TH122}	2.0000
P_{TH11}	496.0000	P_{TH39}	774.0000	P_{TH67}	400.3000	P_{TH95}	978.0000	P_{TH123}	4.0000
P_{TH12}	496.0000	P_{TH40}	769.0000	P_{TH68}	441.2000	P_{TH96}	682.0000	P_{TH124}	15.0000
P_{TH13}	506.0000	P_{TH41}	3.0000	P_{TH69}	130.0000	P_{TH97}	720.0000	P_{TH125}	9.0000
P_{TH14}	509.0000	P_{TH42}	3.0000	P_{TH70}	277.6000	P_{TH98}	718.0000	P_{TH126}	12.0000
P_{TH15}	506.0000	P_{TH43}	211.9000	P_{TH71}	137.0000	P_{TH99}	720.0000	P_{TH127}	10.0000
P_{TH16}	505.0000	P_{TH44}	211.6000	P_{TH72}	315.5000	P_{TH100}	958.0000	P_{TH128}	112.0000
P_{TH17}	506.0000	P_{TH45}	220.9000	P_{TH73}	195.0000	P_{TH101}	1007.0000	P_{TH129}	4.0000
P_{TH18}	506.0000	P_{TH46}	233.3000	P_{TH74}	238.7000	P_{TH102}	1006.0000	P_{TH130}	5.0000
P_{TH19}	505.0000	P_{TH47}	201.9000	P_{TH75}	175.0000	P_{TH103}	1013.0000	P_{TH131}	5.0000
P_{TH20}	505.0000	P_{TH48}	250.0000	P_{TH76}	276.1000	P_{TH104}	1020.0000	P_{TH132}	50.0000
P_{TH21}	505.0000	P_{TH49}	223.5000	P_{TH77}	326.9000	P_{TH105}	954.0000	P_{TH133}	5.0000
P_{TH22}	505.0000	P_{TH50}	247.3000	P_{TH78}	330.0000	P_{TH106}	952.0000	P_{TH134}	42.0000
P_{TH23}	505.0000	P_{TH51}	165.7000	P_{TH79}	531.0000	P_{TH107}	1006.0000	P_{TH135}	42.0000
P_{TH24}	505.0000	P_{TH52}	179.8000	P_{TH80}	531.0000	P_{TH108}	1013.0000	P_{TH136}	41.0000
P_{TH25}	537.0000	P_{TH53}	165.0000	P_{TH81}	386.4000	$P_{THTH109}$	1021.0000	P_{TH137}	17.0000
P_{TH26}	537.0000	P_{TH54}	185.8000	P_{TH82}	56.0000	P_{TH110}	1015.0000	$P_{THTH138}$	7.0000
P_{TH27}	549.0000	P_{TH55}	180.0000	P_{TH83}	115.0000	P_{TH111}	1015.0000	P_{TH139}	7.0000
P_{TH28}	549.0000	P_{TH56}	180.0000	P_{TH84}	115.0000	P_{TH112}	94.0000	P_{TH140}	26.0000
Total Cost	1559336.8098 ($/hr)								

Table 7. Comparison of AVOA with other algorithms for 140 unit system without wind

Algorithms	Max cost ($/hr)	Min cost ($/hr)	Ave cost ($/hr)
AVOA	1560101.1125	1559336.8098	1559454.8769
SDE[25]	NR	1560236.85	NR
CBBO[25]	1560103.2354	1559945.5994	1559994.1265

[NR: Not Reported]

Table 8. AVOA for single objective 140 unit system including wind and Power Demand 49342 MW

Unit No.	Gen. (MW)	Unit No.	Gen. (MW)	Unit No.	Gen. (MW)	Unit No.	Gen. (MW)	Unit No.	Gen. (MW)
P_{w1}	120.0000	P_{29}	501.0000	P_{57}	122.8000	P_{85}	115.0000	P_{113}	94.0000
P_{w2}	240.0000	P_{30}	501.0000	P_{58}	198.0000	P_{86}	207.0000	P_{114}	94.0000
P_3	190.0000	P_{31}	506.0000	P_{59}	179.6000	P_{87}	207.0000	P_{115}	244.0000
P_4	167.8000	P_{32}	506.0000	P_{60}	271.4000	P_{88}	175.0000	P_{116}	244.0000
P_5	94.1000	P_{33}	506.0000	P_{61}	163.0000	P_{89}	175.0000	P_{117}	244.0000
P_6	90.0000	P_{34}	506.0000	P_{62}	95.0000	P_{90}	175.0000	P_{118}	95.0000
P_7	490.0000	P_{35}	500.0000	P_{63}	267.5000	P_{91}	182.8000	P_{119}	95.0000
P_8	490.0000	P_{36}	500.0000	P_{64}	315.2000	P_{92}	580.0000	P_{120}	116.0000
P_9	496.0000	P_{37}	241.0000	P_{65}	243.8000	P_{93}	645.0000	P_{121}	175.0000
P_{10}	496.0000	P_{38}	241.0000	P_{66}	285.9000	P_{94}	984.0000	P_{122}	2.0000
P_{11}	496.0000	P_{39}	774.0000	P_{67}	321.2000	P_{95}	978.0000	P_{123}	4.0000
P_{12}	496.0000	P_{40}	769.0000	P_{68}	338.0000	P_{96}	682.0000	P_{124}	15.0000
P_{13}	506.0000	P_{41}	3.0000	P_{69}	130.0000	P_{97}	720.0000	P_{125}	9.0000
P_{14}	509.0000	P_{42}	3.0000	P_{70}	240.3000	P_{98}	718.0000	P_{126}	12.0000
P_{15}	506.0000	P_{43}	160.2000	P_{71}	180.0000	P_{99}	720.0000	P_{127}	10.0000
P_{16}	505.0000	P_{44}	160.0000	P_{72}	211.8000	P_{100}	964.0000	P_{128}	112.0000
P_{17}	506.0000	P_{45}	161.2000	P_{73}	419.1000	P_{101}	958.0000	P_{129}	4.0000
P_{18}	506.0000	P_{46}	160.0000	P_{74}	285.0000	P_{102}	1007.0000	P_{130}	5.0000
P_{19}	505.0000	P_{47}	160.0000	P_{75}	228.8000	P_{103}	1006.0000	P_{131}	5.0000
P_{20}	505.0000	P_{48}	160.0000	P_{76}	403.7000	P_{104}	1013.0000	P_{132}	50.0000
P_{21}	505.0000	P_{49}	160.0000	P_{77}	251.2000	P_{105}	1020.0000	P_{133}	5.0000
P_{22}	505.0000	P_{50}	180.8000	P_{78}	378.2000	P_{106}	954.0000	P_{134}	42.0000
P_{23}	505.0000	P_{51}	301.0000	P_{79}	470.6000	P_{107}	952.0000	P_{135}	42.0000
P_{24}	505.0000	P_{52}	233.6000	P_{80}	531.0000	P_{108}	1006.0000	P_{136}	41.0000
P_{25}	537.0000	P_{53}	346.9000	P_{81}	432.0000	P_{109}	1013.0000	P_{137}	17.0000
P_{26}	537.0000	P_{54}	283.5000	P_{82}	56.0000	P_{110}	1021.0000	P_{138}	7.0000
P_{27}	549.0000	P_{55}	180.0000	P_{83}	115.0000	P_{110}	1015.0000	P_{139}	7.0000
P_{28}	549.0000	P_{56}	180.0000	P_{84}	115.0000	P_{112}	94.0000	P_{140}	26.0000

Total Cost   1550818.3212 ($/hr)

5   Conclusions

In this paper, ELD problem has been solved for thermal power plant incorporating wind energy by using AVOA algorithm. The effectiveness of the AVOA approach is demonstrated on standard three case examples. For most runs of the algorithm, AVOA is able to determine a global optimum point. Sometimes, it has the tendency to get stuck in local optimum. The results indicate that AVOA has an edge over other algorithms as it performs better. The proposed AVOA has the advantage of not putting no curvature requirements on the properties of the power generated. The AVOA technique has better features, benefits instead of other methods in terms of stability, reduced complex effort, prevent convergence rate, easy applicability, and consistent convergence feature. This technology has a bright future in solving more complex difficulties relating to power systems.

References

1. Chen, C., Qu, L., Tseng, M.L., Li, L., Chen, C.C., Lim, M.K.: Reducing fuel cost and enhancing the resource utilization rate in energy economic load dispatch problem. J. Clean. Prod. **364**, 132709 (2022)
2. Nagaraju, S., Sankar, M.M., Ashok, G., Srinivasareddy, A.: Economic load dispatch considering valve point loading using cuckoo search algorithm. Int. J. Sci. Eng. Dev. Res. **1**, 225–229 (2016)
3. Vinh, Phan Nguyen, et al. Minimize electricity generation cost for large scale windthermal systems considering prohibited operating zone and power reserve constraints. In: International Journal of Electrical and Computer Engineering (2088–8708)11.3(2021)
4. Kumar, A., Thakur, M., Mittal, G.: Planning optimal power dispatch schedule using constrained ant colony optimization. Appl. Soft Comput. **115**, 108132 (2022)
5. Pandya, S.B., Ravichandran, S., Manoharan, P., Jangir, P., Alhelou, H.H.: Multi-objective optimization framework for optimal power flow problem of hybrid power systems considering security constraints. IEEE Access **10**, 103509–103528 (2022)
6. Papi Naidu, T., Balasubramanian, G., Venkateswararao, B.: Optimal power flow control optimization problem incorporating conventional and renewable generation sources: a review. In: International Journal of Ambient Energy, (just-accepted), pp. 1–47
7. Moradian, H., Kia, S.S.: A distributed continuous-time modified Newton-Raphson algorithm. Automatica **136**, 109886 (2022)
8. Takeang, C., Aurasopon, A.: Multiple of hybrid lambda iteration and simulated annealing algorithm to solve economic dispatch problem with ramp rate limit and prohibited operating zones. J. Electr. Eng. Technol. **14**(1), 111–120 (2019)
9. Mahmoudimehr, J., Sebghati, P.: A novel multi-objective Dynamic Programming optimization method: performance management of a solar thermal power plant as a case study. Energy **168**, pp. 796–814 (2019)
10. Deb, S., Abdelminaam, D.S., Said, M., Houssein, E.H.: Recent methodology-based gradient-based optimizer for economic load dispatch problem. IIEEE Access **9**, 44322–44338 (2021)
11. Khan, B.S., Raja, M.A.Z., Qamar, A., Chaudhary, N.I.: Design of moth flame optimization heuristics for integrated power plant system containing stochastic wind. Appl. Soft Comput. **104**, 107193 (2021)

12. Siddiqui, A.S., Sarwar, M.: An Optimum GA-based solution for economic load dispatch for clean energy. In: Proceedings of 3rd International Conference on Machine Learning, Advances in Computing, Renewable Energy and Communication. Springer, Singapore, pp. 325–336 (2022)
13. Parouha, R.P., Nath Das, K.: Economic load dispatch using memory based differential evolution. Int. J. Bio-Inspired Comput. **11**(3), 159–170 (2018)
14. Naama, B., Bouzeboudja, H., Allali, A.: Solving the economic dispatch problem by using tabu search algorithm. Energy Procedia **36**, 694–701 (2013)
15. Saha, B., Roy, P.K., Mandal, B.: Economic load dispatch incorporating wind power using hybrid biogeography-based optimization: salp swarm algorithm. In: Int. J. Appl. Metaheuristic Comput. (IJAMC) **12**(3), 54–80 (2021)
16. Sahoo, A.K., et al.: Dynamic economic dispatch using harmony search algorithm. In: Advances in Machine Learning and Computational Intelligence, Springer, Singapore, pp. 425–435 (2021)
17. Hazra, S., Roy, P.K.: Quasi-oppositional chemical reaction optimization for combined economic emission dispatch in power system considering wind power uncertainties. Renewable Energy Focus **31**, 45–62 (2019)
18. Nematollahi, O., Alamdari, P., Jahangiri, M., Sedaghat, A., Alemrajabi, A.A.: A techno-economical assessment of solar/wind resources and hydrogen production: a case study with GIS maps. Energy **175**, 914–930 (2019)
19. Abdollahzadeh, B., Gharehchopogh, F.S., Mirjalili, S.: African vultures optimization algorithm: a new nature-inspired metaheuristic algorithm for global optimization problems. Comput. Ind. Eng. **158**, 107408 (2021)
20. Kaloop, M.R., et al.: Shear strength estimation of reinforced concrete deep beams using a novel hybrid metaheuristic optimized SVR models. Sustainability **14**(9), 5238 (2022)
21. Zou, D., Li, S., Wang, G.G., Li, Z., Ouyang, H.: An improved differential evolution algorithm for the economic load dispatch problems with or without valve-point effects. Appl. Energy **181**, 375–390 (2016)
22. Jose, J.T.: Economic load dispatch including wind power using Bat Algorithm. In: 2014 International Conference on Advances in Electrical Engineering (ICAEE), pp. 1–4. IEEE (2014)
23. Kaur, A., Singh, L., Dhillon, J.S.: Modified Krill Herd Algorithm for constrained economic load dispatch problem. Int. J. Ambient Energy **43**(1), 4332–4342 (2022)
24. Alkoffash, M.S., Awadallah, M.A., Alweshah, M., Zitar, R.A., Assaleh, K., Al-Betar, M.A.: A non-convex economic load dispatch using hybrid salp swarm algorithm. Arabian J. Sci. Eng. **46**(9), 8721–8740 (2021)
25. Mistri, A., kumar Roy, P., Mandal, B.: Chaotic biogeography-based optimization (CBBO) algorithm applied to economic load dispatch problem. In: 2020 National Conference on Emerging Trends on Sustainable Technology and Engineering Applications (NCETSTEA), pp. 1–5. IEEE (2020)

Grey Wolf Optimization Based Maximum Power Point Tracking Algorithm for Partially Shaded Photovoltaic Modules in Wireless Battery Charging Application

Preet Samanta(✉) , Rishav Roy , Sarthak Mazumder ,
and Pritam Kumar Gayen

Electrical Engineering Department, Kalyani Government Engineering College,
Nadia, West Bengal, India
falsepreetsamantha@gmail.com

Abstract. This paper presents a wireless battery charging scheme for electric vehicle. Here, electrical source can be either conventional power supply or solar photovoltaic power source. During sufficient solar radiation level, charging power is wirelessly fed from solar PV module through the controlling of converter under maximum power point tracking (MPPT) mode. Otherwise, battery is charged from conventional power source via wireless method. Under passing cloudy condition or presence of nearby objects like buildings or trees, partially shaded PV module fails to supply maximum electrical power for charging battery bank. Here, the conventional MPPT algorithm is unable to track the global peak power under presence of multiple peaks on power-voltage characteristic of partially shaded PV module. Thereby, this reduces power conversion efficiency of PV module under partial shading condition. In the context, Grey Wolf Optimization (GWO) based MPPT method is proposed to maximize charging power of battery. This facilitates efficient and rapid charging action of battery bank in EV application.

Keywords: Wireless Battery Charging Scheme · Partially Shaded Photovoltaic Modules · Grey Wolf Optimization Based Maximum Power Point Tracking Algorithm

1 Introduction

The growth of electric vehicles (EVs) [1, 2] and its technologies [3, 4] has tremendously increased in recent times. Different types of EVs are now present in the market. Though most of the EVs are charged through electric cables, EV manufacturing firms like BMW, Tesla has started implementing wireless mode to charge battery bank in EVs. This technology effectively prevents sparking because it does not use any kind of cumbersome cables. It is also possible to charge the battery through wireless charging method [5, 6] while driving on the road. This gives benefits as wide range of driving span and reduction of battery size. Thus, emphasis has been given in wireless battery charging scheme for

K. Dasgupta et al. (Eds.): CICBA 2023, CCIS 1955, pp. 121–134, 2024.
https://doi.org/10.1007/978-3-031-48876-4_10

EV throughout world, particularly in Germany, Korea and UK. In this context, comprehensive works are conducted for efficient and reliable wireless charging technology for EVs. In this connection, the work takes a beneficial approach for the utilization of renewable energy sources such as solar energy [7].

In this context, a wireless charging scheme for battery has been designed and modeled using MATLAB-SIMULINK software. In the model, incremental conductance (INC) type maximum power point tracking (MPPT) algorithm [8, 9] is used to extract maximum solar photovoltaic (PV) power so that efficient and fast charging process occurs. The PV panels in wireless charging schemes, which are mostly situated in cities or megacities, are frequently exposed to shading effects due to nearby objects like buildings and sometimes due to passing clouds. This modifies the power vs voltage (P-V) characteristics of PV modules. Here, it is noticed that P-V characteristic exhibits multiple power peaks. In this regard, the global power peak is not accurately tracked by INC type MPPT method and thereby, this reduces electrical power conversion efficiency of wireless charging scheme. In this regard, some papers propose hybrid [10] or optimization based approach [11]. The work of this paper suggests usage of Grey Wolf Optimization (GWO) [12] based improved MPPT method [13, 14] for solar PV based charging scheme. This assist tracking of global solar power for partially shaded PV panel in the charging scheme and thus, enhances power transfer efficiency from solar PV panel to battery by injecting more charging power to battery. It reduces charging time of battery. The beneficial features of the proposed scheme are:

I. GWO based MPPT method is used for charging the battery in wireless scheme,
II. This method is more effective during partial shading condition of PV modules,
III. Power sharing between conventional power supply and PV modules are done low insolation and partial shading conditions.

2 Fundamentals of Wireless Charging Scheme for Battery

Autonomous electric vehicles are still in development and their full potential has yet to be realized. If autonomous vehicles do not need to stop to charge, then they can continue to travel conveniently. In this regard, wireless charging methods are comparatively new in the field of EV. Wireless charging means charging of battery without using power cables. Unlike regular charging system, wireless electric vehicle charging system does not have a charging port. Here, inductive coupling based wireless charging process is widely adopted in the scheme and the power transfer takes place from transmitter to receiver via magnetic field in air.

Here, the primary coil transmits power wireless to the secondary coil via air. The transmitter coil is normally situated on road and secondary coil in the vehicle. The primary coil can be energized from either an AC source or DC source or both in power sharing mode. Various types of electrical power sources (AC and DC) are connected to a common DC-link. Then DC-link voltage converted to AC via primary-side DC-AC converter and then, this is applied to the primary coil via compensation network. The secondary-side coil receives the power wirelessly and charges the battery bank via secondary-side compensation network and AC-DC converter.

The power sources for the charging scheme can be considered as either conventional power sources or solar PV modules. During non-working periods of solar PV module, the conventional power source supplies charging power of battery.

The power source is normally either nonconventional (renewable) energy source based electrical power or conventional power plant based electrical power or hybrid (combination of conventional and nonconventional power sources), The hybrid one is better option in regard to environment friendly option and cost-effective power source. In the scheme, solar photovoltaic (PV) modules are mostly used as renewable (solar) power conversion source in charging battery bank of electric vehicle. The schematic diagram is presented in Fig. 1.

The key benefits of the wireless charging scheme are mentioned as,

- Charging cable is not required: Wireless charging eliminates the need to use a cable, thus, provides user-friendly and convenient option for charging battery in electric vehicle.
- Feasibility of charging action under dynamic condition of vehicle: Wireless charging provides the flexibility in charging of battery when vehicle moves on road.
- Time saving option: The charging in dynamic condition action provides time saving charging operation.
- Reliable option: The damage and faults in wire are absent. This fact improves the reliability of charging scheme.
- Smaller battery units: Because of the increased charge points, the battery pack's size can be lowered. This reduces the vehicle's cost and weight.

   Also, there are some limitations, which are presented as follows:

- Energy loss: Although 90–93 percent energy efficiency is possible, there will be some energy loss during the transfer. Here, energy is lost in surrounding environment. On a broader scale, this wastes a lot of energy and thus, this raises the overall amount of electricity needed to run the cars.
- Infrastructure issue: When it comes to bringing wireless charging to roadways in place this may not be cost effective. So, in the beginning, it can be built only in hi-tech urban cities.
- Health impacts: Before implementing wireless charging completely, it has to be made sure that it will not cause any health impacts to common people. Research is going on its long-term health impacts and the result is yet to come.

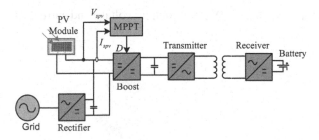

Fig. 1. Inductively coupled wireless charging scheme.

3 Maximum Power Point Tracking (MPPT) of PV Module

The maximum power capture via solar PV module is primary issue in connection with charging of battery bank of electric vehicle. Maximum power point tracking (MPPT) of PV module is the process of extracting maximum power from PV panel. The particular voltage and current combination at terminals of PV module for tracking maximum power under a particular solar radiation and temperature are obtained via MPPT control logic. The MPPT algorithm controls power electronics converter to convert DC voltage output of solar modules to a suitable voltage for maximally charging EV battery. Thus, a MPPT driven solar PV based charge controller helps to supply maximum current to the battery from PV panel. Here, MPPT assists fast charging of battery bank by maximizing power transfer from solar PV module to battery unit.

3.1 MPPT under Normal Solar Radiation

Under normal sunny environment, the has single peak power. The maximum power value is conveniently tracked via any of reputed conventional MPPT algorithm (Perturb & Observe / incremental conductance method). In this work, incremental conductance method is chosen due to its good dynamic performance. The flowchart of the algorithm is given in Fig. 2(a).

3.2 MPPT under Partial Shading Condition

Partial shading of PV module happens if any nearby object or structure shadowed some portions of the module. As a result, the blocked parts of the solar modules becomes fully or partially inactive and this causes overall reduction in the generated power. Here, the P-V terminal characteristic of the PV module is modified, which exhibits multiple peaks instead of single peak. In this context, tracking of global peak power is not possible via conventional algorithm. Therefore, Grey Wolf Optimization (GWO) based MPPT method is suggested under partial shading condition in the renewable energy based charging scheme. The flowchart of the algorithm is given in Fig. 2(b). Here, the fitness function is defined as,

$$P_{spv}(i) > P_{spv}(i-1) \tag{1}$$

In Fig. 1, P_{spv}, V_{spv}, I_{spv} = PV power output, voltage and current. 'D' is duty cycle.

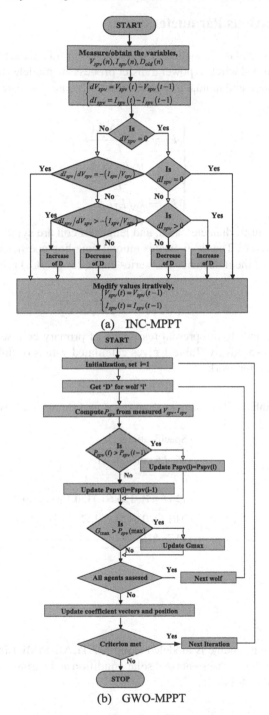

(a)   INC-MPPT

(b)   GWO-MPPT

Fig. 2. INC-MPPT and GWO-MPPT steps.

4 Design of Various Parameters

Various elements used in the modeling of wireless power transfer scheme are designed. The inductively coupled wireless power transfer process are modeled as transformer and its primary, secondary, and mutual inductive parameters are calculated as,

The inductors

$$
\begin{cases}
L_1 = \dfrac{\mu_o \mu_r N_1^2 A}{L} \\[2mm]
L_2 = \dfrac{\mu_o \mu_r N_2^2 A}{L} \\[2mm]
L_m = k\sqrt{L_1 L_2}
\end{cases}
\tag{2}
$$

The number of turns, diameter, area, and length of coil are symbolized as 'N', 'D', 'A', and 'L' respectively. The 'k' indicates mutual coupling coefficient. The resonance frequency in terms of the inductance and series capacitor (C_1/C_2) is expressed as,

$$
f_r = \frac{1}{2\pi\sqrt{L_1 C_1}} = \frac{1}{2\pi\sqrt{L_2 C_2}}
\tag{3}
$$

The 'R_1', 'R_2', and 'R_m' represent resistance of primary coil, secondary coil, and mutual resistance respectively. Table 1 gives calculated values of different parameters used in the model of this work.

Table 1. Table captions should be placed above the tables.

Item	Specifications
N, D, L	25, 7.6 cm, 750 cm
k	0.2
L_1, L_2, C_1, C_2	126.6 μH, 126.6 μH, 0.1 μF, 0.1 μF
R_1, R_2, R_m,	0.01 Ω, 0.01 Ω, 0.1 Ω
fr	44.73 kHz

5 Validation

The wireless charging scheme is modeled using MATLAB-SIMULINK software. The model is tested under both cases - normal solar condition and partially shaded condition. These are described as follows:

5.1 Validation under Normal Solar Condition

The model of charging scheme with hybrid power sources (renewable and convention sources) is presented in Fig. 3. The specifications of devices / components used in the model are listed in Table 2. The characteristics of PV module due to variations of solar irradiance level and temperature are given in Fig. 4. The current output of PV module is provided in Fig. 5, which falls to zero after shutting down of PV module. The responses of battery power, voltage and current are presented in Fig. 6. The rising state-of-charge (SOC) characteristic under charging action is shown in Fig. 7. Here, it is observed that battery's charging power (2.5 kW) equals to maximum power of PV module (0.8 kW/m^2) under action of INC type MPPT before simulation time (t) = 0.2 s. At t = 0.2 s, the solar PV module shuts down due to insufficient solar level. At this instant, charging power is taken from conventional power source diode bridge rectifier. During the transition of power sources, initial transient is appearing in the responses of battery-side variables. Thus, the operation of hybrid power source based wireless charging scheme is tested in this simulation study. Here, PV module is working under normal solar condition.

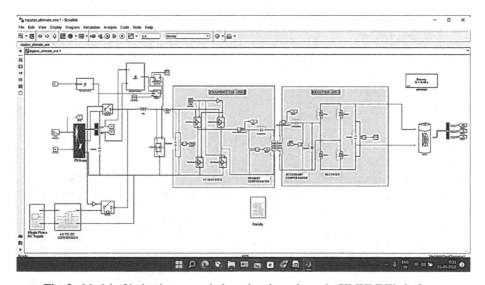

Fig. 3. Model of inductive type wireless charging scheme in SIMULINK platform.

Table 2. Rated values of different items in the model.

Item	Specifications
PV Cell	$V_{oc} = 40V$, $I_{sc} = 8.75A$, $P_{mp} = 250.29$ W, $V_{mp} = 30.9$ V, $I_{mp} = 8.1$ A
Local Supply	Single phase, 230 V (rms), 50 Hz
Battery	Lithium ion, 20 Ah, 325 V

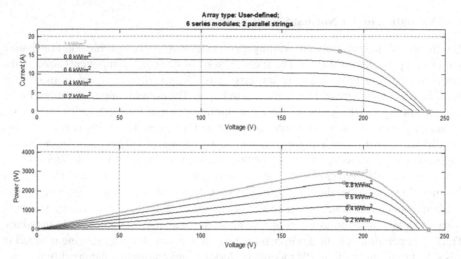

Fig. 4. Characteristics under variations of solar conditions.

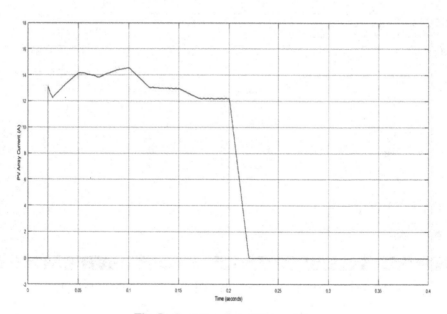

Fig. 5. Current output of PV module.

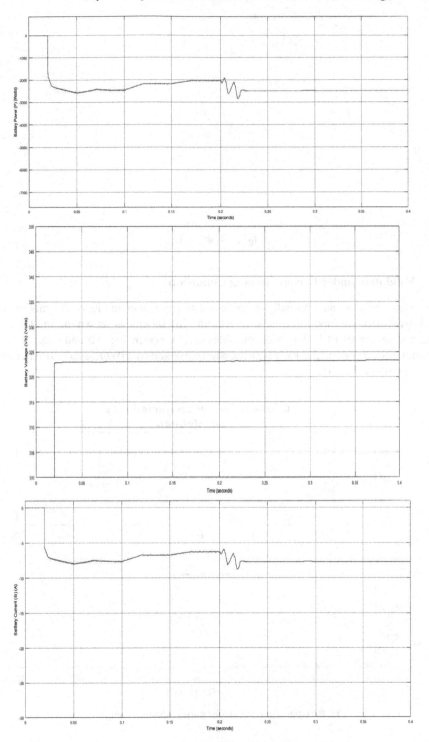

Fig. 6. Battery side variables.

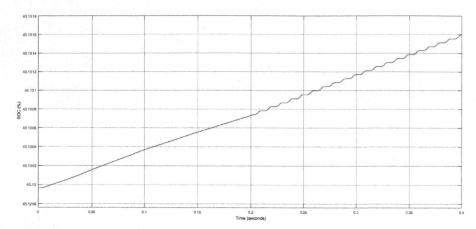

Fig. 7. SOC profile.

5.2 Validation under Partial Shading Condition

The characteristics under partially shaded condition are given in Fig. 8. The model of the partially shaded PV module based wireless charging scheme is shown in Fig. 9. Various obtained responses of battery side variables are shown in Fig. 10 and Fig. 11. Here, accurate global power (2.2 kW) is successfully tracked by GWO based MPPT method for charging the battery.

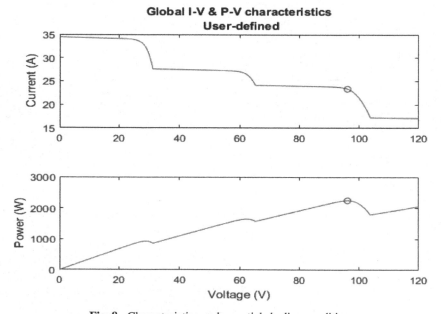

Fig. 8. Characteristics under partial shading condition.

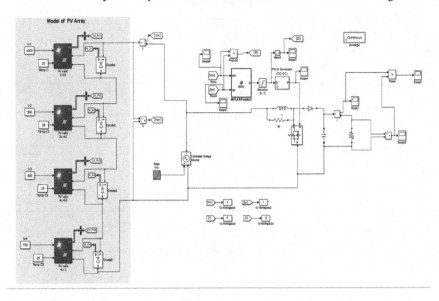

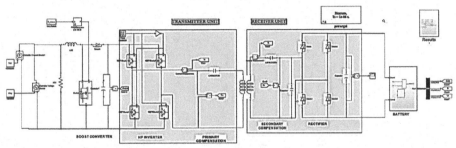

Fig. 9. Model of wireless charging scheme with partially shaded PV module in SIMULINK platform.

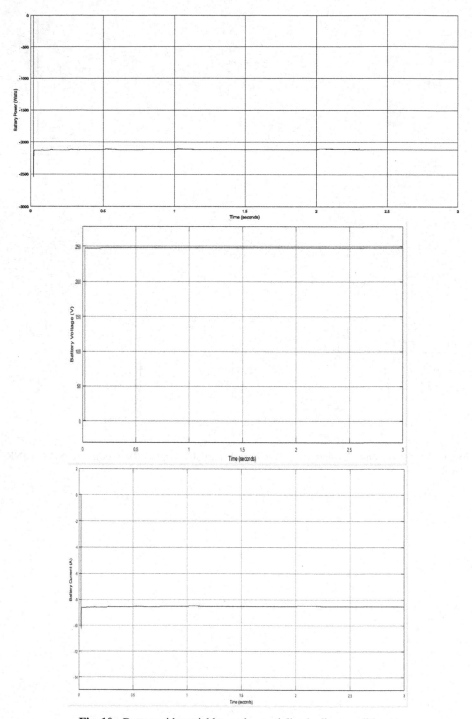

Fig. 10. Battery side variables under partially shading conditions.

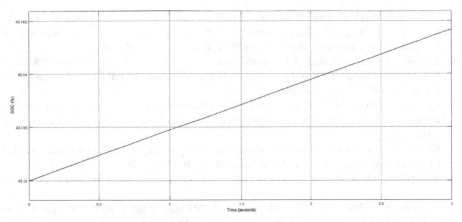

Fig. 11. SOC profile.

6 Conclusion

This paper proposes Grey Wolf Optimization (GWO) based MPPT method for solar PV based battery charging system. The benefits of this proposed scheme are efficient and quick charging of battery under partially shaded solar PV panels, whereas the conventional MPPT based wireless charging method fails to track maximum power under partial shading condition of PV module. The proposed charging system is modeled using MATLAB-SIMULINK software. The obtained results reveal desired performances of the system. However, the comparative performances considering other recent optimization techniques will be done in future works.

References

1. Matharu, H.S., Girase, V., Pardeshi, D.B., William, P.: Design and deployment of hybrid electric vehicle. 2022 International Conference on Electronics and Renewable Systems (ICEARS), pp. 331–334 (2022)
2. Raherimihaja, H.J., Yuan, Z., Wang, J., Zhang, Q.: Fast integrated charger solution for heavy-duty electric vehicles. 2019 IEEE 10th International Symposium on Power Electronics for Distributed Generation Systems (PEDG), pp. 705–710 (2019)
3. Habib, A.K.M.A., Hasan, M.K., Mahmud, M., Motakabber, S.M.A., Ibrahimya, M.I., Islam, S.: A review: Energy storage system and balancing circuits for electric vehicle application. IET Power Electron **14**, 1–13 (2021)
4. Lv, Z., Qiao, L., Cai, K., Wang, Q.: Big data analysis technology for electric vehicle networks in smart cities. IEEE Trans. Intell. Transp. Syst. **22**, 1807–1816 (2021)
5. Jyothi, P., Sudarsana Reddy, K., Kirthika Devi, V.S.: Analysis of wireless power transfer technique for electric vehicle. 2021 2nd International Conference on Smart Electronics and Communication (ICOSEC), pp. 696–701 (2021)
6. Raff, R., Golub, V., Pelin, D., Topić, D.: Overview of charging modes and connectors for the electric vehicles. 2019 7th International Youth Conference on Energy (IYCE), pp. 1–6 (2019)
7. Mobarak, M.H., Kleiman, R.N., Bauman, J.: Solar-charged electric vehicles: a comprehensive analysis of grid, driver, and environmental benefits. IEEE Transactions on Transportation Electrification **7**, 579–603 (2021)

8. Samadhan, M.A., Kamble, S.S.: Introduction of different maximum power point tracking method using photovoltaic systems. 2020 6th International Conference on Advanced Computing and Communication Systems (ICACCS), pp. 752–755 (2020)
9. Jain, K., Gupta, M., Bohre, A.K.: Implementation and comparative analysis of P&O and INC MPPT method for PV system. 2018 8th IEEE India International Conference on Power Electronics (IICPE), pp. 1–6 (2018)
10. Chao, K.-H., Rizal, M.N.: A hybrid MPPT controller based on the genetic algorithm and ant colony optimization for photovoltaic systems under partially shaded conditions. Energies **14**, 2902 (2021)
11. Kraiem, H., et al.: Increasing electric vehicle autonomy using a photovoltaic system controlled by particle swarm optimization. IEEE Access **9**, 72040–72054 (2021)
12. Mirjalili, S., Mirjalili, S.M., Lewis, A.: Grey wolf optimizer. Adv. Eng. Softw. **69**, 46–61 (2014)
13. Mohanty, S., Subudhi, B., Ray, P.K.: A new MPPT design using grey wolf optimization technique for photovoltaic system under partial shading conditions. IEEE Transactions on Sustainable Energy **7**, 181–188 (2016)
14. Millah, I.S., Chang, P.C., Teshome, D.F., Subroto, R.K., Lian, K.L., Lin, J.-F.: An enhanced grey wolf optimization algorithm for photovoltaic maximum power point tracking control under partial shading conditions. IEEE Open Journal of the Industrial Electronics Society **3**, 392–408 (2022)

Regression Analysis for Finding Correlation on Indian Agricultural Data

Somenath Hazra⬤ and Kartick Chandra Mondal$^{(\boxtimes)}$⬤

Department of Information Technology, Jadavpur University, Kolkata, India
kartickjgec@gmail.com

Abstract. Food scarcity will be a threatening problem in front of the global civilization due to huge growth in world population and reduce in world agricultural land covers. Agriculture depends on several factors like climate, soil conditions, irrigation, fertilization, condition of pests. The increase in carbon footprint due to civilization adversely affects the worldwide climate which causes unexpected floods, droughts and increase in pests directly affects the productivity and quality of agricultural products. We can increase the productivity of agricultural sector by analyzing and predicting the data of external parameters like carbon footprint, rainfall information, moisture information, soil information by predicting flood, drought, pest movement and other factors. In this article, we tried to perform the prediction of rainfall and carbon-footprint and used regression analysis for finding the correlation between Indian agricultural data containing carbon footprint and rainfall over Indian geography which can helps to increase the indian agricultural product.

Keywords: Flood and drought monitoring · Indian Agriculture · Climate change monitoring · Carbon footprint · Regression Analysis

1 Introduction

In the 19th century, the most powerful revolution was the industrial revolution which helps to deploy machines to reduce human labour. Though in the late 19th century and early 20th Century (1890–1945s), European countries facilitated the green revolution, India follows the traditional agricultural process. Very soon, Indian government realizes the need for change in the Indian traditional agricultural process as agriculture is the base of the Indian economy. During the 20th century (around the 1960s) in India Green Revolution occurred through the adaption of technology such as the use of High Yielding Variety (HYV) seeds. Mechanize forum tools irrigation facilities, fertilizers, and pesticides. It helps to increase the food grain production in the northern part of India, mainly. Soon after the green revolution, other states in India adopted the model and enjoy the revolution.

This kind of HYV seed requires high irrigation and more availability of other parameters like fertilizers, pesticides, chemicals. However, the chemical fertilizer

K. Dasgupta et al. (Eds.): CICBA 2023, CCIS 1955, pp. 135–151, 2024.
https://doi.org/10.1007/978-3-031-48876-4_11

has been used to get more production which in turn polluted the soil and killed the helpful insects and wildlife. It also affects the biodiversity in the ecological niche. The document from the Government of India [2,3] informs the details information of bio-fertilizer, as well as chemical fertilizer, uses in yearly as well as the state-wise data. The documents also contain the production, import and consumption data information.

So, understanding the pattern of rainfall regions and prediction of rainfall are important issues in agricultural sector. Recent research on rainfall data analysis in several regions in India and neighbouring countries can be found like the Uma Oya Sri Lanka [8], three districts in Orissa [18], Barmer District of Rajasthan [15], West Coast Plain and Hill Agro-Climatic (WCPHAC) [23], Nanded city of Maharashtra [7], Southeast Asia [12], Terengganu, Malaysia [21], Banten, Indonesia [10], Indian subcontinental [19,20] region. These research articles are mostly uses the Mann-Kendall's Test, Sen's Slope Estimator Test, ARIMA model, and Pettitt's test To predict rainfall.

India is a very diverse country. Its climate and pollution differ from one region to another. The Indian Ocean, Arabian Sea, and the Bay of Bengal cover this land from three sides. The Himalayan range is present on the northern side of the country. In this country, one can find high rainfall like Mawsynram which is a town in the East Khasi Hills district of Meghalaya state which is located in North-eastern India as well as the Great Indian Desert, As per source data from the Department of Agriculture, Cooperation & Farmer Welfare, the planning commission decided to divide Indian geography into 15 Agro-Climatic zones; further divided into 72 Sub-Zone. The 15 Zones are shown in the map is given in Fig. 1 which is taken from [3].

Population density and industry measures are different in different parts of India. The carbon footprint is high in the cities in comparison with villages. During the ripping of the crop, the residuals are fired to clean from the field. It also causes an increase in the carbon footprint in rural areas. We can't avoid pollution and carbon footprint as it is part of modern civilization. So, for the deep dive into the carbon footprint, it requires getting in touch with the research paper on the correlation between Rainfall and temperature is indirectly connected to carbon emis-

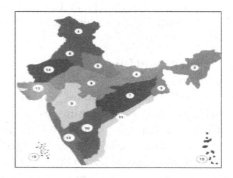

Fig. 1. 15 Agro-Climatic zone in India

sion [6]; Turkey carbon footprint forecasting by measuring CO_2 using time series data mining methods [1]; Impact of carbon emission on GDP of Iran [4]; The Carbon Footprint in The University of Talca in Chile [25]; carbon footprint impact on Agriculture in Northern India [14]; Relationship between GDP and

Carbon dioxide emissions along with energy consumption and urbanisation [17]. The prediction was done through Multiple regression (MR), Linear regression (LR), Vector Auto-Regression (VAR), some statistical models, and WEKA data mining software.

The most recent forecasting methods proposal [11] for the rainfall data analysis are based on the machine learning algorithm such as multivariate linear regression (MLR), random forest (RF), XGBoost gradient descent which is nothing but the specific use of the Gradient Boosting method implements more precise approximations to find the best-fit model. Another recent work [9], where the 'secondary decomposition technology' clubbing with 'ensemble empirical mode decomposition (EEMD)' and 'variational mode decomposition (VMD)' are used. It processes the actual data, and the 'partial autocorrelation function (PACF)' is used to select the optimal model input. The 'long short-term memory network (LSTM)' is chosen for the prediction of the carbon footprint forecasted data. The R-Squared, MAPE, and RMSE error method is involved to find out the error value for the given algorithm. In a nutshell, we are trying to proceed in the prediction process from a very basic for the rainfall and carbon footprint data analysis.

As per the above discussion, in this paper we are going to analyse the climate and pollution data for the diverse country like India. It is generally observed during rainy season in West Bengal region in India, agricultural production is heavily affected due to uneven distribution of rainfall. This uneven nature of the distribution of rain leads us to work on the predictive analysis of it. Several study found that, in most of the cases, carbon is the major determining factor for pollution and climate change which subsequently affect the agricultural production. Hence, in this work, we tried to correlate two major factors to predict a value which will help our agricultural sector to take the decision on their choice of crop or timing of the crop to increase productivity.

The rest of the article is organized as follows: next in Sect. 2 we have presented information on data, data extraction, and preparation of data. Section 3 used to explain the used methodology for regression data analysis. Experimental setup, result and discussion is presented in Sect. 4. At the end, the conclusion future scope is shown in Sect. 5.

2   Indian Agricultural Data

The overall flow of the proposed approach is shown in Fig. 2. It starts the process by collecting the data from sources and end by predicting and finding correlation between carbon footprint and rainfall.

2.1   Source

The 'Indian Agricultural Data' covers climate-related information, soil information, crop information, fertilizer, pesticides, medicines, seed related information. Different departments of the central as well as the state government, are involved

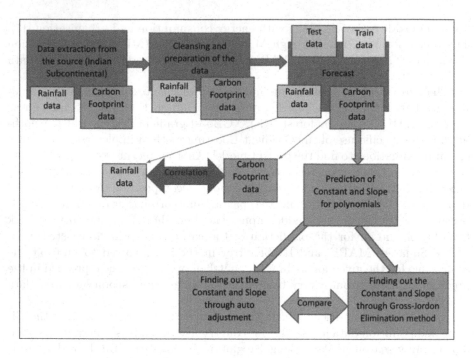

Fig. 2. Overall flow of the proposed work.

in this data collection, some of them like Indian Meteorological department under Ministry of Earth Sciences, Department of Agriculture, Cooperation & Farmers Welfare, other departments which are indirectly associated with the agriculture - National Textile Corporation Limited, Jute Commissioner under Ministry of Textile.

To provide information on weather, climate, ocean and coastal state, hydrology, seismology, and natural hazards the Ministry of Earth Sciences (MoES) formerly named as Department of Ocean Development (DOD). It brought under its administration the Indian Meteorological Department (IMD), Delhi, Indian Institute of Tropical Meteorology (IITM), Pune, and the National Centre for Medium-Range Weather Forecasting (NCMRWF), Noida. Most climate-related data can be accessed for the last century from the Indian Institute of Tropical Meteorology (IITM), Pune.

Year-wise 'national water quality monitoring' data reports are also hosted for the visitor of the site.

2.2   Extraction

The website [5] contains rainfall data for the 1901–2014 year month-wise. Another website [16] contains rainfall data for the 1901–2021 year monthly Monsoon data for June-September and total rainfall data segmented by all India,

North West India (9 Sub-division), North East India (7 Sub-division), Central India (10 Sub-division), South provinces (10 Sub-division). We extracted the data from the cited source in the local table to use in our prediction. All the rainfall data has been captured in millimetres (mm). Figure 3 represent the 1901–2011 rainfall data on monthly basis. Figure 4 represent the all over India monsoon record. Other Figs. 5, 6, 7, 8 represent the data of North West India, North East India, Central India, South provinces in graph, respectively.

The carbon footprint information we collected from the source [24] is listed for CO_2 emission by country in tonnes per capita. The downloadable CSV file is available in the source [22]. The sheet contains the data from 1750 to 2019 depending on the availability of the data with respect to the country. Indian data for CO_2 emission is available from 1885 to 2019. The Fig. 9 represent almost 160 year carbon footprint data for India.

Fig. 3. 1901–2011 rainfall data for monthly basis in the stacked column chart

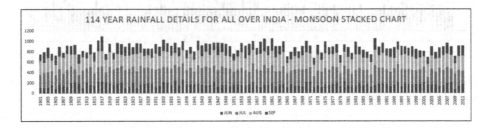

Fig. 4. 1901–2011 all India rainfall data for monsoon month Jun–Sep in the stacked column chart

2.3   Data Cleansing and Preparation

The data was cleansed by replacing, the blank or populated with NA due to the unavailability of data, with zero values to create the continuous data set as well as to avoid the breakage in the algorithm functionalities. In the rainfall data set we got data for 1901–2021; for carbon footprint data we got data for

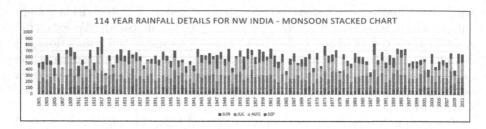

Fig. 5. 1901–2011 North West India rainfall data for monsoon month Jun–Sep in the stacked column chart

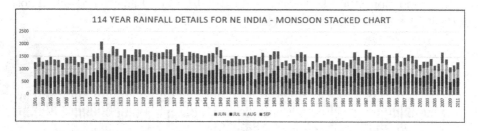

Fig. 6. 1901–2011 North East India rainfall data for monsoon month Jun–Sep in the stacked column chart

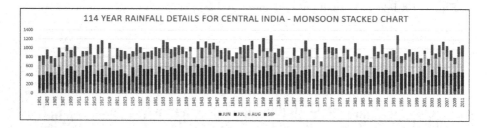

Fig. 7. 1901–2011 Central India rainfall data for monsoon month Jun–Sep in the stacked column chart

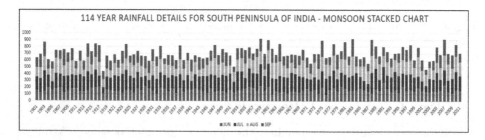

Fig. 8. 1901–2011 South Province of India rainfall data for monsoon month Jun–Sep in the stacked column chart

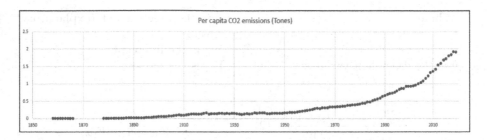

Fig. 9. 1857–2019 per capita CO_2 emission in tons in India

1857–2019. So for co-relation, we consider the 1901–2012 data set. We consider all data without the window detector of any algorithm. Used the data as is only after truncating the blank data set.

We segmented the data into two parts; one is test data on which we can validate or generate the algorithm and another is training data which will be our reference data for comparison with the algorithm output data. We consider the ninety-nine-year data as test data which can be considered as the historical data on which the algorithm operates and generate the predictive output so that we can compare it with training data. Which in turn consists of the rest twelve years of data to get the error calculation and finding the accuracy of the process.

3   Data Analysis Approach

3.1   Methodology

The forecast data has been generated based on historical data collected from different sources and with the help of regression algorithm. Regression analysis is all about estimation or prediction of the relation between one dependent variable and one or multiple independent variables (Fig. 10). We try to do the polynomial regression analysis on the prepared dataset.

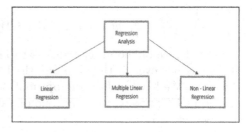

Fig. 10. Different Regression Analysis

3.2   Algorithmic Explanation

Simple linear regression is the correlation between the dependent and independent variables. The equation for simple linear regression is mentioned in Eq. 1.

$$y = W_0 + W_1 x \tag{1}$$

Where

- x is the independent (explanatory) variable
- W_0 is the intercept
- y is the dependent variable
- W_1 is the Slope

$$W_1 = \frac{\sum_{i=1}^{n}(x - \bar{x})(y - \bar{y})}{\sum_{i=1}^{n}(x - \bar{x})^2} \quad (2)$$

$$W_0 = \bar{y} - W_1\bar{x} \quad (3)$$

the calculated value of next y is shown in Eq. 4 based on the Eq. 1.

$$y\prime = W_0 + W_1x \quad (4)$$

The relationship between the dependent and independent variables describes the nature of the graph or correlation of the variables. To describe the non-linearity nature of the variable, we have to add the polynomial terms in the linear regression formula. The polynomial formula can be described as below:

$$y = W_0 + W_1x_1 + W_2x_2 + W_3x_3 \quad (5)$$

where

- y is dependent variable
- x_1, x_2, x_3 are the independent (explanatory) variable
- W_0 is the intercept
- W_1, W_2, W_3 are the Slope

The more non-linearity and turbulence value can be described through the degree of the polynomial.

$$y\prime = W_0 + W_1x_1 + W_2x_1^2 + ... + W_nx_1^n \quad (6)$$

The degree of the order requires to be selected wisely. As the higher order of degree may over fit the data and the lower value of data may be under fitted the data. We have to find the optimal degree of the polynomial. To solve the polynomial expression we have n no of data set of (x, y), so the data set can be represented as in Eq. 7.

$$(x_1, y_1), (x_2, y_2), (x_3, y_3)....(x_n, y_n) \quad (7)$$

To generate the Equation of degree p; the polynomial equation can be generated by the least-square method as mentioned in Eq. 8

$$y = W_0 + W_1x + W_2x^2 + W_3x^3 + ... + W_px^p \ where \ p < n \quad (8)$$

The aim of this method is to downgrade the residual r value for each point.

$$r_i = y_i - W_0 - W_1x_i - W_2x_i^2 - W_3x_i^3 - ... - W_px_i^p \quad (9)$$

This can be represented in 2-D form for the polynomial expression of degree 4.

$$\begin{bmatrix} n & \sum x_i & \sum x_i^2 & \sum x_i^3 & \sum x_i^4 \\ \sum x_i & \sum x_i^2 & \sum x_i^3 & \sum x_i^4 & \sum x_i^5 \\ \sum x_i^2 & \sum x_i^3 & \sum x_i^4 & \sum x_i^5 & \sum x_i^6 \\ \sum x_i^3 & \sum x_i^4 & \sum x_i^5 & \sum x_i^6 & \sum x_i^7 \\ \sum x_i^4 & \sum x_i^5 & \sum x_i^6 & \sum x_i^7 & \sum x_i^8 \end{bmatrix} \begin{bmatrix} w_0 \\ w_1 \\ w_2 \\ w_3 \\ w_4 \end{bmatrix} = \begin{bmatrix} \sum y_i \\ \sum x_i y_i \\ \sum x_i^2 y_i \\ \sum x_i^3 y_i \\ \sum x_i^4 y_i \end{bmatrix} \tag{10}$$

The middle vector of Eq. 10 is calculated through Gauss-Jordan elimination to find the coefficient of Eq. 8. From the Eq. 10, it can be represented as the below representation.

$$\sum_{i=0,n} x_i^{(r+c)} \tag{11}$$

where matrix row = r and matrix column = c, range of the index $0 <= i <= p$, and n = number of data samples. Also it require to be noted that x0 = 1 and x1 = x.

Next step to solve the Eq. 10 a new column eventually add at the right side as below.

$$\begin{bmatrix} n & \sum x_i & \sum x_i^2 & \sum x_i^3 & \sum x_i^4 & 0 \\ \sum x_i & \sum x_i^2 & \sum x_i^3 & \sum x_i^4 & \sum x_i^5 & 0 \\ \sum x_i^2 & \sum x_i^3 & \sum x_i^4 & \sum x_i^5 & \sum x_i^6 & 0 \\ \sum x_i^3 & \sum x_i^4 & \sum x_i^5 & \sum x_i^6 & \sum x_i^7 & 0 \\ \sum x_i^4 & \sum x_i^5 & \sum x_i^6 & \sum x_i^7 & \sum x_i^8 & 0 \end{bmatrix} \tag{12}$$

It is required to keep in mind that in the Eq. 10 the

$$\sum x_i^2 = \sum_{i=0}^{,n-1} x_i^2$$

The next step is required to replace the last vector with the right-hand matrix column of Eq. 10

$$\begin{bmatrix} n & \sum x_i & \sum x_i^2 & \sum x_i^3 & \sum x_i^4 & \sum y_i \\ \sum x_i & \sum x_i^2 & \sum x_i^3 & \sum x_i^4 & \sum x_i^5 & \sum x_i y_i \\ \sum x_i^2 & \sum x_i^3 & \sum x_i^4 & \sum x_i^5 & \sum x_i^6 & \sum x_i^2 y_i \\ \sum x_i^3 & \sum x_i^4 & \sum x_i^5 & \sum x_i^6 & \sum x_i^7 & \sum x_i^3 y_i \\ \sum x_i^4 & \sum x_i^5 & \sum x_i^6 & \sum x_i^7 & \sum x_i^8 & \sum x_i^4 y_i \end{bmatrix} \tag{13}$$

4   Experiment Result and Discussion

4.1   Experimental Set Up

Initially, we used the Google co-lab platform to plot the graph and polynomial expression solution through the python code. Later, we used the online portal [13] which will generate the coefficient value by selecting the degree. Also, we used the Microsoft Excel to generate the graph and coefficient value of the polynomial expression.

4.2   Algorithmic Development

It is clear from the above discussion that we are using the rainfall data and carbon footprint data to predict the forecast value and correlation between rainfall and carbon footprint using regression analysis. During the prediction of rainfall data, we used the trend line by using the weighted moving average with period four. We computed the constant value through the polynomial graph adjusting features in Microsoft excel for carbon data. We captured those constant/coefficient values in the Table 1

Table 1. Constant value from the Polynomial equation

Order	4th Order Polynomial	5th Order Polynomial	6th Order Polynomial
W0	14	−17772221.04	48309905.51
W1	−162754.79	2212066.96	−7215625.705
W2	26828.621	−110132.32	478993.1337
W3	−30693	3289.899	−17885.747
W4	39.749	−6696.5	218730
W5		0.6909	−45.553
W6			0.004

Now the challenge is to find the optimized value of the intercept and slope coefficient as well as the constant term from the polynomial regression expression. So, we tried to improve the algorithm so that we can get a more optimized value of the coefficient of the polynomial. With the help of Eq. 13, it's required to perform the Gauss-Jordan elimination to find out the coefficient of the polynomial of 4th, 5th, and 6th degree as the most suitable degree are decided. Through this method, the polynomial coefficient values are given in Table 2.

Table 2. Coefficient value calculated from Polynomial regression analysis through Gauss-Jordan elimination

Order	4th Order Polynomial	^5th Order Polynomial	6th Order Polynomial
W0	28477217.58	−1778468.358	3178086.467
W1	−2419922.454	6059536.486	4168585.239
W2	207624.5176	−374056.0315	−190633.2204
W3	−4843.838	549.0383223	3306.285106
W4	39.74856418	−132.9765321	2.049415114
W5		0.690900385	−0.494845788
W6			0.003952487

4.3   Result Generation

In the experimental set-up section, we informed that we used the google co-lab platform for our coding through Python as well as used the Microsoft Excel environment to generate the result. The output graph has been shown below on which we discussed the output. The four-period moving average of rainfall has been shown in Fig. 11.

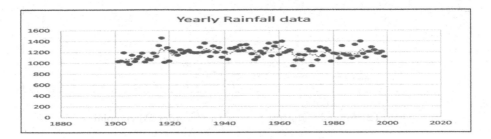

Fig. 11. Annual Rainfall data

We tried to generate the forecast with the help of polynomial regression of 4th (representation graph is shown in Fig. 12), 5th (representation graph is shown in Fig. 13), 6th (representation graph is shown in Fig. 14) order expression to generate the carbon footprint predictive analysis.

The graph from the test data set for carbon footprint data has been generated with help of Gauss-Jordan elimination methods for polynomial expression. We took the service from the [13] online portal to generate the 4th, 5th, and 6th order polynomial graphs, which are given below.

Lastly, we tried to generate the correlation between two different kinds of data that the relation between the Rainfall data and the carbon emission data with the help of a regression model. If we consider the x as rainfall data and y as annual CO_2 emission data then calculate the constant value as per the Eqs. 2 and 3. With the help of this value, the calculated and actual values are shown in the Fig. 18.

4.4   Output Explanation

The above discussion leads us to that the algorithm has been generated on the test data set used for the generation of predictive data set to compare with the train data set. In the below tables, Table 4 and 3, we tried not it down the maximum, minimum, and average percentage error for the graph which was adjusted manually and the Gauss-Jordan Elimination method. We found that the polynomial of 6th order and 5th order is more predictive in comparison with the 4th order polynomial on the test data set of carbon footprint data which is generated from the graph manual adjustment details. For the GJE method, the 4th and 6th order max min and average percentage error are reliable because the related data for 5th order is varying in between the huge range of the max, min, and average percentage error values. It is also observed that for the train data set 4th order Max, Min, and Average percentage error is quite low for both methods in comparison to the 5th order as well as the 6th Order polynomial output (Figs. 15, 16 and 17).

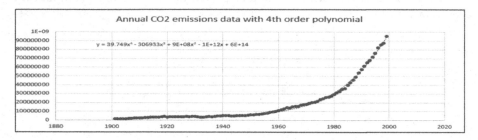

Fig. 12. Annual CO_2 test data with 4th order Polynomial

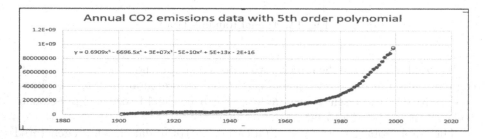

Fig. 13. Annual CO_2 test data with 5th order Polynomial

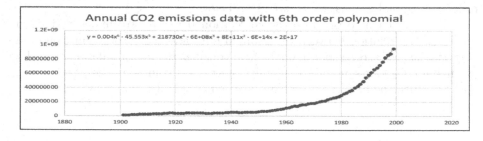

Fig. 14. Annual CO_2 test data with 6th order Polynomial

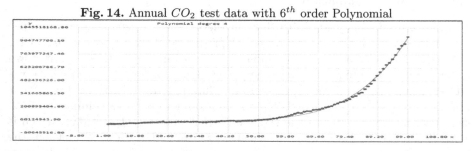

Fig. 15. Annual CO_2 test data with 4th order Polynomial generated by GJE method

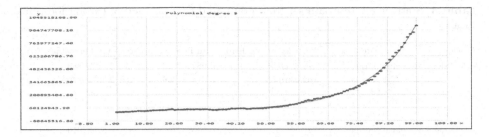

Fig. 16. Annual CO_2 test data with 5th order polynomial generated by GJE method

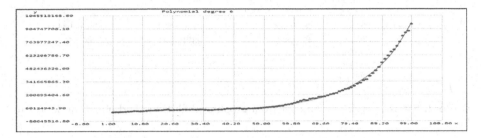

Fig. 17. Annual CO_2 test data with 6th order Polynomial generated by GJE method

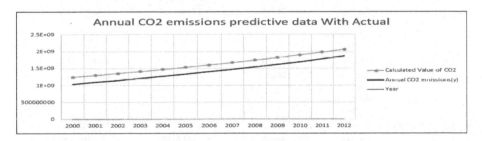

Fig. 18. Correlation Data graph

It is also observed that for polynomial equations, it is required to find the proper degree so that it would not be overshot or undershot. Here we can pick the 6th order as the more predicted polynomial with respect of test and training both data. The maximum, minimum, and average percentage error has been calculated on the test and train data set for the rainfall data which has been predicted through the moving average given below:

Table 3. Statistic on Test data set from graph and GJE method of carbon footprint data

Order	Method	Max Percentage Error	Min Percentage Error	Avg Percentage Error
4th Order Polynomial	Graph	113.6341538	0.082657993	25.80078809
	Gauss-Jordan elimination method	102.0991966	0.649714326	23.87599729
5th Order Polynomial	Graph	72.4548532	0.10525279	8.825970106
	Gauss-Jordan elimination method	2157.591089	0.671540322	1173.008879
6th Order Polynomial	Graph	48.39452298	0.023019894	8.996368034
	Gauss-Jordan elimination method	45.76851381	0.03710404	7.168625574

Table 4. Statistic on Train data set from graph and GJE method of carbon footprint data

Order	Method	Max Percentage Error	Min Percentage Error	Avg Percentage Error
4th Order Polynomial	Graph	13.98049978	0.267422397	7.687687528
	Gauss-Jordan elimination method	13.83676186	0.172987137	7.584363331
5th Order Polynomial	Graph	15.52465559	5.587590115	11.49283947
	Gauss-Jordan elimination method	1028.536428	717.7263201	895.151734
6th Order Polynomial	Graph	21.80585715	13.45489557	17.96627631
	Gauss-Jordan elimination method	17.83763195	9.563179377	14.13160189

Data Set	Max Percentage Error	Min Percentage Error	Average Percentage Error
Test data set	21.67212076	0.058270207	5.59157672
Train data set	15.66628224	0.361539124	5.661058802

The Fig. 18 shows the comparison of the actual data and the predictive data with the help of the regression model. One can observe the trend is predicted almost properly but the absolute value is quite high in comparison with the actual value in the correlations of the yearly rainfall and carbon footprint data.

4.5 Discussion

During the output or result analysis, we found that there are four different segments are considered in the article.

- Prediction or forecast of rainfall data with the help of moving average method
- Prediction or forecast of carbon footprint data with the help of graphical prediction method
- Prediction or forecast of carbon footprint data with the help of the Gauss-Jordan elimination method
- Correlation between the rainfall and carbon footprint data

The annual rainfall data prediction of 1901–1999 i.e., test data set percentage error is varying from 21% to 0.05% whereas the train data set for the year 2000–2012 varies from 15% to 0.36%. The average value of the error is 5.59% and 5.66% for test and train data respectively. Hence, we can say that the predicted data almost follow the trained value.

The percentage error varying 0.08%–114%, 0.1%–72%, 0.2%–48%, respectively, for 4th, 5th, 6th order polynomial for the period of the entire range of data set through manual adjustment in graphical method for test data set. Similarly, these values are varying 0.26%–14%, 6%–16%, 14%–22% for train data set. But, from just before the green revolution of India six-decade 1950 to 2012 the carbon footprint data predictive value generated through graphical method varies 0–40%, 3–14%, 1–20% for 4th, 5th, 6th order polynomials respectively. Similarly, the error is varying from 1–102%, 1–2157%, and 0.02–48% respectively for the 4th, 5th, 6th order polynomials respectively for the Gauss-Jordan elimination method and on test data. Whereas the data varies 0.2–14%, 717–1028%, 10–18% for the train data set.

In the correlation between rainfall and CO_2 emission graph, one can predict the algorithm which we select is predicting the trends but the predicted value is high with respect to the actual. The Relative absolute error on the predictive value from 2000–2012 is 11.14 and the absolute value for this period is 10–20% overshoot with respect to the train set of data.

If one can improve the polynomial equation in such a way that the constant value of the Intercept and the slope are more accurate to predict the algorithm with a lower percentage error. If one can reduce the no of the sample data set might give you a better result in comparison to the larger data set. If the data set is too small you can't predict the value properly. On the other hand, for the rainfall data prediction, if one can choose the single exponential, double exponential, or triple exponential, smoothing algorithm instead of the moving average might provide better results and less error. For the correlation analysis if the test data set can be cleansed properly; i.e. the flood or drought information from the rainfall data; the high rainfall and low rainfall data can be cleansed with the help of substitute missing value, outlier correction, interquartile range (IQR) test or variance test then we might get the nearest value with the actual.

5   Conclusion and Future Scope

A fast economically growing country like India depends on agriculture mostly. The agricultural data is very sensitive to the growth of any country's economy. For a fast-growing country, carbon footfall is also a threatening problem in the world which in turn increase global warming and direct changes in climate. Hence, we have to consider the carbon footfall as well as the growth in the agricultural sector in the evolving situation.

Keeping the discussion section of the experimental result in focus, we found that the 6th order polynomial equation is predicting the more accurate carbon footprint data set. The four-period moving average algorithm is generating similar forecasted values for the Indian yearly rainfall data. Through the correlation algorithm, we found that the trend has been following but the values are a bit overshot in comparison with the exact data.

The future scope of the most popular topic has two aspects; one is the improvement of the equation, and another is the improvement of the topics. One can deep drive the improvement of the ordered polynomial by adjusting the intercept and slope constant value so that the percentage error will be reduced, and the equation will fit with the test value more accurately and also in turn predict the more accurate value on the train data. The researcher can choose the topic which is more relevant with respect to the current scenario and start the research on it. The most relevant last but not the least thing is the data on which one can predict algorithms or analyses.

References

1. Akyol, M., Uçar, E.: Carbon footprint forecasting using time series data mining methods: the case of Turkey. Environ. Sci. Pollut. Res. **28**, 1–11 (2021)
2. Department of Fertilizers, Ministry of Chemical and Fertilizer, Government of India: Fertilizers final annual report 2022. https://fert.nic.in/publication-reports/annual-report. Accessed 21 Jan 2023
3. Department of Fertilizers, Ministry of Chemical and Fertilizer, Government of India: Fertilizers scenario 2018. https://fert.nic.in/publication-reports/fertilizers-scenario. Accessed 21 Jan 2023
4. Hosseini, S.M., Saifoddin, A., Shirmohammadi, R., Aslani, A.: Forecasting of Co2 emissions in Iran based on time series and regression analysis. Energy Rep. **5**, 619–631 (2019)
5. indiaenvironmentportal: 114 year of rainfall data. https://www.tropmet.res.in/lip/Publication/RR-pdf/RR-138.pdf. Accessed 21 Jan 2023
6. Islam, M.M., Alharthi, M., Murad, M.W.: The effects of carbon emissions, rainfall, temperature, inflation, population, and unemployment on economic growth in Saudi Arabia: an ARDL investigation. PLoS ONE **16**(4), 1–21 (2021)
7. Karnewar, K.V.: Analysis of rainfall trends over Nanded of Maharashtra, India. Int. J. Res. **5**(16), 571–581 (2018)
8. Khaniya, B., Jayanayaka, I., Jayasanka, P., Rathnayake, U.: Rainfall trend analysis In Uma Oya Basin, Sri Lanka, and future water scarcity problems in perspective of climate variability. Adv. Meteorol. **2019**, 3636158 (2019)

9. Kong, F., Song, J., Yang, Z.: A novel short-term carbon emission prediction model based on secondary decomposition method and long short-term memory network. Environ. Sci. Pollut. Res. **29**, 1–16 (2022)
10. Kurniawan, D.: Rainfall time series analysis and forecasting, Banten, Indonesia 2019–2020 (2020). https://towardsdatascience.com/rainfall-time-series-analysis-and-forecasting-87a29316494e. Accessed 21 Jan 2023
11. Liyew, C.M., Melese, H.A.: Machine learning techniques to predict daily rainfall amount. J. Big Data **8**(1), 1–11 (2021)
12. Loo, Y.Y., Billa, L., Singh, A.: Effect of climate change on seasonal monsoon in Asia and its impact on the variability of monsoon rainfall in southeast Asia. Geosci. Front. **6**(6), 817–823 (2015)
13. Lutus, P.: Polynomial regression data fit. https://arachnoid.com/polysolve/. Accessed 21 Jan 2023
14. Malhi, G.S., Kaur, M., Kaushik, P.: Impact of climate change on agriculture and its mitigation strategies: a review. Sustainability **13**(3), 1–21 (2021)
15. Mehta, D., Yadav, S.: An analysis of rainfall variability and drought over Barmer district of Rajasthan: Northwest India. Water Supply **21**, 2505–2517 (2021)
16. Additional Director General of Meteorology (Research) Climate Application Group, Ministry of Earth and Science, IMD: 114 year of rainfall data region-wise. https://www.imdpune.gov.in/library/public/e-book110.pdf. Accessed 21 Jan 2023
17. Misra, K.: The relationship between economic growth and carbon emissions in India. Institute for Social and Economic Change (2019)
18. Panda, A., Sahu, N.: Trend analysis of seasonal rainfall and temperature pattern in Kalahandi, Bolangir and Koraput Districts of Odisha, India. Atmos. Sci. Lett. **20**(10), 1–10 (2019)
19. Patel, P., Khan, A.: Changing rainfall patterns in India: a spatiotemporal analysis of trends & impacts. Research Square Preprint (2020)
20. Praveen, B., Talukdar, S., Mahato, S., Mondal, J., et al.: Analyzing trend and forecasting of rainfall changes in India using non-parametrical and machine learning approaches. Sci. Rep. **10**(1), 1–21 (2020)
21. Ridwan, W.M., Sapitang, M., Aziz, A., Kushiar, K.F., Ahmed, A.N., El-Shafie, A.: Rainfall forecasting model using machine learning methods: case study Terengganu, Malaysia. Ain Shams Eng. J. **12**(2), 1651–1663 (2021)
22. Ritchie, H.: Co2 emission by country per capita data download. https://ourworldindata.org/per-capita-co2. Accessed 21 Jan 2023
23. Saini, A.: Advanced rainfall trend analysis of 117 years over west coast plain and hill agro-climatic region of India. Atmosphere **11**(11), 1–25 (2020)
24. Wikipedia, the free encyclopedia: Co2 emission by country per capita. https://en.wikipedia.org/wiki/List_of_countries_by_carbon_dioxide_emissions. Accessed 21 Jan 2023
25. Yañez, P., Sinha, A., Vásquez, M.: Carbon footprint estimation in a university campus: evaluation and insights. Sustainability **12**(1), 1–15 (2020)

Classification of the Chest X-ray Images of COVID-19 Patients Through the Mean Structural Similarity Index

Mayukha Pal[1] and Prasanta K. Panigrahi[2]([✉])

[1] ABB Ability Innovation Center, Asea Brown Boveri Company, Hyderabad 500084, India
[2] Indian Institute of Science Education and Research Kolkata, Mohanpur 741246, India
pprasanta@iiserkol.ac.in

Abstract. The chest X-ray (CXR) images of healthy patients and patients with COVID-19 are clustered into distinct classes using the mean structural similarity index measure (SSIM). SSIM is intrinsically similar to the human visual system (HVS) and has potential for extracting the information for structural changes in the image to perceive the distortions. The proposed approach is based on local statistical parameters like mean, variance etc., to extract structural information through SSIM. This information is subsequently used for CXR image differentiation, akin to the clinician's visual inspection of these images. As a feature extractor, SSIM is found to effectively classify and characterize COVID-19 patients from the healthy ones from analysis of the CXR images. Our approach of classifying CXR images, based on a single comparative parameter with the use of an ensemble tree classifier, leads to an accuracy equivalent to the recently developed methods using a variety of convolutional neural network (CNN) approaches and is computationally faster. We obtained an accuracy of 97.7% for our proposed models. The obtained results are corroborated through the statistically reliable analysis from the receiver operating characteristic (ROC) curve and confusion matrix. The comparative SSIM index enables the effective use of larger data points for the classifier's robust training due to cross-correlation between healthy subjects and diseased ones, yielding higher classification accuracy. Our proposed method may find clinical application for classifying patients of COVID-19 using CXR images.

Keywords: Chest X-ray · Clustering and supervised classification learners · Coronavirus · COVID-19 · Image Classification · SARS-CoV-2 · Structural similarity index measure

1 Introduction

SARS-CoV-2 is a severe acute respiratory syndrome virus first reported in Wuhan, China in December 2019. This disease is highly infectious, contagious and spreads through various means rapidly. From Wuhan, China within two months it spread to the rest of the world (Fan et al. (2020); Chaolin et al. (2020)). The World Health Organization (WHO) declared it a global pandemic as it has affected normal human life like never before and

K. Dasgupta et al. (Eds.): CICBA 2023, CCIS 1955, pp. 152–164, 2024.
https://doi.org/10.1007/978-3-031-48876-4_12

named as Coronavirus disease (COVID-19). Much of the years 2020 and in the year 2021, have created havoc as the medical infrastructure of the world is being severely challenged due to rapid infection of the disease and the requirement of oxygen-supported beds and intensive care units (ICU) for the patients. So far globally 190 million people have been infected with the disease and around 4.1 million mortalities due to the virus. In India from Apr–May 2021 daily infection was reported to be 0.4 million alone. Nearly 1% mortality is reported daily among the total infected patients of the day. Of the infected patients, nearly 20% are reported to be requiring admission to the hospital for oxygen support or ICU. Typical clinical features of COVID-19 are breath shortness, fatigue, headache, loss of taste and smell sense, sore throat, muscular pain, high fever, and heavy cough (Tanu et al. (2020); Anshuman et al. (2020)). With increase in severity of the disease, the oxygen level for patients drops drastically and result in critical situations for the patients.

The initial diagnosis method for the COVID-19 diagnosis is performed in real time by reverse transcription-polymerase chain reaction (RT-PCR) test. In many instances, it is reported that negative RT-PCR test reports still show signs of COVID-19 among patients. As the disease is respiratory-related hence medical practitioners prefer chest radiology to understand and confirm the infection in the lungs. Generally, chest radiological imaging techniques like computed tomography (CT) scans and X-rays are made use of in such cases for early diagnosis and treatment of the disease (Jeffrey et al. (2020)). These tests play a vital role in deciding medical treatment protocols for the patients and executing the same. Generally, it is reported that the RT-PCR results are sensitive up to 60%–70%, patients having negative RT-PCR results were found positive by examining the radiological scans. CXR identifies general abnormality while a chest CT scan help in detecting the precise position and better diagnosis of the infection. CXR provides 2D images, but a chest CT scan develops a 3D view of the organs. X-rays are used to examine dense tissues and is lower in cost, good, preliminary examination with fast test result and is more widely available compared to the CT scan for a mass-scale infection diagnosis. Usually, CT scan is considered as a sensitive method with 100-fold more powerful radiation exposure to the human body hence medical practitioners prefer initially X-rays to detect COVID-19 pneumonia. Recently in India during the wave 2 impact of the virus, doctors recommended an X-ray as a firsthand tool than a CT scan due to various reasons including radiation, medical infrastructure availability when virus infection is on a large scale and the requirement of quick diagnosis result availability for immediate medication etc. Chest imaging is key in detecting the disease and can be analyzed to detect the severity of the disease for the COVID-19 treatment (Harrison et al. (2020); Xingzhi et al. (2020)).

The use of machine learning (ML) techniques for classification, clustering and detection of diseases from medical data has become popular in medical science. Clinicians prefer such methods if they are more accurate and faster as it complements their diagnosis. ML, especially methodologies in deep learning, is more attractive to artificial intelligence (AI) researchers, as it enables the development of end-to-end models giving promising results (Yadu et al. (2020); Dilbag et al. (2020)). The COVID-19 pandemic further demands more accurate diagnostic ML methods and tools for clinicians to use in medical infrastructures. Many ML methods are used for classifying COVID-19 patients like Support Vector Machine, Random Forest, and Artificial Neural Networks (ANN) (Pranav et al. (2017); Ezz et al. (2020); Linda et al. (2020); Ioannis et al. (2020); Ali et al. (2021); Song et al. (2020)). Also, Deep Learning (DL) techniques are used to classify COVID-19 patients from the chest radiology image dataset (Shuai et al. (2020); Chuansheng et al. (2020); Xiaowei et al. (2020); Mücahid et al. (2020); Khalid et al. (2020); Tulin et al. (2020); Yadunath et al. (2020); Prabira et al. (2020); Ferhat et al. (2020); Mesut et al. (2020); Adedigba et al. (2021); Abolfazl et al. (2021)). Classification accuracy of COVID-19 patients based on CXR images using DL techniques largely varies among different methods in a range of 87–98% (Tulin et al. (2020); Soumya et al. (2021); R. Murugan et al. (2021)). The recent research for classifying COVID-19 patients use ML methods has used relatively small sample sizes. This may limit the generalizability of the results and making it hard to provide firm conclusions on the performance of different algorithms. An accurate and efficient ML methods for COVID-19 detection that would be suitable to be used by clinicians in medical infrastructures is needed. The main contributions of this work are as follows:

1. Clinicians generally use their medical knowledge-based memory and human visual system (HVS) to process and classify CXR images for detecting COVID-19 disease. HVS relies on a local approach that analyzes structural parameters such as variance and mean to distinguish characteristics in the CXR images. SSIM is a structural comparative coefficient that can be computed using the mean, variance, and similarity index of two images, similar to the HVS analysis approach.
2. The proposed SSIM-based classification approach could be used as a feature extractor to compare two radiology images of a healthy or a patient, which can be further utilized for clustering and classification using supervised ML-based classifiers.
3. The proposed method is computationally faster than deep learning (DL) networks as it uses basic supervised learning classifiers. The results show that the SSIM-based classification approach for CXR images is comparable to the recently used different DL methods.

Overall, the proposed SSIM-based classification approach for CXR images can aid clinicians in detecting COVID-19 accurately in real time. Furthermore, the approach is suitable to be used as an alternative to DL methods, providing a faster and more efficient solution for COVID-19 detection in CXR images. One demerit of our approach is that it assumes that the CXR images are of high quality and have been acquired using similar imaging protocols. Variations in imaging systems or patient conditions can introduce artefacts or inconsistencies that may affect the accuracy of our proposed approach. Section 2 of the manuscript describes the used dataset for our analysis and details of the proposed method for analyzing CXR images, while Sect. 3 shares the results and discussion. We draw conclusions of our work in Sect. 4 of the manuscript.

2 Materials and Methods

2.1 Description of Dataset

We have obtained CXR images from the most frequently used database for COVID-19 (Joseph et al. (2020)), that accumulated from pneumonia images available readily as open sources (Gabriele et al. (2021); Xiaosong et al. (2017); Paul (2018)). The dataset contains CXR images from 3 categories of patients: those with COVID-19, those with other respiratory diseases, and those without any respiratory disease. The COVID-19 images were taken from a variety of sources, which includes peer-reviewed publications, preprints, and online repositories. The other respiratory disease images were collected from patients with conditions like viral pneumonia, tuberculosis and bacterial pneumonia. The healthy patient's images were collected from sources, including the NIH Chest X-Ray dataset. The dataset also includes metadata for each image, including patient age, sex, and medical history, as well as the date the image was taken, and the imaging modality used. The metadata is intended to help researchers identify trends and patterns in the data and to facilitate the implementation of ML algorithms for the automated diagnosis of respiratory diseases.

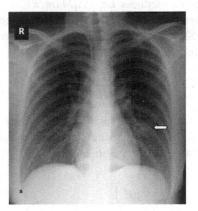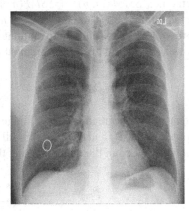

Fig. 1. Sample chest X-ray images, (a) a COVID-19 patient, (b) a healthy subject's chest X-ray image

There are various challenges hosted for detection of COVID-19 patients using CXR image (Brixia GitHub webpage (2020)) and also the COVID-19 disease severity score model (Kaggle webpage (2020)) mostly utilizing this COVID-19 CXR database of Dr Joseph P. Cohen (Sivaramakrishnan et al. (2020); Joseph et al. (2020a, 2020b)). To compare the performance of our proposed method with the recently developed methods based on DL (Tulin et al. (2020); Soumya et al. (2021)), we preferred to use the same public database employed earlier. The database used here is a subset of the CXR image database by Dr Joseph P. Cohen. As the collection of CXR in the master database has grown, we obtained 500 randomly chosen COVID-19 patient's X-ray images from (Joseph et al. (2020a, 2020b)). We also obtained 500 frontal Chest X-rays of healthy subjects chosen randomly from the open-source database (Xiaosong et al. (2017)) for normal images. We choose higher CXR image quantities for our analysis compared to the previous work to add more image variability and randomness in CXR classification for COVID-19 to show the efficacy of our method. Figure 1 shows an image of a COVID-19 and healthy subject obtained from the databases.

2.2 Structural Similarity Index Measure

The images are pre-processed by resizing them all to an equal size of 1024 × 1024 for comparison analysis after converting them to grayscale first. We convert the obtained image matrixes to data type double for our SSIM analysis. If natural image signal's pixels possess spatial similarities, then they are strongly dependent. This feature makes similarity comparison between CXR images very easy. We computed SSIM coefficients using the method discussed below (Zhou et al. (2004); Shahriar et al. (2014); Hai et al. (2018)). The similarity measurement function is computed by combining the three functions where $SSIM(m, n) = f(l(m, n), c(m, n), s(m, n))$. These components are relatively independent i.e., the image structures would not get affected by luminance change and contrast. Similarity measurement function SSIM(m, n) satisfies three conditions: the symmetry i.e., $SSIM(m, n) = SSIM(n, m)$; boundedness i.e., $SSIM(m, n) \leq 1$; the unique maximum i.e., if and only if $m = n$ then only $SSIM(m, n) = 1$. The mathematical expression of each function to compute SSIM is discussed below. The average grey level is used as a luminance measurement estimate for all discrete signals:

$$\alpha_m = \frac{1}{N} \sum_1^N m_i \tag{1}$$

Here m_i is the grayscale image, N is image's size. Hence the luminance function $l(m, n)$ is computed using α_m and α_n values. Similarly, for contrast estimation, the average grey value is removed from the signal making the standard deviation an estimator.

$$\beta_m = \frac{1}{\sqrt[2]{N-1}} \left(\sum_{i=1}^N (m_i - \alpha_m)^2 \right)^{1/2} \tag{2}$$

The $c(m, n)$ is a contrast function, computed using β_m and β_n. Similarly, by dividing the signal with its standard deviation, the $s(m, n)$ is a structural function, computed as a function of $(m - \alpha_m)/\beta_m$ and $(n - \alpha_n)/\beta_n$. The luminance function for comparison is defined as:

$$l(m, n) = \frac{2\alpha_m \alpha_n + C_1}{\alpha_m^2 + \alpha_n^2 + C_1} \tag{3}$$

C_1 is a constant applied for avoiding the instability for $(\alpha_m^2 + \alpha_n^2)$ very close to 0. In particular, $C_1 = (K_1 L)^2$ where L represents a dynamic range of the pixels for the grayscale image while $K_1 << 1$ is a constant. Equation (3) obeys Weber's law, which implies that the HVS is highly sensitive to the relative change in luminance when compared to the absolute change in luminance. Further, the contrast function for comparison is defined as:

$$c(m, n) = \frac{2\beta_m \beta_n + C_2}{\beta_m^2 + \beta_n^2 + C_2} \tag{4}$$

Here, $C_2 = (K_2 L)^2$ with $K_2 \ll 1$ is a constant. Equation (4) obeys the contrast masking feature of the HVS which suggest that it is less sensitive to the case of high-base contrast compared to the low-base contrast with similar contrast change. The structure function for comparison is given as:

$$s(m, n) = \frac{\beta_{mn} + C_3}{\beta_m \beta_n + C_3} \tag{5}$$

Here, $\beta_{mn} = \frac{1}{N-1} \sum_{i=1}^{N} (m_i - \alpha_m)(n_i - \alpha_n)$ and $C_3 = C_2/2$. The similarity measure index SSIM is then defined by combining the three comparison functions as in Eqs. (3)–(5), and the total SSIM is obtained as:

$$SSIM\,(m, n) = [l(m, n)]^\gamma . [c(m, n)]^\mu . [s(m, y = n)]^\delta \tag{6}$$

We could simplify and rewrite Eq. (6) as:

$$SSIM\,(m, n) = \frac{(2\alpha_m \alpha_n + C_1)(2\beta_{mn} + C_2)}{(\alpha_m^2 + \alpha_{y=n}^2 + C_1)(\beta_m^2 + \beta_n^2 + C_2)} \tag{7}$$

Here, $\gamma > 0, \mu > 0, \delta > 0$ are used to bring relative importance of the three functions in Eq. (6). For simplification we use $\gamma = \mu = \delta = 1$. For our analysis, the image components may be either pixel intensities or other extracted features like transformed linear coefficients. We obtained the SSIM index of the 500×500 coefficient matrix by comparing the COVID-19 images among themselves. Similarly, we have also obtained an SSIM index of 500×500 coefficient matrix by comparison of Healthy CXR images among themselves. For further analysis, the diagonal elements of this coefficient matrix which is the image compared with itself having the coefficient value 1 is discarded. The remaining coefficient matrix is concatenated, and the classification label is appended accordingly as 'COVID-19' or 'Healthy'. For both COVID-19 and healthy we have 249500 labelled SSIM coefficients each. Due to correlation, the comparative SSIM index makes large coefficient data points for the classifier's robust training for each class of healthy and diseased individuals, hence leading to higher classification accuracy. We choose 80% of the labelled coefficients for training the ML classifier and use the balance 20% for testing. Then the classifier was trained and further tested for classification accuracy. The choice of SSIM-based feature inherently uses symmetric characteristics to statistically improve the system performance.

2.3 Ensemble Tree Classifier

Ensemble tree classifier is a powerful and flexible ML technique that could help to improve accuracy, reduce overfitting, improve robustness, retain interpretability, and adapt to a wide range of applications. There are several types of ensemble tree classifiers, including Random Forest, AdaBoost, and Gradient Boosting. In each of these methods, a set of decision trees is trained on subsets of the training data, using different features or model parameters. Each tree makes a prediction, and the final prediction is made by aggregating the predictions of all the trees. However, they may incur more computational cost and would need proper hyperparameter tuning for achieving optimum performances.

We optimized the hyperparameters of the ensemble classifier to give the best statistical performances. Hyperparameter search range set for the ensemble method is Bag,

GentleBoost, LogitBoost, AdaBoost, and RUSBoost with 10 to 500 learners at 0.01 to 1 learning rate. Bayesian optimizer is used for 30 iterations to optimize the hyperparameters. The obtained optimized hyperparameters for the classifier are ensemble method – GentleBoost, number of learners – 15, learning rate – 0.0016302 and maximum number of splits - 165145. We obtained an accuracy of 97.7% with a total training time of 2583 s and prediction speed of 69000 observations per second. The total misclassification cost is 2320 out of 99800 observations used to test the classifier. The obtained confusion matrix and ROC curve from the classifier show the efficacy of the method by calculated accuracy and other performance evaluators. We also computed SSIM coefficients by comparing images of COVID-19 with healthy subject images then K-means clustering is used to obtain two clusters. MATLAB classification learner toolbox is used for our ML analysis.

3   Results and Discussion

We used the labelled SSIM index in the ensemble tree classifier after discarding the diagonal coefficients which were self-comparison with coefficient values 1. Due to the correlation among healthy subjects and similarly among the disease, the obtained comparative SSIM index data points become very large from the same input image database for robust training of the ML classifier hence giving higher classification accuracy compared to other standard feature extractors. Figure 2 represents the confusion matrix obtained while evaluating the trained classifier's performance using the test dataset. We used 20% of the total observation i.e., 49900 coefficients of each class for testing the classifier performance. From Fig. 2, we observe the false negative classification is very low compared to the total disease test cases used to evaluate the classifier performance. Figure 3 shows classifier performance accuracy in % for the confusion matrix along with the false negative rate. To further understand the significance of this feature with the use of supervised ML classifiers for classifying CXR images, we computed various statistical performance indicators as shown in Table 1.

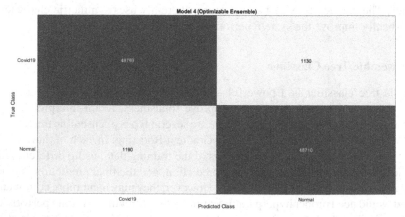

Fig. 2. Confusion Matrix obtained from the classifier with the use of SSIM coefficient

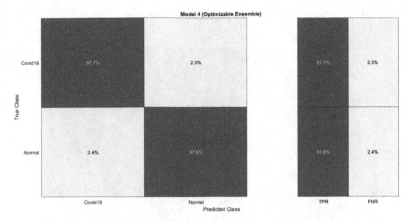

Fig. 3. Confusion Matrix with false negative rate showing classifier performance

Figure 4 shows the performance of the classifier from the ROC curve which is a graphical plot between the true positive rate (TPR) and the false positive rate (FPR) for varying threshold setting. Figure 5 plots the minimum classification error during the classifier optimization iterations process. Figure 6 is the clustering of SSIM coefficients obtained comparing the CXR images between COVID-19 and healthy subjects using K-means. We observe two distinct clusters with no or very less overlapping with the use of comparative SSIM coefficients.

Table 1. Performance Metrics obtained for our proposed method in classifying COVID-19 subjects.

Performance Metrics	Values
Sensitivity in %	97.6152
Specificity in %	97.7354
Precision in %	97.73
Recall in %	97.62
Accuracy in %	97.6753

From Table 1, we could observe 97.7% accuracy for the ensemble tree classifier for using SSIM as a feature extractor to classify CXR images. We also report 97.6% sensitivity for the classifier which is comparable to the deep learning-based classifiers for CXR images. Table 2 shares the comparative study of various deep learning methods with our proposed method. The proposed approach based on the SSIM coefficient with the use of a supervised classifier is computationally very fast in training and prediction with comparable accuracy yield to various DL approaches recently utilized to classify COVID-19 from CXR images. To avoid overfitting our model, we used a relatively small number of parameters in our model. We also employed regularization techniques, such as dropout and weight decay, to further reduce overfitting.

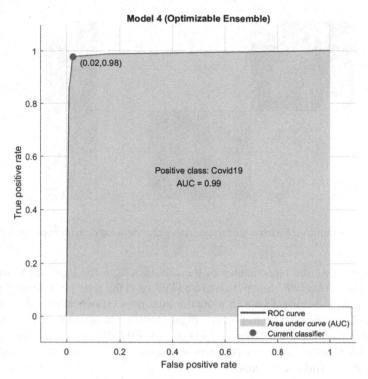

Fig. 4. ROC Curve for the classifier

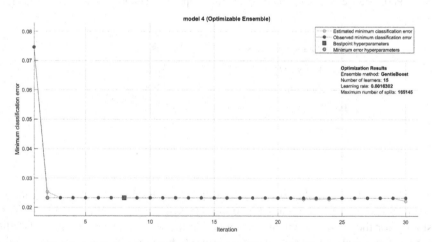

Fig. 5. Minimum classification error plot for the classifier optimization

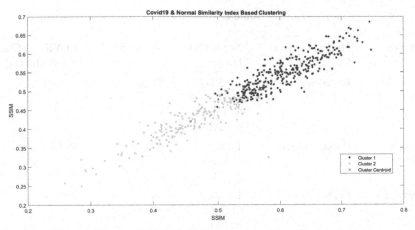

Fig. 6. Clustering using K-mean for SSIM coefficients obtained comparing X-ray images between Healthy and COVID-19 subjects

Table 2. Comparison of the proposed method with existing DL COVID-19 detection methods for CXR images.

Reference	Method Uses for Classification	No. of CXR Images	Accuracy (%)	COVID-19 Class Sensitivity (%)
Ezz et al. (2020)	COVIDX-Net	T – 50 C: 25 N: 25	90.00	100.00
Prabira et al. (2020)	ResNet-50 and SVM	T – 50 C: 25 N: 25	95.38	NA
Ali et al. (2021)	ResNet-50	T – 100 C: 50 N: 50	98.00	96.00
Mesut et al. (2020)	SqueezeNet and MobileNetV2 SMO and SVM	T – 458 C: 295 N: 65 P: 98	98.25	99.32
Linda et al. (2020)	COVID-Net	T – 13870 C: 266 N: 8066 P: 5538	92.60	87.10

(continued)

Table 2. (*continued*)

Reference	Method Uses for Classification	No. of CXR Images	Accuracy (%)	COVID-19 Class Sensitivity (%)
Ferhat et al. (2020)	Bayes-SqueezeNet	T – 5949 C: 76 N: 1583 P: 4290	98.30	100.00
Tulin et al. (2020)	DarkCovidNet	T – 625 C: 125 N: 500	98.08	90.65
Soumya et al. (2021)	ResNet-34	T – 406 C: 203 N: 203	98.33	100.00
Proposed Method	SSIM Coefficient with Ensemble Tree Classifier	T – 1000 C: 500 N: 500	97.7	97.62

[*]Total – T, COVID-19 – C, Normal – N, Pneumonia – P.

4   Conclusion

In conclusion, the SSIM coefficient-based optimized ensemble classifier gives 97.7% classification accuracy even for an increase in test dataset having more image variability and randomness in CXR image. Many recent deep learning-based classifiers using fewer images gave a maximum of 98.3% accuracy (Tulin et al. (2020); Soumya et al. (2021); R. Murugan et al. (2021)) in classifying COVID-19 patients. Our proposed method complements the human visual system approach used by medical practitioners in the diagnosis of radiology images and hence the SSIM index-based ML classifier is capable of automating the classification of COVID-19 patients.

Authors' Contributions. Mayukha Pal conceived the idea and conceptualized it, performed the data analysis, and wrote the manuscript. Prasanta K. Panigrahi contributed to the analysis and discussion of the results, guidance, and review of the manuscript.

Declaration of Competing Interest. The authors declare that they have no known competing financial interests or personal relationships that could have appeared to influence the work reported in this paper. The data obtained for our analysis is from the available public domain database (Brixia GitHub webpage (2020)) made for academic research purposes with approval from the institute's ethical committee. We have appropriately cited the data reference in this work.

References

Narin, A., Kaya, C., Pamuk, Z.: Automatic detection of coronavirus disease (COVID-19) using X-Ray images and deep convolutional neural networks. Pattern Anal. Appl. (2021). https://doi.org/10.1007/s10044-021-00984-y

Padhi, A., Pradhan, S., Sahoo, P.P., Suresh, K., Behera, B.K., Panigrahi, P.K.: Studying the effect of lockdown using epidemiological modelling of COVID-19 and a quantum computational approach using the Ising spin interaction. Sci. Rep. **10**, 21741 (2020). https://doi.org/10.1038/s41598-020-78652-0

Khuzani, A.Z., Heidari, M., Shariati, S.A.: COVID-classifier: an automated machine learning model to assist in the diagnosis of COVID-19 infection in chest X-ray images. Sci. Rep. **11**, 9887 (2021). https://doi.org/10.1038/s41598-021-88807-2

Adedigba, A.P., Adeshina, S.A., Aina, O.E., Aibinu, A.M.: Optimal hyperparameter selection of deep learning models for COVID-19 chest X-ray classification. Intell. Based Med. **5**, 100034 (2021)

Huang, C, Wang, Y., et al.: Clinical features of patients infected with 2019 novel coronavirus in Wuhan, China. Lancet **395**(10223), 497–506 (2020)

Zheng, C., et al.: Deep learning-based detection for COVID-19 from chest CT using the weak label, medRxiv (2020). https://doi.org/10.1101/2020.03.12.20027185

Singh, D., Kumar, V., Vaishali, Kaur, M.: Classification of covid-19 patients from chest CT images using multi-objective differential evolution–based convolutional neural networks. Eur. J. Clin. Microbiol. Infect. Dis., 1–11 (2020)

Hemdan, E.E.D., Shouman, M.A., Karar, M.E.: COVIDX-Net: a framework of deep learning classifiers to diagnose COVID-19 in X-ray images. arXiv (2020). arXiv:2003.11055

Wu, F., Zhao, S., Yu, B., et al.: A new coronavirus associated with human respiratory disease in China. Nature **579** (7798), 265–269 (2020)

Ucar, F., Korkmaz, D.: COVIDiagnosis-Net: deep Bayes-SqueezeNet based diagnosis of the coronavirus disease 2019 (COVID-19) from X-Ray images. Med. Hypotheses **140**, 109761 (2020)

Gabriele, G., et al.: COVID-19:caso 56. https://www.sirm.org/2020/03/21/COVID-19-caso-56/. Accessed 20 July 2021

https://brixia.github.io/. Accessed 15 July 2021

https://www.kaggle.com/c/siim-covid19-detection. Accessed 15 July 2021

Bai, H.X., Hsieh, B., et al.: Performance of radiologists in differentiating COVID-19 from viral pneumonia on chest CT. Radiology (2020). https://doi.org/10.1148/radiol.2020200823

Ni, H.m., Qi, D.w., Mu, H.: Applying MSSIM combined chaos game representation to genome sequences analysis. Genomics **110**(3), 180–190 (2018)

Ioannis, D., Apostolopoulos, T.: Bessiana, COVID-19: automatic detection from X-ray images utilizing transfer learning with convolutional neural networks. Phys. Eng. Sci. Med. **43**, 635–640 (2020). https://doi.org/10.1007/s13246-020-00865-4

Kanne, J.P., Little, B.P., Chung, J.H., Elicker, B.M., Ketai, L.H.: Essentials for radiologists on COVID-19: an update—radiology scientific expert panel. Radiology (2020). https://doi.org/10.1148/radiol.2020200527

Cohen, J.P., et al.: COVID-19 Image Data Collection (2020). https://github.com/ieee8023/COVID-chestxray-dataset. Accessed 15 July 2021

Cohen, J.P., Dao, L., Roth, K., et al.: Predicting COVID-19 pneumonia severity on chest X-ray with deep learning. Cureus **12**(7), e9448 (2020)

Asnaoui, K.E., Chawki, Y.: Using X-ray images and deep learning for automated detection of coronavirus disease (2020). https://doi.org/10.1080/07391102.2020.1767212

Wang, L., Lin, Z.Q., Wong, A.: COVID-Net: a tailored deep convolutional neural network design for detection of COVID-19 cases from chest X-ray images. Sci. Rep. **10**, 19549 (2020)

Barstugan, M., Ozkaya, U., Ozturk, S.: Coronavirus (COVID-19) classification using CT images by machine learning methods. arXiv:2003.09424 (2020)

Toğaçar, M., Ergen, B., Cömert, Z.: COVID-19 detection using deep learning models to exploit social mimic optimization and structured chest X-ray images using fuzzy color and stacking approaches. Comput. Biol. Med., 103805 (2020)

Rajpurkar, P., Irvin, J., et al.: CheXNet: radiologist-level pneumonia detection on chest X-rays with deep learning. arXiv:1711.05225 (2017)

Mooney, P.: Chest X-ray images (pneumonia) (2018). https://www.kaggle.com/paultimothymooney/chest-xray-pneumonia. Accessed 15 July 2021

Sethy, P.K., Behera, S.K.: Detection of coronavirus disease (COVID-19) based on deep features, Preprints (2020). https://doi.org/10.20944/preprints202003.0300.v1

Murugan, R., Goel, T.: E-DiCoNet: extreme learning machine based classifier for diagnosis of COVID-19 using deep convolutional network. J. Ambient Intell. Humaniz. Comput. **12**, 8887–8898 (2021)

Ying, S., Zheng, S., Li, L., et al.: Deep learning enables accurate diagnosis of novel coronavirus (COVID-19) with CT images. IEEE/ACM Trans. Comput. Biol. Bioinform. https://doi.org/10.1109/TCBB.2021.3065361

Wang, S., et al.: A deep learning algorithm using CT images to screen for Corona Virus Disease (COVID-19). Eur. Radiol. **31**, 6096–6104 (2021). https://doi.org/10.1007/s00330-021-07715-1

Rajaraman, S., Sornapudi, S., Alderson, P.O., Folio, L.R., Antani, S.K.: Analyzing inter-reader variability affecting deep ensemble learning for COVID-19 detection in chest radiographs. PLoS ONE **15**(11), e0242301 (2020)

Nayak, S.R., Nayak, D.R., Sinha, U., Arora, V., Pachori, R.B.: Application of deep learning techniques for detection of COVID-19 cases using chest X-ray images: a comprehensive study. Biomed. Signal Process. Control **64**, 102365 (2021)

Akramullah, S.: Digital Video Concepts, Methods, and Metrics: Quality, Compression, Performance, and Power Trade-off Analysis. Springer, Cham (2014). https://doi.org/10.1007/978-1-4302-6713-3

Singhal, T.: A review of coronavirus disease-2019 (COVID-19), Indian. J. Pediatr. **87**, 281–286 (2020)

Ozturk, T., Talo, M., Yildirim, E.A., Baloglu, U.B., Yildirim, O., Acharya, U.R.: Automated detection of COVID-19 cases using deep neural networks with X-ray images. Comput. Biol. Med. **121**, 103792 (2020)

Wang, X., Peng, Y., Lu, L., Lu, Z., Bagheri, M., Summers, R.M.: ChestX-ray8: hospital scale chest x-ray database and benchmarks on weakly-supervised classification and localization of common thorax diseases. In: Proceedings of the IEEE Conference on Computer Vision and Pattern Recognition, pp. 2097–2106 (2017)

Xie, X., Zhong, Z., Zhao, W., Zheng, C., Wang, F., Liu, J.: Chest CT for typical 2019- nCoV pneumonia: relationship to negative RT-PCR testing, Radiology (2020). https://doi.org/10.1148/radiol.2020200343

Xu, X., Jiang, X., Ma, C., Du, P., Li, X., Lv, S., et al.: Deep learning system to screen coronavirus disease 2019 pneumonia. Engineering **6**(10), 1122–1129 (2020)

Pathak, Y.N., Shukla, P.K., Tiwari, A., Stalin, S., Singh, S., Shukla, P.K.: Deep transfer learning based classification model for COVID-19 disease. IRBM (2020)

Pathak, Y., Shukla, P.K., Arya, K.V.: Deep bidirectional classification model for COVID-19 disease infected patients (2020). IEEE/ACM. https://doi.org/10.1109/TCBB.2020.3009859

Wang, Z., Bovik, A.C., Sheikh, H.R., Simoncelli, E.P.: Image quality assessment: from error visibility to structural similarity. IEEE Trans. Image Process. **13**, 4 (2004)

A Religious Sentiment Detector Based on Machine Learning to Provide Meaningful Analysis of Religious Texts

Sourasish Nath[✉], Upamita Das, and Debmitra Ghosh

Computer Science and Engineering Department, JIS University, Kolkata, India
sourasish11042002.jis.cse@gmail.com,
{upamitadas,debmitraghosh}@chalmers.se

Abstract. This paper has the sole purpose of showing the fact that religious sentiment detection holds an important place in the industry and our efforts have been totally concerned with easing the problems of the industry which have been existing to date. Our research has been focused on the shortcomings of various previous methods which have been suggested by previous researchers to classify religious sentiments. There has never been any single application that can classify the sentiments present in a given block of religious text by analyzing only the religious text. We have designed the model in such a way that the users will not have to specify the religious texts and filter them out. The application will reject all the nonreligious texts and provide the desired outcome after analyzing the given religious text which is provided by the user. The model works on the basis of Natural Language Processing and it is able to handle a large amount of data. It is trained using the data sets of the 12 main religions of the world and it is able to perform predictive analysis of the input text since the model is trained using RNN and LSTM algorithms. We have also used the KNN algorithm in the testing phases of the model. A brief analysis of the time complexity along with the comparison of performance evaluation among the different methods have also been discussed in this paper. In the results that we received, it can be clearly seen that we have achieved a minimum loss of 0.083, and the highest accuracy value of the model is found to be 99.8%, This study evaluates the different approaches that can be used to perform sentiment analysis on religious texts and provides a landmark for future researchers to continue improvements in this field. Our research paves the way for future researchers to work more on the untouched portions of sentiment analysis and its applications in real life. In this way, these extensive technologies can be put to better use. We believe that our work and our results might be able to help the people in common to get rid of the harmful and malicious effects of certain religious texts and they would be able to recognize the religious texts which carry good value or provide comfort to them.

Keywords: RNN · LSTM · Sentiment-Analysis · Natural Language Processing

K. Dasgupta et al. (Eds.): CICBA 2023, CCIS 1955, pp. 165–184, 2024.
https://doi.org/10.1007/978-3-031-48876-4_13

1   Introduction

Sentiment refers to an emotional feeling or sensitivity. It also means the affection or passion that an individual feels. There are 5 kinds of sentiment, those are Very positive, Positive, Neutral, Negative, and Very negative. In order to give the users a precise classification of the religious texts entered by the users, we have used the three main sentiment classifications namely Positive, Negative and Neutral. Sentiment analysis involves the use of data mining, machine learning (ML), and artificial intelligence (AI) to mine text for sentiment and subjective information. Sentiment analysis tries to identify sentiment, opinion mining can extract the polarity (or the amount of positively and negativity), subject, and opinion holder within the text. Additionally, other scopes, including document, paragraph, sentence, and sub-sentence levels, can be used with sentiment analysis. "He is not a wise man" - here this kind of sentence is positive or not it will be identified by the system using sentiment analysis step by step.

Sentiment analysis is necessary for classifying the religious texts as good or bad. As we know, religious texts have long been a primary source of mythological education and gaining spiritual knowledge. People tend to heal or inspire themselves mentally by going through different kinds of religious texts. For those who are suffering from depression or trauma, the positively of the religious texts helps them to overcome their feelings and gain composure. People who feel left out or secluded or those who live far from their loved ones find solace and compassion in positive religious texts. Unfortunately, nowadays some transcripts of old religious texts and the modified versions of mythological texts of different religions are sounding more and more negative. This in addition to the fact that a lot of religious negativity is being spread through social media and media articles demands public attention towards the negative aspects of religious texts. If used in the wrong meaning, these religious texts can hurt the feelings of people from different communities and also incur communal hatred. The place where people feel secure will no longer be habitable for finding getting a calm mind. For this reason, people need to be alert about the sentiments associated with different religious texts and which ones they should avoid. Thus, we have decided to build a model in such a way that the users find it easy to use and they can solve their queries related to different religious texts or articles. The rating of the sentiments in the text entered by them would help them to determine whether it imparts any positive value or whether it is harmful to them. The paper is organized from here on as follows: The section Review of Literature discusses some existing research work on the field of sentiment analysis and describes the previous works related to sentiment analysis on religious texts. This section brings out the shortcomings of the previous research works and the parts which have been untouched to date. Therefore, Sect. 2 provides us with the necessary limitations of the previous works and the ideas we can incorporate. Section 4 elaborates on our proposed model stating the proposed algorithm and explaining the overall workflow of the model. A detailed analysis of the results and the comparison between different methods which have been applied to the model for testing and qualitative analysis have been discussed in Sect. 5. The applications and conclusion of our study and how it can be used to solve real-world problems have been discussed in Sect. 6. Finally, we have concluded our research in this paper on sentiment analysis in religious texts with the references.

2 Review of Literature

In the paper Medhat, W., Hassan, A., & Korashy, H. (2014). Sentiment analysis algorithms and applications: A survey. Ain Shams engineering journal, 5(4), 1093–1113, the authors have briefly discussed the various Sentiment Analysis applications and investigated the contributions of various Sentiment Analysis techniques. The survey mainly deals with the pre-existing sentiment analysis methods and how they can be improved to get better results and apply them in different fields. It focuses on the recent trends of research in sentiment analysis using the improvised versions of orthodox techniques. It does not suggest any new approach toward solving the different problems which exist in the domain or any new strategy which might be useful. In the paper Asif, M., Ishtiaq, A., Ahmad, H., Aljuaid, H., & Shah, J. (2020), the main topic of their research is the method of using textual data, sentiment analysis of extremism on social media. Telematics and Informatics, 48, 101345, the authors have discussed their research on the sentimental analysis of multilingual textual data in order to discover the intensity of extremism showcased by the textual data. The data has been incorporated from social media, primarily from Twitter. The model proposed by the authors classifies the incorporated textual views into four categories of extremism. This is a strategy that has been followed widely by researchers all over the world and the primary source of data for all of them is Twitter. This creates some problems in classifying the broader sentiments because extremism is not the only negative sentiment of religious views and the researchers have also omitted the positive aspects of religious texts or comments which are helpful spiritually as well as scientifically to human beings. In the paper Hemalatha, I., Varma, G. S., & Govardhan, A. (2013). Sentiment analysis tool using machine learning algorithms. International Journal of Emerging Trends & Technology in Computer Science (IJETTCS), 2(2), 105–109, the authors have described their sentiment analysis tool which primarily focuses on data received from tweets and analyzes them to classify into three categories, positive, negative, and neutral. The objective of the research is to find out the sentiments from the tweets which can be of any topic with the focus on tweets from media houses and improvising future strategies depending on the market trends. This caters to a broad variety of topics which does not have any primary focus and maintaining such a huge load of data is time-consuming. Analyzing the tweets from all categories and then implementing the improved strategies based on the classification is not viable for every genre. So, solving the problem of spreading religious hatred and classifying the good and bad religious texts will not be done accurately. In the paper Gautam, G., & Yadav, D. (2014, August), they have discussed about Twitter data sentiment analysis utilising machine learning techniques and semantic analysis. The authors have described their model which they have designed to carry out customers' review classification which is able to analyze the information given to it and return a meaningful result from an unstructured input.

The primary source of data is tweets from Twitter. The authors have extracted the adjective, which is also known as a feature vector, and applied machine learning algorithms such as Naive Bayes, Maximum entropy, and SVM. The semantic orientation-based WordNet has also been used which is able to extract synonyms of words and similarity for the content features. In the paper Zhou, X., Tao, X., Yong, J., & Yang, Z. (2013, June). Sentiment analysis on tweets for social events. It had been brought out to the public in International Conference on Computer Supported Cooperative Work in Design, Proceedings of the 2013 IEEE, which was the 17th International conference. IEEE, the authors have described the working of their Tweets Sentiment Analysis Model (TSAM). The model is designed in such a way that it is able to detect societal interest and general peoples' opinions in case of any social event. The model's effectiveness is checked using the detection of interest regarding the sentiment of the specific political candidates, Julia Gillard and Tony Abbot. In the paper Balahur, A., Steinberger, R., Kabadjov, M., Zavarella, V., Van Der Goot, E., Halkia, M., ... & Belyaeva, J. (2013). Sentiment analysis in the news. arXiv preprint arXiv:1309.6202, the authors have presented their idea of sentiment analysis on news articles where they have identified three subtasks under the main task, the definition of the target, separating the good and bad news content from the good and bad sentiment which is showed by the model. The model is meant for mining opinions about entities in the news. It will check the relative suitability of various sentiment dictionaries and separate positive and negative opinions from good or bad news. In the paper Pandarachalil, R., Sendhilkumar, S., & Mahalakshmi, G. S. (2015), the main topic of discussion is unsupervised Twitter sentiment analysis for large-scale data Cognitive Computation, 7(2), 254–262, the authors have described their model in which the polarity of tweets is evaluated using three sentiment lexicons - SenticNet, SentiWordNet, and SentislangNet. The F-score has been calculated by the authors and when a good score is achieved, the model has been tested in parallel python framework. A large volume of data can be handled by using the model which significantly reduces the space complexity. In the paper Bleich, E., & van der Veen, A. M. (2021), the topic for the research being discussed is Muslim stereotypes in the media: a comparison of reader attitude in American, with the time frame being within 1996–2015. Politics, Groups, and Identities, 9(1), 20–39, the authors have shown their research based on American newspapers about the tone of media articles towards Muslims. The authors have brought out the fact that the tone of the articles is considerably more negative towards Muslims than both the baseline set by them and the other groups which have been compared. This research primarily focuses on one religious community, that is the Muslims, and it fails to take into account the negativity that might be spread against other communities too. Religious hatred in media articles is more prevalent in every country more or less, and if we analyze the religious groups in all the countries we would be able to find different ratios of negativity that are being spread against different religious groups or communities. So, after reviewing all these previous works in the field of sentiment analysis, we came to the conclusion that the sentiment analysis on religious texts has not been left incomplete by the previous researchers due to their primary focus being a particular religious community, region, or the approach taking into account huge loads of data. Hence, we have structured our model in such a way that it analyzes the sentiments of the religious texts which can be of any religion, and shows all the sentiments attached to that text. We have given the users the monopoly to enter any kind of religious text. The model will classify its rate of positivity, neutrality, and negativity and return the overall rating of the text entered by the user. There is no need to handle huge amounts of data because the model is trained using the datasets of the 12 main religions present in the world and it will analyze the sentiments accordingly. It is also able to analyze the sentiments of articles, media journals, and social media posts as and when required by the user.

3   Background

LSTM: Long Short Term Memory networks, popularly known as LSTM, are a special kind of recurrent neural network which are able to sort out long-term dependencies. LSTMs have the ability to perform better when the situation comes to long-term learning patterns. This is because apart from the normal neural layers, LSTM has the additional hidden state layer which can store the results of previous values given to it. For this reason, LSTMs are highly valuable for analyzing sequential predictions on a particular set of data. LSTM is made up of four gates which are its main components - Forget gate, Input gate, Output gate, and Cell gate. Each gate has its own function which is summarized as follows:

Forget Gate: The forget gate is our first step towards training the model with useful information for predictive analysis. When working with a long-term memory network, the bits of the cell state are incorporated into the forget gate which helps in deciding the usefulness of the given data. The network takes into account the data from the hidden layer. This network (inside the forget gate) is trained to output a value near 0 when an input component is regarded as irrelevant and a value closer to 1 when the input component is deemed important. It is helpful to think of each component of this vector as a sort of filter or sieve that lets through more data as the value approaches 1.

Input Gate: The input gate is responsible for determining the new information which needs to be added to the long-term memory, also known as cell state. It receives the data from the hidden states which are used for predictive analysis of the current input and ultimately yields the most likely outcome which has to be incorporated into the output layer. The previously hidden state data and new input data is combined by a special vector known as new memory update vector which is part of a tanh activated neural network.

Output Gate: The primary task of the output gate is to decide the next hidden state. In order to determine the new hidden test for the upcoming prediction, the newly updated cell state after the previous prediction, the hidden state from the previous inputs, and the new data from the current input are taken into account.

Cell Gate: The cell gate is responsible for determining the cell states to be given to the output gate. It takes into account the forget vector from the forget gate and multiplies its value with the previous cell state. If the result comes out to be 0, then the values will be dropped by the cell gate. In that case, the cell gate takes the input vector and performs point-by-point addition on it which gives rise to a new cell state with the ability to predict values based on the new outcomes.

Working with LSTM in Our Model: In our model, we have used LSTM in order to reduce the time complexity significantly as it increases the chances of our model to provide accurate outcomes to the users through predictive analysis. The model is trained using a variety of inputs and the hidden layers of the neural network are able to store the inputs from the previous timestamps. These are analyzed and the model retains all the information from these past inputs as the data is fetched from the hidden layers when the current input is taken and then the output layers receive the final value which is a combination of the data from both the previous and current timestamps. The LSTM algorithm is able to analyze data sequentially as it takes into account all the information that is stored in the memory and it works as a good classifier. The required information is filtered and sent to the output layers in a refined way which also increases the efficiency of our model. The values turned out to be pretty promising as the predictions started to improve with the addition of more inputs as the model is able to learn from the previous input values which get stored in the hidden layers. Hence, we can deduce that the model will be able to maintain consistency in its predicted values.

RNN: RNN stands for Recurrent Neural Network. RNN is a special kind of algorithm and the fact which makes it unique is that it possesses internal memory, which is not present in any other neural network. This makes RNN one of the most promising algorithms for predictive analysis and classification works since it offers a robust environment to users with a variety of applications. With the help of the internal memory, RNN is able to store the inputs which are given to it and then consider these values when a new input is given. Thus, it analyzes the patterns of the inputs which it fetches from the user by reconstructing the previous inputs and provides an efficient predictive analysis of the values that it works with and ultimately gives the desired outcome to the users. The working procedure of an RNN is similar to the human brain. For this reason, it is widely used in the case of machine learning models. As the human brain retains the information that is once given to it, in the same way, RNN is capable of storing the information given to it in the form of inputs and then using these values from the previous inputs to incorporate into the analysis o the present input which is given to it. Every time the user enters a query, the recent past value is considered and the model predicts the most likely outcome for the user after comparing that value with the present input. So, for sequential classifications, RNN is highly viable as it capable of handling two inputs simultaneously and thus reduces the time complexity to a great extent. If we set the maximum permissible limit of the error margin we can see that the right information is given as output and the model can determine what information the user is likely to need next, thus ascertaining that the accuracy of the model maintains the saturation level.

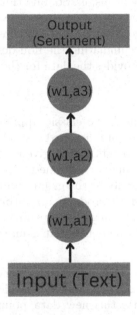

Fig. 1. Workflow of RNN used in the model.

In Fig. 1, we can see the working procedure of an RNN for a sentiment analysis model. Here, (w1,a1), (w1,a2), and (w1,a3) are the values from the load matrix which contains the positions of the weights according to their timesteps. The load matrix keeps on varying and the weights show an increasing trend when new inputs are added as a lot of timestamps need to be considered in every timestep. In this way, the model deduces the actual sentiments attached to the concerned inputs.

Working with RNN in Our Model: In our model, we have used RNN in order to increase the model's perceptibility of different sentiments contained in the users' texts. The presence of internal memory in RNN makes it easier to store the previous inputs provided by the user so that it can be used in the analysis of the current input provided by the user and predict the correct outcomes. It has helped us to use our training models efficiently by producing new results in various test cases and arrive at a better predictive output by comparing the results of the testing phases with other methods too. The main approaches used with RNN in our model are summarized as follows:

Backpropagation - It takes into account the time series of the data that is given as input. Generally, we get one output for every input. In this approach, the previous inputs which are stored in the internal memory are also considered as inputs for the present scenario. So, both the current and previous inputs are analyzed to get a viable conclusion. So, one timestep determines the output from the inputs of the current timestamp along with the inputs of the previous timestamps coming up to it. One timestep consists of data from numerous timestamps. This helps in accumulating the non-desirable outcomes from every timestamp and this further provides the data for the training models to be aware of the mistakes.

One to Many RNN - This is the classic approach for a sentiment analysis model in which a single input containing text is analyzed and the output consists of the score of different sentiments in the given text. In our model, the RNN predicts the values of the sentiments contained within the input text in order to come to the conclusion as it analyzes the given input with the inputs of all other timestamps. After the analysis, it produces an output that shows the percentage values of Positive, Neutral, and Negative sentiments in the given text and also shows the overall rating of the sentence that is entered.

KNN: The KNN algorithm is based on a supervised learning technique. It stands for k-Nearest Neighbour. It mainly classifies a new data point in the given data and then it inserts this new data point into the existing data-set based on the similarity of that particular data point to the data within the data-set. KNN does not evaluate the predictions which are done by RNN or LSTM, mainly due to the fact that it is non-parametric in nature. Hence, it is better suited to classification. KNN classifies the positive, negative, and neutral sentiments contained in the input text based on the polarities of the words after comparing the new data point created by it with the previous data.

Working with KNN in Our Model: In our model, kNN has been used primarily during the testing phases. It has provided us with an environment that is ideal to compare the accuracy values that we received from the different methods that we used. Since kNN does not perform predictive analysis, the accuracy values do not shoot up as they can do in the case of RNN or LSTM. There is no internal memory in kNN and as a result, it only compares the values of the current input with the previous inputs based on the new data point that has to be calculated by measuring the Euclidean distance between the two nearest data points of the input that is given by the user. After performing the analysis on the input, the comparison yields the most likely sentiment values which match with the data given in the dataset. Thus, after taking into account the results provided by using the kNN approach, we are able to conduct a performance analysis of our training models and check which training model gives the highest accuracy and is suitable to be used in the final application.

4 Proposed Model

The model has been designed in such a way that it reciprocates the inputs from the user and provides a meaningful result as output after processing the data according to the values with which it is trained. When the user enters a religious text, or any word resembling religious fundamentals, the model will analyze the polarity of the text entered. It undergoes polarity checking under the positive and negative polarity counter and then the values of the positive and negative polarities of the text are stored in the program. The program uses the outcome of the positive and negative polarities to generate the percentage of positive and negative sentiment in the provided text. The following steps are an example of the working of our model:

Step 1: Extraction of text from mythological novels or social media or media articles.
Step 2: The polarity of the text will be determined.
Step 3: The intensity and the strength of the opinion will be determined.
Step 4: The text is Positive or Negative or Neutral which will be specified by Sentiment Analysis.
Step 5: The rating of the text will be returned as output.

The positive sentiment score is determined by the formula given in the following equation:

$$PositiveSentimentScore = \frac{\text{No. of Positive words} - \text{No. of Negative words}}{\text{Total no. of words}}$$

As we can see in the above equation, the Positive Sentiment score can be calculated by dividing the result of the difference between the number of positive words and the number of negative words by the total number of words. The negative sentiment score is determined using the formula in the following equation:

$$NegativeSentimentScore = \frac{\text{No. of Negative words} - \text{No. of Positive words}}{\text{Total no. of words}}$$

As we can see in the above equation, the Negative Sentiment score can be calculated by dividing the result of the difference between the number of negative words and the number of positive words by the total number of words. The model calculates the overall sentiment of the given word in percentage using the formula given in the following equation.

$$OverallScore = \frac{\text{Negative Sentiment Score} + \text{Positive Sentiment Score}}{2}$$

The model then produces the output in the layout which shows the values of the positive sentiment rating, neutral sentiment rating, negative sentiment rating, and the overall rating of the sentence.

Whenever the user enters any input which does not cater to any religious fundamentals and does not show any religious feelings attached to it, the model treats it as a false alarm and ignores the specific sentiments associated with the sentence. As a result, the model produces an output in such a way that it contains the mixed sentiments shown by the sentence. Since it is not religious

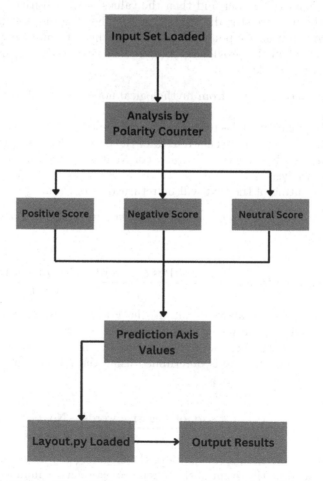

Fig. 2. Data Flow Diagram representing the working of the model.

in nature, the model shows all the ratings of positive, negative, and neutral sentiments together because it is treated as an undesirable outcome. The Data Flow Diagram of the overall religious text analysis system is shown in Fig. 2.

The overall sentiment rating produced by the model is aspect based. It takes into account the previous inputs of the user and whether the aspects of the inputs showcase any religious sentiments or not. The model remembers the polarities of the positive and negative values of the sentences that it receives as input from the user. Since the model functions based on the LSTM algorithm, the values can be stored in the memory temporarily and the output is generated after the previous values are analyzed with the new inputs given to the model. The aspect-based analysis enables the model to scrutinize the actual feeling being established by the texts which are entered simultaneously. Sometimes, the inputs might be the same qualitatively but they might differ quantitatively. If such a condition occurs, the model is able to predict the missing values and it shows the output taking into account the polarity values of both the possible outcomes, which finally gives more accurate outputs.

5   Result Analysis and Discussion

All the codes have been written in Python and the Integrated Development Environment (IDE) used for developing the model is VS Code. Apart from that, text editors such as Notepad++ and IDLE have also been used. The application and its layout have been designed using the Tkinter GUI interface of Python. It is comfortable for any kind of personal computer and the layout is compatible with all operating systems. The testing of the model with the initial and final demo work has been completed using the hardware configuration mentioned below: Processor - Intel core i3 RAM - 8 GB DDR4 HDD - 1 TB SSD - 240 GB Operating System - Windows 10 The application has been tested in other systems as well with different operating systems and hardware configurations. It functions perfectly under the following different configurations too:-

1. **Linux Operating System**
   Processor - Intel core i5
   RAM - 12 GB DDR4
   HDD - 1 TB
   SSD - 120 GB
   Operating System - Arch Linux
2. **Mac Operating System**
   Processor - Apple M1
   RAM - 8 GB
   SSD - 512 GB
   Operating System - macOS Monterey Version 12.6.

So, we have observed that our model is able to produce the correct outputs under different environments. It works seamlessly in all operating systems, without any delay or lagging. The outputs that we received in Windows match the outputs received in Linux and macOS. Hence, it can be deduced that when the application is designed for the android framework, it will function correctly in the Android operating system too. An exe demo file has to be tested in the android devices and matched with the functioning in desktop computers to get the measure of the accuracy. The working model of the religious text analysis system is shown below in the following pictures:

In Fig. 3, we can see the main interface of the Religious Sentiment Detector which will show the output to the users once they enter the input text in the designated area.

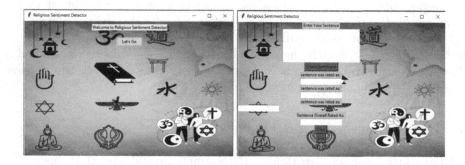

Fig. 3. Application interface of the model.

In the above picture, it can be seen that the layout of the application has been designed extensively using the Tkinter library of Python. The layout consists of two windows with the primary window showing a label that contains the text "Welcome to Religious Sentiment Detector". It is followed by a button that reads "Let's Go". The user has to click on this button in order to move to the main layout from the primary layout. If the user wishes to discontinue and close the application, he can do so by clicking on the close button of the primary Tkinter window. The Let's Go button is connected to the python file layout.py which contains the main layout of the application and runs the application by assembling all the programs from the trained model. Once the user opens the main layout by clicking on the Let's Go button, the user will be able to enter the input in the area provided which is named "Enter your Sentence". The user has to click on the "Check Sentiment" button in order to analyze the religious sentiment associated with the text entered by him. The application will show the result in the dedicated boxes below for each sentiment and ultimately shows the overall rating of the text entered by the user. The following images show the behavior of the model according to different types of inputs which are positive, negative, or neutral. Each time it shows the perfect output after correctly analyzing the sentiments of the entered sentences (Fig. 4):

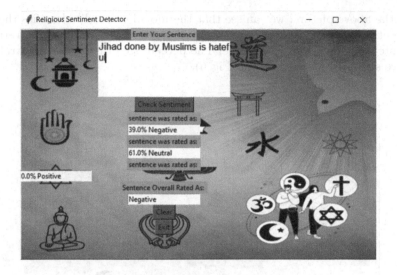

Fig. 4. Negative Sentiment Detection.

In the above picture, we can see that the model correctly identifies the negative sentiment of the sentence entered by the user. Hence, the overall rating of the sentence is produced as Negative. The percentage of Negative, Neutral, and Positive sentiments is also shown (Fig. 5).

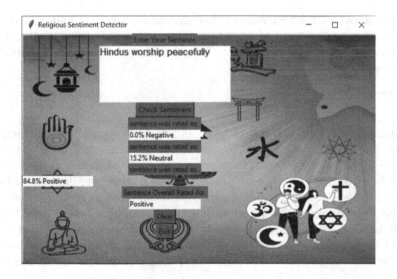

Fig. 5. Positive Sentiment Detection.

In the above picture, we can see that the model correctly identifies the positive sentiment of the sentence entered by the user. Hence, the overall rating of the sentence is produced as Positive. The percentage of Negative, Neutral, and Positive sentiments is also shown (Fig. 6).

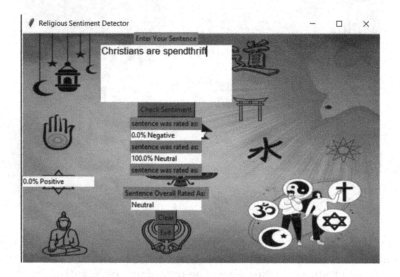

Fig. 6. Neutral Sentiment Detection.

In the above picture, we can see that the model correctly identifies the neutral sentiment of the sentence entered by the user. Hence, the overall rating of the sentence is produced as Neutral. The percentage of Negative, Neutral, and Positive sentiments is also shown.

Features:

Tagging of Parts of Speech (POS) - Parts of Speech (POS) tagging is an efficient way of annotating text. In this strategy, each text from the provided sentence or data is tagged with Parts of Speech. A POS Tagger is used to mark the words with their corresponding parts of speech which are denoted as tokens. In our training model, we have taken the six basic parts of speech - noun, verb, adjective, adverb, preposition, and conjunction. They have been tagged from the dataset to identify the required aspects and their polarity scores. In this way, the user does not need to see the background of the detection, and the model also identifies the grammatical errors which might be present in the sentence.

Dependency Parsing - The grammatical structure of a sentence can be analyzed using dependency parsing. The "Main" words present in the sentence are identified and the model then checks the relationships between these "Main" words and the words which modify the "Main" words in order to give a meaningful structure to the sentence. The relationship thus obtained with the help of the dependency parser is used to extract the aspects which might be critical in determining the sentiments of the sentence since the words are being modified and the sentiments can also be changed during the modification.

Score Analysis - Let us consider the aspect ratio to be ri. If there are n number of aspects that are to be analyzed, then the formula for the score analysis, Score(ri) is:

$$\sum_{i=1}^{n}(score(adj) + score(adj, adj) + score(adv, adj) + score(neg) + score(acro) + score(punc))$$

5.1 Training and Testing Phases

The model has to be prepared by loading the data-set and splitting it into separate sets for training and testing. The training model contains the CSV or XML file with all the required data showing religious sentiments. The training model helps the final application predict the correct result based on the input given by the user. If the training model gains a high accuracy and is able to provide correct results based on its analysis, we can say that it is fit to be used for the final application. So, before using it in the final application, we have to look after the training and testing phases which give us the outcome of the functioning of the model. The loss and accuracy percentage of the model have to be checked and based on the values that we get, we can decide whether the model is feasible or not. We can check the accuracy and a loss percentage of our training model from the table given below (Table 1):

Table 1. Lowest accuracy of training model.

Training model	Epoch	Batchsize	Loss	Accuracy
Sentiment model1.0	150/150	25	0.52	81

In this table, the training model, Sentiment model 1.0 is used which has a batch size of 25. After analyzing the sentiments from the provided dataset, the model gives an accuracy of 81% which is significantly lower than the required value. We tested the other training models as well and gradually the accuracy value began to increase which ultimately rose to 99.8% in our final training model, Sentiment model 3.0 The accuracy and loss of the final training model are shown in the table below (Table 2):

Table 2. Highest accuracy of training model

Training model	Epoch	Batchsize	Loss	Accuracy
Sentiment model 3.0	300/300	30	0.083	99.8

In this table, we can see that our training model has achieved the highest accuracy which is 99.8%. After undergoing 300/300 epochs with a batch size of 30, the training model has seen a decrease in loss and an increase in accuracy percentage. This means that the analysis and prediction of the model have become higher and more accurate. It is able to recognize the sentiments correctly and it will be helpful to the users since it provides the correct outcome. If the accuracy of the model remains low, it will create problems for the user if the model is applied to the final application because the prediction might not be always correct in case of a model with low accuracy, as a result of which, the user might get the wrong outcome. The model becomes unstable in that case and it may provide unexpected results to the user. In the above table, the highest accuracy is shown on epoch 300/300. Here, we have the minimum loss which is 0.083, and the highest accuracy percentage which is 99.8%. In order to get the required results, we have used the algorithm LSTM. It has four different components, namely, Forget gate, Input gate, Output gate, and Cell gate. All the gates within LSTM have their respective functions to perform and their roles are important for getting the overall result. The forget gate helps to determine which information from the cell gate we are going to throw away. The "forget gate layer," which is a sigmoid layer, helps us to arrive on a concluding decision on this. It examines ht1 and xt, and for each number in the cell state Ct1, it labors a number between 0 and 1. A 1 means "entirely keep this," and a 0 means "entirely get relief of this." The forget gate works according to the following equation: When the sigmoid function is applied, the ft is expressed as a number, 0 or 1. This ft will be multiplied by the cell state of the previous timestamp. We can understand from the image below: The Cell gate is responsible for combining all the information from the Input gate and Forget gate that is meant to be kept after getting 1 as a result, which means keep. The equation for the cell gate is shown below: The input gate looks after the analysis of the previous inputs and decides which values should be updated. The equation of the input gate is shown below: The output gate predicts the relevant outcome according to the inputs from the previous timestamp. It includes the output from the current timestamp and adds the output from the previous inputs as well after applying Softmax activation on the hidden state. The equation for the output gate is shown below: When these gates are combined in the LSTM, they help to make a perfect training model by applying this strategy simultaneously to the models and they undergo different loss and accuracy.

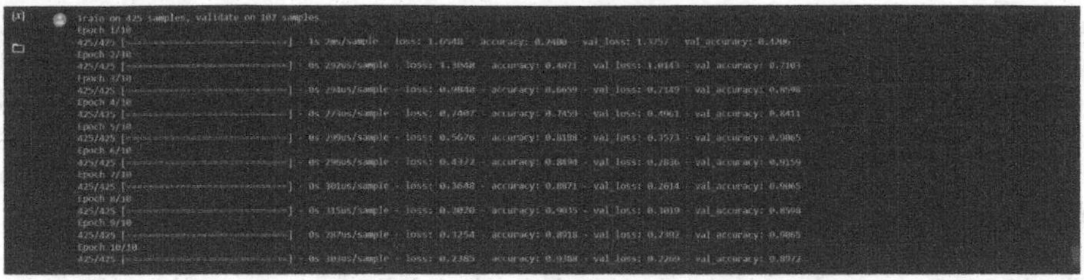

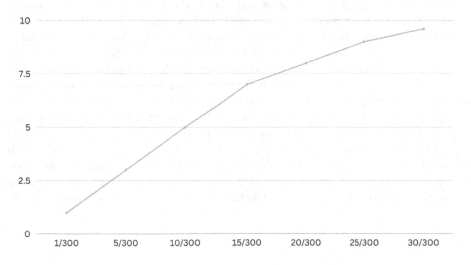

Fig. 7. Increase in Accuracy of the model.

In Fig. 7, we can see that the trends in the accuracy values of our model have been increasing along with the introduction of new test cases. From here, it can be deduced that with the passage of the epochs, the accuracy of the model improves due to the training it had received previously that is applied to the testing phases. In our model, it has been observed that the accuracy has been increasing consistently per epoch. When the epoch is 1/300 to 5/300, the accuracy progresses slowly and the loss starts decreasing. When the epoch is 10/300 to 20/300, the accuracy becomes steady and there is a stable increasing rate seen at this point. When the epoch is 30/300 and moves ahead further, it is seen that the accuracy percentage increases at a high rate, and till the last epoch, it keeps on increasing with a steady decrease in the loss. So, when the model is used, the user gets a perfect response since the accuracy has been increasing with each epoch. The performance of the model is stable for any kind of input. If the accuracy of the model is low and it experiences a lower proficiency rate, the results after analyzing the inputs from the user will not be closer to his expectations or it might even be inconvenient to the user. Hence,

Fig. 8. The Accuracy vs Epoch graph.

in order to get a closer prediction of the sentiments after analyzing the input, a high accuracy percentage has to be maintained. The higher accuracy levels of the model suggest that a good and proficient sigmoid layer is working and all the hidden state information have been checked and perceived correctly. In this way, the data is utilized in a constructive way and the loss can be limited to a negligible minimum (Fig. 8).

In the above graph, we can see a steady increase in accuracy with each epoch. The hidden state values play a great role in the higher accuracy values. It stores the values after the inputs are provided from the previous timestamps and take into account the values from the current timestamp as well. In order to calculate the loss and accuracy from the sigmoid layer, a Soft-max activation is applied to the hidden state. It allows the hidden layers to send accurate values and the output layer analyzes values from all the timestamps correctly thus giving a great performance.

6   Discussion and Conclusions

We used real-time tests and "questionnaire" techniques to perform the usability of the voice-chat-agent when this application is further developed. Also, the AI Agent gathers expected information from students so that we could make accurate predictions. Our model works on the scalable features of the voice available in audio format which it converts into text. The amplitude and decibel log is compared from the coordinates of the starting and end points of the input as can be observed from the text. These labels are read as tokens by the model and the spectrogram generated from these values gives us an idea of how far the prediction of the sentiments can go according to the given threshold of the model. For the calling agent, we will add more flexibility so that it can handle multiple international calls at once and speak the user's preferred regional or other languages. Even so, every time a user sends a "request," it will be activated as a call. As for free hosting, we utilize Streamlit, which is both free and simple to use, but in the future, we'll use it for its own domain because it allows for one-click communication with users all over the world. The calling agent will be immensely helpful to any educational organization because the primary cause of concern for every institute is the analysis of students' attitudes. Students are always worried about which institute is going to be right for them and making a perfect choice would be easier once their queries are resolved. The institutes would be able to predict which way a particular student wants to go and which stream they want to join and also ascertain if they have any negative attitude towards any religion since the agent will analyze their sentiments and provide a result that would help to ascertain whether they want to take admission or not.

References

1. Du Preez, S.J., Lall, M., Sinha, S.: An intelligent web-based voice chat bot. In: IEEE EUROCON 2009, pp. 386–391. IEEE, May 2009
2. Sehgal, R.R., Agarwal, S., Raj, G.: Interactive voice response using sentiment analysis in automatic speech recognition systems. In: 2018 International Conference on Advances in Computing and Communication Engineering (ICACCE), pp. 213–218. IEEE, June 2018
3. Prabha, M.I., Srikanth, G.U.: Survey of sentiment analysis using deep learning techniques. In: 2019 1st International Conference on Innovations in Information and Communication Technology (ICIICT), pp. 1–9. IEEE, April 2019
4. Mammen, J.R., Java, J.J., Rhee, H., Butz, A.M., Halterman, J.S., Arcoleo, K.: Mixed-methods content and sentiment analysis of adolescents' voice diaries describing daily experiences with asthma and self-management decision-making. Clin. Exp. Allergy 49(3), 299–307 (2019)
5. Silviya Nancy, J., Udhayakumar, S., Pavithra, J., Preethi, R., Revathy, G.: Context aware self learning voice assistant for smart navigation with contextual LSTM. In: Luhach, A.K., Jat, D.S., Hawari, K.B.G., Gao, X.-Z., Lingras, P. (eds.) ICAICR 2019. CCIS, vol. 1075, pp. 441–450. Springer, Singapore (2019). https://doi.org/10.1007/978-981-15-0108-1_41
6. Alexander, J.: A photo-realistic voice-bot (Master's thesis, Universitat Politècnica de Catalunya) (2019)
7. Megalingam, R.K., Sathi, S.R., Pula, B.T., Chandrika, D., Reddy, N.S.: Cloud computation based urban management system using Ros. In: 2019 3rd International Conference on Trends in Electronics and Informatics (ICOEI), pp. 764–769. IEEE, April 2019
8. Shukla, S., Maheshwari, A., Johri, P.: Comparative analysis of ML algorithms & stream lit web application. In: 2021 3rd International Conference on Advances in Computing, Communication Control and Networking (ICAC3N), pp. 175–180. IEEE, December 2021
9. Khorasani, M., Abdou, M., Hernández Fernández, J.: Streamlit use cases. In: Web Application Development with Streamlit, pp. 309–361. Apress, Berkeley, CA (2022)
10. Kumari, S., Naikwadi, Z., Akole, A., Darshankar, P.: Enhancing college chat bot assistant with the help of richer human computer interaction and speech recognition. In: 2020 International Conference on Electronics and Sustainable Communication Systems (ICESC), pp. 427–433. IEEE, July 2020
11. Esposito, A., Raimo, G., Maldonato, M., Vogel, C., Conson, M., Cordasco, G.: Behavioral sentiment analysis of depressive states. In: 2020 11th IEEE International Conference on Cognitive Infocommunications (CogInfoCom), pp. 000209–000214. IEEE, September 2020
12. Alsaeedi, A., Khan, M.Z.: A study on sentiment analysis techniques of Twitter data. Int. J. Adv. Comput. Sci. Appl. 10(2), 361–374 (2019)
13. Liu, B.: Sentiment analysis: a multi-faceted problem. IEEE Intell. Syst. 25(3), 76–80 (2010)
14. Jayashree, D., Pandithurai, O., Prasad, S., Suresh, A.S., Vigneshwaran, S.: Sentimental analysis on voice based reviews using fuzzy logic. In: 2021 International Conference on Advancements in Electrical, Electronics, Communication, Computing and Automation (ICAECA), pp. 1–6. IEEE, October 2021
15. Vanmassenhove, E., Cabral, J.P., Haider, F.: Prediction of emotions from text using sentiment analysis for expressive speech synthesis. In: SSW, pp. 21–26 (2016)

16. Manna, D., Baidya, S., Bhattacharyya, S.: Sentiment analysis of audio diary. In: Nath, V., Mandal, J.K. (eds.) Proceedings of the Fourth International Conference on Microelectronics, Computing and Communication Systems. LNEE, vol. 673, pp. 99–111. Springer, Singapore (2021). https://doi.org/10.1007/978-981-15-5546-6_9
17. Wooldridge, M.: Intelligent agents. In: Multiagent Systems: A Modern Approach to Distributed Artificial Intelligence, vol. 1, pp. 27–73 (1999)
18. Nwana, H.S.: Software agents: an overview. Knowl. Eng. Rev. **11**(3), 205–244 (1996)
19. Wooldridge, M., Jennings, N.R.: Intelligent agents: theory and practice. Knowl. Eng. Rev. **10**(2), 115–152 (1995)
20. Maes, P., Kozierok, R.: Learning interface agents. In: AAAI, vol. 93, pp. 459–465, July 1993
21. Ramya, P., Sindhura, V., Sagar, P.V.: Testing using Selenium web driver. In: 2017 Second International Conference on Electrical, Computer and Communication Technologies (ICECCT), pp. 1–7. IEEE, February 2017
22. Bruns, A., Kornstadt, A., Wichmann, D.: Web application tests with Selenium. IEEE Softw. **26**(5), 88–91 (2009)
23. Holmes, A., Kellogg, M.: Automating functional tests using Selenium. In: AGILE 2006 (AGILE 2006), pp. 6-pp. IEEE, July 2006
24. Feigl, F., West, P.W.: Test for Selenium based on catalytic effect. Anal. Chem. **19**(5), 351–353 (1947)
25. Ranoliya, B.R., Raghuwanshi, N., Singh, S.: Chatbot for university related FAQs. In: 2017 International Conference on Advances in Computing, Communications and Informatics (ICACCI), pp. 1525–1530. IEEE, September 2017
26. Batish, R.: Voicebot and Chatbot Design: Flexible Conversational Interfaces with Amazon Alexa, Google Home, and Facebook Messenger. Packt Publishing Ltd., New York (2018)
27. Tran, D.C., Nguyen, D.L., Hassan, M.F.: Development and testing of an FPT. AI-based VoiceBot. Bull. Electr. Eng. Inform. **9**(6), 2388–2395 (2020)
28. Liesenfeld, A., Huang, C.R.: NameSpec asks: What's Your Name in Chinese? A voice bot to specify Chinese personal names through dialog. In: Proceedings of the 2nd Conference on Conversational User Interfaces, pp. 1–3, July 2020
29. Ma, Y., Drewes, H., Butz, A.: Fake moods: can users trick an emotion-aware Voice-Bot?. In: Extended Abstracts of the 2021 CHI Conference on Human Factors in Computing Systems, pp. 1–4, May 2021

Automated Detection of Melanoma Skin Disease Using Classification Algorithm

Manisha Barman[1](✉), J. Paul Choudhury[2], and Susanta Biswas[3]

[1] Department of Information Technology, Kalyani Government Engineering College, Kalyani, Nadia, WB, India
memanisha5@gmail.com
[2] Department of Computer Science and Engineering, Narula Institute of Technology, Sodepur, Kolkata, India
[3] Department of Engineering and Technological Studies, University of Kalyani, Kalyani, Nadia 741235, India

Abstract. The advancement of modern technology has enabled the diagnosis of various skin diseases through image processing. Researchers face significant challenges when it comes to utilize image processing tools for skin disease analysis. One particularly serious disease is Melanoma, a type of cancer originating from melanocytes. The primary objective of this research article is to develop a machine learning classification-based algorithm for melanoma detection.

The complexities associated with analyzing melanoma skin disease can be mitigated by employing an effective classification technique. In this proposed model, two machine learning (ML) classification algorithms, namely the Probabilistic Neural Network (PNN) and Support Vector Machine (SVM), are utilized for disease detection. These algorithms are employed to differentiate between melanoma-affected skin and normal skin.

To establish the machine learning algorithms, feature selection is performed using Factor Analysis (FA), and the dermenetNZ.org dataset is utilized. The performance of the two classification algorithms is compared using standard performance metrics. Through comparative analysis, it is demonstrated that the Probabilistic Neural Network classifier outperforms the Support Vector Machine in the classification of melanoma skin disease. Overall, this research article showcases the efficacy of a machine learning-based approach for melanoma detection, with the Probabilistic Neural Network exhibiting superior results compared to the Support Vector Machine classifier.

Keywords: Digital image · color channel conversion · mean value · standard deviation · GLCM · probabilistic neural network · Support vector machine · confusion matrix

1 Introduction

We face a significant obstacle in predicting a skin disease using modern technology. In this setting, making use of an intelligent system is a real challenge. To meet this challenge, numerous researchers have proposed various strategies.

K. Dasgupta et al. (Eds.): CICBA 2023, CCIS 1955, pp. 185–198, 2024.
https://doi.org/10.1007/978-3-031-48876-4_14

1.1 Background Study

Arfika Nurhudatiana [1] has proposed a method which use an RGB image as input, use Fuzzy C-Mean clustering for segmenting skin from the background, use YCbCr and RGB color space for separating depigmented skin and normal skin into two clusters, and then depigmentation ratio is calculated. In their study, Nibanran Das et al. [2] successfully identified various diseases from skin images by employing a combination of well-known texture and frequency domain features. These features included Local Binary Pattern, Gray Level Co-occurrence Matrix, Discrete Cosine Transform, and Discrete Fourier Transform. To classify the diseases, they utilized Support Vector Machines (SVM) as the underlying classifier. Their proposed technique achieved remarkable recognition accuracies, with a maximum accuracy of 89.65%. In their research, Nowrin Akter Surovi et al. [3] have created an intelligent computer algorithm that demonstrates a high level of accuracy in making diagnostic decisions. To achieve this, feature extraction plays a crucial role in assisting doctors or enabling computer algorithms to automatically identify specific skin diseases among the numerous possibilities. The researchers utilized an artificial intelligence-based computer algorithm specifically designed to make accurate diagnostic decisions.

In their study, Li-sheng Wei, Quan Gan, and Tao Ji [4] have presented a computational technique capable of identifying three types of skin diseases: herpes, dermatitis, and psoriasis. They employed a novel cognition method for this purpose. Initially, to eliminate noise and irrelevant background, the skin images underwent preprocessing using filtering and transformation techniques. Furthermore, the researchers introduced the Grey-level Co-occurrence Matrix (GLCM) as a means of segmenting the skin disease images, facilitating the accurate identification and analysis of the specific diseases. In their research, Seema Kolkur, Vidya Kharkar, and colleagues [5] developed a system that employs input symptoms to identify diseases. The team gathered symptom data for 10 skin diseases with the assistance of an expert doctor in the field. Various classifiers, including Support Vector Machines (SVM), Artificial Neural Networks (ANN), Random Forest, Decision Tree, and K-Nearest Neighbors (KNN) algorithm, were trained using the symptom data. The trained classifiers demonstrated an accuracy of 90% or higher, showcasing the effectiveness of the system in disease identification.

Most of the skin disease detection algorithm use traditional segmentation and feature extraction methods that are highly depends on threshold. This threshold requires a huge experience and poor generalization ability leeds to unsatisfactory classification result [6]. Here to overcome the problem Probabilistic Neural Network (PNN) has been used. The main advantage of PNN is trained quickly, decision surface shape can be made as complex as necessary and sparse samples are enough for network performance. These features are very important to identify skin disease [7]. New technologies and analysis are effectively guide physicians approaches for advanced genetic analysis [7–10] but there are few numbers of research works have been executed out for detecting melanoma skin. Authors develop a hybrid algorithm to detect melanoma skin disease. Here we use different color model, extract different color channels, compute statistical data, and use PNN and SVM for detecting melanoma skin disease. Authors have organized the paper in following manner-first introduction, section two represents description of models and parameters used in proposed method. Section three presents algorithm and finally section four represents results and conclusions.

1.2 Methodology

Image Filtering

A median filter is a common filtering technique used to reduce impulsive or "salt-and-pepper" noise in images while preserving useful features and edges. It operates by replacing each pixel in an image with the median value of its neighboring pixels within a defined neighborhood or kernel.

Here's how a median filter works:

1. Define the size of the kernel, typically a square matrix. For example, a 3 × 3 kernel means a 3-pixel by 3-pixel neighborhood.
2. Starting from the top-left corner of the image, move the kernel across the entire image.
3. For each pixel position, collect the pixel values within the kernel.
4. Sort the collected pixel values in ascending order.
5. Replace the current pixel value with the median value from the sorted list. In other words, select the middle pixel value if the kernel size is odd or take the average of the two middle values if the kernel size is even.
6. Move the kernel to the next position and repeat steps 3–5 until the entire image is processed.

By using the median value instead of the original pixel value, the median filter effectively reduces the impact of sporadic noise while preserving the overall image structure and edges. This is because the median value is less likely to be influenced by outliers compared to other statistical measures such as the mean.

It's important to note that the median filter is not defined as erosion followed by dilation using the same structuring element. Erosion and dilation are morphological operations that are distinct from the median filter. Erosion is a morphological operation that shrinks or erodes the boundaries of objects in an image, while dilation expands or grows the boundaries. These operations are commonly used for tasks such as noise removal, image segmentation, and feature extraction, but they are not directly related to the median filter [18].

Support Vector Machine

The Support Vector Machine (SVM) is a well-defined machine learning tool widely used for classification tasks. It belongs to the family of classifiers based on universal feed forward networks. SVM is capable of separating data points using either linear or nonlinear boundaries.

SVM is particularly known for its ability to provide good generalization performance in pattern classification problems. This classifier constructs a surface, known as a hyperplane, that effectively separates data points into distinct sections or classes. The hyperplane is determined by considering the data points that are closest to it, referred to as support vectors. These support vectors have the most influence on determining the hyperplane, while data points further away have lesser importance.

The goal of SVM is to find the hyperplane that maximizes the margin between the classes. The margin refers to the distance between the hyperplane and the nearest data points from each class. By maximizing this margin, SVM aims to achieve the best separation between the classes.

In summary, SVM is a powerful machine learning technique used for classification tasks. It constructs a hyperplane to separate data points, with support vectors playing a crucial role in determining the hyperplane. The objective of SVM is to find the hyperplane that maximizes the margin between classes, leading to effective classification results.

Suppose we have a set of n training examples.

$$(x_i y_i) y_i = \pm 1, i = 1, 2, 3, 4 \ldots \ldots \ldots n \tag{1}$$

The goal of SVM is to find a hyperplane, represented by the equation w.x + b = 0, that effectively separates the positive and negative training examples using the decision function:

$$f(x) = sign(w.x + b), \text{ where } sign(x) : \begin{cases} -1, & \text{if } x < 0 \\ 0, & \text{if } x = 0 \\ 1, & \text{if } x > 0 \end{cases} \tag{2}$$

In this context, the weight vector w represents the normal to the hyperplane, and b is referred to as the bias. It can be observed that:

$$y_i(w_i x_i + b) > 0 \quad \forall i = 1\,2\,3\,4 \ldots \ldots .. n \tag{3}$$

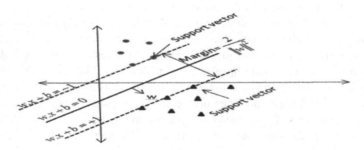

Fig. 1. SVM structure

Implicitly define (w, b) Given the conditions (w.x + b) = 1 for the positive class and (w.x + b) = -1 for the negative class, depicted in Fig. 1, two hyperplanes can be identified. The region between these hyperplanes is known as the margin band. The margin band is determined by the expression $\frac{2}{\|w\|} 2$ which is to be maximize or minimize

$$\frac{1}{2} \|w\|^2$$

subject to the constraints:

$$yi(wx_i + b) \geq 0 \quad \forall i = 1\,2\,3\,4 \ldots \ldots .. n \tag{4}$$

Most real-life datasets contain noise, which can negatively affect the performance of a classifier. One way to mitigate the impact of outliers and noise is by introducing a soft margin in Support Vector Machines (SVM). The soft margin allows for a certain degree of error in classification, accommodating misclassifications and making the classifier more robust.

By incorporating the soft margin with a marginal error term £i, the objective function of the SVM changes. The new objective is to minimize this error term while still maximizing the margin and finding an optimal hyperplane that separates the classes effectively. The objective function aims to strike a balance between minimizing classification errors and maintaining a reasonable margin between the classes.

$$\frac{1}{2}\|W\|^2 + C \sum_{i=1}^{n} \epsilon_i \; with \; y_i(v_i x_i + b_i) \geq 1 - \epsilon_i \quad \xi \geq 0, \forall i = 1, 2, 3 \ldots n \quad (5)$$

The tradeoff between the marginal error and testing error is determined by the parameter C.

The Karush-Kuhn-Tucker (KKT) conditions serve as necessary conditions for non-linear optimal problems. By converting the primal problem into a dual problem and applying the KKT conditions, we can derive valuable insights and solutions.

$$w = \sum_{i=1}^{n} \propto_i w_i x_i \quad (6)$$

Using kernel function decision function becomes

$$f(x) = sign \; (\Sigma_{i \in sv} \propto_i w_i K(x, x_i) + b \quad (7)$$

with the objective function: Maximize

$$W(\propto) = \sum_{i=1}^{n} \propto_i - \frac{1}{2} \sum_{i,j=1}^{n} \propto_i \propto_j y_i y_j K(x_i, x_j) \quad \forall i = 1, 2, ..n \; with \; a_i \geq 0 \; \sum \propto_i y_i = 0 \quad (8)$$

where $K(x_i, x_j)= \S (x_i), \S(x_j), \S(x)$, is called kernel function, The specific knowledge about the inner product in the feature space is not required, as it is the defining characteristic. Therefore, the feature space is expected to be an inner product space, commonly referred to as a Hilbert space. The Mercer's kernels, known for being positive semi-definite, play a crucial role in achieving the global optimum. The objective function corresponds to a Quadratic Optimization Problem that can be effectively addressed using the Sequential Minimal Optimization (SMO) algorithm [16].

Probabilistic Neural Network
Probabilistic neural network (PNN) is a feed forward neural network. In early 1990's it is initiated by D.F. Specht [14]. The basic operations of PNN are contained four layers. They are Input layer, Hidden layer, Simulation layer and Output layer.

Figure 2 describes the working procedure of PNN. Features are applied to M number of input layer. From input layers these features are branched into each node of hidden layers. Hidden layers are collected into groups in simulation layer. In the simulation layer, the number of groups is equal to the number of distinguishable classes determined by the Probabilistic Neural Network (PNN). This means that each group in the simulation layer corresponds to a distinct class identified by the PNN algorithm. The grouping of data in the simulation layer aligns with the classification capabilities of the PNN, allowing for accurate class separation and prediction. Gaussian function is calculated for each feature vector in hidden layer. Functional values of all the Gaussians in a class group feed them to the same output layer node.

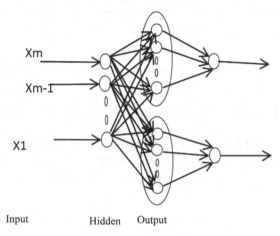

Fig. 2. PNN structure

Applied Parameter

Texture Feature Extraction
The Gray Level Co-occurrence Matrix (GLCM) operates on the concept of contiguity in images. It focuses on identifying pairs of neighboring pixel values that appear in an image and records their occurrences throughout the entire image. GLCM stands out as an effective tool for recognizing texture features, surpassing traditional methods in this regard. By utilizing GLCM, various textures associated with different skin epithelial diseases can be extracted, including contrast, correlation, entropy, homogeneity, and energy. For the purposes of this paper, four commonly selected features are employed from the GLCM.
   Contrast

$$I_1 = \sum_{i}^{I-1} \Sigma_j^{i-1}(i-j)^2[g(i,j)] \tag{9}$$

In this context, the term $|i - j|$ represents the difference in gray levels between adjacent pixels. The function $g(i, j)$ denotes the probability distribution of these gray level differences. Specifically, the variable $I1$ represents the contrast, which is primarily employed to assess the depth of image textures and grooves.
   Correlation

$$I_2 = \frac{\sum\sum(i-x)(j-y)g(i,j)}{\delta_x\delta_y} \tag{10}$$

In this context, the term I2 represents correlation. The variables x and y denote the mean values of the sums of elements in each column and row, respectively, within a given square. The variables i and j correspond to the specific row and column. The standard deviation of the sum of elements in each column is denoted as σx, while σy represents the standard deviation of the sum of elements in each row. Correlation is primarily utilized to analyze the details of relevant elements in both rows and columns during the vertical image segmentation process.

Entropy

$$I_3 = - \sum_i^{1-1} \Sigma_j^{i-1} [g(i,j) \text{Log } g(i,j)] \tag{11}$$

In this context, I3 represents entropy, a metric that quantifies the amount of information present within an image and is influenced by different textures. As the value of I3 increases, the speck textures in the image become more scattered or sparse. Conversely, as I3 decreases, the textures of specks tend to be more densely arranged.

Homogeneity

$$I_4 = \sum_i^{l-1} \sum_j^{l-1} \frac{1}{(i-j)^2 + 1} g(i,j) \tag{12}$$

In this context, I4 represents homogeneity, a measure that evaluates the proximity of the distribution of elements in the Gray Level Co-occurrence Matrix (GLCM) to the GLCM diagonal. Homogeneity provides insight into how closely the elements are distributed along the diagonal, indicating the level of uniformity or similarity within the texture being analyzed.

1.3 Implementation

Step 1: Skin images have been collected from the specific database dermnetnz.org. Which are recycled for research. Block diagram of Snap shot of the selected sample input images in the original RGB form have been furnished in Fig. 4.

Step 2: Primarily a selection of spot pixels from a 100 × 100 pixel-based image has been made as the region of interest. In our proposed method we use two different classification model one is probabilistic neural network and another is support vector machine. In both the cases we use different types of input data. First input images convert into HSV and YCbCr color model. Then computes statistical and texture parameters to train and test Support vector machine (SVM) and Probabilistic neural network (PNN). Pictorial representation of our proposed model has been discussed in Fig. 3.

Color pattern of melanoma affected skin and normal skin is different. Fundamental properties of color are main issues for melanoma detection. Color space is very important mathematical model that represents color information. For skin disease classification choosing appropriate color model is very important [15]. Our detection algorithm we use HSV and YCbCr color model. For training and testing we collects different melanoma images from dermnetnz.org. Our proposed algorithm consists of three phases, preprocessing, training and testing phases.

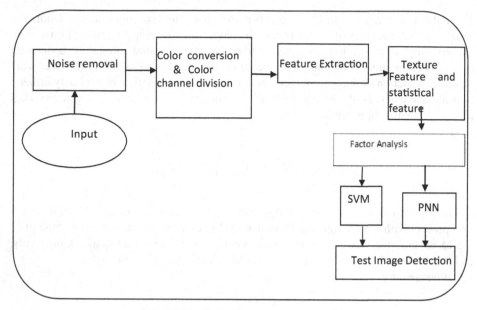

Fig. 3. Block diagram of proposed work

Step3:

In preprocessing capture images are converted into different color models, secondly necessary parameters are computed for proper classification model construction and lastly a set of images are applied to that model for result.

3.1 Preprocessing

1.1 For training purpose RGB images classify into two categories I_a & I_n where I_a. represent set of affected images and I_n represent set of normal image.

1.2 Read the input RGB images of both sets.

1.3 Passes the RGB images through median low pass filter.

1.4 Convert each RGB image into the HSV and YCbCr color models, the following formulas are utilized:

$$I = (I_{hsv}, I_{Ybr})$$

HSV (Hue, Saturation, Value) conversion:

- Calculate the normalized red, green, and blue values (R, G, B) by dividing them by 255.
- Find the maximum (max) and minimum (min) values among R, G, and B.
- Compute the hue (H) as follows:
- If max = min, set H to 0 (undefined).
- If max = R, set H to (60 * (G − B)/(max − min) + 360) % 360.
- If max = G, set H to (60 * (B − R)/(max − min) + 120).
- If max = B, set H to (60 * (R − G)/(max − min) + 240).
- Calculate the saturation (S) as (max − min)/max if max ≠ 0; otherwise, set S to 0.

– The value (V) is the maximum among R, G, and B.

  YCbCr conversion:

– Calculate the luminance (Y) as $Y = 0.299 * R + 0.587 * G + 0.114 * B$.
– Compute the chrominance blue (Cb) as $Cb = (B - Y)/(2 * (1 - 0.114))$.
– Compute the chrominance red (Cr) as $Cr = (R - Y)/(2 * (1 - 0.299))$.

  By applying these formulas, the RGB images can be effectively transformed into the HSV and YCbCr color models, allowing for different color space representations.

1.5 After conversion we obtain six different channels form every image.

$$I(channel) = \{I(h)I(s)I(v): I_{hsv}\}$$
$$I(y)I(b)I(r): I_{ybr}$$

  Step4:

3.2 Training phase: -
   3.2.1 for every channel (i.e H channel, S channel V channel and Y channel Cb channel and Cr channel) we compute mean and standard deviation.
   3.2.2 For every color models (i.e HSV and YCbCr) compute correlation, contrast, energy and homogeneity.
   3.2.3 For each image we have twenty different types of features (statistical and texture feature) (Table 1).
   3.2.4 Factor analysis technique has been applied for combining all features into a single value.
   3.2.5 The equation of factor analysis represented by $Z = FP + UD$ where UD represents a unique variance of a variable. UD contains both unreliable variance of measurement error and reliable variance which does not overlap with a common variance. F is the normalized factor score matrix and P is the factor by variable weight matrix.

  In our proposed method we trained Support vector machine and probabilistic neural network techniques the output values of factor analysis.

3.3 Tasting phase: -
   3.3.1 A set that contain both normal image and affected image have been chosen for testing.
   3.3.2 To remove noise, tested images are passed through median filter.
   3.3.3 Tested images have been converted into HSV and YCbCr color model.
   3.3.4 Compute twenty different features (describe in Table 1) for each tested image and multiple each feature with specified factors obtained for factor analysis.
   3.3.5 Apply these values to previously trained appropriate SVM and PNN for detection.
   3.3.6 Thus outcomes of different SVM and PNN confirms the disease.

1.4 Results

In our proposed method 250 images of affected and normal image have been used to train and for testing we use 100 different image. These images are converted into different color model. A step wise output of color conversion presents in figure [4]. Different values of each parameter have been furnished in Table 1. Twenty different parameters have been computed for more accurate result and these parameters ae converted into single effective value by using factor analysis. After applying trained SVM and PNN to tested images we can detect the proper disease. To analysis the performance of two classification algorithm we use confusion matrix that has been furnished in Table 2.

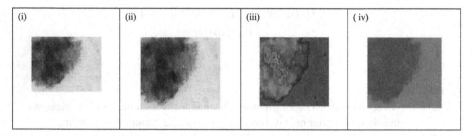

| (i) | (ii) | (iii) | (iv) |

Fig. 4. i) affected image ii) filtered image iii) conversion to hsv iv) conversion to ycbcr

Data repository: All the images taken from (http://www.dermnetnz.org.). In our proposed method 250 images of affected and normal image have been used to train and for testing we use 100 different image.

Our proposed algorithm's performance has been evaluated using four crucial measurements: accuracy, sensitivity, specificity, and precision. These measures play a vital role in assessing the effectiveness and precision of our algorithm.

$$Accuracy = \frac{T_p + T_n}{T_p + T_n + F_p + F_n}$$

$$Sencitivity = \frac{T_p}{T_p + F_n}$$

$$Specificity = \frac{T_n}{T_n + F_p}$$

$$Precision = \frac{T_p}{T_p + F_p}$$

In order to analyze the performance of our proposed method, a dataset of 200 input images was utilized. The method involved the detection of vitiligo using both Support Vector Machine (SVM) and Probabilistic Neural Network (PNN). The outcomes of the proposed method have been presented in Table 3. The table includes the values for true positive (TP), true negative (TN), false positive (FP), and false negative (FN), which are essential for evaluating the accuracy and efficacy of our approach.

Table 1. Values of input Parameter

	Extracted Features	HSV MODEL							YCbCr MODEL						
		H CHANNEL	S CHANNEL	V CHANNEL	CO RELATION	ENERGY	HOMOGENITY	CONTRAST	Y CHANNEL	Cb CHANNEL	Cr CHANNEL	CO RELATION	ENERGY	HOMOGENITY	CONTRAST
Sample1.jpg	Mean	0.9263	0.1966	0.7980					168.9299	129.7656	144.3650				
	Std.dev.	0.0407	0.0219	0.1073	0.7610	0.7114	0.9729	0.0580	22.3634	2.5749	2.5903	0.7669	0.9177	0.9922	0.0156
Sample2.jpg	Mean	0.0615	0.2571	0.8597					183.6666	114.1028	144.4260				
	Std.dev	0.0054	0.0305	0.0298	0.8138	0.7231	0.9781	0.0438	7.0547	1.5519	1.7052	.2993	0.9966	0.9993	0.0014
Sample3.jpg	Mean	0.0578	0.3553	0.9331					184.6097	107.5632	153.5520				
	Std.dev	0.0071	0.0339	0.0291	0.7274	0.4562	0.9969	0.0061	8.2305	2.1435	2.2677	0.4702	0.9803	0.9966	0.0068
Sample4.jpg	Mean	0.0853	0.3188	0.8683					184.3239	107.0682	145.3695				
	Std dev	0.0057	0.0421	0.0618	0.6425	0.9984	0.9985	0.0031	12.0910	2.0014	1.1938	0.6730	0.8480	0.9811	0.0378

Table 2. Confusion Matrix of two classification algorithm.

PNN	Predicted		Actual	
			Has mela-noma	Does not has melanoma
		Has Melanoma	97	9
		Does not has melanoma	15	79

SVM	Predicted		Actual	
			Has mela-noma	Does not has melanoma
		Has Melanoma	88	13
		Does not has melanoma	24	75

Table 3. Values of confusion matrix.

	Accuracy (%)	Sensitivity (%)	Specificity (%)	Precision (%)
SVM	81.5	78.57	85.22	87.12
PNN	88	86.61	89.77	91.50

1.5 Conclusion

It has been observed that effected area of melanoma has high contrast in all color space. So it is almost easy to detect the melanoma effected area. But our proposed scheme it has been proven that Probabilistic Neural network has 88.68% accuracy whereas Support Vector Machine has 81.5% of accuracy so it has been concluded that in this method PNN is more efficient than SVM. In future we should apply more classification algorithm to our proposed technique to detect more types of skin diseases.

References

1. Nurhudatiana, A.: A computer-aided diagnosis system for vitiligo assessment: a segmentation algorithm. In: Intan, R., Chi, CH., Palit, H., Santoso, L. (eds.) ICSIIT 2015. CCIS, vol. 516, pp. 323–331. Springer, Heidelberg (2015). https://doi.org/10.1007/978-3-662-46742-8_30
2. Das, N., Pal, A., Mazumder, S., Sarkar, S., Gangopadhyay, D., Nasipuri, M.: An SVM based skin disease identification using Local Binary Patterns 978-0-7695-5033-6/13 $26.00. In: Third International Conference on Advances in Computing and Communications. IEEE (2013). https://doi.org/10.1109/ICACC.2013.48
3. Surovi, N.A., Kiber, A., Kashem, A., Babi, K.N.: Study and development of algorithm of different skin diseases analysis using image processing method. Asian J. Biomed. Pharm. Sci. **7**(60), 1–3 (2017)
4. Wei, L., Gan, Q., Ji, T.: Skin disease recognition method based on image color and texture features. Hindawi Comput. Math. Methods Med., 1–10 (2018). Article no. 8145713, 10 p.
5. Kolkur, S., Kalbande, D.R., Kharkar, V.: Machine learning approaches to multi-class human skin disease detection. Int. J. Comput. Intell. Res. **14**(1), 29–39 (2018). ISSN 0973-1873
6. Kumar, S., Singh, A.: Image processing for recognition of skin diseases. Int. J. Comput. Appl. **149**(3), 37–40 (2016)
7. Lu, J., Kazmierczak, E., Jonathan, H.: Automatic segmentation of scaling in 2-D psoriasis skin images. IEEE Trans. Med. Imaging **32**(4), 719–730 (2013)
8. Arivazhagan, S., Shebiah, R.N., Divya, K., Subadevi, M.P.: Skin disease classification by extracting independent components. J. Emerg. Trends Comput. Inf. Sci. **3**(10), 1379–1382 (2012)
9. Cui, Q., McIntosh, S., Sun, H.: Identifying materials of photographic images and photorealistic computer-generated graphics based on deep CNNs. CMC Comput. Mater. Continua **055**(2), 229–241 (2018)
10. Suer, S., Kockara, S., Mete, M.: An improved border detection in dermoscopy images for density based clustering. BMC Bioinform. **12**(S10) (2011)
11. Amaliah, B., Fatichah, C., Rahmat Widyanto, M.: ABCD feature extraction for melanoma skin cancer diagnosis. Int. J. Med. Imaging, 1–8
12. Relethford, J.H.: Human skin color diversity is highest in sub-Saharan African populations. Hum. Biol. Int. Rec. Res. **72**(5), 773–80 (2000)
13. Nguyen, N.H., Lee, T.K., Stella Atkins, M.: Segmentation of light and dark hair in dermoscopic images: a hybrid approach using a universal kernel. Int. J. Comput. Technol., 42–50
14. Specht, D.F.: Probabilistic Neural Networks. Neural Netw. **3**(1,1990), 109–118 (1990)
15. Yasir, R., Rahman, Md.A., Ahmed, N.: Dermatological disease detection using image processing and artificial neural network. In: 8th International Conference on Electrical and Computer Engineering, December 2014, Dhaka, Bangladesh, pp. 687–690 (2014)
16. Parikha, K.S., Shahb, T.P.: Support vector machine – a large margin classifier to diagnose skin illnesses. In: 3rd International Conference on Innovations in Automation and Mechatronics Engineering, ICIAME 2016 (2016). https://doi.org/10.1016/j.protcy.2016.03.039

17. Burges, C.J.C.: A tutorial on support vector machines for pattern recognition. Data Min. Knowl. Discov. **2**(2), 121–167 (1998)
18. Zanaty, E.A.: Support vector machine versus multilayer perception (MLP) in data classification. Egypt. Inform. J., 177–183 (2012)
19. Vapnik, V.N.: The Nature of Statistical Learning Theory. Springer, New York (1995). https://doi.org/10.1007/978-1-4757-2440-0
20. JaseemaYasmin, J.H., Mohamed Sadiq, M.: An improved iterative segmentation algorithm using canny edge detector with iterative median filter for skin lesion border detection. Int. J. Comput. Appl. (IJCA) **50**(6), 37–42 (2012). ISSN: 0975-8887
21. Übeyli, E.D., Doğdu, E.: Automatic detection of erythemato-squamous diseases using k-means clustering. J. Med. Syst. **34**(2), 179–184 (2010)
22. Relethford, J.: Human skin color diversity is highest in sub-Saharan African populations. Hum. Biol. Int. Rec. Res. **72**(5), 773–80 (2000)

Identification of Cloud Types for Meteorological Satellite Images: A Character-Based CNN-LSTM Hybrid Caption Model

Sanjukta Mishra[1]([⊠]) and Parag Kumar Guhathakurta[2]

[1] University of Engineering and Management, Kolkata, India
sanjuktamish@gmail.com
[2] CSE Department, NIT Durgapur, Durgapur, India
paragkumar.guhathakurta@cse.nitdgp.ac.in

Abstract. Satellite Clouds have a significant role in the weather system and climate change, and the distribution of clouds is always strongly tied to a particular meteorological phenomenon. In this paper, an automatic identification of cloud types is proposed using a hybrid approach of convolution neural network (CNN) and bidirectional character based long short-term memory (LSTM). The large-scale cloud image database for meteorological research (LSCIDMR) of the ground truth images related to weather types is used as the input for the proposed work. Three types of CNN models, such as inception v3 network, Vgg-16 and Alexnet, are used separately and subsequently, the results are compared, in terms of precision, recall, and F1 score, to obtain the best among them. The LSTM is trained with our self-trained dictionary having tokens. The image features and single character are merged into a single step. It produces the output as the next character to come and so on.

Keywords: Satellite cloud image · caption generation · CNN · LSTM · accuracy

1 Introduction

Cloud images are very essential for weather forecasting and the study of climate change. The brief information about the cloud arrangements is provided by meteorological satellite images [2]. The weather forecast would be efficient enough if the correct distribution of clouds can be located. Hence, the cloud images can play an important role to predict different weather phenomena. Nowadays, the meteorologists can perfectly forecast the day-to-day weather changes. However, it is still difficult to predict the extreme climate, such as typhoons, cyclones etc.

Cloud types that dominate satellite imagery are stratiform clouds and convective clouds. Cloud images can be of satellite-based or ground-based. Visual sensors positioning on the ground are used to record ground-based cloud images. On the other hand, the cloud, atmosphere, and ocean data can be found in satellite photos which are captured by the weather satellites. For weather analysis and future warning, the weather

K. Dasgupta et al. (Eds.): CICBA 2023, CCIS 1955, pp. 199–212, 2024.
https://doi.org/10.1007/978-3-031-48876-4_15

satellites are important as they are primarily used to track earth's weather and climate. More studies show that deep learning [4, 9] may significantly enhance meteorological research as the fields of meteorological study deal with enormous volumes of data. But most of the deep learning - based research on Cloud datasets are typically based on the class of the cloud. But sometimes more detailed descriptions helps for understanding the climate. Hence if we can able to generate captions for cloud images, we can provide a more comprehensive description of the cloud type, which can aid meteorologists in their weather forecasting efforts. In such a case, one of the most challenging tasks is, creating a model that can decipher the details of input and output them as captions. This automatic retrieval system can assist the meteorologists for the efficient prediction of the climate with the help of the cloud contents. Thus, it motivates us to design an automatic classification and identification of satellite cloud images using deep learning technology.

In this paper, an automatic identification of cloud types is proposed using a hybrid approach of convolution neural network (CNN) and bidirectional character based long short-term memory (LSTM). The large-scale cloud image database for meteorological research (LSCIDMR) database for the ground truth images related to weather types is used as the input for the proposed work. Initially, the size of the input image is pre-processed by using segmentation. In the proposed work, a pre-trained network is used for the image recognition. Three types of CNN models, such as inception v3 network, Vgg-16 and Alexnet, are used separately to extract the features from the images and subsequently, the results are compared to obtain the best among them. Meanwhile, the LSTM is trained with our self-trained dictionary having tokens. Here, the tokens are character sized and the text will be generated one character at a time. The image features and single character are merged into a single step. It produces the output as the next character to come and so on. This procedure is executed for multiple iterations. Finally, the word caption of the corresponding image is obtained.

The rest of the paper organized as follows: the related work is presented in Sect. 2. Some preliminaries related to the proposed work is discussed in Sect. 3. The problem description is introduced in Sect. 4. The proposed methodology is shown in Sect. 5. Various simulation results are shown in Sect. 6 followed by a conclusion in Sect. 7.

2 Related Work

Currently, there are basically three categories of common cloud classification techniques, such as supervised methods, unsupervised methods and artificial neural network (ANN) methods. Liang Ye et al. [1] proposed a ground-based cloud image classification using Deep neural network (DNN). However, the main drawback is that deep cloud consumes a considerable amount of memory. Wei Jin et al. [2] developed a model to determine the type of cloud image from a meteorological satellite. Van Hiep et al. [3] experimented a classification algorithm for cloud image patches on the small datasets. However, it is applied only for whole-sky images, not tested on the satellite images. Jacob Høxbroe Jeppesena et al. [4] developed a deep learning model on cloud detection method for satellite imagery. Michal Segal Rozenhaimera et al. [5] presented an algorithm for cloud detection using CNN. Seema Mahajan et al. [6] showed a quick overview of various satellite image cloud detection techniques from 2004 to 2018. Ceri Ahendyarti et al.

[7] discussed a method for cloud classification. Tashin Ahmed et al. [8] proposed the cloud classification method by utilizing a segmentation. Cong Bai et al. [9] developed a large database of satellite cloud images for the meteorological research. W. Jiao et al. [10] developed a cloud detection method using transformer technology. It gives the global information but the validation test accuracy is 85.92% which needs to increase. Gupta R et al. [11] given an overview of different techniques used for identifying clouds and their applications, including recognizing cloud shadows, distinguishing between different types of clouds, and eliminating clouds from images captured by multispectral satellites. Lv, Q et al. [12] performs a fine tune supervised method to identify the cloud but is incapable of identifying the wide range of cloud shapes and forms. And the method is not tested on satellite images. P. Romero Jure et al. [13] creates an algorithm that generates a tabular output consisting of pixels extracted from multiband images and each of these tagged with the specific cloud type they depict. A summary of the related work is provided in Table 1.

Table 1. Summary of Related Work

Sl no	Reference	Year	Proposed	Positive Aspect	Negative Aspect
1	Liang Ye et al. [1]	2017	ground-based cloud image classification using DNN	Outperforms than previous methods	Consumes a considerable amount of memory
2	Wei Jin et al. [2]	2019	Model to find the type of cloud image	Better than traditional method	Need more improvement
3	Van Hiep et al. [3]	2019	Classification algorithm	Good for small datasets	Not tested in Satellite images
4	Jacob Høxbroe Jeppesena et al. [4]	2019	Deep learning model	Good result for spatial patterns	Not for multiclass classification
5	Michal Segal Rozenhaimera et al. [5]	2020	Algorithm using CNN	Focus in both spectral and spatial context	Need to generalize
6	Seema Mahajan et al. [6]	2020	Quick overview of satellite images	Detailed overview	No suggestive proposed method
7	Ahendyarti et al. [7]	2020	Cloud Classification Algorithm	Fuzzy set tested	Not good Accuracy 83.33%

(*continued*)

Table 1. (*continued*)

Sl no	Reference	Year	Proposed	Positive Aspect	Negative Aspect
8	Tashin Ahmed et al. [8]	2020	Cloud Segmentation Algorithm	Good result with pre- trained model	No new CNN model
9	Cong Bai et al. [9]	2022	Cloud detection Algorithm	Provides a good dataset and research baseline	No new architecture
10	W. Jiao et al. [10]	2022	Transformer Technology	Provides global information	Validation test accuracy needs to improve
11	Gupta R et al. [11]	2022	A brief review	Good overview	Need to tested
12	Lv, Q et al. [12]	2022	Fine tune supervised method	Better than Normal Supervised method	Not identify the wide range of cloud shapes and forms
13	P. Romero Jure et al. [13]	2022	Tabular Output	good output on deep convective clouds	Need to lessen complexity and need an improvement for other clouds

Thus, most of the existing literature worked for satellite images which are mainly concentrated on the classification of cloud or no cloud, snow or cloud, cloud mask, high cloud, low cloud and middle cloud. But if we can make a system where image itself can talk then it will help the meteorologists in early detection of the climate forecast. So, for this we need to focus on making a model which can generate the caption with the image automatically. In the proposed work, for an advancement over the existing works, an automatic system is proposed to obtain the identification of the cloud type along with its caption as an output. Here we just concentrate on the small caption.

3 Preliminaries

3.1 Convolutional Neural Network (CNN)

The CNN is a type of deep neural network which has vast application in the field of computer vision. It learns to automatically extract the properties of the inputs to for a specified goal, such as image classification, face identification, or image semantic segmentation, given a sequence of real-world images or videos. A general block diagram of CNN architecture with convolution layers is shown in Fig. 1. In addition, some of the CNN models [14] are introduced in Table 1 for ease of understanding the proposed work.

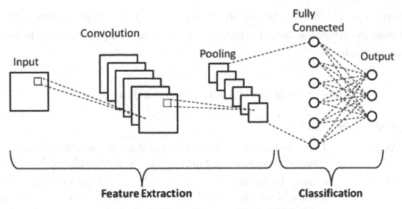

Fig. 1. Different layers of basic CNN

3.2 Bidirectional LSTM

An exclusive form of recurrent neural network (RNN) architecture is the long short-term memory (LSTM). It has a memory cell that keeps track of the input, output, forget gate, and value. The three gates managed the cell's entry and exit. A bidirectional LSTM uses both past and future data. The incoming patterns are processed by the following using two sub-layers towards the front and back directions [15].

$$\overrightarrow{h}_t = H_A(W_{h\overrightarrow{i}}x_t + W_{\overrightarrow{hr}}\overrightarrow{h}_{t-1} + bi_{\overrightarrow{hl}}) \tag{1}$$

$$\overleftarrow{h}_t = H_A(W_{h\overleftarrow{i}}x_t + W_{\overleftarrow{hr}}\overleftarrow{h}_{t+1} + bi_{\overleftarrow{hl}}) \tag{2}$$

$$y_t = W_{\overrightarrow{ho}}\overrightarrow{h}_{ft} + W_{\overleftarrow{ho}}\overleftarrow{h}_t + b_{ol} \tag{3}$$

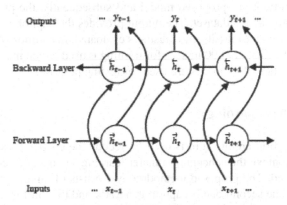

Fig. 2. BLSTM Architecture

Where b_{hl} is the bias vector of the hidden layer, b_{ol} is the bias vector of the output layer, W_{hi}, denotes the weight matrix between the input and hidden layer, W_{hr} denotes the recurrent weight matrix, the outcome and hidden layer's weight matrix is W_{ho} and H_A denotes the activation task of hidden level. $\overrightarrow{h}_t$ is hidden pattern towards front and $\overleftarrow{h}_t$ towards back.

Table 2. Overview of Alexnet, VGG16 and Inception -V3

Slno	Model Types	Description
1	Alexnet	The convolutional layers, such as two dropout layers, three fully connected layers, and one max-pooling layer can make up AlexNet
2	VGG-16	In analyzing the image with a size of 224 × 224, the VGG-16 is trained to a deeper structure of 16 layers, comprising of 13 convolutional layers and 3 fully connected layers
3	Inception-V3	A CNN architecture from the Inception family called Inception-v3 which includes a number of advances, such as employing label smoothing, factorized 7 × 7 convolutions, and the inclusion of an auxiliary classifier to transfer label information lower down the network

4 Problem Description

An efficient cloud satellite image identification is necessary for the weather forecasting. Hence, an automatic retrieval is required to speed up the process. In order to obtain automatic cloud satellite image identification along with its caption, the single-label annotation database LSCIDMR-S, having a large-scale cloud image is considered as the input of the proposed work. We have taken here 8 categories of the cloud images as shown in Table 2. This input is divided into the training and the testing dataset. The training dataset is used to train our proposed model and subsequently, the proposed model is tested by the testing image dataset. The output provides the caption of the image type. Next, the accuracy on the classification result is evaluated. In addition, it is significant to mention here that a total of 4000 images for training is used which includes 500 images for 8 classes. Another 4000 images are used for testing purpose.

5 Proposed Methodology

In this paper, a hybrid architecture is used to decode the encoded text and the image features. In this context, the concept of transfer learning and the character-based LSTM techniques are used. The proposed methodology consists of three parts. One is image feature extractor, the second one is caption generator and the third is merging which is shown in Fig. 2. We have used here three CNN models, such as InceptionV3 model, VGG-16 and Alexnet, for image feature extraction. In the caption generator, an own dictionary has been buildup to train the LSTM. We have not used any type of pre-trained word or character embedding model. In this work feature vectors are extracted from image

Table 3. Criteria of different Category

Category	Captions	Criteria
Weather system	Tropical-cyclone	It is a vortex of low pressure that develops on the surface of a tropical or subtropical ocean. It is seen in the satellite cloud image as a blue counterclockwise spiral cloud system
	Extratropical-cyclone	These are elliptic baroclinic cyclones that are active at temperate mid-high latitudes
	Frontal-surface	It is the boundary between hot and cold air masses with distinct physical characteristics, such as temperature, humidity, or a transition zone
	Snow	Individual ice crystals that make up snow grow floating in the atmosphere, typically within clouds, before falling and accumulating on the ground. On the map, snow is depicted in dark blue
Cloud system	High ice cloud	These clouds, which comprise cirrus, cirrocumulus, cirrostratus, and high-level clouds in high latitudes throughout the winter, have a temperature below 0 degrees Celsius. On the satellite cloud image, high ice clouds have a blue appearance
	Low-water cloud	It is typically found at greater temperatures and lower altitudes. Pink, the color of the low water cloud, makes it simple for us to tell them apart from high ice clouds
Terrestrial system	Ocean	70% of the surface of the planet, are covered by the ocean, which has an average depth of 3793 m
	Dessert	It appears brown on the satellite cloud image; however, the tint of light brown will vary depending to the slice's varying geographic position and timing

data using CNN. After that we apply hybrid or merge architecture. The model combines these two components before decoding them to produce the subsequent character in the pattern. During training, captions or words are divided into several tokens and every token being transformed into a fixed-sized vector. To retain the previously produced character, LSTM is utilized. Figure 2 shows the encoded and decoded model architecture. Image and developed caption are loaded first in this instance. With the assistance of training set's images and annotations, we trained the model. The model will only produce a single character at a time, never an entire word. Thus, the input is a string of characters that were previously generated. The primary focus of this work is the development of a captioning model and assessing its effectiveness on cloud images. Specifically, we investigate how well the model performs on cloud images by training it using our own dictionary and without utilizing any pre-existing word or character embedding models.

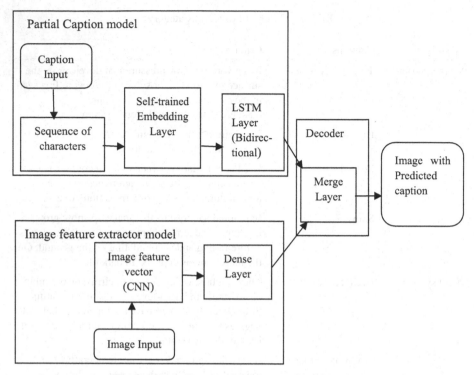

Fig. 3. Block diagram of the proposed Methodology

The character-based model predicts the next character of the sequence based on the particular character that comes before on that sequence. It is shown in Fig. 3. If the caption is small, then the character-based model is very useful. We develop our input-output sequences, where each input sequence consists of a certain number of characters and each output character creates a series of characters, in order to train the model. The model accepts a character and an image vector as inputs, and it outputs the next character. The next result is obtained by using two characters and image vectors as input, and so forth. The suggested model is trained in this way. Here, each distinct character represents an integer value, so every series of characters is encoded as an integer sequence (Fig. 4).

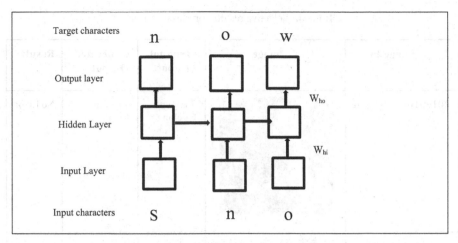

Fig. 4. Character Based LSTM model

6   Experimental Results

In order to determine the results on the test images, a training database consisting of photos and captions are used to train the model. A predictive output, or probability distribution function which is applied in the caption dictionary, will be the outcome. The output is therefore based on Maximum Likelihood Estimation [16]. In Table 3, some of the selective results which provides the output in terms of the classes, such as no error and error. However, it is observed that the error count is much less than the "no error". In addition, all the experiments are carried out on a machine having 1.6-GHz Intel Core i5-8250U CPU and 8-GB RAM. The code has been written in Python in Jupiter notebook.

In order to obtain the best one among three CNN models used in the proposed work, a comparison has been made by evaluating them in terms of the precision, recall and F1 score [9]. Hence, we evaluate the precision, recall and F1 score individually for each class and then, calculate the average of all the evaluation metrics. The comparison char along with comparison graph are shown in Table 4 (Table 5).

Table 4. Selective results for classification

Image Id	Image	Original Output	Generated Output	Result
20190101_10_7.png		Tropical Cyclone	Tropical Cyclone	No Error
20190101_11_7.png		Tropical Cyclone	Tropical Cyclone	No Error
20190101_1_10.png		Snow	Snow	No Error
20190104_3_7.png		Dessert	Dessert	No Error

(*continued*)

Table 4. (*continued*)

20190101_7_4.png		Low Water Cloud	Dessert	Error
20190104_1_22.png		High Ice Cloud	Snow	Error

Table 5. Comparison Chart along with comparison graph

Model Name	Comparison Chart				Comparison Graph
Inception-V3	**Class**	**preci-sion**	**re-call**	**f1-score**	
	Dessert	0.833333	1.0	0.909091	
	Extra Tropical-Cyclone	1.000000	1.0	1.000000	
	Frontal Surface	1.000000	1.0	1.000000	
	HighIce Cloud	1.000000	1.0	1.000000	
	LowWa-terCloud	1.000000	0.8	0.888889	
	Ocean	1.000000	1.0	1.000000	
	Snow	1.000000	0.8	0.888889	
	Tropical Cyclone	1.000000	1.0	1.000000	
	Avg Precision: 0.97916625 Avg Recall: 0.95 Avg F1 Score: 0.96085887				
Alexnet	Class	preci-sion	re-call	f1-score	
	Dessert	0.833333	1.0	0.909091	
	Extra-Tropical Cyclone	1.000000	1.0	1.000000	
	Frontal Surface	1.000000	1.0	1.000000	
	High IceCloud	1.000000	0.8	0.888889	
	Low Water-Cloud	1.000000	0.8	0.888889	
	Ocean	1.000000	1.0	1.000000	
	Snow	0.833333	1.0	0.909091	
	Tropical Cyclone	1.000000	1.0	1.000000	
	Avg Precision: 0.9583333333333334 Avg Recall: 0.95 Avg F1 Score: 0.9494949494949495				

(*continued*)

Table 5. (*continued*)

	Class	preci-sion	re-call	f1-score	
VGGNET -19	Dessert	0.7142 86	1.0	0.8333 33	
	Extra Tropical Cyclone	1.0000 00	1.0	1.0000 00	
	Frontal Surface	1.0000 00	1.0	1.0000 00	
	High IceCloud	1.0000 00	0.8	0.8888 89	
	Low Water-Cloud	1.0000 00	0.8	0.8888 89	
	Ocean	1.0000 00	1.0	1.0000 00	
	Snow	0.8333 33	1.0	0.9090 91	
	Tropical Cyclone	1.0000 00	1.0	1.0000 00	
	Avg Precision: 0.9434523809523809 Avg Recall: 0.925 Avg F1 Score: 0.9226641414141414				

7 Conclusion

The paper proposes hybrid architecture of CNN model with character-based LSTM layer. It provides a comparison to find the best CNN model in terms of various evaluation metrics. It is found that Inception V3 model is performing better in terms of accuracy. Thus, the proposed automatic cloud detection can reduce the amount of time needed for the meteorologists to assess the upcoming weather. But according to the result we find that some of the outputs provide wrong results which need to focus in the near future.

In future, we can explore with the following points to increase the result accuracy.

- We can use other probability algorithms such as beam search algorithm for predicting the output.
- We can train the same with multiple sentences and long words.
- We can use attention module to increase the quality of the result.
- We can find other important details as caption from the image itself according to the problem definition of the work

References

1. Ye, L., Cao, Z., Xiao, Y.: DeepCloud: ground-based cloud image categorization using deep convolutional features. IEEE Trans. Geosci. Remote Sens. **55**(10), 5729–5740 (2017)
2. Jin, W., Gong, F., Tang, B., Wang, S.: Cloud types identification for meteorological satellite image using multiple sparse representation classifiers via decision fusion. IEEE Access **7**, 8675–8688 (2019)

3. Phung, V.H., Rhee, E.J.: A high-accuracy model average ensemble of convolutional neural networks for classification of cloud image patches on small datasets. Appl. Sci. **9** (2019)
4. Jeppesen, J.H., Jacobsen, R.H., Inceoglu, F., Toftegaard, T.S.: A cloud detection algorithm for satellite imagery based on deep learning. Remote Sens. Environ. **229**, 247–259 (2019). ISSN 0034-4257
5. Segal-Rozenhaimer, M., Li, A., Das, K., Chirayath, V.: Cloud detection algorithm for multi-modal satellite imagery using convolutional neural-networks (CNN). Remote Sens. Environ. **237** (2020)
6. Mahajan, S., Fataniya, B.: Cloud detection methodologies: variants and development—a review. Complex Intell. Syst. **6**, 251–261 (2020)
7. Ahendyarti, C., Wiryadinata, R., Rohana, N., Muhammad, F.: Cloud classification from NOAA satellite image using learning vector quantization method. In: 2020 2nd International Conference on Industrial Electrical and Electronics (ICIEE), pp. 97–100 (2020)
8. Ahmed, T., Sabab, N.: Classification and understanding of cloud structures via satellite images with EfficientUNet (2020). https://doi.org/10.1002/essoar.10507423
9. Bai, C., Zhang, M., Zhang, J., Zheng, J., Chen, S.: LSCIDMR: large-scale satellite cloud image database for meteorological research. IEEE Trans. Cybern. **52**(11), 12538–12550 (2022)
10. Jiao, W., Zhang, Y., Zhang, B., Wan, Y.: SCTrans: a transformer network based on the spatial and channel attention for cloud detection. In: IGARSS 2022 - 2022 IEEE International Geoscience and Remote Sensing Symposium, Kuala Lumpur, Malaysia, pp. 615–618 (2022). https://doi.org/10.1109/IGARSS46834.2022.9883360
11. Gupta, R., Nanda, S.J.: Cloud detection in satellite images with classical and deep neural network approach: a review. Multimed Tools Appl. **81**, 31847–31880 (2022). https://doi.org/10.1007/s11042-022-12078-w
12. Lv, Q., Li, Q., Chen, K., Lu, Y., Wang, L.: Classification of ground-based cloud images by contrastive self-supervised learning. Remote Sens. **14**, 5821 (2022). https://doi.org/10.3390/rs14225821
13. Romero Jure, P., Masuelli, S., Cabral, J.: A labeled dataset of cloud types using data from GOES-16 and CloudSat. In: 2022 IEEE Biennial Congress of Argentina (ARGENCON), San Juan, Argentina, pp. 1–6 (2022). https://doi.org/10.1109/ARGENCON55245.2022.9940053
14. Alzubaidi, L., Zhang, J., Humaidi, A.J., et al.: Review of deep learning: concepts, CNN architectures, challenges, applications, future directions. J Big Data **8**, 53 (2021)
15. Alawneh, L., Mohsen, B., Al-Zinati, M., Shatnawi, A., Al-Ayyoub, M.: A comparison of unidirectional and bidirectional LSTM networks for human activity recognition. In: 2020 IEEE International Conference on Pervasive Computing and Communications Workshops (PerCom Workshops), pp. 1–6 (2020)
16. Balasingam, B., Bar-Shalom, Y., Willett, P., Pattipati, K.: Maximum likelihood detection on images. In: 2017 20th International Conference on Information Fusion (Fusion) (2017)

Prediction and Deeper Analysis of Market Fear in Pre-COVID-19, COVID-19 and Russia-Ukraine Conflict: A Comparative Study of Facebook Prophet, Uber Orbit and Explainable AI

Sai Shyam Desetti[1] and Indranil Ghosh[2]

[1] Institute of Management Technology, Hyderabad, Telangana, India
[2] IT and Analytics Area, Institute of Management Technology, Hyderabad, Telangana, India
fri.indra@gmail.com

Abstract. Tracking market fear in distress periods is a highly challenging and essential task of paramount practical relevance. If the future figures of market fear can be predicted in conjunction with explaining the dependence structure on predictor variables, market players at different levels can be benefited. The current work endeavors to model the Chicago Board Options Exchange's Volatility Index (CBOE VIX) of the US, reflecting the extent of market fear in the futures market through the lens of applied predictive modeling and explainable artificial intelligence (AI). The methodological framework deploys two advanced forecasting tools, namely, Facebook Prophet and Uber Orbit, to gauge the temporal pattern of the CBOE VIX. The exercises have been carried out across different regimes characterized by varying degrees of volatility and uncertainty. It is revealed that the market fear in the US was relatively more predictable during the Pre-COVID-19 phase. The outcome of explainable AI analysis using Shapley additive explanations (SHAP) and accumulated local effect (ALE) plots indicates the past information of CBOE VIX exerts significant predictive influence, which largely explains the variation.

Keywords: Market Fear · CBOE VIX · Facebook Prophet · Uber Orbit · Explainable AI

1 Introduction

The CBOE volatility index, CBOE VIX, regarded as a barometer of stock market anxiety levels in the US, has long been recognized as the most commonly accepted gauge of fear in the futures market [3, 14]. The CBOE VIX has been argued to be the key determinant of the abrupt fluctuations of the market outlook [5]. It is closely interlinked with investors' sentiment during the normal and Black Swan phases [9]. Due to the turbulent external factors and rising global geo-political conflicts, tracking the dynamics of CBOE VIX is highly arduous yet practically relevant. Fear is also directly related to people's ability to

K. Dasgupta et al. (Eds.): CICBA 2023, CCIS 1955, pp. 213–227, 2024.
https://doi.org/10.1007/978-3-031-48876-4_16

take risks. As traders enter and exit the markets in significant numbers due to this fear, stock price movements will change dramatically. In this research, we strive to fathom the predictability and dependence structure of CBOE VIX during the normal, COVID-19, and the ongoing Russia-Ukraine conflict regimes.

The current research leverages state-of-the-art forecasting frameworks, namely, Facebook's Prophet and Uber's Orbit algorithm, to carry out granular forecasting exercises to ascertain the degree of predictability across the select regimes. It should be noted that despite the practical implications, uncovering the deeper dynamics of CBOE VIX in highly volatile time horizons has seen very little attention in the literature. The majority of the existing research has primarily been confined to predictive modelling of conventional financial variables [2, 6, 7, 15, 18]. Thus, precise estimation of future figures of CBOE VIX is of paramount practical relevance. We simultaneously contribute to the methodological front by adopting two highly promising forecasting methods, which have been documented to be highly effective for non-financial complex time series [5, 19]. As the lack of past research on the same is imminent, choosing appropriate explanatory variables is challenging. We resort to the cognate literature, wherein the nexus of CBOE VIX with economic uncertainty and fear in commodity assets has been reported [10, 20]. Accordingly, we deploy US economic policy uncertainty (EPU), Crude OIL VIX, and GOLD VIX as key exogenous variables. Additionally, 5-lagged observations of CBOE VIX itself are used as predictor variables to account for the autoregressive effect. Nevertheless, Facebook's Prophet and Uber Orbit are designed to estimate future figures with minimal interpretability, which acts as a significant roadblock to uncovering the dependence structure of the CBOE VIX. To resolve the issue, we apply explainable artificial intelligence (AI) methodologies to explain the hidden interplay. The SHAP (Shapley additive explanations) values and accumulated local effect (ALE) plots are used to accomplish the objective. Although explainable AI has been deployed successfully for interpreting complex AI models in different contexts [4, 12, 21], the present research is the first of its kind to employ the same for critically gauging the dependence structure of CBOE VIX in distress and chaotic regimes. The principal endeavor of the existing research lies in delving into the predictability of the US market fear manifested by CBOE VIX, vis-à-vis discovering the dependence structure of the same on different macroeconomic indicators to facilitate strategic interventions at critical circumstances. The novelty of the underlying work is basically reflected in the regime-wise granular prediction of CBOE VIX and in comprehending the complex predictive interplay simultaneously. The lack of cognate literature truly rationalizes the positioning of the present research.

We contribute to the existing literature in the following ways. First, we strive to track CBOE VIX, a little-known but crucial financial variable. Second, we have identified the set of explanatory factors capable of driving CBOE VIX. These are the CRUDE OIL VIX, the EPU, the GOLD VIX, and the five lagged values of CBOE VIX. Finally, we employ explanatory AI to interpret the results. Predicted graphs and other statistical data, such as accuracy, RMSE values, and so on, have been included in XAI. Finally, the data was separated into three phases: Pre-COVID-19 (standard), COVID-19, and the Russia-Ukraine war. The CBOE VIX values were trained, tested, and predicted in each stage, and the applicable interpretations have been drawn and tabulated.

The remainder of the manuscript is designed as follows. We describe the variables, data sources, partitions, and critical statistical properties of underlying variables in Sect. 2. We briefly enunciate the utilized methodological components subsequently in Sect. 3. The detailed results and thorough analyses are then documented in Sect. 4. Finally, the paper is completed in Sect. 5, highlighting the significant findings, limitations, and scopes for future research.

2 Data Description

We compiled the daily data of CBOE VIX from December 2017 to November 2022 for simulation from the data repository of the Federal Reserve Bank, St. Louis, and collected it from its official portal, https://fred.stlouisfed.org/. The lagged variables are computed from the original CBOE VIX series. The current work considers 1-day lag (LAG1), 2-day lag (LAG2), 3-day lag (LAG3), 4-day lag (LAG4), and 5-day lag (LAG5) as explanatory features. The daily observations of the macroeconomic predictors, CRUDE OIL VIX, GOLD VIX, and EPU, are collated from the same repository. The predictive exercises have been carried out on stipulated data partitions. Firstly, we assess the overall predictability across the entire data samples, which we define as the aggregate period. Secondly, data samples from December 2017 to December 2019 comprise the Pre-COVID-19 phase. Thirdly, samples spanning January 2020 to December 2021 set the predictive modeling for the COVID-19 phase. Finally, the predictive exercises from March 2022 to November 2022 evaluate the forecasting performance explicitly during the ongoing Russia-Ukraine conflict. Tables 1, 2, 3 and 4 present the descriptive statistics of the critical variables.

Table 1. Key Statistics for the Aggregate Data

Series	CBOE VIX	Crude Oil VIX	EPU	Gold VIX
Minimum	9.34	17.86	4.05	8.89
Maximum	82.69	325.15	861.1	48.98
Mean	21.4216	43.612	166.6895	16.3227
Median	19.6	37.705	120.795	15.885
Std. Dev	8.9201	26.1239	133.909	5.2137
JB Test	4825.2***	38581***	1357.8***	1341.4***
ADF Test	−1.291#	−2.300***	−3.8614***	−0.899#
Treasvirta's NN Test	773.25***	2492.3***	694.84***	1097.3***
Hurst Exponent	0.8157***	0.7706***	0.8400***	0.8468***

#Not Significant, *Significant at 10% Level of Significance, **Significant at 5% Level of Significance, ***Significant at 1% Level of Significance, JB Test: Jarque-Bera Test, ADF Test: Augmented Dickey-Fuller Test, Terasvirta's NN Test: Terasvirta's Neural Network Test.

It can be seen that the underlying samples strictly adhere to nonparametric properties and nonlinear movements, as apparent from the JB and Terasvorta's NN test, respectively. CBOE VIX has emerged to be nonstationary alongside Gold VIX, whereas Crude Oil VIX and EPU have shown a stationary trend as manifested by the outcome of the ADF test. Finally, Hurst exponent figures indicate strong dominance of long-memory dependence structure in CBOE VIX, which justifies the rationale of choosing lagged values as predictor variables. Other series also display a long-memory dependence structure.

Table 2. Key Statistics for the Pre-COVID-19 Phase

Series	CBOE VIX	Crude Oil VIX	EPU	Gold VIX
Minimum	9.34	17.86	4.05	8.89
Maximum	37.32	56.73	272.42	18.72
Mean	15.6607	30.9545	93.1022	12.1194
Median	14.75	29.935	84.81	11.595
Std. Dev	4.0461	6.6633	44.1842	2.0972
JB Test	518.39***	176.42***	103.18***	68.652***
ADF Test	−1.0773#	−0.5869#	−3.2111***	−0.4525#
Treasvirta's NN Test	1031.3***	954.56***	654.87***	848.09***
Hurst Exponent	0.7022***	0.8192***	0.6562***	0.8140***

#Not Significant, *Significant at 10% Level of Significance, **Significant at 5% Level of Significance, ***Significant at 1% Level of Significance, JB Test: Jarque-Bera Test, ADF Test: Augmented Dickey-Fuller Test, Terasvirta's NN Test: Terasvirta's Neural Network Test.

The behavioral pattern of CBOE VIX during the Pre-COVID-19 phase also suggests assertive nonlinear and nonstationary behavior. The distribution emerges to be strictly nonparametric too. The value of the Hurst exponent is reduced but adequate to infer the presence of long-memory dependence. The pattern of Gold VIX remained unchanged, while Crude Oil VIX completely resumed nonstationary traits.

During the COVID-19 in phase, CBOE VIX resembled strictly nonparametric behavior coupled with a high degree of nonlinearity and nonstationary movements. The magnitude of the Hurst exponent indicates that the long-memory behavior did not change in the new normal. The properties of Gold VIX remained unaltered too. Crude Oil VIX and EPU, nonetheless, exhibited stationary trends.

The behavior of CBOE VIX amidst the armed military conflict fueled by invasion rhetoric has emerged to be nonparametric, nonstationary, and nonlinear. Interestingly, the value of the Hurst exponent for CBOE VIX has transpired to be minimum across all four phases indicating growing chaotic behavior in the presence of external volatility. Thus, estimating high and low fluctuations reflecting different quantum of market fear is arduous and challenging. Except for EPU, all variables are nonstationary. In a nutshell, it is evident that the underlying variables do not abide by the normal distribution and are characterized by high nonlinearity and varying degrees of the nonstationary pattern. Therefore, the deployment of state-of-the-art forecasting models and subsequent

Table 3. Fundamental Statistics for the COVID-19 Phase

Series	CBOE VIX	Crude Oil VIX	EPU	Gold VIX
Minimum	12.1	28.6	19.85	10.91
Maximum	82.69	325.15	861.1	48.98
Mean	24.9758	52.9891	236.0512	19.4253
Median	22.21	39.515	178.24	17.935
Std. Dev	10.8465	37.0544	169.3164	5.4951
JB Test	1288.6***	3581.4***	91.338***	703.38***
ADF Test	−0.8263#	−1.7787*	−2.1643**	−0.6803#
Treasvirta's NN Test	772.33***	1494.8***	867.06***	1113.2***
Hurst Exponent	0.8074***	0.7956***	0.8408***	0.8179***

#Not Significant, *Significant at 10% Level of Significance, **Significant at 5% Level of Significance, ***Significant at 1% Level of Significance, JB Test: Jarque-Bera Test, ADF Test: Augmented Dickey-Fuller Test, Terasvirta's NN Test: Terasvirta's Neural Network Test.

Table 4. Fundamental Statistics for the Russia-Ukraine Phase

Series	CBOE VIX	Crude Oil VIX	EPU	Gold VIX
Minimum	18.57	42.06	20.63	15.22
Maximum	36.45	78.91	699.78	31.7
Mean	26.5774	52.0538	164.2353	19.1024
Median	26.17	50.27	142.39	18.91
Std. Dev	4.0284	7.0414	6.2449	2.5473
JB Test	4.9681***	141.64***	694.93***	246.16***
ADF Test	−0.7576#	−0.8067#	−2.1521**	−0.7327#
Treasvirta's NN Test	704.98***	920.31***	810.19***	791.51***
Hurst Exponent	0.6971***	0.7780***	0.7185***	0.7461***

#Not Significant, *Significant at 10% Level of Significance, **Significant at 5% Level of Significance, ***Significant at 1% Level of Significance, JB Test: Jarque-Bera Test, ADF Test: Augmented Dickey-Fuller Test, Terasvirta's NN Test: Terasvirta's Neural Network Test.

explainable AI methodologies to model complex time series are justified. The figures of the Hurst exponent rationalize the usage of the lagged information as additional predictor variables.

3 Methodology

This section briefly elucidates the working principles of different methodologies to meet the research objectives.

3.1 Facebook Prophet

The core data scientists [17] at Facebook developed an applied predictive modeling algorithm named Facebook Prophet. It has recently gained more popularity in time series forecasting operations. Through accurate segregation of trends, abrupt regime shifts, seasonality, etc., it can achieve remarkable forecasts for complicated daily, weekly, monthly, and yearly time series observations. The equation used to describe the prophet model is as follows:

$$y(t) = g(t) + s(t) + h(t) + x(t) + \epsilon_t \tag{1}$$

where y(t) stands for the desired framework or time series, g(t) represents the trend component accounting for linear or nonlinear effects, s(t) for periodic components, h(t) for holiday effects resulting from erratic schedules, x(t) for the influence of exogenous features, and ϵ_t for the error term. In this research, the growth part of the model is approximated using a piece-wise constant function, which has been reported to be highly effective for complex time series [5, 8]. It can be mathematically represented as:

$$g(t) = \left(k + a(t)^T \delta\right)t + \left(m + a(t)^T \gamma\right) \tag{2}$$

Here, k accounts for the rate of growth, $\delta(\in \mathbb{R}^S)$ denotes the adjustment parameter enabling the S change points to be integrated for drawing prediction, m represents the offset parameter, and finally, γ governs the quantum of the rate of change. Seasonality is modelled leveraging the Fourier series as:

$$s(t) = \sum_{n=1}^{N} \left(a_n cos\left(\frac{2\pi nt}{P}\right) + b_n sin\left(\frac{2\pi nt}{P}\right)\right) \tag{3}$$

where the scale of the underlying series, i.e., daily, weekly, monthly, etc., is denoted by P (Yearly, Weekly, Daily, etc.). Hence, estimating seasonality requires determining values of 2N parameters, $\beta = [a_1 b_1 \ldots a_N b_N]^T$.

3.2 Uber Orbit

Orbit stands for Object-Oriented Bayesian time series. For Bayesian time series forecasting and inference, Uber developed Orbit, a Python framework, which is based on PyStan and Pyro, its own probabilistic programming library [13]. Kernel-based Time-varying Regression (KTR) has been implemented in our research. This was done to address the complex-seasonality pattern and time-varying regression coefficients. KTR makes use of the latent variables to define a smooth time-varying representation of model coefficients. KTR uses the latent variables to provide a smooth representation of the model coefficients that change over time. KTR considers a time-series y(t) as the linear combination of three parts which are the local-trend l(t), seasonality s(t), and regression r(t) terms. Mathematically,

$$y(t) = l(t) + s(t) + r(t) + x(t) + \epsilon(t) \tag{4}$$

Here, $\epsilon(t)$ is the standard random error.

3.3 Performance Measurement

To evaluate the accuracy of forecasting exercises, three metrics, namely, mean squared error (MSE), root mean squared error (RMSE), and R squared value (R2), are utilized. They are computed as:

$$MSE = \frac{1}{N} \sum_{i=1}^{N} \left(Y_i - \hat{Y}_i \right)^2 \tag{5}$$

$$RMSE = \sqrt{\frac{1}{N} \sum_{i=1}^{N} \left(Y_i - \hat{Y}_i \right)^2} \tag{6}$$

$$R^2 = 1 - \frac{\sum_{i=1}^{N} \left(Y_i - \hat{Y}_i \right)^2}{\sum_{i=1}^{N} \left(Y_i - \overline{Y}_i \right)^2} \tag{7}$$

$$NSE = 1 - \frac{\sum_{i=1}^{N} \left\{ \hat{Y}_i - Y_i \right\}^2}{\sum_{i=1}^{N} \left\{ Y_i - \overline{Y} \right\}^2} \tag{8}$$

where Y_i and $\hat{Y}_i$ denote the actual and predicted values on the ith data sample, N refers to the total sample size, and $\overline{Y}$ represents the average of original observations. The values of MSE and RMSE should be as low as possible, while the R^2 coefficient and NSE figures should be close to 1 to establish the efficiency of any framework in deriving highly accurate predictions.

3.4 Explainable AI

The present work uses two explanatory AI tools, SHAP and ALE plots, to interpret the influence of the select predictor variables on the forecasting process. The model outcome for individual data points is determined by aggregating. The measure SHAP was originally incepted by [16] to estimate the contribution of individual entities in the collaborative game. Of late, development and work on XAI have opened up new avenues to leverage the SHAP metric for feature evaluation [11]. Conceptualized by [1], the accumulated local effect (ALE) plot aims to determine the average impact of the independent variable on the predictions by deciphering the black box operations of utilized ML models. It is computationally swift and capable of extracting accurate interpretations of predictive contributions in the presence of correlated features.

4   Results and Analyses

4.1 Outcome of Forecasting

To conduct predictive modelling, the respective datasets are portioned into training (85%) and test (15%) segment in sequential forward-looking orientation, which is primarily used for time series forecasting [6]. Forecasting on the training segment refers to in-sample predictions, whereas the predictability assessment on the test segment is known as out-of-sample forecasting. Table 5 reports the results.

Table 5. Comparison of Facebook Prophet and Uber Orbit

	MSE	RMSE	R^2	NSE
In-Sample				
Facebook Prophet	4.8322	2.1982	0.9429	0.9394
Uber Orbit	5.2596	2.2934	0.9389	0.9089
Out-of-Sample				
Facebook Prophet	1.9706	1.4038	0.8590	1.0000
Uber Orbit	40.1518	6.3366	0.1292	0.9862

On the training segment of the aggregate series, the performance of both Facebook Prophet and Uber Orbit in predicting future movements of CBOEVIX has appeared to be highly effective, as manifested by the estimated figures of the performance indicators. Uber Orbit's performance degrades heavily in the test segment, as indicated by substantially high MSE and RMSE values and low R^2 figures. On the other hand, the predictive accuracy of forecasts obtained by the Facebook Prophet algorithm for the test segment can be classified to be highly precise as the same is linked with considerably low MSE and RMSE values and reasonably high R^2 and NSE figures. Hence, an inference can be drawn that Facebook Prophet is relatively more efficient than Uber Orbit in accurately determining the extent of market fear. Figures 1 and 2 display the prediction process.

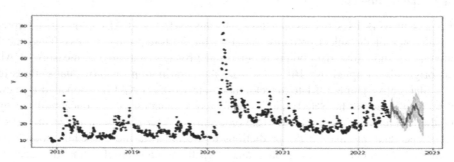

Fig. 1. Predictions by Facebook Prophet

The black segments on both figures represent the prediction on in-samples, while the blue segments account for the out-of-samples predictions by respective models. Table 6 reports the outcome of forecasting exercises across different regimes.

Rigorous predictive assessments across the phases suggest that the performance of the Facebook Prophet has turned out to be best in the Pre-COVID-19 phase on training and test segments. The values of MSE and RMSE resemble a minimum, while R2 and NSE values are maximum when compared to the other two phases. The outcome is expected considering relatively low market uncertainty and external chaos during

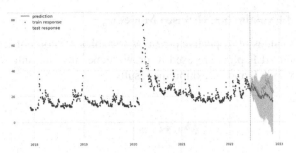

Fig. 2. Predictions by Uber Orbit

Table 6. The Outcome of the Forecasting by Facebook Prophet in Different Phases

	MSE	RMSE	R^2	NSE
In-Sample				
Pre-COVID-19 Phase	2.5605	1.6002	0.8536	0.9482
COVID-19 Phase	5.0741	2.2526	0.9599	0.9231
Russia-Ukraine Conflict Phase	1.2889	1.1353	0.9243	0.9894
Out-of-Sample				
Pre-COVID-19 Phase	1.4342	1.1976	0.7022	1.0000
COVID-19 Phase	8.1160	2.8489	0.5861	0.9340
Russia-Ukraine Conflict Phase	62.3116	7.8938	0.6883	0.9048

the Pre-COVID-19 phase. The computed performance metrics imply that the predictive performance during the COVID-19 phase is not poor either, considering the external vagaries. The predictive performance on the test segment marginally deteriorated in this phase compared to the training accuracy. Finally, the in-sample predictive performance of the Facebook Prophet during the Russia-Ukraine conflict is highly encouraging. However, the framework's accuracy suffers substantially when subjected to test data samples. The said phenomenon is not completely unexpected considering the rapid increase in disruptions in commodity markets, supply chains, etc., owing to the armed conflicts, which induce a high degree of fluctuations in the implied market volatility of the US. The findings also suggest how the US market reacts to the ongoing uncertainty of military conflict directly. Hence, market fear is relatively more efficient in this phase. Despite the level of accuracy of the predictive exercises, the models offer very little insight into the influence structure of the select explanatory variables. The contribution of the present work, thus, involves the deployment of sophisticated explainable AI frameworks to accomplish the task.

4.2 Outcome of Explainable AI-Based Modeling

As stated, SHAP values of respective predictor variables are computed to rank the features globally, and ALE plots are used to draw deeper insights into critical features. Figures 3, 4, 5, 6, 7, 8, 9 and 10 exhibit the results.

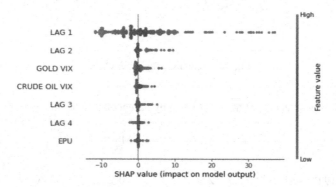

Fig. 3. Feature Importance Ranking on the Aggregate Dataset

At the aggregate level, it can be noticed that immediate past information of the CBOE VIX played a critical role in explaining its futuristic movements, as LAG1 and LAG2 occupy the top two essential feature spots. The influence of the macroeconomic counterparts, GOLD VIX and CBOE OIL VIX We introspect the impact of LAG1 and the joint contribution of LAG1 and LAG2 using the one-dimensional (1D) and two-dimensional (2D) ALE plots, respectively.

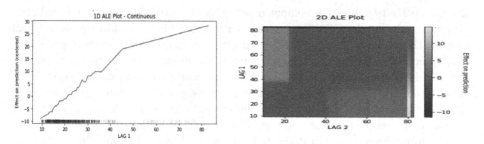

Fig. 4. ALE Plots on the Aggregate Dataset

It can be seen that as the values of LAG1 increase, its predictive prowess on the target increases rapidly. The said finding basically conforms to the long-memory dependence structure of the underlying variable detected earlier. The 2D plot reveals how the co-movement of both LAG1 and LAG2 affects the temporal pattern of the CBOE VIX. The insights are helpful for closely tracking the future figures of the CBOE VIX.

Similar to the aggregate phase, the impact of the LAG1 and LAG2 on the movements of CBOE VIX has become significant. The influence of GOLD VIX is critical as well. We next attempt to uncover the dependence structure using the ALE plots.

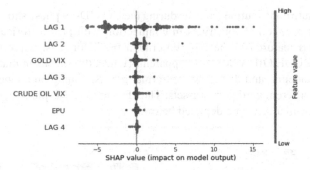

Fig. 5. Feature Importance Ranking for the Pre-COVID-19 Phase

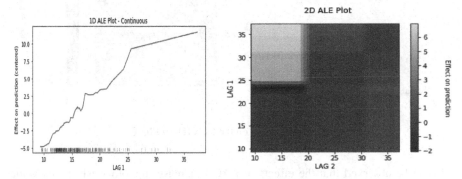

Fig. 6. ALE Plots on the Pre-COVID-19 Phase

The 1D ALE plot conforms to the long-memory dependence pattern of the CBOE VIX. On the flip side, an explanation of the joint contribution through the lens of the 2D ALE plot reveals that LAG1 exerts comparatively more predictive influence on CBOE VIX than LAG 2.

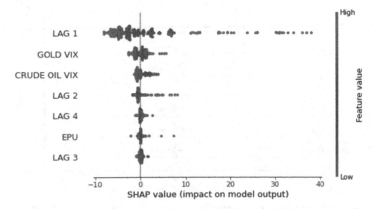

Fig. 7. Feature Importance Ranking for the COVID-19 Phase

Global feature contribution analysis during the COVID-19 phase shows an increased impact of macroeconomic constructs in conjunction with past historical information. GOLD VIX has featured in the top two critical predictor lists, while the significant influence of CRUDE OIL VIX is also apparent. Hence, the shocks in market fear at the onset of the pandemic and disruption of normal regime contagion connectedness with uncertainty in different commodity assets. The 1D and 2D ALE plots to analyze impact patterns at a granular scale are depicted below.

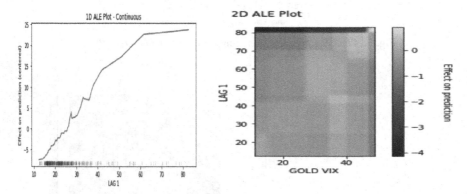

Fig. 8. ALE Plots on the COVID-19 Phase

It can be observed that the effects of LAG1 increase monotonously as its values experience a bullish phase. Therefore, when the previous day's market fear is high during the new normal time regime, market fear is also expected to remain high the next day. The Joint contribution uncovers an exciting outcome. It has emerged that if GOLD VIX attains higher figures, the effects of LAG1 cannot heavily influence the movements of CBOE VIX. The aforesaid result is an indication of hedge possibility in uncertain regimes.

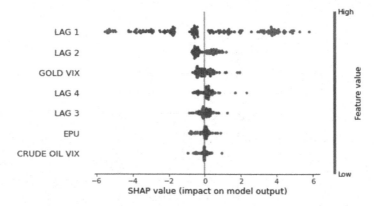

Fig. 9. Feature Importance Ranking for the Russia-Ukraine Conflict Phase

During the Russia-Ukraine military conflict phase, the strong dependence of CBOE VIX on its own historical information is amply apparent. GOLD VIX exerts reasonable predictive prowess, while the impact of CRUDE OIL VIX, unlike the previous phases, has seen subdued effects. The direct implication simply suggests the presence of steep uncertainty in the conflict phase has vehemently induced turbulence in the Crude Oil market. As a consequence, its control over other assets has been marginalized. The 1D and 2D ALE plots to decode the dependence structure at a deeper level are presented below.

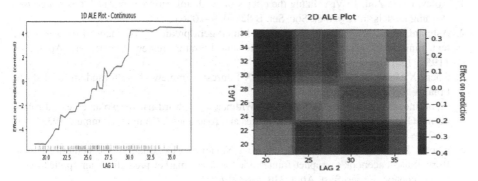

Fig. 10. ALE Plots on the Russia-Ukraine Conflict Phase

The unitary effects of LAG1 during the Russia-Ukraine conflict are similar to other phases, which support the evidence of a long-memory dependence structure. As the degree of predictability during the current invasion regime is relatively low, the presence of subdued unitary and joint effects is imminent.

5 Conclusions

The findings of our study reveal the dominance of past information on market fear in predicting the future figures of CBOE VIX. Thus, it is crucial to monitor the market fear in the futures market closely. Market anxiety primarily hinges on prior knowledge. We advance a novel methodological framework to estimate future figures of future market fear of the US, vis-a-vis decoding the exact dependence structure. Our results indicate that during the pre-COVID-19 phase, market fear may be anticipated with superior accuracy under normal circumstances. The presence of long-memory behavioral traits is exemplified. In COVID-19, market fear is more predictable than the ongoing Russia-Ukraine conflict. As the quantum of distress increases, the persistent behavior of CBOE VIX diminishes steadily. High external distress induces chaotic traits in temporal movements of the CBOE VIX. The GOLD VIX and CRUDE OIL VIX emerge to exert significant predictive influence, while the impact of EPU appears to be relatively low. The results and methodological framework propounded in this work can be leveraged for risk mitigation and trading effectively. The overall findings espouse the efficiency of the Facebook Prophet algorithm as the superiority of the same over Uber Orbit in accurately forecasting the CBOE VIX in out-of-sample data segments has been found.

We have used a limited number of variables in this study. We intend to expand the present work to include new features. The research can be expanded to track how much market fear exists in emerging and developing economies. The current research is confined to two methodological structures. In the future, a comparative study encompassing the well-known ensemble and deep learning models will be carried out.

References

1. Apley, D.W., Zhu, J.: Visualizing the effects of predictor variables in black box supervised learning models. J. Roy. Stat. Soc. Ser. B **82**, 1059–1086 (2020)
2. Ashtiani, M.N., Raahemi, B.: News-based intelligent prediction of financial markets using text mining and machine learning: a systematic literature review. Expert Syst. Appl. **217**, 119509 (2023)
3. Chen, X., Feng, J., Wang, T.: Pricing VIX futures: a framework with random level shifts. Finance Res. Lett. **52**, 103501 (2023)
4. Fiandrino, C., Attanasio, G., Fiore, M., Widmer, J.: Toward native explainable and robust AI in 6G networks: current state, challenges and road ahead. Comput. Commun. **193**, 47–52 (2022)
5. Ghosh, I., Datta Chaudhuri, T.: Integrating Navier-Stokes equation and neoteric iForest-BorutaShap-Facebook's prophet framework for stock market prediction: an application in Indian context. Expert Syst. Appl. **210**, 118391 (2022)
6. Ghosh, I., Datta Chaudhuri, T., Alfaro-Cortés, E., Gámez, M., García, N.: A hybrid approach to forecasting futures prices with simultaneous consideration of optimality in ensemble feature selection and advanced artificial intelligence. Technol. Forecast. Soc. Change **181**, 121757 (2022)
7. Jana, R.K., Ghosh, I., Das, D.: A differential evolution-based regression framework for forecasting Bitcoin price. Ann. Oper. Res. **306**, 295–320 (2021)
8. Jana, R.K., Ghosh, I., Wallin, M.W.: Taming energy and electronic waste generation in bitcoin mining: insights from Facebook prophet and deep neural network. Technol. Forecast. Soc. Change **178**, 121584 (2022)
9. John, K., Li, J.: COVID-19, volatility dynamics, and sentiment trading. J. Bank. Finance **133**, 106162 (2021)
10. Lu, X., Ma, F., Wang, J., Wang, J.: Examining the predictive information of CBOE OVX on China's oil futures volatility: evidence from MS-MIDAS models. Energy **212**, 118743 (2020)
11. Lundberg, S., Lee, S.I.: A unified approach to interpreting model predictions. arXiv:1705.07874 (2017)
12. Mi, J., Wang, L.F., Liu, Y., Zhang, J.: KDE-GAN: a multimodal medical image-fusion model based on knowledge distillation and explainable AI modules. Comput. Biol. Med. **151A**, 106273 (2022)
13. Ng, E., Wang, J., Chen, H., Yang, S., Smyl, S.: Orbit: probabilistic forecast with exponential smoothing. arXiv:2004.08492, https://doi.org/10.48550/arXiv.2004.08492 (2020)
14. Qiao, G., Jiang, G., Yang, J.: VIX term structure forecasting: new evidence based on the realized semi-variances. Int. Rev. Financ. Anal. **82**, 102199 (2022)
15. Shahparast, H., Hamzeloo, S., Safari, E.: An incremental type-2 fuzzy classifier for stock trend prediction. Expert Syst. Appl. **212**, 118787 (2023)
16. Shapley, L.S.: Stochastic games. PNAS **39**, 1095–1100 (1953)
17. Taylor, S.J., Letham, B.: Forecasting at scale. Am. Stat. **72**, 37–45 (2018)
18. Toochaei, M.R., Moeini, F.: Evaluating the performance of ensemble classifiers in stock returns prediction using effective features. Expert Syst. Appl. **213C**, 119186 (2023)

19. Wang, J., Lu, X., He, F., Ma, F.: Which popular predictor is more useful to forecast international stock markets during the coronavirus pandemic: VIX vs EPU? Int. Rev. Financ. Anal. **72**, 101596 (2020)
20. Wei, Y., Liang, C., Li, Y., Zhang, X., Wei, G.: Can CBOE gold and silver implied volatility help to forecast gold futures volatility in China? Evidence based on HAR and Ridge regression models. Finance Res. Lett. **35**, 101287 (2020)
21. Yang, G., Ye, Q., Xia, J.: Unbox the black-box for the medical explainable AI via multi-modal and multi-centre data fusion: a mini-review, two showcases and beyond. Inf. Fus. **77**, 29–52 (2022)

ANN for Diabetic Prediction by Using Chaotic Based Sine Cosine Algorithm

Rana Pratap Mukherjee[1]([✉]), Rajesh Kumar Chatterjee[2],
and Falguni Chakraborty[3]

[1] Tata Consultancy Services, Kolkata, India
ranapratapmukherjee15@gmail.com
[2] Usha Martin University, Ranchi, India
[3] Dr. B. C. Roy Engineering College, Durgapur, India

Abstract. The use of AI is becoming increasingly widespread in medical diagnosis. Recently, many decision-making systems have used the Artificial Neural Networks (ANN) model to train the ANN's weight and biases to get the lowest error function and highest accuracy. In this concern meta-heuristic based optimization technique play an important role. Already various optimization techniques have been applied to train an ANN's weight and bias. But due to improper balancing between exploration and exploitation they fail to give the global optima. To overcome this issues, this study used a new stochastic-based optimization algorithm the Sine Cosine Algorithm (SCA). The mathematical formulation of SCA is based on trigonometric functions, sine and cosine. However, sometimes slow convergence is the main disadvantage of the basic SCA algorithm. This paper proposes a modified SCA optimization technique called Chaotic SCA(CSCA) to train the control parameters like weights and biases of a single-layer ANN by integrating chaotic into SCA to expedite the convergence speed. The performance of the above algorithm is examined and verified using The Pima Indian data set. The experiment revealed the outperformance of CSCA than the other algorithms.

Keywords: Diabetic prediction · Neural network · Sine cosine algorithm (SCA) · Chaotic Theory

1 Introduction

Diabetes occurs when the pancreas does not release enough hormone insulin, a gland behind the stomach, or the body is unable to use insulin properly. It also happens when the blood glucose level, or blood sugar, becomes too high. Nowadays, approximately 450 million people suffering from diabetes worldwide. Diabetes diagnosis with accurate data is a significant classification problem. World health organisations show that nearly 1.6 million deaths in 2015 were caused by diabetic disease. Therefore, many supervised and unsupervised machine learning techniques have already been applied to detect diabetes in the early stages.

MK Hasan et al. [1] used the same dataset and proposed a robust framework for diabetic prediction. The Multilayer Perceptron (MLP) and other Machine Learning (ML) classifiers were used in this literature. Researchers of [2] applied the Logistic Regression (LR) classification technique, and SVM works well for diabetic prediction. However, due to a lack of searching capabilities, traditional machine learning algorithms may fail to locate the optimal solutions. Some deep learning techniques are also used to categorise people with diabetes in various ways to address the abovementioned problem. The authors of [3] compared conventional machine learning with deep learning approaches.

ANN can solve these types of classification problems in an artificial intelligence system. A Feed-forward Neural Network(FNN) is one type of ANN. It has been broadly used in fields like stock market analysis, Price prediction, data mining, image classification, etc. An ANN is built up by the input, hidden, and output layers. It may have more than one hidden layer(s). Every layer(s) is interconnected with its weights and biases. Recently ANN has been applied in various domains, including the medical field, due to its exceptional self-learning capabilities and high accuracy in mapping complicated nonlinear relationships. ANN has been commonly used to detect tumours, cancers, hepatitis, lung diseases, etc. Various architectures of ANN have recently been used in the medical field to diagnose several diseases. Nasim Ghadami et al. [4] forecast the consumption of electrical energy in summer and winter periods with predicted 99 percent accuracy. Researchers [5] showed the application of ANN and SVM on Stock market analysis. Basavaraj Amarapur et al. [6] used adaptive ANN (AANN) methodology to increase classification accuracy. The researcher [7] predicts the survival rate for 13 different cancer using CNN. However, objective functions aren't always differentiable because of the nonlinearity of the data. Therefore, these strategies are sometimes inappropriate, and they occasionally fail to identify a global optimum. Heuristic algorithms are the most encouraging replacement for classical optimization to overcome the drawbacks above. This is the main driving force behind many scientific communities' quest to solve a particular issue. The main advantage of using this algorithm is that there is a chance that it can get global minima. Fevrier et al. [8] integrated Ant Colony Optimization (ACO) and Particle Swarm Optimization (PSO) to optimize a neural network. Parviz et al. [9] have used Whale Optimization Algorithm (WOA) and ANN to predicts West Texas Intermediate (WTI) petroleum prices.

Eslam. M. Hassib et al. [10] proposed WOA and BRNN to classify big data. Experimental findings demonstrated that the algorithm had achieved high local optima avoidance and accuracy. The author of [11] introduced a hybrid parallel Harris Hawks Optimization (HPHHO) algorithm to solve the RLV trajectory optimization problem. The main goal of the proposed algorithm was to enhance the performance of the existing Harris Hawks Optimization (HHO) algorithm. Tradition whale optimization algorithm (WOA)-trained artificial neural network (ANN) have been used in the literature [12], and the authors showed that the proposed method could address the challenges of attacks, failure prediction, and failure detection in a power system. Kanagasabai Lenin [13] integrated both Duponchelia Fovealis Optimization (DFO) algorithm and enriched squirrel search optimization (ESSO) in the literature algorithm to solve optimal reactive power problem.

The SCA [14] algorithm has been recently developed to solve optimisation problems. Nabil et al. [15] used swarm based sine cosine algorithm for feature selection. Rozita Talaei Pashiri et al. [16] proposed a feature selection-based method to reduce spam detection errors. But due to lack of exploration, this algorithm gets stuck in local optima and fails to determine global optima. To overcome the above mentioned issues, researchers integrated chaotic systems into optimization algorithms, which helped explore the search domain to accelerate the convergence speed. Previously, like PSO [17], WOA [18], DE [19], ACO [20] etc., have used chaos to increase the searching ability. By motivating the previous research, in this study, we have integrated the chaotic system with the SCA and named as Chaotic SCA(CSCA) to identify the accurate chaotic mapping combined with the original SCA in the current study to speed up convergence mobility. Today, there is a vast amount of medical data available. We need an accurate approach to diagnose the disease before we can anticipate it. The main goal of this research is to develop a method for predicting Diabetes disease classification using ANN. This algorithm's primary objective is calculating the optimum NN architecture's hyper-parameter values. We have optimize the hyperparameters (weights and biases) using the Pima dataset by the proposed algorithm and compare the result with the other algorithms based on the fitness function, Convergence mobility and a few well-known quality indicators are used to illustrate how effective the suggested CSCA is at locating the global optimum solution to the problems above.

2   Mathematical Model of the Diabetic Prediction Problem

In the Fig. 1(a), we have shown n input single layer neural network.

The weighted sum with bias is represented by the following equation:

$$v_l = \sum_{i=1}^{n} M_i X_i + b \tag{1}$$

Figure 1 shown the structure of multilayer feed forward NN. Where $(X_1, X_2, ..., X_n)$ and $(Y_1, Y_2, ..., Y_r)$ represents the input and output nodes and $(H_1, H_2, ..., H_k)$ represents as hidden nodes.

following is the output of the jth hidden node

$$H_j = f(\sum_{i=1}^{n} X_i W_{ij} + b_j), j = 1, 2, ..., k \tag{2}$$

Similarly, following is the output of the lth output node is as follows

$$Y_l = f(\sum_{i=1}^{k} H_i V_{il} + e_l), l = 1, 2, ..., r \tag{3}$$

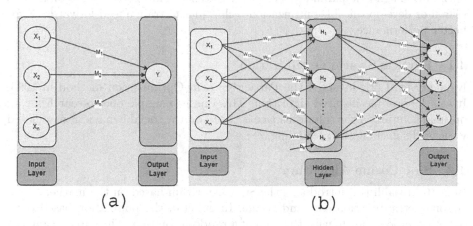

(a)   (b)

Fig. 1. (a) Single layer (b) Multi layer NN

where $f()$ is the activation function.

The following equation is used to calculate the learning error

$$E_l = \sum_{i=1}^{m} (Y_l^i - C_l^i)^2 \tag{4}$$

Where C_l^i corresponds to i^{th} sample for l^{th} output. Total number of samples is m for the given classification problem.

3   Dataset Description

The data used in this experiment are collected from The National Institute of Diabetes and Digestive and Kidney Diseases. This Pima Indians Diabetes Database consists of 768 instances, including age, the patient's BMI and insulin level and many other factors of 21 years old female patients. The goal of this dataset is to diagnostically forecast whether a patient has diabetes based on specific diagnostic metrics present in the dataset.

4   Optimization Algorithms

The main aim of applying the optimization process in neural networks is to get the best combination of weight and biases to increase the network speed. And for this, several optimization strategies have been employed in the past. This research aims to predict the survival chances of diabetic patients based on the optimally diagnostic parameters from the dataset. This leads the researchers to search or develop suitable optimzation techniques to train a feed-forward NN for better performance.

4.1   Particle Swarm Optimization

Kennedy et.al [21] invented the Particle Swarm Optimization method in 1995. It was a novel bio-inspired algorithm. This one is a simple one to search for an optimal solution in the solution space is based on the social behaviour associated with bird's flocking, fish schooling, etc.

4.2   Sine Cosine Algorithm

In 2016 Mirjalili [14] introduced the SCA algorithm based on the mathematical trigonometric function sine and cosine. In general, the population-based optimization process starts with the help of a random solution. The exploration and exploitation are both common phases in stochastic-based and population-based algorithms. The functions (Sine and Cosine) are implemented in this algorithm to maintain the appropriate balance between exploration and exploitation, as they are crucial in determining the ideal solution.The SCA employs two equations that can be formulated as follows to balance the phases above.

$$Q_v^{(j+1)} = Q_v^j + z_1 * sin(z_2) * |z_3 P_v^j - Q_v^j| \tag{5}$$
$$Q_v^{(j+1)} = Q_v^j + z_1 * cos(z_2) * |z_3 P_v^j - Q_v^j| \tag{6}$$

In the $(j+1)^{th}$ and j^{th} iteration the vth dimensional position of the current solution is Q_v^{j+1} and Q_v^j respectively. Random numbers with the threshold [0,1] are z_1, z_2 and z_3. P_v^j is position of vth particle at j^{th} generation. The 5) and (6 combinedly rewritten as:

$$Q_v^j = \begin{cases} Q_v^j + z_1 * sin(z_2) * |z_3 P_v^j - Q_v^j| \ , \ z_4 < 0.5 \\ Q_v^j + z_1 * cos(z_2) * |z_3 P_v^j - Q_v^j| \ , \ z_4 > 0.5 \end{cases} \tag{7}$$

the following function are used to modify the Eq. (5) to (6)

$$z_1 = a - m.(a/M) \tag{8}$$

where M signifies the maximum iteration, m denotes the current iteration, and a denotes a constant.

As mentioned earlier, the algorithm's four primary parameters are z_1, z_2, z_3 and z_4. The parameter z_2 lies between 0 to 2π. z_1 and z_3 are the gives random variable used to control the direction of the movement.Finally, z_4 switches of functions from sine to cosine and vise versa.

5   Chaos Theory

It has been observed that the different scientific community have been used the application of chaos theory for more than two decades. M. Farahani et al. [22] used chaos to address the load-frequency control (LFC) problem. Sankalap Arora et al. [23] integrated chaotic with grasshopper optimization algorithm. The chaos is integrated into the SCA to improve the performance of the algorithm. Sometime traditional optimization algorithms are trapped in local optima which causes poor convergence rate. Consequently, by using this technique the capability of the other two phases i.e. exploration and exploitation are enhanced. In general, optimization algorithms essentially begin with random initialization, which causes them to reach global or almost global optimums more slowly. In this study, we have proposed a CSCA algorithm that combines chaos with the fundamental SCA algorithm. Chaos is used as random number generator, used to update the population in each iteration. The Various chaotic maps are incorporated with the general SCA. The starting point, which was taken to be 0.7, can be lowered to any number between 0 and 1. The adjustment of SCA's parameters involves looking at several chaotic maps. Later, a suitable chaotic map is chosen and mapped throughout the remainder of the simulation study through both iteration cycles and startup of the method.

6   Proposed Chaotic Sine Cosine Algorithm

As previously mentioned, we have tested the efficiency of the suggested CSCA using several chaotic maps. It has been found that the Gaussian maps outperforms the other variants of chaotic maps among the ten various 1-D chaotic maps. The Gaussian maps is define as

$$x_{n+1} = e^{-a x_n^2} + \beta \qquad (9)$$

where α and β are real number and $a > 0$. $-1 \leq \beta \leq 1$ gives better chaotic behaviour.

The details of the proposed algorithm are stated below:

- **Step 1:** Initially, ANN network is created with the randomly initialized weights and biases as the input of this system. The weights and biases connected with the input, hidden and, output nodes are refereed as control parameters.

- **Step 2:** Evaluate the current population by calculating their fitness value using learning error equation (4) of the neural network.

- **Step 3:** With the help of the (5) of SCA, update the population at the starting of each iteration.

- **Step 4:** Non-repeating dynamic random numbers are generated by the chaotic map and employed to expedite the convergence speed and escape to stuck into the local solutions.

- **Step 5:** Select the best fifty solutions for the next iteration.

- **Step 6:** Each of the fifty fittest solutions' weights and biases is examined for duplication and, if any are discovered, replaced with random values.

- **Step 7:** To train the ANN model repeat the steps 3 to step 6 are as per the number of iterations. In the simulation study for the suggested CSCA technique, 100 iterations are assumed to be the maximum number.

- **Step 8:** Stop the iteration if reach the termination condition. Otherwise, go to step 4.

Pictorial representation of the proposed work is shown in Fig. 2

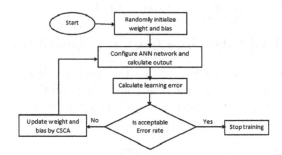

Fig. 2. Flowchart of the proposed system

7   Result and Discussion

The experimental work extended the original benchmark problem known as the diabetes prediction problem to demonstrate the resilience of the suggested CSCA algorithm. The Pima Indian Diabetes Dataset, divided into two portions, was used for the experiment. Seventy percent of the data is used for training, while the remaining thirty percent is used for testing. As a result, out of 768 instances, about 538 data were used for training and 238 for testing. We used the (8-H-1) structure in NN, where "H" is the number of hidden nodes. Tables 1, 2, and 3 show that the proposed algorithm performs best among all other techniques. From the statistical view, It has also been observed that the different statistical measures obtained by the CSCA method are remarkably similar, demonstrating the method's resilience. Figure 3 shows the box plot of the various statistical variables.

Table 1. Optimum weight and bias of diabetic classification

Control Variables	CSCA	CPSO	SCA	PSO	Control Variables	CSCA	CPSO	SCA	PSO
Wt_1^i	-5.65E+00	-5.25E+04	4.76E-01	2.57E+01	Wt_{29}^i	-1.39E-01	-1.93E+00	1.05E+00	-2.61E-02
Wt_2^i	-1.27E+00	3.55E-01	-2.82E+00	6.13E+00	Wt_{30}^i	3.66E-01	-1.36E+00	-4.42E-02	-8.92E-01
Wt_3^i	-9.88E-01	7.09E-01	3.90E-02	-3.97E-02	Wt_{31}^i	4.11E-01	1.07E-01	4.60E-03	-3.65E-01
Wt_4^i	-2.66E-02	-3.30E-01	-3.27E-02	8.09E-02	Wt_{32}^i	8.44E-02	7.81E-03	7.49E-03	1.03E-01
Wt_5^i	-2.69E-03	8.12E+00	2.10E-01	-9.95E-01	Wt_{33}^i	-2.57E-01	-6.74E-01	1.05E+00	-1.69E-02
Wt_6^i	-5.66E-01	-1.62E+00	4.74E-02	-4.24E+00	Wt_{34}^i	2.43E-02	-1.73E+00	-4.42E-02	-3.87E-03
Wt_7^i	-1.30E+00	4.98E+00	4.39E-01	4.11E+00	Wt_{35}^i	-2.94E-03	-5.66E-01	4.60E-03	-4.84E-01
Wt_8^i	4.62E-02	-3.41E+00	-1.54E+00	-1.85E+01	Wt_{36}^i	3.18E-02	2.82E-01	7.49E-03	-1.55E+00
Wt_9^i	-1.64E+00	-5.80E-02	1.87E-02	-4.31E-01	Wt_{37}^i	-2.56E-02	4.59E-01	7.49E-03	-3.59E+00
Wt_{10}^i	2.07E-03	1.72E+00	1.89E-01	-3.04E+00	Wt_{38}^i	2.08E+00	2.50E-01	1.70E+00	-5.83E-02
Wt_{11}^i	-6.68E-03	-2.25E+00	5.22E-07	-2.41E+00	Wt_{39}^i	-5.20E-01	-1.70E+00	-1.16E-03	-1.74E+01
Wt_{12}^i	-1.50E-02	-1.95E+01	-5.61E-02	1.99E-01	Wt_{40}^i	-8.44E-03	-1.78E+00	4.46E+01	-3.54E+00
Wt_{13}^i	9.29E-04	9.11E-02	-5.61E-02	-3.05E+00	Wt_{41}^i	6.38E-02	-2.84E-01	-5.46E-01	-2.21E-01
Wt_{14}^i	2.08E-02	8.33E-02	9.58E-01	-5.10E-00	Wt_{42}^i	-5.25E+00	1.16E+00	-3.03E-01	-1.01E-00
Wt_{15}^i	4.23E+00	4.03E-01	1.27E+00	3.94E-01	Wt_{43}^i	-4.18E+01	-2.24E-01	1.31E-01	4.49E-02
Wt_{16}^i	2.56E-00	9.91E+01	3.14E-01	-6.94E-00	Wt_{44}^i	4.70E-04	1.82E+00	-2.59E-02	-2.93E+00
Wt_{17}^i	-2.38E-01	-1.21E-02	-3.31E-02	5.47E-01	Wt_{45}^i	4.41E-01	1.62E+00	4.87E-01	-1.96E+00
Wt_{18}^i	-6.98E-01	7.96E-01	1.74E-01	-9.44E-01	Wt_{46}^i	-1.57E-03	5.71E-01	6.25E-01	-4.82E+00
Wt_{19}^i	3.83E-01	-6.16E+00	4.45E-01	-3.80E-01	Wt_{47}^i	3.70E-01	1.21E-01	-6.11E-01	1.78E+00
Wt_{20}^i	-2.49E-02	1.35E+00	9.58E-01	-4.78E+00	Wt_{48}^i	-3.01E-02	2.07E-01	-4.83E+00	-2.83E+00
Wt_{21}^i	6.35E+01	-1.65E-01	1.27E+00	4.27E+01	Wt_{49}^i	8.45E+01	5.23E+00	1.30E-02	5.03E-01
Wt_{22}^i	-6.65E-03	-2.13E-01	3.14E-01	-9.17E+01	Wt_{50}^i	2.59E+00	-4.87E+00	1.60E-03	-2.83E-02
Wt_{23}^i	-9.26E-04	-1.76E+00	3.74E-01	-2.96E-01	Wt_{51}^i	-3.35E-03	2.10E-01	2.37E+00	-1.41E-02
Wt_{24}^i	-4.18E-05	7.69E-00	5.29E-07	-5.77E-01	Wt_{52}^i	2.19E-01	-4.51E+00	-6.81E-03	-1.02E-01
Wt_{25}^i	5.86E-01	7.43E-00	2.42E-02	1.03E-02	Wt_{53}^i	8.20E-02	1.17E+00	3.83E-01	-2.67E+00
Wt_{26}^i	-1.67E-02	8.14E+00	-5.84E-02	-7.89E-01	Wt_{54}^i	-3.86E-01	-8.26E-01	2.79E-01	1.43E-02
Wt_{27}^i	4.18E-01	1.30E-02	9.00E+01	-1.44E+00	Wt_{55}^i	-2.83E-01	-4.37E+00	7.58E-01	-1.14E+02
Wt_{28}^i	8.94E+00	-2.77E-01	3.61E-03	-5.76E-01	Wt_{56}^i	6.35E-02	5.91E-01	1.03E-01	-1.22E+00
B_1^i	-3.85E+00	7.28E-03	1.85E-01	2.03E-01	Wt_1^o	-6.67E-01	-4.38E-01	6.90E-01	-3.68E+01
B_2^i	1.85E-05	-2.00E+00	-1.77E-02	1.35E-01	Wt_2^o	-4.52E+00	-1.63E-02	-1.21E+00	-6.55E-01
B_3^i	-8.02E-02	-5.82E-01	4.75E-01	-7.41E-02	Wt_3^o	2.85E+00	-7.33E-02	6.94E-02	-2.24E-01
B_4^i	1.08E+01	-1.47E+00	1.78E-03	2.48E-01	Wt_4^o	1.56E-03	1.84E+00	1.95E-03	-1.59E+00
B_5^i	-5.81E+00	3.63E-01	9.90E-03	5.11E-02	Wt_5^o	-5.26E-03	-2.91E+00	-1.54E-02	-6.07E+00
B_6^i	5.51E-01	1.05E-02	3.23E-03	5.75E+00	Wt_6^o	-4.04E-02	-2.57E+00	-6.10E-01	-3.24E+00
B_7^i	-8.02E-02	1.11E+00	-8.46E-03	-3.57E+00	Wt_7^o	5.01E-03	-5.55E-01	2.03E-01	-4.36E-01

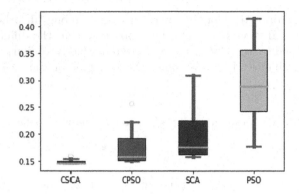

Fig. 3. Boxplot of diabetic classification

Table 2. Performance metrics of CSCA, CPSO, SCA and PSO for diabetic classification

Algorithms	Fitness values	Accuracy	Computational time
CSCA	0.1461	95.2124	17.91
CPSO	0.1507	78.5421	18.20
SCA	0.1584	72.1456	19.65
PSO	0.1689	61.6576	20.16

Table 3. Performance evaluation of CSCA, CPSO, SCA and PSO for diabetic classification

Algorithms	CSCA	CPSO	SCA	PSO
Best	0.1461	0.1507	0.1584	0.1689
Mean	0.1489	0.1779	0.1993	0.2963
Worst	0.1633	0.2864	0.3210	0.4212
Median	0.1465	0.1576	0.1759	0.2888
Standard	0.0043	0.0366	0.0467	0.0731
Variance	1.9045	0.0013	0.0021	0.0053

8   Conclusion and Future Direction

In this research, we suggested a brand-new algorithm called CSCA that combines the recently created optimization method known as SCA with chaotic behaviour. We have used the Pima Indian diabetic dataset to test the performance of the proposed algorithm. The simulation analysis suggests that the CSCA method is better than other algorithms. Additionally, the simulation's findings suggest that chaos has a stronger ability to locate global optimums quickly. The limitations of this study may be that there is no assurance that the classification techniques used in this study, which have acceptable accuracy for the Pima Indian Diabetes Dataset, will also have the same coherency for other datasets of this type. Despite the offered method's many benefits, researchers should adapt and use new optimization techniques to continuously improve the present answers.

References

1. Hasan, M.K., Alam, M.A., Das, D., Hossain, E., Hasan, M.: Diabetes prediction using ensembling of different machine learning classifiers. IEEE Access **8**, 76516–76531 (2020)
2. Khanam, J.J., Foo, S.Y.: A comparison of machine learning algorithms for diabetes prediction. ICT Express **7**(4), 432–439 (2021)
3. Yahyaoui, A., Jamil, A., Rasheed, J., Yesiltepe, M.: A decision support system for diabetes prediction using machine learning and deep learning techniques. In: 2019 1st International Informatics and Software Engineering Conference (UBMYK), pp. 1–4. IEEE (2019)
4. Ghadami, N., et al.: Implementation of solar energy in smart cities using an integration of artificial neural network, photovoltaic system and classical delphi methods. Sustain. Cities Soc. **74**, 103149 (2021)
5. Kurani, A., Doshi, P., Vakharia, A., Shah, M.: A comprehensive comparative study of artificial neural network (ann) and support vector machines (svm) on stock forecasting. Annals Data Sci. **8**, 1–26 (2021)
6. Amarapur, B., et al.: Computer-aided diagnosis applied to MRI images of brain tumor using cognition based modified level set and optimized ANN classifier. Multimedia Tools Appl. **79**(5), 3571–3599 (2020)
7. Ramirez, R., et al.: Prediction and interpretation of cancer survival using graph convolution neural networks. Methods **192**, 120–130 (2021)
8. Valdez, F., Vazquez, J.C., Melin, P.: A new hybrid method based on ACO and PSO with fuzzy dynamic parameter adaptation for modular neural networks optimization. In: Castillo, O., Melin, P. (eds.) Fuzzy Logic Hybrid Extensions of Neural and Optimization Algorithms: Theory and Applications. SCI, vol. 940, pp. 337–361. Springer, Cham (2021). https://doi.org/10.1007/978-3-030-68776-2_20
9. Sohrabi, P., Dehghani, H., Rafie, R.: Forecasting of WTI crude oil using combined ANN-whale optimization algorithm. Energy Sources Part B: Econ. Plann. Policy **17**(1), 2083728 (2022)
10. Hassib, E.M., El-Desouky, A.I., Labib, L.M., El-Kenawy, E.-S.M.: WOA + BRNN: an imbalanced big data classification framework using whale optimization and deep neural network. soft Comput. **24**, 5573–5592 (2020)
11. Ya, S., Dai, Y., Liu, Y.: A hybrid parallel Harris hawks optimization algorithm for reusable launch vehicle reentry trajectory optimization with no-y zones. Soft. Comput. **25**, 14597–14617 (2021)
12. Haghnegahdar, L., Wang, Y.: A whale optimization algorithm-trained artificial neural network for smart grid cyber intrusion detection. Neural Comput. Appl. **32**, 9427–9441 (2020)
13. Lenin, K.: Real power loss reduction by duponchelia fovealis opti- mization and enriched squirrel search optimization algorithms. Soft. Comput. **24**(23), 17863–17873 (2020)
14. Mirjalili, S.: SCA: a sine cosine algorithm for solving optimization problems. Knowl.-Based Syst. **96**, 120–133 (2016)

15. Neggaz, N., Ewees, A.A., Elaziz, M.A., Mafarja, M.: Boosting salp swarm algorithm by sine cosine algorithm and disrupt operator for feature selection. Expert Syst. Appl. **145**, 113103 (2020)
16. Pashiri, R.T., Rostami, Y., Mahrami, M.: Spam detection through feature selection using artificial neural network and sine-cosine algorithm. Math. Sci. **14**(3), 193–199 (2020)
17. Tian, D., Zhao, X., Shi, Z.: Chaotic particle swarm optimization with sigmoid-based acceleration coefficients for numerical function optimization. Swarm Evol. Comput. **51**, 100573 (2019)
18. Sayed, G.I., Darwish, A., Hassanien, A.E.: A new chaotic whale optimization algorithm for features selection. J. Classification **35**(2), 300–344 (2018)
19. Gao, S., Yang, Yu., Wang, Y., Wang, J., Cheng, J., Zhou, M.C.: Chaotic local search-based differential evolution algorithms for optimization. IEEE Trans. Syst. Man Cybern. Syst. **51**(6), 3954–3967 (2019)
20. Yang, L., Xin, H., Wang, H., Zhang, W., Huang, K., Wang, D.: An ACO-based clustering algorithm with chaotic function mapping. Int. J. Cogn. Inf. Nat. Intell. (IJCINI) **15**(4), 1–21 (2021)
21. Kennedy, J., Eberhart, R.: Particle swarm optimization. In: Proceedings of ICNN1995-International Conference on Neural Networks, vol. 4, pp. 1942–1948. IEEE (1995)
22. Farahani, M., Ganjefar, S., Alizadeh, M.: PID controller adjustment using chaotic optimisation algorithm for multi-area load frequency control. IET Control Theory Appl. **6**(13), 1984–1992 (2012)
23. Arora, S., Anand, P.: Chaotic grasshopper optimization algorithm for global optimization. Neural Comput. Appl. **31**(8), 4385–4405 (2019)

A Deep CNN Framework for Oral Cancer Detection Using Histopathology Dataset

Mahamuda Sultana[1]([✉]) [iD], Suman Bhattacharya[1] [iD], Ananjan Maiti[1], Adarsh Pandey[1], and Diganta Sengupta[2] [iD]

[1] Guru Nanak Institute of Technology, Kolkata 700114, India
`falsesg.mahamuda@gmail.com`
[2] Meghnad Saha Institute of Technology, Kolkata 700150, India
`sg.diganta@ieee.org`

Abstract. One of the most common oncological types is oral cancer. Although medical technology has advanced at a phenomenal rate, high fatality has been observed in developing countries due to the lack of early stage diagnosis of the disease. The most fundamental symptom being the prolonged inflammation in the mouth areas. Cancers in the tongue, lips, cheeks, the floor of the mouth, hard and soft palates, sinuses, and pharynx (throat) are all considered oral cancers. This study focuses on early stage diagnosis of the disease using deep learning frameworks. It will offer a more thorough understanding of the disease and help experts make judgments about diagnostic and treatment options that are well-versed. We have used a deep learning framework based on the modified Convolutional Neural Network (CNN) that uses different sizes of hidden layers. The dataset comprised histopathology images. Histopathology datasets have the potential to transform the field of medical research. By feeding a histopathology dataset into a deep-learning framework, researchers can rapidly and precisely classify patterns in the data that would otherwise be difficult or impossible to detect. It could lead to faster diagnosis of diseases and more effective treatments. A total of 8000 images (4000 for each category of the cancers) are used for result analysis. Per epoch, the testing loss likewise diminishes gradually. As a final result, at 30 epochs, it has reached the highest accuracy of 97.6%. The convolutional neural network exhibits result which fare better than peer proposals in literature.

Keywords: Oral Cancer · Convolution Neural Network · Histopathology dataset · Deep learning

1 Introduction

The 6th most widespread cancer worldwide is oral cancer [1]. The World Health Organization estimates more than 3 30,000 fatal cases and 6 57,000 new cancers of the oral cavity and pharynx per year [2] Oral cancer (OC) is one of the most common cancers in India accounting for a mortality rate of 50–70% of total cancer fatalities, and Asian countries [3] have the highest incidence record. Lesions can be observed in the floor of

© The Author(s), under exclusive license to Springer Nature Switzerland AG 2024
K. Dasgupta et al. (Eds.): CICBA 2023, CCIS 1955, pp. 239–248, 2024.
https://doi.org/10.1007/978-3-031-48876-4_18

the mouth, tongues, cheek, gingiva, and any other oral cavity. There is a significant difference in cancer incidence in the oral cavity at the global scale. The primitive symptom of oral cancer can be the inflammation or swelling of the mouth.

It could be life-threatening if not detected and treated right away. The first detection makes treating oral cancer considerably simpler for medical professionals. But for most patients, the diagnosis comes too late for effective treatment. This invention aims to identify Oral Cancer as early as possible so that there are negligible chances of any severity and maximum time for treatment. Oral cancer has a high mortality rate mainly because of its late detection. We have tried to reduce the workload on our health workers and give faster results than the present methods. This study presents a workable and practical solution to detect oral cancer using histopathologic images. As we know that histopathology datasets has the potential to revolutionize the field of medical research. By feeding a histopathology dataset into a deep-learning framework, researchers can quickly and accurately identify patterns in the data that would otherwise be difficult or impossible to detect. It could lead to faster diagnosis of diseases and more effective treatments. Additionally, it could help researchers better understand diseases' underlying biology and develop new therapies. Deep learning can also help reduce costs associated with medical research, as it reduces the need for manual labor and increases efficiency.

We have developed a modified CNN algorithm to identify oral cancer patients using a validated dataset of verbal histopathologic images. This study also aims to create a deep-learning model that can reliably identify malignancies in people with oral cancer. It will provide a more thorough understanding of the disease and help professionals make judgments about diagnostic and treatment options that are more informed. Additionally, this study will shed light on the efficiency of convolutional neural networks for medical image interpretation applications.

A deep CNN framework will determine whether the image is cancerous or non-cancerous. The modified CNN model is responsible for cancer detection. We have trained the model for detecting oral cancer using Kaggle Oral Cancer Dataset [4]. This model exhibits fair better than the previous model and is economically more advantageous. Next, we take the dataset we want to test and send it to the server where the proposed model classifies the wound as cancerous or non-cancerous. A total of 8000 images are fed to the system, 4000 images for cancerous and 4000 for non-cancerous, and the train test ratio is 80%–20%. Also, we observe an accuracy of 97.6%. Rest of the paper are as follows: Related Work, Proposed Work, Experimental Results and Conclusion.

2 Related Work

This section provides the latest literary proposals in detection of oral cancer. The authors in [5] have constructed automated systems using deep learning frameworks where bounding box annotations are tackled through Two image processing algorithms using computer vision have been used for automatic detection of the oral wounds and subsequent categorization of the same.

In [6], Primary attention is received in the literature on image-based automatic oral cancer diagnosis using specialized imaging methods. On the other hand, several studies have been carried out using white-light photographic pictures, most of which concentrate on detecting particular categories of oral lesions. This study evaluated the prospects of an automated system for recognizing potentially oral malignant illnesses. In [7], a survey is carried out. These nine publications are taken for analysis. The research reporting on using A.I. for Oral Cancer diagnosis and outcome prediction revealed a tendency toward a progressive increase. Patients can be guided by sound information, and well-informed choices can drive professionals. The authors in [8] clip the tissue-index transmission patches from the sub-epithelium region. The images of these regions are then processed generating the spatial-deformation dynamics. The intrinsic anisotropic geometry and the local contour connectivity are kept within clinically acceptable limits. The prediction model's accuracy is tested on a corpus of TITP samples, gathered experimentally, and confirmatory data statistics and analysis support its inter-class segregation effectiveness. In [9], the authors predicted the survival chances of patients through analysis of oral squamous cell carcinoma using deep learning frameworks. The used a dataset comprising of data collected form 255 patients through 2000 and 2017. Analysis of tongue cancer using deep learning was done in [10] using a dataset generated through oral endoscopy. Several deep learning models using convolutional neural networks were used for predicting the likelihood of the cancer. The authors observed that DenseNet169 produced the best results. Convolutional neural networks have been used in [11] too.

The authors in [12] evaluated the salivary fern pattern for oral cancer assessment. The evaluation was based on multifractal-based statistical method. Images for the fern pattern of the dried saliva formed the dataset. The images were captured using stereo-zoom microscope. Studies in [13] and [14] examined the use of artificial intelligence in diagnosis of early stage oral cancer including gender bias. The authors in [15] focused on image acquisition for better use of artificial intelligence models. The authors studied different types of imagery based on low cost cameras to smartphone-based imaging. A similar approach has been done in [16] where the authors use smartphone-based imaging to feed into the deep learning frameworks. The research work [17] of Mohammed Shamim contributes in three different ways. First, an AI-based technology can automatically identify oral pre-cancerous tongue wounds from medical annotated taken images. Pre-trained deep convolutional neural networks such as VGG19, and ResNet50 have exhibited appreciable results in classifying tongue wounds. Other notable contributions in oral cancer diagnosis have been proposed in [18] and [19], where the authors compare multiple machine learning models for classifying oral cancer.

3   Proposed Work

In this study, we have found different ways to explore oral cancer diseases to make effective computer-aided diagnoses. There are various ways to design deep learning models. The model was designed to identify the histopathological images of oral cancers. Here we have preprocessed images acquired from the available data set. The data set consisted of 4000 images of each type of cancer and non-cancer histopathological images. Designing this model was challenging because there can be many image variations here.

Here these methods are used automatically; each technique has been tested repeatedly and used the appropriate amount of hyperparameters.

The architecture of CNN systems is made up of three layers: input, hidden, and output. The input layer consists of the images that the system will analyze. The output layer then converts this representation into an action or prediction. The hidden layer is a set of artificial neurons that process input data. The output layer is connected to all hidden layers. Appropriately organizing the hidden layers is a challenging endeavor. When using the approach, there are numerous hyperparameters. The test was conducted by varying the number and order of such Activation layers, Batch sizes, and different combinations of layer kinds. The proposed model is implemented from a convolution neural network model by adding different hidden layers, activation functions, and kernel filters by varying input with neurons. This CNN model can recognize patterns in oral cancer images through convolutional layers that extract features from the input image by applying filters. These filters are then followed by pooling layers that reduce the feature map's size while preserving vital elements from the input image. Finally, the output from these layers is fed into fully-connected layers, which classify the extracted features.

This model consists of convolutional layers, pooling layers, and fully-connected layers, which are connected in a specific way. The convolutional layers are responsible for extracting features from the input image. The pooling layers reduce the dimensionality of the feature maps. The fully-connected layers are then used to map these features to their corresponding oral cancer classes.

This paper uses a histopathology dataset fed into a deep-learning framework for oral cancer detection. The proposed framework is based on the Convolutional Neural Network (CNN) and uses different sizes of hidden layers. Those layers are visible below Fig. 1.

3.1 Data Augmentation

Data or image augmentation is a critical part where images are reformed and altered according to the requirement of the problem. Oral cancer images have distinct patterns between cancer and noncancerous images. First, image augmentations are done on cancer and noncancerous images. The steps are listed below.

1 Center crop the images
2 There's also some randomness introduced on where and how it crops for data augmentation
3 Color space augmentations
4 Image resize

3.2 Conv2D Layer

It is the convolutional layer, the Conv2D layer, operating on two oral cancer image dimensions. The advantage of this layer is that it works by filtering the image outputs from the layer above it. It has helped process an oral cancer feature map used in multi-channel image classification that records features in various parts of the oral cancer images. This oral cancer image filter's parameters, or "weights," are determined by the data collected during the training phase.

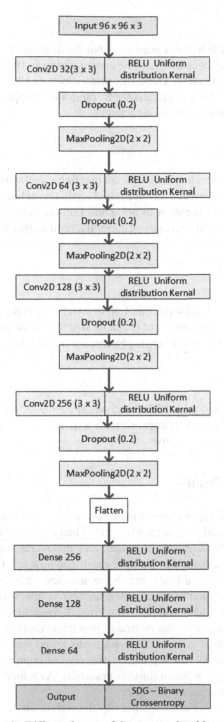

Fig. 1. Different layers of the proposed architecture

3.3 Drop-Out Layer

During the training of CNN, it has been seen that the dropout layer is an essential part of the neural network. It has been used to prevent over-fitting and improve generalization for oral cancer image classification. There are various reasons CNN has a higher chance of generalizing, and that has to reduce variance by randomly dropping out a few information of nodes from the hidden layers during training.

3.4 Max Pooling Layer

The proposed CNN architecture is significant and helps deal with information extracted from each hidden layer. Researchers have relied on this layer because this layer has some functionalities. This layer is robust to noise and outliers in the oral cancer data, which means it does not need clean data to work correctly, unlike other layers like convolutional or fully-connected layers.

3.5 Flatten

It is an essential part of developing this CNN model. It accepts a vector of oral cancer images as input and returns a vector of the same size in a single column. It can transform a fully-connected network into a single channel for dense node connectivity.

3.6 Dense

Input nodes are processed with RELU activation functions during deep learning; the model is typically a deep neural network with a dense layer. Here, the input image of oral cancer is output to a dense layer.

4 Experimental Results

Using a variety of techniques, researchers have discovered a CNN-modified alternative. Nonetheless, it is only a question of time. Thus a handful of solutions have been evaluated. The computer hardware is tested, and the average result is determined by repeatedly executing the software. We have examined how this CNN has read and processed each epoch. Described below are the various test findings. The suggested CNN model's accuracy is assessed in epochs. Researchers have verified the accuracy, which is the likelihood that a model's output would match the actual outcome. Compared to other models, this one has a higher degree of precision, despite not being evaluated on real-time photos. The total number of photographs tested was 4000 for each category. Passing of epochs across all training data is observed to improve accuracy steadily. Per epoch, the testing loss likewise diminishes gradually. As a final result, at 30 epochs, it has reached the highest accuracy of 97.6%.

The performance of this model is heavily dependent on the hyperparameters used to train them. Therefore, tuning these hyperparameters to achieve optimal performance from the model is essential.

This paper will explore different hyperparameter tuning techniques and optimizers that can use for deep learning models, such as the popular Oral Cancer Detection CNN Model. We have studied these techniques can be applied to improve the model's accuracy and reduce its training time. Furthermore, we will look at best practices for choosing an appropriate optimizer for a given deep-learning task (Fig. 2), (Fig. 3), (Table 1)

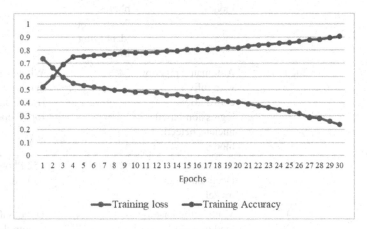

Fig. 2. Cross entropy loss and accuracy obtained per epochs passed during the training phase

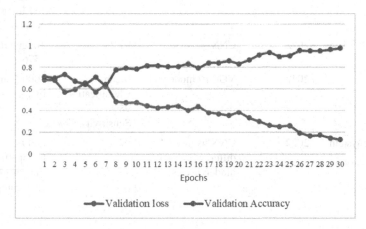

Fig. 3. Cross entropy and accuracy obtained per epochs passed during the validation phase

Table 1. Comparison with existing models

References	Year of publication	Framework Used	Accuracy	Dataset Used
[5]	2020	ResNet-101and Faster R-CNN model	87.07% for identifying photos 78.30% for identifying images	1433 Oral images
[18]	2020	Automated pipeline with fully convolution regression-based nucleus detection model	84%	Whole side cytology images (Batch size of 512 for 50 epochs)
[6]	2021	Two stage Deep-learning model	92.9%	652 Photographic images
[12]	2021	Multifactral based methodology	-	Dried Saliva captured by stereo-zoom microscope and 151 images are generated
[10]	2022	CNN	91.7%	Tongue images of 5576
[17]	2022	VGG19 model	Mean Classification 98% Sensitivity 89%	1000 Tongue images
Proposed System	2022	CNN using different sizes of hidden layers	97.6%	8000 histopathology images (4000 of each category)

5 Conclusion

This study detects oral cancer using histopathology data. The model automatically assists the classifiers in determining the image state by deriving a set of features. We also applied several artificial intelligence techniques to the datasets and compared the results. This study proposed a deep learning-based approach to identify and categorize 8000 oral cancer histopathology pictures. This method compares the results of classifying the produced features using a CNN with 16 hidden layers. Also, it shows that oral cancer stages can be reliably categorized within 30 epochs. Therefore, this new CNN model is more effective at classifying the various forms of oral cancer.

To summarize, it has been reported this CNN's oral cancer screening has surpassed the previous standard of 5% accuracy and is continuing to improve. The current experiment used the oral cancer dataset and was successful to the tune of 97.6%. In addition, we have evaluated the performance of our model on different datasets and compared it with existing methods. Our results indicate that CNNs can effectively detect oral cancer with a high accuracy rate. Furthermore, we have discussed some potential limitations of this approach and how they can be addressed in future research. With improved feature engineering and a more efficient method of CNN learning, oral cancer prognosis predictions will improve in the future. This work will provide valuable insights into the possible use of CNNs for oral cancer detection.

References

1. Boring, C.C., Squires, T.S., Tong, T.: Clin, J.: Cancer Statistics, in CA Cancer **42**, 19–38 (1992)
2. Oral health, The WHO, 18 November 2022. https://www.who.int/news-room/fact-sheets/det ail/oral-health. Accessed 2 Dec 2022
3. SP, K., PS, B., RR, T.: Oral cancer and some epidemiological factors: a hospital based study. Indian J Community Med (2006)
4. www.kaggle.com, Kaggle (2018). https://www.kaggle.com/competitions/histopathologic-cancer-detection/overview. Accessed 1 Nov 2022
5. Welikala, R.A., et al.: Automated detection and classification of oral lesions using deep learning for early detection of oral cancer. IEEE **8**, 132677–132693 (2020)
6. Tanriver, G., Tekkesin, M.S., Ergen, O.: Automated detection and classification of oral lesions using deep learning to detect oral potentially malignant disorders. Cancers **13**(11), 1–13 (2021)
7. Khanagar, S.B., et al.: Application and performance of artificial intelligence technology in oral cancer diagnosis and prediction of prognosis: a systematic review. Diagnostics **11**(1004), 1–12 (2021)
8. Nawn, D., et al.: Multiracial alterations in oral sub-epithelial connective tissue during progression of pre-cancer and cancer assessment. IEEE J. Biomed. Health Inform. **25**(1), 1–10 (2021)
9. Kim, D.W., Lee, S., Kwon, S., Nam, W., Cha, I.-H., Kim, H.J.: Deep learning-based survival prediction of oral cancer patients. Sci. Rep. **9**(6994), 1–10 (2019)
10. Heo, J., et al.: Deep learning model for tongue cancer diagnosis using endoscopic images. Sci. Rep. **12**(6281), 1–10 (2022)
11. Zhang, H., Li, W., Zhang, H.: An image recognition framework for oral cancer cells. J. Healthcare Eng. **2021**(2449128), 1–8 (2021)
12. Sharma, N., et al.: Multifractal texture analysis of salivary fern pattern for oral pre-cancers and cancer assessment. IEEE Sens. J. **21**(7), 9333–9340 (2021)
13. Al-Rawi, N., et al.: The effectiveness of artificial intelligence in detection. Int. Dent. J. **72**(4), 436–447 (2022)
14. Alzabibi, M.A., et al.: Oral cancer knowledge and practice among medical students: a cross-sectional study during the Syrian crisis. Ann. Med. Surg. **77**, 1–6 (2022)
15. Ilhan, B., Lin, K., Wilder-Smith, P.: Improving oral cancer outcomes with imaging and artificial intelligence. J. Dent. Res. **99**(3), 241–248 (2020)
16. Lin, H., Chen, H., Weng, L., Shao, J., Lin, J.: Automatic detection of oral cancer in smartphone-based images using deep learning for early diagnosis. J. Biomed. Opt. **26**(8), 1–16 (2021)

17. Shamim, M., Syed, S., Shiblee, M., Usman, M., Ali, S.: Automated detection of oral pre-cancerous tongue lesions using deep learning for early diagnosis of oral cavity cancer. Comput. J. **65**(1), 91–104 (2022)
18. Lu, J., Sladoje, N., Stark, C.R., Ramqvist, E.D., Hirsch, J.M., Lindblad, J.: A deep learning based pipeline for efficient oral cancer screening on whole slide images in ICIAR (2020). https://doi.org/10.1007/978-3-030-50516-5_22
19. Palaskar, R., Vyas, R., Khedekar, V., Palaskar, S., Sahu, P.: Transfer learning for oral cancer detection using microscopic images. Comput. Vis. Pattern Recognit. **1**, 1–8 (2021)

AntiNuclear Antibody Pattern Classification Using CNN with Small Dataset

Munakala Lohith, Soumi Bardhan, Oishila Bandyopadhyay(✉)(iD),
and Bhabotosh Chanda

Indian Institute of Information Technology Kalyani, Kalyani, India
{lohith_bt18,soumi_bt18,oishila}@iiitkalyani.ac.in

Abstract. Antinuclear antibody patterns are used as an important screening technique to diagnose autoimmune disorders. The rising prevalence of autoimmune conditions, such as connective tissue diseases, has resulted in an increase in the production of antinuclear antibodies (ANA). Unavailability of expert pathologist delay the analysis and interpretation of ANA patterns in many places. Automated analysis of ANA pattern can reduce the time of pathological investigation and help doctors to plan for the treatment. This work proposes a convolutional neural network based model that can classify the ANA pattern into four different categories - mitotic, nuclear, cytoplasmic, and negative. The model trained with relatively fewer number of samples has performed satisfactorily while being trained and tested with ANA dataset. It exhibits a relatively good F1 score of 0.97.

Keywords: Antinuclear antibody · Deep learning · Convolutional Neural Network · Autoimmune disorder · Immunofluorescence · ResNet50

1 Introduction

Antibodies are produced by an individual's immune system to protect the body from foreign viruses and bacteria in the blood stream. An antinuclear antibody attacks the cell's nucleus and destroy the body's healthy cells instead [16]. Antinuclear antibodies (ANA) illuminated by indirect immunofluorescence (IIF) serve as a gold standard for screening of individuals suspected with autoimmune disease. These antibodies develop against proteins bound to DNA, RNA and cytoplasm and can reflect the disease activity state [16]. International Consensus on ANA Patterns (ICAP) have classified the ANA patterns observed in indirect immunofluorescence assay in twenty nine subcategories grouped under four major categories [5]. The major categories includes - Negative (AC-0), Nuclear (AC-1 to AC-14, AC-29), Cytoplasmic (AC-15 to AC-23), and Mitotic (AC-24, AC-28). ANA screening process can be performed by expert pathologists and biochemists only. Unfortunately the availability of such experts to analyze, interpret and diagnose these patterns is not sufficient.

With the advancement in medical image processing and computer vision in the past few years, ANA patterns can be classified using deep learning models. Development of an automated pattern recognition system through validated deep learning models would help recognize the ICAP patterns and may reduce the subjectivity factor and harmonize

K. Dasgupta et al. (Eds.): CICBA 2023, CCIS 1955, pp. 249–260, 2024.
https://doi.org/10.1007/978-3-031-48876-4_19

this technique. This would also help in getting reports within a reasonable time limit as there are only a few experts available in India. The main objective of this work is to develop a convolutional neural network based model to classify ANA pattern into four major categories - Mitotic, Nuclear, Cytoplasmic, and Negative. The proposed classifier is developed based on the images collected from https://www.anapatterns.org/ [15]. As the size of the dataset is relatively small and data imbalance is also present among different categories and subcategories, image entropy based pre-processing algorithm is developed to reduce data imbalance. The proposed architecture has exhibited a relatively good accuracy of 0.97 with test data.

2 Literature Survey

Antinuclear antibody (ANA) patterns play an important role in diagnosis and monitoring of several autoimmune diseases, particularly systemic autoimmune diseases (SAIDs). Automated analysis and classification of ANA patterns and development of diagnostic algorithms can help in fast diagnosis and monitoring of SAIDs. In the past few years, different research groups have proposed machine learning and artificial neural network (ANN) based classification models to identify ANA patterns.

Several clinical experts and biochemists all over the world have carried out detailed study on ANA patterns for the past few decades. Indirect ImmunoFluorescence (IIF) technique has been widely used for ANA determination. Detection of ANA positive cases and identification of different sub-patterns along with their clinical correlations are the main objective of most of these studies. The first International Consensus on ANA Patterns (ICAP), a subcommittee of Auto antibody Standardization Committee (ASC) was developed during the 12th International Workshop on Auto antibodies and Autoimmunity (IWAA) which was held in São Paulo, Brazil in 2014. Chan et al. [4] have reported the first consensus on the standardized nomenclature of ANA Hep-2 cell patterns. Development of gold standards to establish inter-laboratory standardization in ANA and identification of disease specific auto antibody testing are the main challenges to the researchers.

Automated classification of ANA patterns have gained interest among researchers working in the domain of medical image analysis and computer vision problems. The International Conference on Pattern Recognition (ICPR) arranged challenge on Hep-2 cell classification in 2012 and 2014. The ANA dataset published after these challenges are now used by researchers to develop the machine learning and AI based ANA classifiers. Qi et al. [17] have proposed a special shape index descriptor (SSID) for Hep-2 cell classifications. SSID utilized a texture classifier (local orientation adaptive descriptor) to capture spatial layout information of second-order structures. They have used the ICPR 2014 dataset for that work.

Nanda et al. [14] have reported the classification of ANA patterns and their relation with different SAIDs. The study of ANA patterns in the Indian population is reported by Gupta et al. [7,8]. Cascio et al. [2] have used a multi-layer deep neural network to extract the features of the segmented cell pattern. The extracted features are used by six support vector machines (SVM) followed by a K-nearest neighbour classifier to classify the ANA patterns. Hep-2 pre-segmented cells have been used for this work. They have reported an overall accuracy of 81.93% and mean class accuracy of 82.16% at cell level. Lin et al. [12] have proposed a deep neural network based on InceptionV3 architecture with 21 layers. They have used ANA images of Rheumatoid patients (81822 ANA images from 8839 patients) to train and test the model. The model successfully classified speckled, mitotic, nucleolar, centromere, dense fine speckled, cytoplasmic and mitochondrial patterns. Unavailability of different categories of ANA pattern is a major challenge for developing Convolutional Neural Network (CNN) based classification models. Gupta et al. [6] have proposed a CNN based feature extraction followed by SVM based classification of ANA patterns. Some approaches have also used deep network based model for feature extraction and SVM or random forest model for classification [3,6,11]. Mengchi et al. [13] have proposed a model that used pretrained VGGNet-A based feature extractor followed by SVM classifier to classify the HEp-2 stained patterns. They have reported 92% and 98% accuracy on ICPR2012 and ICPR2014 dataset respectively. It can be concluded that several ANA pattern classification techniques have been proposed based on different CNN based classifier models [3,6,10,11,19].

3 Methodology

The proposed approach includes dataset preprocessing, development of CNN model, training of the model with labeled dataset and finally, classification of ANA patterns using that model.

3.1 Dataset

Most of the ANA images are collected from https://www.anapatterns.org/ [15]. A dataset of 221 images are labeled under four categories-

- Nuclear: 112
- Cytoplasmic: 60
- Mitotic: 32
- Negative: 17

Figure 1 shows the sample image of each category. Dataset pre-processing algorithm is developed to prepare a balanced dataset that can be used to train and test the proposed model.

3.2 Dataset Preprocessing

The collected dataset has severely imbalanced images for each class, with the maximum number of images are available for Nuclear (112) and the minimum for Negative (17) category. Hence, to create a more balanced dataset, following algorithm is adopted.

   In Algorithm 12, each image (size $H \times W$, i.e. 700×400) is cropped into smaller windows (wdh $\times$ wdw with stride, i.e. 200×200 with stride 100) and entropy of each cropped part is computed. Entropy represents the measure of randomness associated with pixel intensity values belonging to a region. As per Shanon's definition and Pun's

---

Algorithm 1. Generate Dataset

1: **procedure** GENDATA(*Img*)
2:     Read Img
3:     Resize (Img,h,w)
4:     Entropy← Entropy(Img)
5:     imdata[]← Crop(Img, wdh, wdw, stride)
6:     j=0
7:     **for** (i=0 to size(imdata)) **do**
8:         loc_entropy← Entropy(imdata[i])
9:         **if** (loc_entropy > Entropy/4) **then**
10:             imres[j]← imdata[i]
11:             j← j+1
12:     return imres[]

---

representation of image entropy, for an image having G number of gray levels and probability of ith gray level P_i, the image entropy E can be computed as

$$E = \sum_{i=0}^{G-1} P_i log_2 \left(\frac{1}{P_i}\right) = -\sum_{i=0}^{G-1} P_i log_2 (P_i) \tag{1}$$

where $P_i = \frac{n_i}{H \times W}$ and n_i is the number of pixels with gray level i and H × W is the size of the image [1]. The cropped region with very low entropy value represents very little change in intensity values (homogeneous region). For ANA slides with black background, cropped widows with low entropy value represent the black region of original image with no change in intensity, i.e. without any useful cell information. Hence, the cropped images with very low entropy value (less than one-fourth of entropy of the input image) are removed from the final dataset. A total of 306 cropped images belonging to the Negative Class are generated using this approach. A balanced dataset of 1124 images is thus generated with each class having a total of 306 images. Different augmentations techniques such as rotation, scaling, shear, horizontal flip etc. are applied on each of the image of the dataset.

3.3 Proposed Architecture

In order to design an efficient convolutional neural network based classifier, experiments are performed with few modifications in layers of VGG16 [18] (model I) and Residual Network (ResNet) based model II and model III (ResNet50 and ResNet152 respectively) [9,18].

Model I. VGG16 [18] is a convolutional neural network with 16 layers depth. The model is pretrained with more than a million images from the ImageNet database [5]. While designing the CNN using VGG16 model (model I), the pretrained ImageNet weights for VGG16 [18] head with following variations in the final layers (as shown in Fig. 2) are introduced. In each case, ReLU is used as activation function and dropout of 0.3 and 0.5 are used to check the classification accuracy.

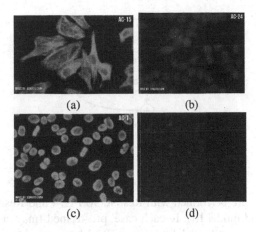

Fig. 1. ANA patterns (anapatterns.org): (a) Cytoplasmic, (b) Mitotic, (c) Nuclear, (d) Negative

- 512, 256, 128 dense layers with dropout
- 256, 128 dense layers with dropout
- 512, 256 dense layers with dropout
- 512, 128 dense layers with dropout

A triangular cyclic learning rate between 10^{-6} to 10^{-4} is used as learning rate to train the model. Categorical cross-entropy is used as the loss function. In each case, a dense 4 neuron layer with SoftMax as the activation function is used as final layer to classify 4 categories of ANA pattern (Cytoplasmic, Mitotic, Nuclear, and Negative).

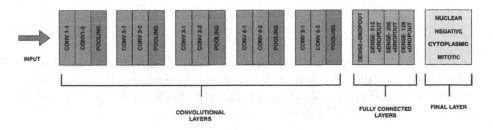

Fig. 2. Architecture of model I

Model II and Model III. Residual Network (ResNet) [9] relieved the problem of training very deep networks with the introduction of residual blocks with skip connections Fig. 3. Skip connection enables the network to move deeper without affecting the performance. Different variants of ResNet model are made up of these blocks.

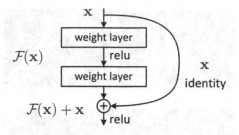

Fig. 3. Residual block

The experiments are performed with RestNet50 Fig. 4 and ResNet152 based CNN models (model II and model III). In each case, pre-trained Imagenet weights are used keeping the head of the each model the same. Final layer in each case is replaced with 512, 256, 128 dense layers with dropout (similar to changes in model I mentioned in Sect. 3.3.

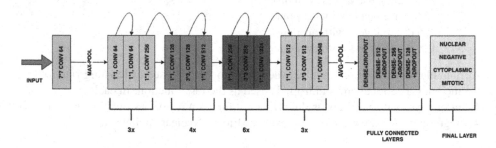

Fig. 4. Architecture of model II

Each model is trained for 40 epochs using a cyclic learning rate which varied between 10^{-6} and 10^{-4}. The best result was obtained from model II with a F1 Score of 0.97. Hence, in the proposed architecture, model II (ResNet50) based CNN model is used as the classifier for ANA patterns.

4   Experimental Result

Experiments have been performed on the dataset mentioned in Sect. 3.1. Pre-processing techniques are used to create a balanced dataset, as the distribution of collected images among different categories was imbalanced. After the balanced dataset is created, three different classifiers models (model I, model II, and model III respectively are trained on the augmented data using transfer learning. Stratified K-fold cross validation is applied for each of the split. The dataset is divided into 75% train and 25% test data which achieved the best results.

4.1   Results for Model I

Table 1 shows the results generated by model I. The training accuracy and the validation accuracy achieved by the model with K=6 fold are 0.688 and 0.80 respectively.

Table 1. Training results on model I (Best fold 6)

Class	Precision	Recall	F1-score
Cytoplasmic	0.94	0.98	0.96
Mitotic	0.90	0.71	0.79
Negative	0.89	0.96	0.92
Nuclear	0.84	0.92	0.88
Test Accuracy			0.89
Micro Avg	0.89	0.89	0.89
Weighted Avg	0.89	0.89	0.89

The Precision and Recall are best for the Cytoplasmic class at 0.94 and 0.96 respectively. The overall F1 score achieved here is 0.97.

Table 2. Confusion matrix for model I

	Cytoplasmic	Mitotic	Negative	Nuclear
Cytoplasmic	50	1	0	0
Mitotic	2	36	4	9
Negative	1	1	49	0
Nuclear	0	2	2	47

Table 2 shows the Confusion Matrix for the trained model I. The Mitotic cells are detected the worst as they get mis-classified into Nuclear images, while the other classes detect cells with good accuracy.

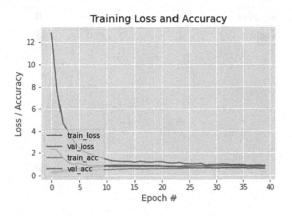

Fig. 5. Training Metrics for Model I

Figure 5 shows the training loss and accuracy curve for model I. The training accuracy of 0.6828 and validation accuracy of 0.8039 are achieved by this model.

4.2   Results for Model II

Table 3 shows the results generated by model II. The stratified K fold cross validation with K = 3 has shown the best results. The training Accuracy and the validation accuracy for the model are 0.922 and 0.825 respectively.

Table 3. Training results on model II (Best fold 3)

Class	Precision	Recall	F1-score
Cytoplasmic	0.93	1.00	0.96
Mitotic	0.98	0.94	0.96
Negative	1.00	1.00	1.00
Nuclear	0.98	0.94	0.96
Test Accuracy			0.97
Micro Avg	0.97	0.97	0.97
Weighted Avg	0.97	0.97	0.97

Table 4 shows the confusion matrix for the trained model II. The Mitotic cells are detected the worst as they get mis-classified into Nuclear images, while the other classes detect cells with good accuracy. Figure 6 shows the training loss and accuracy curve for the model. Training accuracy of 0.8273 and validation accuracy of 0.8627 are achieved with this model.

Table 4. Confusion matrix for model II

	Cytoplasmic	Mitotic	Negative	Nuclear
Cytoplasmic	51	0	0	0
Mitotic	2	48	0	1
Negative	0	0	51	0
Nuclear	2	1	0	48

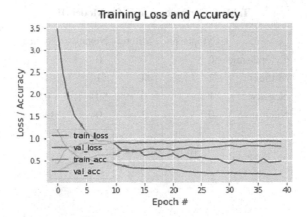

Fig. 6. Training Metrics for model II

4.3 Results for Model III

Table 5 shows the results generated by model III. The best performance has been observed with 3 fold data-split. The training accuracy and the validation accuracy achieve by the model are 0.8307 and 0.8824 respectively.

The Table 5 shows the confusion matrix for model III. The Mitotic cells are detected the worst as they get mis-classified into Nuclear images, while the other classes are detected with good accuracy.

Figure 7 shows the training loss and accuracy curve for the model. A training accuracy of 0.8262 and validation accuracy of 0.9020 are exhibited by this model.

As shown in these results, the model II has achieved best result with a Precision of **0.97**, Recall of **0.97** and F1 Score of **0.97** (Table 6).

Table 5. Training results on model III (Best fold 3)

Class	Precision	Recall	F1-score
Cytoplasmic	0.94	0.98	0.96
Mitotic	0.96	0.86	0.91
Negative	0.98	0.98	0.98
Nuclear	0.91	0.96	0.93
Test Accuracy			0.57
Micro Avg	0.95	0.95	0.95
Weighted Avg	0.95	0.95	0.95

Table 6. Confusion matrix for Model III

	Cytoplasmic	Mitotic	Negative	Nuclear
Cytoplasmic	50	0	0	1
Mitotic	2	44	1	4
Negative	1	0	50	0
Nuclear	0	2	0	49

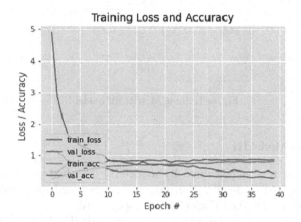

Fig. 7. Training Metrics for Model III

5   Conclusion

In this work, a CNN based model is proposed to perform classification of ANA pattern into four major categories - nuclear, cytoplasmic, mitotic and negative. Out of all the experiments, the ResNet50 based CNN Model has shown best performance in classifying ANA patterns. In order to resolve the data imbalance issue, image entropy based pre-processing technique is adopted. In the proposed design, the initial layers of ResNet50 pre-trained with the large ImageNet dataset, is used with modifications in final layer. This helps to overcome the problem arise with small dataset. To improve the current results, a more diverse mitotic cell distribution can be taken to train the model as mitotic patterns get classified as nuclear type because of the existence of similar looking cells between mitotic and nuclear. This work may be extended in future to classify subcategories of ANA pattern.

Acknowledgements. Ana pattern images are collected from http://www.anapatterns.org. Several clinical details and valuable suggestions regarding ANA pattern classification are received from Prof. Kalyan Goswami of AIIMS Kalyani and Prof. Rachita Nanda of AIIMS Raipur. We acknowledge them with thanks.

References

1. Bandyopadhyay, O., Chanda, B., Bhattacharya, B.B.: Entropy-Based Automatic Segmentation of Bones in Digital X-ray Images. In: Kuznetsov, S.O., Mandal, D.P., Kundu, M.K., Pal, S.K. (eds.) PReMI 2011. LNCS, vol. 6744, pp. 122–129. Springer, Heidelberg (2011). https://doi.org/10.1007/978-3-642-21786-9_22

2. Cascio, D., Taormina, V., Raso, G.: Deep CNN for IIF images classification in autoimmune diagnostics. Appl. Sci. **9**(8), 1618 (2019). https://doi.org/10.3390/app9081618

3. Cascio, D., Taormina, V., Raso, G.: Deep convolutional neural network for HEp-2 fluorescence intensity classification. Appl. Sci. **9**(3), 408 (2019). https://doi.org/10.3390/app9030408

4. Chan, E., et al.: Report of the first international consensus on standardized nomenclature of antinuclear antibody HEp-2 cell patterns 2014–2015. Front. Immunol. **6**, 412 (2015). https://doi.org/10.3389/fimmu.2015.00412

5. Damoiseaux, J., Andrade, L., Carballo, O., Conrad, K., Francescantonio, P., Fritzler, M., et al.: Clinical relevance of HEp-2 indirect immunofluorescent patterns. The international consensus on ANA patterns (ICAP) perspective. Ann. Rheum. Dis. **78**(7), 879–889 (2019). https://doi.org/10.1136/annrheumdis-2018-214436

6. Gupta, K., Bhavsar, A., Sao, A.: CNN based mitotic HEp-2 cell image detection. In: International Conference on Bioimaging (2018). https://doi.org/10.5220/0006721501670174

7. Gupta, P., et al.: Antinuclear antibody profiling in patients of a tertiary care centre in central India. Indian J. Clin. Biochem. **36**(3), 345–352 (2021). https://doi.org/10.1007/s12291-020-00925-2

8. Gupta, P., Priya, R., Nanda, R., Patel, S., Mohapatra, E.: A hospital-based insight into the antinuclear antibody patterns in autoimmune disorders. J. Lab. Phys. **12**, 115–120 (2020)

9. He, K., et al.: Deep residual learning for image recognition. arXiv:1512.03385 [Cs] (2015). https://doi.org/arxiv.org/abs/1512.03385

10. Li, H., Huang, H., Zheng, W.S., Xie, X., Zhang, J.: HEp-2 specimen classification via deep CNNs and pattern histogram. In: 23rd International Conference on Pattern Recognition (ICPR), pp. 2145–2149 (2016)

11. Li, H., Shen, L., Zhou, X., Yu, S.: HEp-2 specimen classification with fully convolutional network. In: 23rd International Conference on Pattern Recognition (ICPR), pp. 96–100 (2016). https://doi.org/10.1109/ICPR.2016.7899615

12. Lin, C., et al.: Development and validation of a deep learning algorithm for classifying antinuclear antibody patterns in indirect immunofluorescence images. Ann. Rheum. Dis. **77**(2) (2018). https://doi.org/10.1136/annrheumdis-2018-eular.6635

13. Mengchi, L., Long, G., Xifeng, G., Qiang, L., Yin, J.: HEp-2 cell image classification method based on very deep convolutional networks with small datasets. In: Ninth International Conference on Digital Image Processing (ICDIP), vol. 10420 (2017). https://doi.org/10.1117/12.2282033

14. Nanda, R., Gupta, P., Patel, S., Shah, S., Mohapatra, E.: Uncommon antinuclear antibody patterns as diagnostic indicators. Clin. Biochem. **90**, 28–33 (2021). https://doi.org/10.1016/j.clinbiochem.2021.01.008

15. Ana Patterns (2022). https://www.anapatterns.org/trees-2021.php. Accessed 08 Jan 2022

16. Pisetsky, D., Lipsky, P.: New insights into the role of antinuclear antibodies in systemic lupus erythematosus. Nat. Rev. Rheumatol. **16**(10), 565–579 (2020). https://doi.org/10.1038/s41584-020-0480-7

17. Qi, X., Zhao, G., Chen, J., Pietikäinen, M.: Exploring illumination robust descriptors for human epithelial type 2 cell classification. Pattern Recogn. **60**, 420–429 (2016). https://doi.org/10.1016/j.patcog.2016.05.032

18. Simonyan, K., Zisserman, A.: Very deep convolutional networks for large-scale image recognition. arXiv:1409.1556 [Cs] (2015). https://doi.org/arxiv.org/abs/1409.1556

19. Gao, Z., et al.: HEp-2 cell image classification with deep convolutional neural networks. IEEE J. Biomed. Health Inform. **21**(2), 416–428 (2017). https://doi.org/10.1109/JBHI.2016. 2526603

Classification of Offensive Tweet in Marathi Language Using Machine Learning Models

Archana Kumari[1], Archana Garge[1], Priyanshu Raj[1], Gunjan Kumar[1(✉)],
Jyoti Prakash Singh[1], and Mohammad Alryalat[2]

[1] Department of Computer Science and Engineering,
National Institute of Technology Patna, Patna, Bihar, India
{archanak.ug19.cs,gargea.ug19.cs,priyanshur.ug19.cs,
gunjank.phd20.cs,jps}@nitp.ac.in
[2] Al-Balqa Applied University, Salt, Jordan

Abstract. Offensive language identification is essential to make social media a safe and clean place to share one's view. In this work, a model is proposed to automatically classify offensive tweets into offensive and not offensive classes of low-resource language. Marathi is spoken in Western India. Marathi being a low-resource language, lacks a comprehensive list of stopwords and proper stammer. To fill this gap, we created a list of stopwords for stopword removal and a list of suffixes to identify the root word in the Marathi language. Two different methods, Label Vectorizer and *term frequency-inverse document frequency* (TF-IDF) Vectorizer, are used to extract features from the text and then these features are used with six different conventional machine learning classifiers to classify a Marathi tweet into offensive or non-offensive.

Keywords: Offensive language · machine learning · stemmer · NLU · NLP · Low-Resource Language

1 Introduction

Social media platforms are widely used by many people to communicate their ideas and opinions. However, a significant portion of the content on these sites is negative and hateful, making them harmful to users. The ease of use and keyboards in various languages has resulted in tweets in one's regional language, such as Bengali, Odia, and Marathi. Therefore, it is essential to curb the spread of offensive language on these platforms. Marathi is the official language of the Indian state of Maharashtra. It ranks as the third most spoken language in India and is spoken by 83 million people nationwide. So people started posting posts in the regional language, and it automatically became easier for people to express their respective options. This language is also popular on social media platforms for better expression of thoughts and opinions by the local Marathi-speaking population. Despite having so much popularity, major technical work

K. Dasgupta et al. (Eds.): CICBA 2023, CCIS 1955, pp. 261–273, 2024.
https://doi.org/10.1007/978-3-031-48876-4_20

like analyzing sentiments and detecting hate speech is only concentrated on the English language. But as the usage of comments in these low-resource languages are being increasing it is high tune to develop tools and modules which can identify the negative and offensive comments in these languages. Pre-processing a comment written in any language is an essential task. One of the major pre-processing steps is the removal of stop words, which eliminates the words which are very frequently used and do not add any value to the classification task. Most of the high-resource languages, such as English, Hindi etc. have a comprehensive list of stop words. However, low-resource languages such as Marathi do not have a comprehensive list of stopwords. This motivated us to make a comprehensive list of stop words for Marathi. The second major pre-processing step is stemming the words to their root words, as many words in natural languages. According to Porter et al. [16], stemming involves converting the words back to their root form. Consider the word "play" it has different forms, like "playing" and "played". The different form of a single word is required to support grammatical correctness during human interaction on social media. However, this does not mean that they add any values, meaning or extra support in terms of root words. As for the literature survey, some stammers are created for the Devanagari script and Hindi language, whereas the Marathi language at minimal importance. The reason behind the availability of stammers for the Marathi language is its peculiar characteristics which are challenging for transfer learning as the fine-tuning-based approach. Considering the need for a proper stemmer and its Marathi language. We enhanced the existing stemmer with some more rules. After adding stopword lists and stemmer, we have tried to classify offensive tweets in Marathi. The major contributions are stated below.

– Created a list of stopwords for Marathi to remove the stopwords from Marathi tweets.
– Created a stemmer to get the proper root word from Marathi text.
– Classify the hate and offensive tweets in the Marathi language.

The rest of the paper is organised as follows: The relevant literature is presented in Sect. 2, and the approach is explained in Sect. 3. Section 4 contains a list of the experiment outcomes. Section 5 includes a description of the paper's discussion and conclusion.

2   Related Work

Much work has been done in the identification of hate speech in the English language [3,10–13] and Hinglish language [2,15,21,23,24]. Very few works have been done to identify the hate speech in regional languages such as Marathi, Gujrati and Maithili, so stemming in regional language [4–6,19,20,27] is not available. Several scholars proposed various methods for assessing the effectiveness and similarity of stemming algorithms. One of these was used by Saharia et al. [20]they propose the WSF to measure the strength of the stemming algorithm; they also propose the CSF and AWCF metrics to measure its accuracy. The study evaluated the robustness and precision of four alternative affix elimination-based stemming techniques to discover that all the techniques mentioned in their work are robust and heavy but less precise. But the Paice/Husk stemmer does not do as well as the other stemmers when it comes to getting the right stemmed words back to their root words and not mixing up different words in the same group. Patil et al. [16] surveyed the stemmers available for Indic languages. The building of stemmers for languages like Hindi, Marathi, Tamil, etc. is frequently done using rule-based and light-stemming techniques. To avoid the limitations of using just one technique, several researchers also employ hybrid approaches. For some Indian languages, the hybrid strategy is more accurate than the other methods. The techniques like dictionary lookup or hybrid approach need to be evaluated for the languages like Marathi, Hindi, etc. For effective information retrieval, they plan to create a stemmer for the Marathi language. Velankar et al. [25] has worked on the low-resource (Marathi and Hindi) languages and detected hate speech in these languages. The lack of data, particularly for regional languages in India such as Hindi, Tamil, and Marathi makes it difficult to detect hate and offensive speech. They focus on detecting hate speech and offensive language in Marathi and Hindi texts. They investigated several Deep Learning (DL) models such as Convolutional Neural Network (CNN), *Bidirectional Encoder Representations from Transformers* (BERT), and *Long Short-Term Memory* (LSTM). They evaluated these classifiers using the HASOC-2021 Marathi and Hindi hate-speech datasets. They showed that the best performances come from transformer-based models, but even the simplest models and fast-text embeddings achieve satisfactory outcomes. Similarly, with the normal hyper-parameter setting, the fundamental models outperform as compared to the BERT-based approach on the Hindi dataset. Velankar et al. [26] focus on the Marathi language languages. They have presented L3-CubeMahaHate a dataset on hate-speech with 25000 samples evenly distributed across four classes. They also conducted studies to gather baseline results on various DL models, such as CNN, BiLSTM, LSTM, and transformer models such as mBERT, IndicBERT, and RoBERT. The dataset is also examined using MahaBERT, MahaALBERT, and MahaRoBERTa, which are the three monolingual Marathi BERT models. For the LSTM-based and CNN-based approaches, the pre-train fast-text model performs best with its trainable counterpart both in four-class and two-class classifications. Giri et al. [8] For effective and precise data modelling, they change the words to the original form. They create an MTStemmer, a brand-new Marathi stemmer that focuses on removing suffixes in order to get to the base word form. Their created stemmer uses a multilevel method by taking into account both an auxiliary verb and gender-based suffixes. It is simple but still able to be efficient without disregarding the Marathi language's grammatical nuances. Regarding mapping to the base words, the stemmer's stemming appears to be extremely precise. Its work shows promising signs of developing similar engines for other Indic languages. Stemming is an important processing step that transformed the inflected words into base or root words before the morphological examination. Patil et al. [17] proposed a hybrid stemmer to analyze the sentiment of the political tweets in the Marathi language, which was developed using the look-up table, linguistic dictionary and rules. The average accuracy of 0.89 is obtained when examined on ten randomly selected samples of 1000 words in each sample. The tremendous increase in the performance of the proposed approach is due to the flawless prefix removal rules and optimal covering of all the rules used for the dataset in this task. The under and over-stemming error rates are less due to the ample size of entries in the work-stem dictionary. Compared to the abundance of text-based social media data analysis for offensive language, only a few studies have analyzed the content of social media in the regional language of India.

3   Methodology

This section outlines the proposed approach for creating the classification models to classify offensive language tweets in the Marathi language. The flow diagram of the proposed approach is shown in Fig. 1.

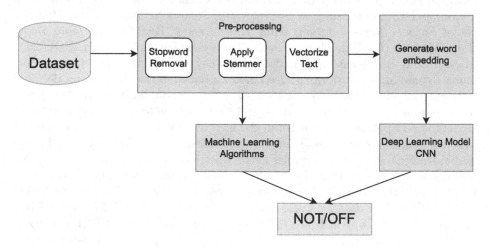

Fig. 1. Flow diagram of the proposed methodology

3.1   Data Description and Pre-processing

In this work, we used the dataset made available by Hate Speech and Offensive Content (HASOC) 2022 in Forum for Information Retrieval Evaluation (FIRE)[1]. One of the key goals connected with the dataset was to separate offensive and non-offensive Marathi language messages. Threats, insults, and remarks including any sort of untargeted vulgarity are examples of offensive postings. The tweets in the dataset are divided into two categories: OFF (posts having any

---

[1] https://hasocfire.github.io/hasoc/2022/dataset.html.

sort of offensive language (profanity) or a targeted offence, which can be veiled or direct) and NOT (posts that do not contain offence or profanity). The dataset contains a unique id for every tweet, having tweets in the Marathi language with their corresponding labels. Some sample of tweets along with their label is shown in Fig. 2. We perform classification into two classes NOT and OFF where NOT means non-offensive language and OFF means offensive language. The dataset contains a total of three tasks but our focus was only on subtask-a. The detailed description of the dataset is given in Table 1.

id	tweet	subtask_a
967	भाऊ संगमनेर तालुक्यातील गाव माझी साली जमीन बँक...	NOT
2389	मरू द्यात लोक नालायक	OFF
2169	ज्या एकाचा डोळा लाल झाला पूर्व नौसैनिक समजू शक...	OFF
1563	भाजपचे अंडभक्त आयटी सेल ह्यांना अत्यंत खालच्या...	OFF
1152	सिनियर पत्रकार एल्गार व्यक्त अव्यक्त भाग १ भेट...	NOT

Fig. 2. Sample of dataset

Table 1. Data statistics used in this study

Tweet Categories	No. of tweet per class
NOT	2029
OFF	1068
Total	3097

In the pre-processing step, to remove the stopwords from the text, we created the list of stopwords which is shown in Fig 3. We have used Label Encoder to encode target labels with values 0 and 1. Then we implemented logic for stemming Marathi words. We compiled a dictionary of Marathi words where each word is associated with its root word and suffix shown in Fig. 4. Using a list of gender-based and verb-based suffixes, we extracted the root word for each word of the dataset by slicing the possible suffix present in the word. The suffix of the Marathi word is sliced using Algorithm.1, and replacing the word with the root word. Then we transformed text to feature vectors that can be used as input to the estimator using TF-IDF and Label Vectorizer, then applied padding to the sequences for uniformity. In TF-IDF text data is converted into a vector form using the text vectorizer. The term frequency (TF) of a word refers to how frequently it appears in a document. The inverse document frequency (IDF), which attempts to lower the weight of a term if its occurrences differ from those in all the documents, determines the weight of a term.

आले,होते,तर,करत,असते,आहे,तो,एका,क,पल्लवी,काही,करावी,भी,हा,होऊन,होणार,जर,ह्या,जे,पाहिजे,ते,हे,व,पण

,जिथून,होत,तिथून,गेले,ठरेल,म्हणजे,एक,आता,म्हणे,आणि,तेच,आता,अँड,या,तरी,त्या,वा,यांना,त्याचं,झालेलं,ना,यांची

,करत,देणाऱ्या,जाताना,करून,येते,का,इथे,मिळाले,जेव्हा,या,का,की,असावे,आहेत,तो,कारण,करता,असे,लागल्यात,

ला,वर,असलेल्या,च,व,चे,व्हावे,पाहा,बघू,येतो,आपण,अशी,झालेलं,जातो,त्यात,मिळणार,अजून,बरं,मग,राहिला,काही,

कसली,समजणे,करत,ह्या,घेऊन,तिला,अन्,रे,तू,का,काय,मी,अरे,येते,यार,मात्र,मध्ये,फक्त,ज्यांनी,त्यांनी,आधी,किंवा,

परंत,सुद्धा,कसे,बापरे,बद्दल,प्रमाणे,वरून,असा,काढले,दे,झाली,कारण,किती,नक्कीच,एवढ्या,जरा,उर्फ,घेतला,जरी,

जाईल,जा,असेल,अहो,आता,जेव्हा,तेव्हा,असू,घ्या,द्या,नंतर,ऐवजी,एखादे,माहित,म्हणून,केले,करायची,नुसती,केल्याव

र,सुरू,होती,त्यामुळे,आली,तसेच,सर्व,न,येणार

Fig. 3. list of stop words in the Marathi language

3.2   Machine Learning Models

After preprocessing, we applied many algorithms for classifying the offensive tweet in Marathi Language and evaluated the results. We have applied various ML and DL models to obtain the baseline result on two-class (NOT and OFF) classification. We implemented six ML models (i) Random Forest (RF), (ii) AdaBoost (AB), (iii) Logistic Regression (LR), (iv) Support Vector Classifier (SVC), (v) Gradient Boosting (GB), and (vi) XGBoost (XGB), with two different methods of Vectorization TF-IDF and Label Vectorizer. To train the ML classifier, we split the dataset with 80% data taken as training data and 20% taken as testing data. The SVC model uses the "Radial basis function" (rbf) kernel with a random-state value of 1, and the RF Classifier model with a random-state value of 42, the n-jobs value of 1, the max-depth value of 5, the n-estimators value as 100, OOB-score value as True. The GB Classifier model uses the n-estimators value of 200, a learning-rate value of 1, max-depth value of 20. In contrast, the Decision Tree (DT) Classifier, which makes use of the "entropy" criterion and a max-depth value of 1, is the AB Classifier model with a base estimator from which the boosted ensemble was constructed. The classifier has an n-estimators value of 200 learning-rate value as 1. The XGB Classifier model with a base estimator from which the boosted ensemble is built is a DT Classifier that uses the "entropy" criterion and max-depth value as 1. The classifier has an n-estimators value of 200 learning-rate value as 1.

Word	Root-word	Suffix
दरबारात	दरबार	त
जिल्ह्यातील	जिल्हा	तील
चाळीसगावचे	चाळीसगाव	चे
भाजपचे	भाजप	चे
कविताच	कविता	च
इतिहासातील	इतिहास	तील
औरंगजेबशी	औरंगजेब	शी
आमच्याकडे	आमच्या	कडे
महाराष्ट्राची	महाराष्ट्र	ची

Fig. 4. Examples of suffixes in the Marathi language

3.3   Deep-Learning Models

In DL algorithms we have used CNN [22] with two types of embedding GloVe [18] of 100 dimensions for Marathi Language and fasttext [1] [14] (non-trainable) for the Marathi language and applied CNN with a combination of different size of filters and kernels ranging in the range of 100–500 filters and 2-5 filters respectively.

After that, we analyzed all combinations and chose the best model result to report. The CNN [9] model has an embedding layer with an output dimension of 100 and an input length of 30. Weight is set as an embedding matrix of 100 dimensions generated by the Word2vec technique. The embedding layer is followed by a 1-dimensional convolution layer having 300 filters of size 3. It used ReLU as an activation, with a global Max-pooling 1-D layer, and the dropout is 0.3 in each layer. The layer is followed by ReLU activation and a dense layer of size 50. In the final layer, we used one node, and the activation function is sigmoid. Binary cross entropy and adam optimizer were used during the compilation of the model. The hyper-parameter tuning of the CNN model is shown in Table 2.

Algorithm 1: Gender and verb-based suffix in the Marathi Language

---

Data: Marithi language words

Result: Root-word

begin

> 1. Define a function called *'marathi − stemmer'* that takes a sentence as input.;
> 2. Define a list of suffixes for each possible stem length.;
> 3. Define a maximum stem length.;
> **for** *Loop over each word in the sentence* **do**
>> a. Get the length of the word.;
>> b. Determine the starting point for stemming.;
>> **for** *Loop over possible stem lengths* **do**
>>> i. Set a flag to indicate if a suffix has been found.;
>>> ii. Get the list of suffixes for this stem length.;
>>> **for** *Loop over possible suffixes:* **do**
>>>> 1. Check if the word ends with the current suffix.;
>>>> 2. If a suffix is found, remove it from the word and store the result in *'stemmed − word'*.;
>>>> 3. Set the *'suffix − found'* flag to True.;
>>>> 4. Print a message indicating whether the suffix is verb-based or gender-based.;
>>>> 5. Stop looping over suffixes for this stem length.;
>>> **end**
>>> iv. If a suffix was found and removed, update the value of 'word' to be the stemmed version and move on to the next stem length.;
>> **end**
>> d. Update the value of the current word in the sentence to be the stemmed version.;
> **end**
> 5. Return the stemmed sentence.;

end

---

4   Result

The classification report of the conventional ML models is measured in terms of weighted Precision, Recall, and F_1-score. CNN is used for DL classification, while different classifications such as (i) SVC, (ii) LR, (iii) RF, (iv) GB, (v) AB, and (vi) XGB are used for traditional ML classification. The results for the ML models without stemming and with stemming are shown in Table 3, Table 4, Table 5 and Table 6, respectively. In the case of the Label-Vectorizor, AB performed best with the F_1-score of 0.92 for class 1 and 0.96 for class 0. In the case of a TF-IDF Vectorizer, XGB Boosting performed best with a F_1-score of 0.89 and 0.65 for classes 0 and 1, respectively. After applying the stemmer on the tweets extract the feature with the Label-Vectorizor and TF-IDF Vectorizer.

AB performs best among all with F_1-score of 0.95 and 0.90, respectively. In the case of TF-IDF Vectorizer, AB and RF performed best with a F_1-score of 0.93 and 0.85 for the class 0 and 1, respectively. We do not include the result of the CNN model because it did not perform well as compared to the ML models.

Table 2. Hyper-parameter tuning for training the CNN model

Parameters	Value
Optimizer	Adam
Activation function	Sigmoid, Relu
Loss	binary cross-entropy
Dropout	0.3
Epochs	100
Batch size	10
GlobalMaxPooling	1D

Table 3. Results without stemming with Label-Vectorizor

Models (Label Vectorizer)	class	Precision	Recall	F_1-score
Logistic	0	0.85	0.67	0.75
	1	0.28	0.50	0.36
SVM	0	0.81	0.75	0.78
	1	0.51	0.61	0.56
Random Forest	0	0.93	0.97	0.95
	1	0.95	0.87	0.90
XGB Boosting	0	0.91	0.97	0.94
	1	0.95	0.83	0.88
AdaBoost	0	**0.94**	**0.97**	**0.96**
	1	**0.95**	**0.89**	**0.92**
Gradient Boosting	0	0.95	0.94	0.95
	1	0.90	0.91	0.90

5   Discussion

Table 4. Results without stemming with TF-IDF Vectorizer

Models (TF-IDF Vectorizer)	class	Precision	Recall	F_1-score
Logistic	0	0.93	0.78	0.85
	1	0.48	0.78	0.60
SVC	0	0.94	0.79	0.86
	1	0.51	0.81	0.62
Random Forest	0	0.75	0.99	0.85
	1	0.96	0.31	0.47
XGB Boosting	0	**0.80**	**1.00**	**0.89**
	1	**0.98**	**0.49**	**0.65**
AdaBoost	0	0.80	0.87	0.83
	1	0.68	0.57	0.62
Gradient Boosting	0	0.85	0.82	0.83
	1	0.61	0.67	0.64

Table 5. Results after stemming with Label-Vectorizor

Models (Label Vectorizer)	class	Precision	Recall	F_1-score
Logistic	0	0.97	0.90	0.93
	1	0.78	0.94	0.85
SVC	0	0.83	0.78	0.80
	1	0.55	0.62	0.58
Random Forest	0	0.97	0.90	0.93
	1	0.78	0.94	0.85
XGB Boosting	0	0.94	0.92	0.93
	1	0.85	0.88	0.87
AdaBoost	0	**0.97**	**0.93**	**0.95**
	1	**0.87**	**0.93**	**0.90**
Gradient Boosting	0	0.95	0.93	0.94
	1	0.86	0.89	0.88

Table 6. Results after stemming with TF-IDF Vectorizer

Models (TF-IDF Vectorizer)	class	Precision	Recall	F_1-score
Logistic	0	0.95	0.81	0.87
	1	0.53	0.84	0.65
SVM	0	0.95	0.81	0.87
	1	0.53	0.84	0.65
Random Forest	0	**0.97**	**0.90**	**0.93**
	1	**0.78**	**0.94**	**0.85**
XGB Boosting	0	0.85	0.80	0.83
	1	0.56	0.65	0.60
AdaBoost	0	**0.97**	**0.90**	**0.93**
	1	**0.78**	**0.94**	**0.85**
Gradient Boosting	0	0.89	0.83	0.86
	1	0.89	0.83	0.86

The significant finding of this research is that the Label Vectorizer performed best before and after applying stemmer, which can be seen from Table 3 and Table 5. Another finding of this research is that the use of conventional ML classifiers such as SVC, LR, RF, AB, XGB, and GB, as compared to the DL model is better with AB outperforming best among all. In this research work, we only compared different ML and DL (CNN) approaches on Marathi datasets to identify the hate and offensive language available in the shared task HASOC-2021. The shared task consists of two-class and three-class classifications. In preprocessing part stopwords dictionary was created and used on dataset tweets, then stemming was done with the stemming algorithm proposed in this paper, and then a vectorizer was applied to tweets to convert them into the numerical format. For text vectorization, two techniques are used, Label vectorizer and TF-IDF vectorizer. For binary classification in Marathi task-1, CNN and ML-based models were used along with Glove 100-D Marathi embedding and FastText embeddings. CNN worked best with 100-D Glove embedding with an accuracy of 0.85 for the Marathi language. In the case of ML models, Boosting models were performing better, and the best model was the AB Classifier model, which gave us an accuracy of 0.94 for subtask-a. Label vectorizer gave us a better result than TF-IDF for our dataset because our dataset is small, and the context is domain specific. The context is extremely domain-specific, so it may not produce a suitable vector using pre-trained word embedding methods (GloVe, FastText, etc.). This is also why our ML Models are performing better than CNN. One of the limitations of this work is we are only trying to identify the root words after removing the verb-based and gender-based suffixes. We created the list of stopwords over the particular offensive dataset.

6   Conclusion

Analyzing tweets in a low-resource language is challenging because the stop-words and stemmer are unavailable in a low-resource language like Marathi. In this research, we created a stop word list and develop suffix and prefix-based rules to convert an inflated Marathi word to its root form. We used TF-IDF Vectorizer and Label Vectorizer to extract relevant features from the Marathi text. Conventional ML classifiers are used to classify whether the tweet is offensive or not. We found that AB performed better among all the ML classifiers and CNN. In the future, the proposed model can be tested with some other DL models. A generalized stemmer in the Marathi language can be developed and apply it to see the performance of the models in classifying offensive and hate text in the Marathi language from social media.

References

1. Athiwaratkun, B., Wilson, A.G., Anandkumar, A.: Probabilistic fasttext for multi-sense word embeddings. arXiv preprint arXiv:1806.02901 (2018)
2. Baruah, A., Das, K.A., Barbhuiya, F.A., Dey, K.: Iiitg-adbu@ hasoc-dravidian-codemix-fire2020: Offensive content detection in code-mixed Dravidian text. arXiv preprint arXiv:2107.14336 (2021)
3. Das, A., Wahi, J.S., Li, S.: Detecting hate speech in multi-modal memes. arXiv preprint arXiv:2012.14891 (2020)
4. Frakes, W.B., Baeza-Yates, R.: Information retrieval: data structures and algorithms. Prentice-Hall, Inc. (1992)
5. Frakes, W.B., Fox, C.J.: Strength and similarity of affix removal stemming algorithms. In: ACM SIGIR Forum, vol. 37, pp. 26–30. ACM, New York(2003)
6. Gaikwad, S., Ranasinghe, T., Zampieri, M., Homan, C.M.: Cross-lingual offensive language identification for low resource languages: The case of Marathi. arXiv preprint arXiv:2109.03552 (2021)
7. Gajbhiye, D., Deshpande, S., Ghante, P., Kale, A., Chaudhari, D.: Machine learning models for hate speech identification in Marathi language. In: Forum for Information Retrieval Evaluation (Working Notes)(FIRE), CEUR-WS. org (2021)
8. Giri, V., et al.: Mtstemmer: a multilevel stemmer for effective word pre-processing in Marathi. Turkish J. Comput. Mathem. Educ. (TURCOMAT) **12**(2), 1885–1894 (2021)
9. Jogin, M., Madhulika, M., Divya, G., Meghana, R., Apoorva, S., et al.: Feature extraction using convolution neural networks (CNN) and deep learning. In: 2018 3rd IEEE International Conference on Recent Trends in Electronics, Information & Communication Technology (RTEICT), pp. 2319–2323. IEEE (2018)
10. Kumar, G., Singh, J.P., Kumar, A.: A deep multi-modal neural network for the identification of hate speech from social media. In: Conference on e-Business, e-Services and e-Society, pp. 670–680. Springer (2021)
11. Kumari, K., Singh, J.P.: Identification of cyberbullying on multi-modal social media posts using genetic algorithm. Trans. Emerging Telecommun. Technol. **32**(2), e3907 (2021)
12. Kumari, K., Singh, J.P., Dwivedi, Y.K., Rana, N.P.: Multi-modal aggression identification using convolutional neural network and binary particle swarm optimization. Futur. Gener. Comput. Syst. **118**, 187–197 (2021)

13. Kumari, K., Singh, J.P., Dwivedi, Y.K., Rana, N.P.: Towards cyberbullying-free social media in smart cities: a unified multi-modal approach. Soft. Comput. **24**(15), 11059–11070 (2020)
14. Kuyumcu, B., Aksakalli, C., Delil, S.: An automated new approach in fast text classification (fasttext) a case study for Turkish text classification without pre-processing. In: Proceedings of the 2019 3rd International Conference on Natural Language Processing and Information Retrieval, pp. 1–4 (2019)
15. Pathak, V., Joshi, M., Joshi, P., Mundada, M., Joshi, T.: Kbcnmujal@ hasoc-dravidian-codemix-fire2020: using machine learning for detection of hate speech and offensive code-mixed social media text. arXiv preprint arXiv:2102.09866 (2021)
16. Patil, H.B., Pawar, B., Patil, A.S.: A comprehensive analysis of stemmers available for indic languages. Int. J. Nat. Lang. Comput **5**(1), 45–55 (2016)
17. Patil, R.S., Kolhe, S.R.: Inflectional and derivational hybrid stemmer for sentiment analysis: a case study with Marathi tweets. In: International Conference on Recent Trends in Image Processing and Pattern Recognition, pp. 263–279. Springer (2022). https://doi.org/10.1007/978-3-031-07005-1_23
18. Pennington, J., Socher, R., Manning, C.D.: Glove: global vectors for word representation. In: Proceedings of the 2014 conference on empirical methods in natural language processing (EMNLP), pp. 1532–1543 (2014)
19. Prajitha, U., Sreejith, C., Raj, P.R.: Lalitha: a lightweight Malayalam stemmer using the suffix stripping method. In: 2013 International Conference on Control Communication and Computing (ICCC), pp. 244–248. IEEE (2013)
20. Saharia, N., Konwar, K.M., Sharma, U., Kalita, J.K.: An improved stemming approach using HMM for a highly inflectional language. In: Gelbukh, A. (ed.) CICLing 2013. LNCS, vol. 7816, pp. 164–173. Springer, Heidelberg (2013). https://doi.org/10.1007/978-3-642-37247-6_14
21. Saumya, S., Kumar, A., Singh, J.P.: Offensive language identification in Dravidian code mixed social media text. In: Proceedings of the First Workshop on Speech and Language Technologies for Dravidian Languages, pp. 36–45 (2021)
22. Simonyan, K., Zisserman, A.: Very deep convolutional networks for large-scale image recognition. arXiv preprint arXiv:1409.1556 (2014)
23. Sreelakshmi, K., Premjith, B., Soman, K.: Detection of hate speech text in Hindi-English code-mixed data. Proc. Comput. Sci. **171**, 737–744 (2020)
24. Swaminathan, S., Ganesan, H.K., Pandiyarajan, R.: Hrs-techie@ dravidian-codemix and hasoc-fire2020: sentiment analysis and hate speech identification using machine learning deep learning and ensemble models. In: FIRE (Working Notes), pp. 241–252 (2020)
25. Velankar, A., Patil, H., Gore, A., Salunke, S., Joshi, R.: Hate and offensive speech detection in Hindi and Marathi. arXiv preprint arXiv:2110.12200 (2021)
26. Velankar, A., Patil, H., Gore, A., Salunke, S., Joshi, R.: L3cube-mahahate: a tweet-based Marathi hate speech detection dataset and BERT models. arXiv preprint arXiv:2203.13778 (2022)
27. Zhang, W.: Neural dependency parsing of low-resource languages: a case study on Marathi (2022)

An Integrative Method for COVID-19 Patients' Classification from Chest X-ray Using Deep Learning Network with Image Visibility Graph as Feature Extractor

Mayukha Pal[1]([✉]) [ID], Yash Tiwari[1,2], T. Vineeth Reddy[1,3], P. Sai Ram Aditya[1,4], and Prasanta K. Panigrahi[5]

[1] ABB Ability Innovation Center, Asea Brown Boveri Company, Hyderabad 500084, India
mayukha.pal@in.abb.com
[2] Department of Physics, IIT Hyderabad, Telangana 502285, India
[3] Department of Mechanical and Aerospace Engineering, IIT Hyderabad, Telangana 502285, India
[4] Department of Artificial Intelligence, IIT Hyderabad, Telangana 502285, India
[5] Indian Institute of Science Education and Research Kolkata, Mohanpur 741246, India

Abstract. We propose a method by integrating image visibility graph and deep learning (DL) for classifying COVID-19 patients from their chest X-ray images. The computed assortative coefficient from each image horizonal visibility graph (IHVG) is utilized as a physical parameter feature extractor to improve the accuracy of our image classifier based on Resnet34 convolutional neural network (CNN). We choose Resnet34 CNN model for training the pre-processed chest X-ray images of COVID-19 and healthy individuals. Independently, the preprocessed X-ray images are passed through a 2D Haar wavelet filter that decomposes the image up to 3 labels and returns the approximation coefficients of the image which is used to obtain the horizontal visibility graph for each X-ray image of both healthy and COVID-19 cases. The corresponding assortative coefficients are computed for each IHVG and was subsequently used in random forest classifier whose output is integrated with Resnet34 output in a multi-layer perceptron to obtain the final improved prediction accuracy. We employed a multilayer perceptron to integrate the feature predictor from image visibility graph with Resnet34 to obtain the final image classification result for our proposed method. Our analysis employed much larger chest X-ray image dataset compared to previous used work. It is demonstrated that compared to Resnet34 alone our integrative method shows negligible false negative conditions along with improved accuracy in the classification of COVID-19 patients. Use of visibility graph in this model enhances its ability to extract various qualitative and quantitative complex network features for each image and enables the possibility of building disease network model from COVID-19 images which is mostly unexplored. Our proposed method is found to be very effective and accurate in disease classification from images and is computationally faster as compared to the use of multimode CNN deep learning models, reported in recent research works.

Keywords: COVID-19 and SARS Coronavirus · Chest X-ray and Image classification · Haar wavelet and Image Visibility Graph · Assortative coefficient

K. Dasgupta et al. (Eds.): CICBA 2023, CCIS 1955, pp. 274–287, 2024.
https://doi.org/10.1007/978-3-031-48876-4_21

and Classification learners · Resnet34 and Convolutional neural network · Multilayer perceptron classifier

1 Introduction

SARS-CoV-2 virus is highly infectious and spreads fast, affecting the respiratory organs like lungs, with the respiratory tracks developing various breath related symptoms in the patients. The severity of the disease in the humans is based on the spread of the infection to the respiratory organs. Patients suffer with heavy cough, high fever, muscle/body pain, sore throat, loss of sensation for taste and smell, headache, fatigue, and shortness of breath. In case of severe infection, the patient's oxygen saturation level drops drastically bringing more medical complications requiring immediate oxygen support and/or intensive medical care. The disease is named as COVID-19 by the World Health Organization which declared it as a pandemic [1–3]. Across the globe, it is observed that proper social distancing, wearing of masks covering nose and mouth, and proper sanitization effectively controls the spread. It is also consistently observed that breaking the chain of the infection by imposing lockdown restricting human movement and imposing COVID-19 containment protocol effectively controls the spread in case of an infection outbreak [4].

Continuous lockdown adversely affects the economic activities and GDP of a nation. It also severely impacts the livelihood of the population working as daily wage laborers, in unorganized sectors, self-employment businesses and for the citizens below poverty line. Hence it is essential to balance the economic activities ensuring all sections of the society are able to sustain their lives, while the nation effectively manages and controls the virus spread. More scientific approaches like early detection, test automation and other tools would help administration effectively manage and control the situation [5, 6]. Various nations have also started vaccination programs to increase the human body immunity to fight against the coronavirus and its mutant strain variants. Another approach of effectively fighting against the virus is to test and diagnose the disease early so that self-isolation is maintained to further stop the virus spread and also effective medication is started early for the patient to stop the infection spread within the body [7]. Nearly 251 million people across the globe have been infected with the coronavirus with more than 5 million deaths. During surge in the virus inspection, healthcare infrastructures face acute shortage of medicines, radiology test facilities, medical oxygen, medical equipment and ICU beds to cater the surge in the high demand challenging test and hospital facility. Generally rapid antigen test (RAT), reverse transcription-polymerase chain reaction (RT-PCR) tests are performed for initial diagnosis of COVID-19. Many instances these tests showed false negatives hence are not much reliable [8–10]. Hence clinicians prefer chest radiology tests to check the lungs image for the COVID-19 Pneumonia. As computed tomography (CT) scans subject more radiation exposure for the patients with limited available facilities compared to X-ray hence X-ray is preferred for initial investigation. For a mass scale community infection, chest X-ray is a good, low-cost, first-look diagnostic tool with quick results. Also, availability of handheld X-ray devices allows easy access and early diagnosis in rural areas hence improves test penetration for effective control of infection spread through early detection.

Various machine learning and deep learning tools are used for classification of COVID-19 patients from their chest X-ray images like Random Forest, Support Vector Machine, Artificial Neural Networks (ANN), convolutional neural network [11–20]. Generally, accuracy of various deep learning methods varies from 78–98% for classifying the COVID-19 patients based on their X-ray images [21–31]. Recently proposed mean structural similarity index measure (MSSIM) based method with the use of a simple classification learner showed 97.7% accuracy for detecting COVID-19 X-ray images with lower false negative case [32]. As the method is comparing between two images to quantify the differences hence generates large data points due to cross-correlation analysis while using the same given dataset, making robust and accurate training for the classification learner. In the present study, we aim to use X-ray images of the patients to find characteristic features for classification using DL without use of comparison-based analysis as used in MSSIM method. Inspired by this, we propose here a new method by integrating CNN and visibility graph for faster computation and accurate classification with low false negative compared to currently used deep learning algorithms for identification of COVID-19 patients from X-ray image. Our choice of Resnet34 is due to the fact that, it is the most optimized and recently analyzed deep convolutional neural networks [33, 34] that is used for image classification, object detection, image segmentation applications as it resolves the inherent problem of degrading gradient descent through residual blocks adding the skip connections in the identity mapping.

The main contribution of the paper is that an integrative method is proposed combining convolutional neural networks and 2D visibility graphs through a multilayer perceptron, for effective classification of COVID-19 patients from the chest X-ray images. In our study, the computed assortative coefficient from the horizontal visibility graph of each wavelet filtered X-ray image is used as a physical feature extractor. We demonstrate that compared to Resnet34 alone, our proposed integrative approach shows significant reduction in false negative conditions and higher accuracy in the classification of COVID-19 patients. The method is computationally fast and with use of visibility graph in the proposed model, it enables to extract complex network based qualitative and quantitative parameters for each subject creating the possibility of disease network model development and its structures, etc. The rest of the paper is organized as follows: Sect. 2 of the manuscript details the chest X-ray data and the methods used in the analysis while Sect. 3 of the manuscript discusses the results from our analysis. Section 4 of the manuscript gives our conclusion and inference to the work.

2   Materials and Methods

The COVID-19 X-ray image database [35] is used to obtain 500 X-ray images of patients diagnosed with COVID-19. 500 healthy subject's chest X-rays is obtained from the open-source database [36]. These pre-processed images are used for our CNN analysis. Further for our visibility graph analysis, these X-ray images are resized to make them of equal pixel size after converting to grayscale first. The images were then resized to 1024×1024 and these image matrices are of data type double. We applied 3-label Haar wavelet decomposition and considered the approximation coefficients for our visibility graph analysis. Here to compress the image, we used 2D Haar discrete wavelet transform

(HDWT). Generally, Haar wavelet transform is used to perform lossy image compression to ensure the compressed image retains its quality. This is one of the efficient procedures to perform lossless and lossy image compression as it uses averaging and differencing values in an image matrix to produce a matrix which is mostly sparse having less non-zero element in the matrix [37]. Haar wavelet transform utilizes a rectangular window for sampling. In the first label decomposition, a window width of two is used and the width doubles at each step until the window encompasses the entire data on hand. Each decomposition generates a new time series and a set of coefficients where the new time series is the average of the previous label time series over the sampling window and the coefficients represent the average change in the sampling window. Let us assume a time series $\{x_i, x_{i+1}, x_{i+2},\}$ then the Haar wavelet coefficient is defined as:

$$c_i = \frac{x_i - x_{1+1}}{2} \tag{1}$$

The Haar scaling function is written as

$$a_i = \frac{x_i + x_{1+1}}{2} \tag{2}$$

The Haar wavelet coefficient, c_i at position i represents the average change in the sampling window between data points x_i and x_{i+1}. The Haar scaling function, a_i at position i represents the average value of the data points x_i and x_{i+1} within the sampling window and is half the size of the input time series. As the analysis procedure is recursive, the average or the smoothed data becomes the input for the next label of the wavelet transform. Unlike other wavelet functions, in Haar wavelet transform, it preserves the average in the smoothed values. The obtained average coefficient from Haar wavelet in our visibility graph analysis contains all information about the image and reduces matrix dimension to 128×128 size allowing extreme fast computation by reducing months of time required in the computation for such image visibility graph analysis to a few hours. Figure 1 shows X-ray images of a COVID-19 subject obtained from the database along with a healthy chest image. Figure 2 represents the sample plot of the approximation coefficient obtained from 2D Haar wavelet for COVID-19 and healthy subjects.

Further these obtained approximation coefficient matrices from Haar wavelet for each image are considered in image visibility graph analysis [38]. If the analyzing matrix is a $N \times N$ for the X-ray image I where $I_{ij} \in \mathbb{R}$ then the image visibility graph (IVG) will have N^2 nodes. Now each node can be labelled by the indices of its corresponding datum I_{ij} in a manner that two nodes ij and $i'j'$ are linked if $(i = i')$ $V(j = j')V[(i = i' + p) \wedge (j = j' + p)]$, for some integer p, and if I_{ij} and $I_{i'j'}$ are linked in the visibility graph defined over the ordered sequence which includes ij and $i'j'$. . We define the visibility graph (VG) as an undirected graph of n nodes, where each node i is lalabeledccording to the time order of its corresponding datum x_i. For visibility graph, two nodes i and j where $i < j$ are connected by an undirected link if and only if a straight line connecting x_i and x_j can be drawn without intersecting any intermediate datum x_k for $i < k < j$ and also the convexity criterion is fulfilled: $x_k < x_i + ((k - i)/(j - i))[x_j - x_i]; \forall k : i < k < j$. For horizontal visibility graph (HVG) the two nodes i, j where $i < j$ is connected by a link if and only if a horizontal line can be drawn connecting x_i and x_j such that it does not intersect any intermediate datum x_k for $i < k < j$. Also, we connect i and j in the HVG if ordering criterion is fulfilled: $x_k < inf(x_i, x_j)$, $\forall k : i < k < j$. The image horizontal visibility graph obeys the same set of conditions like IVG [39–41].

We computed graphs from the coefficient matrices of the images using IHVG, where pixels are considered as nodes and the nodes are connected if they lie in a specific direction i.e. rows, columns, diagonals as per the defined HVG visibility criteria. We obtained 500 IHVG graphs for COVID-19 patients and 500 for the healthy subjects. Then from each IHVG graph the assortative coefficient is computed as a physical feature extractor and used along with our earlier obtained Resnet34 results through a multilayer perceptron (MLP) to obtain the final classification results. As the graph for each image is available, we could obtain qualitative and quantitative characteristics like degree distribution, image descriptor patch frequency, assortative coefficient etc. from the graph for characterization studies and further for possible disease network model development.

In our Resnet34 model, we normalized the pixel values of the input images using mean values [0.485, 0.456, 0.406] and the standard deviation values [0.229, 0.224, 0.225] then further the values were rescaled in range of −2 to 2. In CNN, image normalization is employed for faster convergence, easy training hence faster learning speed with stable gradient descent. Image augmentation is used in CNN models to improve the network generalization ability, however we didn't use in Resnet34 model to avoid data bias due to its use in our integrative model with image visibility graph.

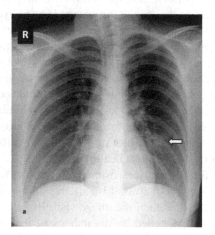 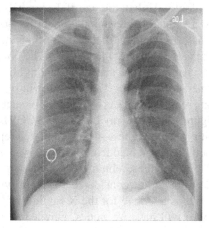

(a) Sample of a COVID-19 Patient chest X-ray image	(b) Sample of a healthy subject chest X-ray image

Fig. 1. Sample chest X-ray images of different subject types.

We used random forest classifier for the assortative coefficients obtained from visibility graph and integrating with Resnet34 results through MLP. The classifier was chosen based on the performance from host of different classifier learners. Among various CNN models analyzed like Resnet18, Resnet50, we found Resnet34 to be performing better. We used 224 × 224 × 3 input layers with 50 epochs in our Resnet 34 model. We modified the bottom fully connected (fc) layer of our Resnet34 model with a two-neuron fc

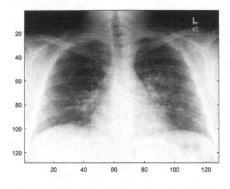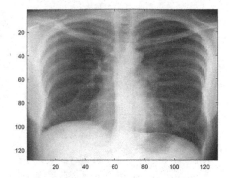

(a) Sample of a COVID-19 Patient 2D Haar approximation coefficient

(b) Sample of a healthy subject 2D Haar approximation coefficient

Fig. 2. Sample chest X-ray images from the 2D Haar approximation coefficient after label 3 decomposition of the images.

layer followed by a softmax activation output layer for computing the probabilities. The learning rate of the Resnet34 model is set to 0.001 and uses cross-entropy validation. For integrating the Resnet34 with visibility graph, we made use of an MLP classifier having ReLU activation function, Adam optimizer with 100 hidden layers for maximum iteration of 500.

3 Results and Discussion

From the visibility graph analysis, IHVG graphs were obtained for all preprocessed image matrices. A sample IHVG graph is shown in Fig. 3. To understand various qualitative and quantitative properties of these graphs, we counted the repetitions of small subgraphs in the IHVG associated to a given input image data matrix which is referred to as visibility patches (VPs). The computed patch frequency is a local image property descriptor. Visibility patch of order p is defined as, VP_p which is any subgraph from the IHVG formed by a set of p^2 nodes $\{ij\}_{i=s,j=s'}^{s+p-1,s'+p-1}$ for arbitrary s, s' satisfying the condition $1 \leq s, s' \leq N - p$. N equal to 128 is the size of $N \times N$ data matrix in our visibility graph analysis. In the analysis, lowest order $p = 3$ yields nontrivial visibility patches. Visibility patches are detected when sliding a 3×3 pixel cell of stride 1 in the image extracting the corresponding IHVGs within the cell. It enables reduced checking of different combination of visibility graph motifs presence or absence hence mathematically enables tractability of visibility patches for computation. Figure 4 shows the visibility patches for 3 randomly selected X-ray images of both healthy and COVID-19 subjects.

We analyzed the degree distribution P(k) where $P(k) \sim k^{-\lambda}$ to understand statistical properties of the networks where k is the degree of a node and is defined as the number of edges connected to a node. If the degree distribution of the network follow a power law distribution then we call it a scale-free network which is characterized by the nodes of the networks that are linked to a significant fraction of the total number of edges of

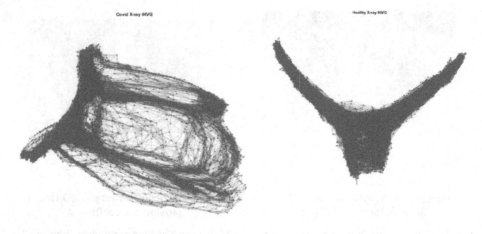

(a) COVID-19 Sample IHVG   (b) Sample of a healthy subject IHVG

Fig. 3. A Sample IHVG graphs for a COVID-19 patient and a healthy subject.

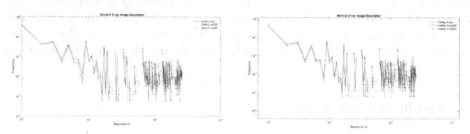

(a) Visibility patches for 3 randomly chosen   (b) Visibility patches for 3 randomly chosen
COVID-19 patients as image descriptor   healthy subjects as image descriptor

Fig. 4. Visibility patches for both COVID-19 and healthy subjects.

the network. Log-log plot of the degree distributions P(k) for a sample IHVG is shown in Fig. 5. We observe that for both healthy and COVID-19 patients the obtained network is scale free.

We computed assortative coefficients for each obtained IHVG which is used along with Resnet34. A complex network is defined as assortative mixing if higher degree nodes of the network tend to be connected to other higher degree nodes whereas in disassortative mixing the high degree nodes attach to low degree nodes only. Computationally, these assortative complex networks remove its highest degree nodes efficiently compared to the disassortative networks. For an undirected network, the assortative coefficient is computed as:

$$r = \frac{M^{-1} \sum_i j_i k_i - \left[M^{-1} \sum_i \frac{1}{2}(j_i + k_i) \right]^2}{M^{-1} \sum_i \frac{1}{2}(j_i^2 + k_i^2) - \left[M^{-1} \sum_i \frac{1}{2}(j_i + k_i) \right]^2} \tag{3}$$

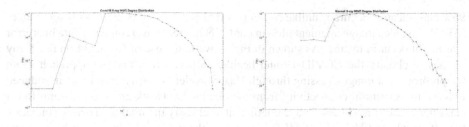

(a) Degree distribution for a sample COVID-19 IHVG

(b) Degree distribution for a sample healthy IHVG

Fig. 5. The degree distribution from the IHVG graph for sample COVID-19 and healthy subjects.

where j_i, k_i are the degrees of the two nodes at the ends of the ith edge where $i = 1, 2$, up to M. Assortative coefficient values vary between -1 to 1 where assortative networks have positive r values while disassortative networks have negative r values. For both COVID-19 and healthy subjects in our analysis, the obtained assortative coefficient values are always positive indicating that all the networks for disease and healthy are assortative.

The obtained 1000 assortative coefficients for both COVID-19 and healthy are labeled with its attribute category for random forest classifier and are further used along with Resnet34 in a MLP classifier as a quantitative physical parameter feature extractor for improving classification performance of standalone Resnet34 as visualized from the confusion matrix. Figure 6 illustrates our system study approach.

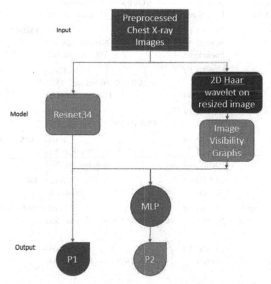

Fig. 6. Our proposed integrative method (P2) in analyzing COVID-19 X-ray images for classification. P1 is the results obtained from only Resnet34 model.

It is worth emphasizing that when the sample size of chest X-ray images increases as in our case to 1000 images, the resnet34 model without image augmentation gives

96% classification accuracy unlike earlier reported accuracy of 98.33% with 406 images [33]. We avoided image augmentation in our CNN model to overcome the data bias error that might occur in testing. As shown in Fig. 6, we make use of Resnet34 on the X-ray images to classify the COVID-19 and healthy subjects. In a parallel approach, from the preprocessed images passing through Haar wavelet visibility graph was introduced to learn the structural connectivity from the obtained network and then random forest classifier is used on VG assortative coefficient to classify the images. Then we integrate both Resnet34 and VG using a MLP considering the predicted labels from both for the final classification result of MLP.

Table 1. Comparison of our proposed method with state-of-the-art deep learning COVID-19 detection approaches using chest X-ray (CXR) images

Article Reference	Classification Method	Used Class	Number of CXR Images		Accuracy (%)	COVID-19 class Sensitivity (%)
Ref [13]	COVIDX-Net	COVID-19 Normal	Total – 50	COVID-19: 25 Normal: 25	90.00	100.00
Ref [42]	ResNet-50 and SVM	COVID-19 Normal	Total – 50	COVID-19: 25 Normal: 25	95.38	NA
Ref [16]	ResNet-50	COVID-19 Normal	Total – 100	COVID-19: 50 Normal: 50	98.00	96.00
Ref [43]	SqueezeNet and MobileNetV2 SMO and SVM	COVID-19 Normal Pneumonia	Total – 458 COVID-19: 295 Normal: 65 Pneumonia: 98		98.25	99.32
Ref [14]	COVID-Net	COVID-19 Normal Pneumonia	Total – 13800 COVID-19: 183 Normal: NA and Pneumonia: NA		92.60	87.10
Ref [44]	Bayes-SqueezeNet	COVID-19 Normal Pneumonia	Total – 5949 COVID-19: 76 Normal: 1583 Pneumonia: 4290		98.30	100.00
Ref [23]	DarkCovidNet	COVID-19 Normal	Total – 625 COVID-19: 125 Normal: 500		98.08	90.65
		COVID-19 Normal Pneumonia	Total – 1125 COVID-19: 125 Normal: 500 Pneumonia: 500		87.02	
Ref [33]	ResNet-34	COVID-19 Normal	Total – 406 COVID-19: 203 Normal: 203		98.33	100.00
Ref [32]	SSIM Coefficient with Ensemble Tree Classifier	COVID-19 Normal	Total – 1000 COVID-19: 500 Normal: 500		97.7	97.62
Proposed Method	Resnet34 with Visibility Graph	COVID-19 Normal	Total – 1000 COVID-19: 500 Normal: 500		98	97.87

In our model, we used 1000 chest X-ray images of which 500 were for COVID-19 while 500 of healthy. We used 800 of these images equally from both the class for training the Resnet34 model and the random forest classifier using assortative coefficient from visibility graph. The remaining 200 is used for validation. The predicted labels from random forest and Resnet34 were fed to the MLP classifier in which 100 data points were used for training while 100 were used for testing to obtain the final accuracy of our model. Table 1 summaries performance of our proposed multi-mode ensemble model with recently developed models. We observe our proposed multi-mode ensemble with introduction of VG as a unique characteristic feature that increases the accuracy by 2% compared to use of Resnet34 model alone. Similarly, the F1-score, sensitivity is increased by almost 1.8% compared to the Resnet34 model alone. We can observe the performance measures of the confusion matrix for both Resnet34 (P1) and our pro-posed integrative method (P2) in Fig. 7. Importantly, from the confusion matrix as shown in Table 2 we also observe our integrative model decreases false negative cases proportionately. The Fig. 8 shows our proposed method training and test accuracy and loss. Our integrative model loss against epoch is very close to 0 while it is 0.4 for Resnet34. The Fig. 9 shows the receiver operating characteristic (RoC) curve for our newly proposed model.

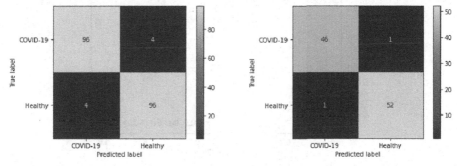

(a) Confusion matrix for Resnet34 alone (P1)   (b) Confusion matrix for our proposed integrative method (P2)

Fig. 7. Performance measures of the confusion matrix for both Resnet34 (P1) and our proposed integrative method (P2).

Table 2. Confusion matrix for the classifiers with its performance measures.

	P1	P2
Accuracy	96	98
Sensitivity	96	97.87
Specificity	96	98.11
Precision	96	97.87
F1 Score	96	97.87

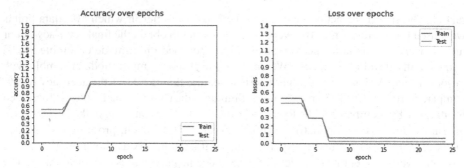

Fig. 8. Our proposed integrative method training and test accuracy, loss over epochs

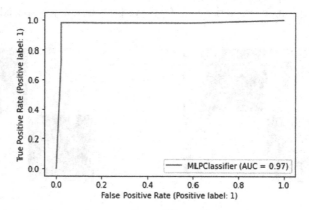

Fig. 9. The RoC curve for our newly proposed model

4   Conclusion

In conclusion, we have shown our integrative multi-model ensemble method combining Resnet34 CNN model and 2D visibility graph helps in better classification of COVID-19 chest X-ray images compared to a CNN model alone or in combinations as reported in prior research work. Also, our method is computationally very fast and with introduction of Haar wavelet it significantly reduced the computation time for image visibility graph and its associated parameter calculation while improving classification performance. With introduction of visibility graph various complex network qualitative and quantitative parameters for the subject image could be obtained and a disease network model could be built for future research on COVID-19.

Authors' contributions. MPal conceived the idea and conceptualized it, developed the model concept and its code, performed the data pre-processing and image processing analysis, wrote and reviewed the manuscript. YT performed the CNN and MLP related code enhancement, analysis, model optimization and contributed to the manuscript writing. TVR developed primary model framework and code. PSRA debugged the code and performed CNN analysis. PKP conceptualized the idea of using haar wavelet with visibility graph, mentored the work and reviewed the manuscript.

Funding:. This research work did not receive any specific grant from funding agencies in the public, commercial, or not-for-profit sectors. The author alone is responsible for the content and writing of the paper.

Competing interests:. The authors declare that they have no known competing financial inter-est or personal relationships that could have appeared to influence the work reported in this paper.

Ethical approval:. The data obtained for our analysis is from the available public domain database made for academic research purpose with approval from origi-nal researcher's insti-tute ethical committee. Same approval is mentioned in their database DOI link from which we had obtained the data for our analysis in this work. We have obtained the data from two sources and appropriately cited the data reference in this work.

References

1. Wu, F., Zhao, S., Yu, B., et al.: A new coronavirus associated with human respiratory disease in China. Nature **579**(7798), 265–269 (2020)
2. Huang, C., Wang, Y., et al.: Clinical features of patients infected with 2019 novel coronavirus in Wuhan. China, Lancet **395**(10223), 497–506 (2020)
3. Singhal, T.: A review of coronavirus disease-2019 (COVID-19). Indian J. Pediatr.Pediatr. **87**, 281–286 (2020)
4. Padhi, A., Pradhan, S., Sahoo, P.P., Suresh, K., Behera, B.K., Panigrahi, P.K.: Studying the effect of lockdown using epidemiological modelling of COVID-19 and a quantum compu-tational approach using the Ising spin interaction. https://doi.org/10.1038/s41598-020-786 52-0
5. Pal, M.: Genomic sequence data analysis using chaos game representation and mean structural similarity index measure to understand COVID-19 strains impacting wave 2 pandemic in India. https://doi.org/10.13140/RG.2.2.16342.78401
6. Pal, M.: A Novel integrative method for genomic sequence classification detecting mutant variants–A case study using the method applied to understand COVID-19 strains impacting wave 2 pandemic in India. https://doi.org/10.13140/RG.2.2.14379.16168
7. Kanne, J.P., Little, B.P., Chung, J.H., Elicker, B.M., Ketai, L.H.: Essentials for radiologists on COVID-19: an update—radiology scientific expert panel. Radiology (2020). https://doi.org/10.1148/radiol.2020200527
8. Bai, H.X., Hsieh, B., et al.: Performance of radiologists in differentiating COVID-19 from viral pneumonia on chest CT. Radiology (2020). https://doi.org/10.1148/radiol.2020200823
9. Xie, X., Zhong, Z., Zhao, W., Zheng, C., Wang, F., Liu, J.: Chest CT for typical 2019- nCoV pneumonia: relationship to negative RT-PCR testing. Radiology (2020). https://doi.org/10.1148/radiol.2020200343
10. Schnuriger, A., Perrier, M., et al.: Caution in interpretation of SARS-CoV-2 quantification based on RT-PCR cycle threshold value. https://doi.org/10.1016/j.diagmicrobio.2021.115366
11. Singh, D., Kumar, V., Kaur, V.M.: Classification of covid-19 patients from chest CT images using multi-objective differential evolution–based convolutional neural networks, European Journal of Clinical Microbiology & Infectious Diseases, pp. 1–11 (2020)
12. Rajpurkar, P., Irvin, J., et al.: Chexnet: Radiologist-Level Pneumonia Detection on Chest X-Rays with Deep Learning, 2017 arXiv preprint arXiv:1711.05225
13. Hemdan, E.E.D., Shouman, M.A., Karar, M.E.: COVIDX-Net: A Framework of Deep Learn-ing Classifiers to Diagnose COVID-19 in X-Ray Images, 2020 arXiv preprint arXiv:2003.11055

14. Wang, L., Lin, Z.Q., Wong, A.: COVID-Net: a tailored deep convolutional neural network design for detection of COVID-19 cases from chest radiography images, 2020 arXiv preprint arXiv:2003.09871

15. Apostolopoulos, I.D., Bessiana, T.: COVID-19: Automatic Detection from X-Ray Images Utilizing Transfer Learning with Convolutional Neural Networks. arXiv:2003.11617

16. Narin, A., Kaya, C., Pamuk, Z.: Automatic Detection of Coronavirus Disease (COVID-19) Using X-Ray Images and Deep Convolutional Neural Networks, 2020 arXiv preprint arXiv: 2003.10849

17. Song, Y., et al.: Deep learning enables accurate diagnosis of novel coronavirus (COVID-19) with CT images, medRxiv (2020)

18. Wang, S., et al.: A deep learning algorithm using CT images to screen for Corona Virus Disease (COVID-19), medRxiv (2020)

19. Zheng, C., et al.: Deep learning-based detection for COVID-19 from chest CT using weak label, medRxiv (2020). https://doi.org/10.1101/2020.03.12.20027185

20. Xu, X., Jiang, X., Ma, C., Du, P., Li, X., Lv, S., et al.: Deep learning system to screen coronavirus disease 2019 pneumonia, 2020 arXiv preprint arXiv:200209334

21. Barstugan, M., Ozkaya, U., Ozturk, S.: Coronavirus (COVID-19) Classification using CT images by machine learning methods, 2020 arXiv preprint arXiv:2003.09424

22. Asnaoui, K.E., Chawki, Y.: Using X-ray images and deep learning for automated detection of coronavirus disease. https://doi.org/10.1080/07391102.2020.1767212

23. Ozturk, T., Talo, M., Yildirim, E.A., Baloglu, U.B., Yildirim, O., Acharya, U.R.: Automated detection of COVID-19 cases using deep neural networks with X-ray images. Comput. Biol. Med. Biol. Med. **121**, 103792 (2020)

24. Pathak, Y., Shukla, P.K., Arya, K.V.: Deep bidirectional classification model for COVID-19 disease infected patients. https://doi.org/10.1109/TCBB.2020.3009859, IEEE/ACM

25. Adedigba, A.P., Adeshina, S.A., Aina, O.E., Aibinu, A.M.: Optimal hyperparameter selection of deep learning models for COVID-19 chest X-ray classification; Intelligence-Based Medicine 5, 100034 (2021)

26. Khuzani, A.Z., Heidari, M., Shariati, S.A.: COVID-Classifier: an automated machine learning model to assist in the diagnosis of COVID-19 infection in chest X-ray images. https://doi.org/10.1038/s41598-021-88807-2

27. Chaudhary, P.K., Pachori, R.B.: FBSED based automatic diagnosis of COVID-19 using X-ray and CT images. https://doi.org/10.1016/j.compbiomed.2021.104454

28. Pathan, S., Siddalingaswamy, P.C., Ali, T.: Automated detection of Covid-19 from Chest X-ray scans using an optimized CNN architecture. https://doi.org/10.1016/j.asoc.2021.107238

29. Toraman, S., Alakuş, T.B., Türkoğlu, İ.: Convolutional CapsNet: a novel artificial neural network approach to detect COVID-19 disease from X-ray images using capsule networks. https://doi.org/10.1016/j.chaos.2020.110122

30. Li, J., Zhao, G., Tao, Y., Zhai, P., Chen, H., He, H., Cai, T.: Multi-task contrastive learning for automatic CT and X-ray diagnosis of COVID-19

31. Demir, F.: DeepCoroNet: a deep LSTM approach for automated detection of COVID-19 cases from chest X-ray images. https://doi.org/10.1016/j.asoc.2021.107160

32. Pal, M., Panigrahi, P.K.: Effective clustering and accurate classification of the chest X-ray images of COVID-19 patients from healthy ones through the mean structural similarity index measure. https://doi.org/10.13140/RG.2.2.33801.57441

33. Nayak, S.R., Nayak, D.R., Sinha, U., Arora, V., Pachori, R.B.: Application of deep learning techniques for detection of COVID-19 cases using chest X-ray images: a comprehensive study. https://doi.org/10.1016/j.bspc.2020.102365

34. Mei, X., Lee, H.-C., et al.: Artificial intelligence–enabled rapid diagnosis of patients with COVID-19. https://doi.org/10.1038/s41591-020-0931-3

35. Cohen, J.P.: COVID-19 Image Data Collection (2020). https://github.com/ieee8023/COVID-chestxray-dataset
36. Wang, X., Peng, Y., Lu, L., Lu, Z., Bagheri, M., Summers, R.M.: Chestx-ray8: hospital scale chest x-ray database and benchmarks on weakly-supervised classification and localization of common thorax diseases. In: Proceedings of the IEEE Conference on Computer Vision and Pattern Recognition, pp. 2097–2106 (2017)
37. Vaidelienė, G., Valantinas, J.: The use of Haar wavelets in detecting and localizing texture defects. 105566/ias.1561
38. Iacovacci, J., Lacasa, L.: Visibility graphs for image processing. IEEE Trans. Pattern Anal. Mach. Intell. https://doi.org/10.1109/TPAMI.2019.2891742
39. Lacasa, L., Iacovacci, J.: Visibility graphs of random scalar fields and spatial data. Phys. Rev. E **96**, 012318 (2017)
40. Lacasa, L., Luque, B., Ballesteros, F., Luque, J., Nunoe, J.C.: From time series to complex networks: the visibility graph, PNAS. https://doi.org/10.1073/pnas.0709247105
41. Zhu, D., Semba, S., Yang, H.: Matching intensity for image visibility graphs: a new method to extract image features. IEEE Access. https://doi.org/10.1109/ACCESS.2021.3050747
42. Sethy, P.K., Behera, S.K.: Detection of Coronavirus Disease (COVID-19) based on deep features. Preprints (2020). https://doi.org/10.20944/preprints202003.0300.v1
43. Toğaçar, M., Ergen, B., Cömert, Z.: COVID-19 detection using deep learning models to exploit social mimic optimization and structured chest X-ray images using fuzzy color and stacking approaches, Comput. Biol. Med., 103805 (2020)
44. Ucar, F., Korkmaz, D.: COVIDiagnosis-Net: Deep Bayes-SqueezeNet based diagnosis of the coronavirus disease 2019 (COVID-19) from X-Ray images. Med. Hypotheses **140**, 109761 (2020)

Identification and Multi-classification of Several Potato Plant Leave Diseases Using Deep Learning

Arpita Paria[✉], Saswati Roy, Pramit Brata Chanda, and Deepak Kumar Jha

Computer Science and Engineering, Kalyani Government Engineering College, Kalyani, West Bengal, India
arpitaporia11@gmail.com

Abstract. Today Potato becomes most well-known crops in world. Now Plant crop disease detection has transferred as an operative research domain. As per enhancement of requirements of methods and demands for detection of diseases of crops are crucial part of agriculture. Many disease affects the perfect enhancement of plants of potatoes. Some Observable problems are very much visible in potato plants leaf areas of affected regions As Early (EB) and Late (LB) Blight. Particularly, image based approach offers the way of gathering knowledge regarding plants for quantitative analysis. In case of other side, manual detection of crop diseases needs more work effort, expert domain persons, execution time higher. Therefore, integration of image processing and machine learning is required to enable the diagnosis of leaf images with disease. CNN is used for image Detection and Analysis of potato diseases and gives the best result than other classifier. Here some classifiers are used for this research paper such as SVM, Random Forest, Logistic Regression & Sequential model. In this proposed work, the model validation, training is done using CNN to identifying and extraction of necessaryinformation of used datasets and for determining that leaf are affected or not. This model achieved accuracy of 97.92% that indicates the suitable outcomes for identifying the crop diseases.

Keywords: Machine Learning · Image Processing · SVM · Potato Disease · CNN · Early Blight (EB) · Late Blight (LB)

1 Introduction

Today Potato is become most necessary food items in our country. Potato is now become a crucial food crops in agriculture areas after rice, maize, wheat. India become one of the biggest nation of making of potatoes. This crops provides good potassium level, vitamins like C & B6 and carbohydrates in our daily diet. However, now a days potato producing is too much hampered for several kinds of diseases, that damages the potato plants. Several disease may attack potato plant leaves and those symptoms are very much changing the several areas that may affects plant. The main causes agricultural disorders are microorganisms, several disorders, agents infected as bacteria viruses. One of the mainly responsible viruses for plants diseases are Fungi, bacteria. Late, early blight diseases of fungal infection. Some diseases on the potato leaves like blight disease, brown spotting shows as shapes like oval, circular etc. So, appropriate spotting and diagnoses of leaf diseases of potato vegetation's like potato plants insists us of creating a proper system that may meliorate plants, betterment of farmer's condition, significant betterments of economy of country. Previous days people in areas of agriculture worked on computational intelligence, and also creates some conventional approach of image processing as LBP, K-means to identify leaf diseases of potato plants.

1.1 Background Study

Now a days India is become one of the major agricultural nation and agriculture is become our back bone of economy. It is the major earner and also locally providing food for the citizens. Farmers can diversify their ranges identifying appropriate crop. Diversification in crops responsible of diseases that limits plants growth, quality, productivity of crops. Here quality control is required for more production of good crops. Diseases due to pandemic organisms, can destroy the plant leaves. Eye observation is one crucial used techniques. Here continuous monitoring is required by an expertise person having prior knowledge of regarding plants and their disease. Moreover requirement of an experienced person needs higher cost. Here expert should be required in time otherwise there may be chances of loss of information.

1.2 Scope

This research attempted to identify Early blight, late blight, and healthy class leaf diseases. All of the diseases above belong to fungal, viral and bacteria type of diseases. We used secondary sources of data like the PlantVillage dataset containing more than thousands of leaf images from Kaggle website for the designing the machine learning model.

1.3 Disease Categories

Several stages of disease of potato plant disease detection are-

1.3.1 A. Early Blight

Early blight's may appear as lesions like small and black.

1.3.2 B. Late Blight

Late may be viewed in case of blistered as if hot water requires for scaling and sometimes it may dry out.

2 Literature Review

2.1 Related Work

In current periods many researchers took model that is ML based of Plant Leaf Detection. Here the collected PlantVillage dataset taken from kaggle. The study is performed on few current papers cases for plant disease prediction, identification. Some related works are discussed here.

Md. Khalid RayhanAsif et al. [1] compared work between CNN and transfer learning.

In their paper they have used five types of transfer learning algorithm. These are VggNet, ResNet, AlexNet, LeNet, Sequential model. For detection of the disease CNN model gives the best result than others. It gives 97% accuracy.

Md. Asif Iqbal1 et al. [2] They classified the disease in their article by using image processing and machine learning for the detection and analysis of potato plant leaf diseases. A variety of machine learning classifiers have been employed to predict and identify the disease. These include the Support Vector Machine (SVM), Naive Bayes (NB), Decision Trees (DT), k-Nearest Neighbors (KNN), Logistic Regression (LR), and Random Forest (RF), with Naive Bayes providing an 84% result and Logistic Regression 94% accuracy. But the best result, 97%, is provided by the Random Forest classifier.

VinayKukreja et al.[3] built a CNN based model for classifying multi-level framework using potato crop plant images. They used binary and multi classification. Binary classification gives 90.77% accuracy. They compared binary classification with multi-classification. The result showed that the multi classification gives better result than binary classification.

Monzurul Islam [4] In their paper they have worked on method that accommodate ML, image processing both that allow to detect the diseases from plant leaf images. They demonstrated the disease classification with a 95% accuracy rate using image segmentation and multiclass support vector machines.

RizqiAmaliatus Sholihati1 et al. [5] Based on leaf conditions built a Deep Learning (DL) for classifying to different diseases in potato plant. Using VGG16, VGG19 CNN based architecture they have achieved 91% accuracy. DivyanshTiwari et al. [6] In their paper a pre-trained models is uses like VGG19 to extraction of features within the sets of images. Multiple classifiers are used. Among which logistic regression better and gives a 97.8% accuracy rate on the test dataset.

mehul.mishra12@gmail.com et al. [7] In agricultural field using AI and Deep Learning Approach disease may be detected for potato leaves that is required of damages reduction process. They used a proposed model which has been needed of train, validate. CNN (Convonutional Neural Network) has required to detect the appropriate information. This approach got the accuracy of 99.84% of test images.

Imran Khan et al. [8] In their paper a multi-level deep learning model has been utilized to detect potato leaf disease. On the dataset for potato leaf disease, they achieved 99.75% accuracy after creating a multi-level deep learning model.

Trong-Yen Lee1 et al. [9] In their paper For the purpose of detecting potato disease, they have utilized CNN (convolutional neural network) architecture. They used different parameters for the proposed CNN. And the outcomes predicts that the methods identify disease and they achieved 99.53% accuracy.

PriyadarshiniPatil, NagaratnaYaligar et al. [10] Comparing the performance of the classifiers using machine learning and image processing methods is illustrated. Artificial neural networks (ANN), random forests (RF), and support vector machines (SVM) were utilized for comparison. On the same test using data sets from potato leaves, they compared these classifiers. The outcome indicated that RF had an accuracy of 79% and SVM had an accuracy of 84%. The best performance, 92%, comes from ANN.

Abdul JalilRozaqi et al. [11] In their paper they have used image processing to solve the disease identification problem in potato plant leaves. To identify this convolutional neural network is used. As a result, those are divided into several segments, and 70:30 division produces better results than 80:20 split. The accuracy obtained is 92% for testing on verified data with a batch size of 20, and 97% for training, using 10 epochs. Utpal Barman et al. [12] proposed a model a self-build CNN is utilized to identify potato disease. For non-augmented and augmented data, the best SBCNN training accuracy is 99.71% and 98.75%, and for orderly data, the best validation rates are 96.98% and 96.75%. The SVCNN model performs effectively in the enhanced dataset without being over fit. The outcome demonstrated that the potato plant image dataset in SBCNN (augmented) offers superior results to SBCNN (non augmented).SBCNN (Augmented) is chosen as the best model after comparison studies between SBCNN and MobileNet.

Sunayana Aryal et al. [13] In their paper For image classification, they have employed Convolutional Neural Networks (CNN). Compared work with CNN and AlexNet The outcomes demonstrate that AlexNet's accuracy outperforms CNN's architecture. Farabee Islam et al. [14] In their paper they have used transfer learning technique for quick detect of plant leaf diseases. The experiments showed that transfer learning of accuracy rate of 99.43% for test with 80% train data, 20% test data. After comparing sequential model with transfer learning the result showed that transfer learning gives best result than sequential deep learning.

Kumar Sanjeev[1] et al. [15] They have usedFeed Forward Neural Network (FFNN) Model of classifying unknown leaf. The framework gives accuracy of 96.5%.

3 Proposed Methodologies

3.1 Dataset Collection

We have collected "PlantVillage" dataset from kaggle. This set consists mostly 56,000 labeled of healthy and contaminated leaves of several kinds of vegetables and fruits like potato, tomato, orange, pepper, blueberry, apple, cherry, grapes etc. Each folder of the vegetable and fruit consist two categories of data as gray, color based image. We have look over 2152 images data, that has several class Early blight, Late blight, Healthy leaf.

3.2 Pre-processing

Here basically data is separated to several classes. This approach takes a crucial role as this is required of processing of data cleaning that consists with noise data and irrelevant features setsthat are not needed for research based work. The requirements is for pre-processing of image dataset collected for creation of uniformity of size of images, as resolution, sizes of data are different types of images. Due to scaling, all images of dataset are resized and dimensions of those data are altered accordingly. Here entire pre-processing jobs are done on framework supported by Machine Learning.

3.3 Filtering

Actually Filtering requires to remove unwanted noise from image data. Several categories of filtering process use reduce the noise and getting good quality of image for the process.

3.4 Visualizing the Images

We have visualized some of the images from our image PlantVillage dataset (Fig. 1).

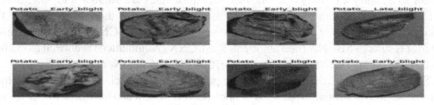

Fig.1. Visualize images

3.5 Model Creation

The sequential model is created here once the CNN algorithm is applied. To build the model Convolutional layers is used, max pooling 2D layers, dense layers. Convonutional, max pooling 2D, dense layers recompense as hidden layer. This outputs of layer is passes through activation function. Here network's capacities are enhanced with activation to allow for learn complex datasets. In this study RELU requires as activation for hidden layer. So Max pooling is needed to reserve those features and size of data is compressed. It is the layer which requires to process for getting matrix data in highest ranges. Dense layer depicts that their previous weight value may be required as input in next consecutive layer. The number of classes with the softmax activation function is contained in the final layer.

3.6 Compiling the Model

To compile the model "adam" optimizer is used. This is a crucial too for optimize the results to get changes rate of learning. Regarding loss function for getting realization easier, 'categorical cross-entropy' requires for train and with help of 'accuracy' metrics related outcomes have been calculated.

3.7 Training and Testing

In our model, 'fit ()' function requires to train. Regarding Validation Testing of image requires. Here fit function are needed to set no of iteration which rhythms the entire process of the system. So Testing is performed after train the particular model. It accept the CNN based framework that is used for training (Fig. 2).

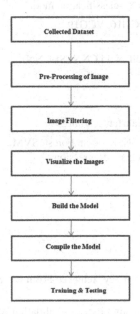

Fig. 2. Proposed Methodology

4 Results and Analysis

In our proposed model here 2152 image data are collected from datasets as "PlantVillage". It is considered as for training 80%, for validation 10%, and for testing10%. CNN has been applied for detection of proper information of this data for classify those images as un healthy or healthy. Thus, regarding this work 15 Epochs are selected that gives 97.92% accuracy, in case data loss lesser for training, validation purposes consecutively.

We have used different classifiers algorithm. We have calculated Accuracy score. And the resultant accuracy of several classifiers are shown in Table 4.

Table 1. Comparison Analysis with Existing Works with Proposed Work

Author Name	Methodologies	Accuracy
Md.KhalidRayhanAsif et. al. [1]	CNN, VggNet, ResNet, AlexNet	97%
VinayKukreja et al.[3]	CNN Based Deep learning multi-classification model	90.77%
RizqiAmaliatus Sholihati1 et al. [5]	VGG16, VGG19	91%
Utpal Barman et al. [12]	Self-build CNN (SBCNN)	Validation accuracy of non-augmented and augmented datasets 96.98% and 96.75%,
Farabee Islam et al. [14]	Transfer Learning	99.43%
Our Used Approach	CNN, Random Forest, SVM, Logistic Regression	Validation Accuracy for CNN for 97.92% Random Forest for 88.6% SVM for 86.54% & for Logistic Regression 77.70%

Table 2. Accuracy Achieved From Different Epochs

Epoch	Train Accuracy	Train Loss	Validation Accuracy	Validation Loss
3	0.8212	0.4567	0.8802	0.3641
6	0.9300	0.1661	0.9271	0.1768
9	0.9757	0.0807	0.9583	0.0774
12	0.9867	0.0314	0.9635	0.1138
15	0.9826	0.0552	0.9792	0.0592

Table 3. Training Testing & Validation Accuracy from CNN

Train Accuracy	Testing Accuracy	Validation Accuracy
0.9635	0.9804	0.9792

In case of different classifier algorithm, parameters such as recall, precision are calculated. These results are displayed in Table 5, 6, 7.

Table 4. Several Classifiers Accuracy

Algorithm/Classifier	Validation Accuracy	Training Accuracy
Convolutional Neural Network (CNN)	97.92%	98.26%
Random Forest (RF)	88.63%	100%
Support Vector Machine (SVM)	86.54%	77%
Logistic Regression (LR)	77.70%	99%

Table 5. SVM Classifier Accuracy Score

Class labels	Precision	Recall	F1score	Support	Sensitivity	Specificity
0	0.93	0.86	0.90	190	86.31	94.90
1	0.89	0.94	0.88	219		
2	0.58	0.18	0.28	23		
accuracy			0.87	432		
Macro average	0.8	0.66	0.68	432		
Avg. Weighted	0.874	0.87	0.86	432		

Table 6. Results Of Logistic Regression Classifier

Class labels	Precision	Recall	F1score	Support	Sensitivity	Specificity
0	0.84	0.78	0.81	300	78.52	85.94
1	0.74	0.84	0.79	312		
2	0.38	0.15	0.21	34		
accuracy			0.79	646		
average. Macro	0.66	0.59	0.60	646		
Avg. Weighted	0.78	0.79	0.78	646		

- **Recall:** Locating the cases that are pertinent to a given set of data. Therefore, recall is the sum of the number of true positives and false negatives divided by the number of true positives (Fig. 3).
- **Recall** = TP /(TP + FN) (Fig. 4)
- **Precision:** Mathematically, ratio of no of true positives by true positives added to the no of false positives. **Precision** = TP/(TP + FP) (Fig. 5), (Fig. 6)

We estimated our model after getting accuracy, loss plots as below which showed the model performance with curves for easy visualization (Fig. 7).

Table 7. Random Forest Classifier Results

Class labels	Precision	Recall	F1score	Support	Sensitivity	Specificity
0	0.88	0.97	0.93	197	97.46	91.95
1	0.88	0.92	0.89	199		
2	0.00	0.00	0.00	36		
accuracy			0.87	432		
Macro average	0.59	0.63	0.60	432		
Avg. Weighted	0.80	0.87	0.83	432		

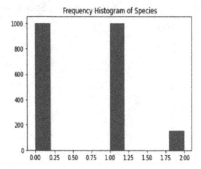

Fig. 3. Freuency Histogram species of CNN

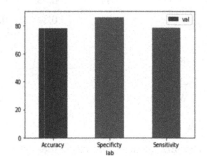

Fig. 4. Results of the SVM classifier for classification

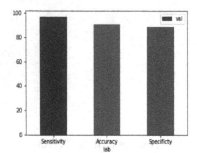

Fig. 5. Classification Results of Logistic Regression classifier

Fig. 6. Random forest classifier

4.1 Model's Accuracy and Loss Graph on the Dataset without Data Augmentation

The accuracy results predict, in the figure below, the model's behaviours on specific data irrespective of using augmentation approaches are used on particular set for training (Fig. 8).

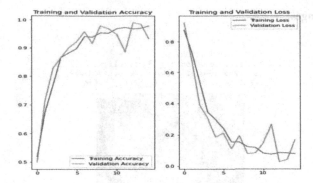

Fig. 7. For training and validation, use the accuracy and loss graph.

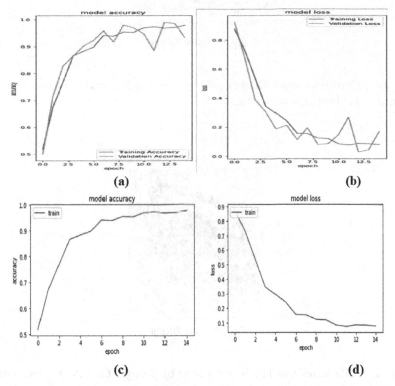

Fig. 8. (a) Accuracy plot of without augmented data (b) Loss plot of model of non augmentation. (c) plot of model accuracy. (d) model loss graph

4.2 Classification

This task is performed using Kaggle environment. At first different infected potato plant leaf images are needed for computing for classify. When we give the path of an image for detection, the results of classification given.

Predicted Images:

first image to predict
actual label: Potato___Early_blight
[9.9999845e-01 1.5920588e-06 6.8490010e-12]
predicted label: Potato___Early_blight

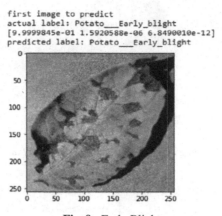

Fig. 9. Early Blight

Figure 9 Depicts the Early Blight Leaf Detected. Large spots can occasionally cause the entire leaf to turn yellow and die.

first image to predict
actual label: Potato___Late_blight
predicted label: Potato___Late_blight

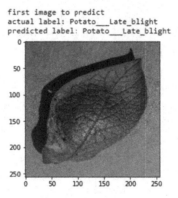

Fig. 10. Late Blight

Figure 10 Illustrates that late blight affects on foliage. Leaf flecks start with tiny, dark green, spots that non-regular way

Figure 11 Shows that it is a Healthy leaf. So, this task identifies disease prone area and views as Healthy Leaf. Here the comparison is performed with other existing work is shown here.

first image to predict
actual label: Potato___healthy
predicted label: Potato___healthy

Fig. 11. Healthy.

5 Conclusion

Today detection of leaf diseases are performed with deep learning based model to improve crop quality and productivity which may losses the crops yield. In this paper, a classification system for plant leaf diseases is developed as a model for learning plant disease detection. Also other approaches like Random Forest, SVM based classifier gives more than 86% of validation accuracy of leaf disease identification. A CNN was subsequently created to categorise early blight, late blight, and healthy class from the leaf images, using the sequential model initially used to extract leaves from potato plants. It considered the effect of environmental factors on potato plant leaf images. Our CNN-based model's performance is assessed using a cross-dataset, where the model's performance on the dataset for Potato Plant Leaf Disease out performed that of PlantVillage because it was trained with no additional data and achieved an overall accuracy of 97.92%.

Acknowledgement. We would like to express our very much appreciation to Mr. Pramit Brata Chanda faculty of department of Computer Science and Engg. Of Kalyani Govt. Engg. College and also the other faculty members of department for their suggestions during this research study on plant diseases. His willingness to provide us valuable time that is very much appreciated.

References

1. Asif, M.K.R., Rahman, M.A., Hena, M.H.: CNN based disease detection approach on potato leaves. In: 2020 3rd International Conference on Intelligent Sustainable Systems (ICISS), pp. 428–432. IEEE (2020)
2. Iqbal, M.A., Talukder, K.H.: Detection of potato disease using image segmentation and machine learning. In: 2020 International Conference on Wireless Communications Signal Processing and Networking (WiSPNET), pp. 43–47. IEEE (2020)
3. Kukreja, V., Baliyan, A., Salonki, V., Kaushal, R.K.: Potato Blight: deep learning model for binary and multi-classification. In: 2021 8th International Conference on Signal Processing and Integrated Networks (SPIN), pp. 967–672. IEEE (2021)

4. Islam, M., Dinh, A., Wahid, K., Bhowmik, P.: Detection of potato diseases using image segmentation and multiclass support vector machine. In: 2017 IEEE 30th Canadian Conference on Electrical and Computer Engineering (CCECE), pp. 1–4. IEEE (2017)
5. Sholihati, R.A., Sulistijono, I.A., Risnumawan, A., Kusumawati, E.: Potato leaf disease classification using deep learning approach. In: 2020 International Electronics Symposium (IES), pp. 392–397. IEEE (2020)
6. Tiwari, D., Ashish, M., Gangwar, N., Sharma, A., Patel, S., Bhardwaj, S.: Potato leaf diseases detection using deep learning. In: 2020 4th International Conference on Intelligent Computing and Control Systems (ICICCS), pp. 461–466. IEEE (2020)
7. Baranwal, A., Mishra, M., Goyal, A.: Potato plant disease classification through deep learning. In: 2022 International Conference on Machine Learning, Big Data, Cloud and Parallel Computing (COM-IT-CON), Vol. 1, pp. 673–681. IEEE (2022)
8. Rashid, J., Khan, I., Ali, G., Almotiri, S.H., AlGhamdi, M.A., Masood, K.: Multi-level deep learning model for potato leaf disease recognition. Electron. **10**(17), 2064 (2021)
9. Lee, T.Y., Lin, I.A., Yu, J.Y., Yang, J.M., Chang, Y.C.: High Efficiency Disease Detection for Potato Leaf with Convolutional Neural Network. SN Comput. Sci. **2**(4), 1–11 (2021)
10. Patil, P., Yaligar, N., Meena, S.M.: Comparision of performance of classifiers-SVM, RF and ANN in potato blight disease detection using leaf images. In: 2017 IEEE International Conference on Computational Intelligence and Computing Research (ICCIC), pp. 1–5. IEEE (2017)
11. Rozaqi, A.J., Sunyoto, A.: Identification of disease in potato leaves using Convolutional Neural Network (CNN) algorithm. In: 2020 3rd International Conference on Information and Communications Technology (ICOIACT), pp. 72–76 IEEE (2020)
12. Barman, U., Sahu, D., Barman, G. G., Das, J.: Comparative assessment of deep learning to detect the leaf diseases of potato based on data augmentation. In: 2020 International Conference on Computational Performance Evaluation (ComPE), p. 682687. IEEE (2020)
13. Arya, S., Singh, R.: A comparative study of CNN and AlexNet for detection of disease in potato and mango leaf. In: 2019 International Conference on Issues and Challenges in Intelligent Computing Techniques (ICICT), Vol. 1, pp. 1–6. IEEE (2019)
14. Islam, F., Hoq, M.N., Rahman, C.M.: Application of transfer learning to detect potato disease from leaf image. In: 2019 IEEE International Conference on Robotics, Automation, Artificial-intelligence and Internet-of-Things (RAAICON), p. 127130. IEEE (2019)
15. Sanjeev, K., Gupta, N.K., Jeberson, W., Paswan, S.: Early prediction of potato leaf diseases using ANN classifier. Orient. J. Comput. Sci. Technol. **13**(2, 3), 129–134 (2021)
16. Chanda, P.B., Sarkar, S.K.: Cardiac MR images segmentation for identification of cardiac diseases using fuzzy based approach. In: International Conference on Smart Systems and Inventive Technology, IEEE ICSSIT (2020). https://doi.org/10.1109/ICSSIT48917.2020.9214080
17. Chanda, P.B., Sarkar, S.K.: Medical image based approach for classification of several stages for retinopathy disease using machine learning methodology, October 2020, IET, 978–1–83953–272–6
18. PramitBrataChanda, S.K., Sarkar,: Efficient identification and classification of blood vessels and exudates in retinal images for diabetic retinopathy analysis. Adv. Appl. Math. Sci. **18**(9), 909–917 (2019)
19. Dataset Used. https://www.kaggle.com/datasets/abdallahalidev/plantvillage-dataset

A GUI-Based Approach to Predict Heart Disease Using Machine Learning Algorithms and Flask API

Sayan Kumar Bose, Shinjohn Ghosh, Sibarati Das, Souhardya Bhowmick, Arpita Talukdar, and Lopamudra Dey[✉]

Department of Computer Science and Engineering, Heritage Institute of Technology, Kolkata, India
lopamudra.dey1@gmail.com

Abstract. Heart conditions are classified as diverse illnesses with numerous subgroups. To make patient clinical treatment easier, early heart disease diagnosis and prognosis are crucial. Although much research has been done to predict the cause of heart disease. We have tried to build a heart disease detection system using machine learning algorithms. The basic goal of work is to detect whether a person is suffering from heart disease or not. We have also built a GUI using HTML and CSS for our front end and integrated both using flask for the back end. The user interface is available at https://github.com/SayanKumarBose/FinalYear Project.git.

Keywords: Decision Tree · Naive Bayes · Support Vector Machine · KNN · Heart Disease Prediction

1 Introduction

Heart disease is the leading cause of death globally over the past few decades. It includes a variety of disorders that have an impact on the heart. Numerous risk factors for heart disease are linked to the requirement for timely access to accurate, trustworthy, and practical methods for early diagnosis and disease management. In several areas, machine learning (ML) techniques have been utilized extensively to forecast cardiac problems.

In [1], a model for studying and keeping track of the human cardiovascular system was developed by Gavhane et al. This model was developed to identify patients with coronary artery disease. The authors used different machine learning algorithms like Support Vector Machine (SVM), Bayesian classifier and functional trees (FT). Compared to FT-based tests, which were only 81.5% correct, where SVM gives 83.8% accuracy. A hybrid strategy involving wrapper-based feature selection was suggested by Tan et al. [2]. It made use of Genetic Algorithm (GA) and Support Vector Machine (SVM) approaches. A technique for anticipating heart illness was put forth by Rairikar et al. [3]. Thirteen clinical traits from a dataset on UC heart disease were used to construct this approach. Heart disease was diagnosed using algorithms based on the Learning Vector Quantization (LVQ) method and Artificial Neural Networks (ANNs). A composite of the

K. Dasgupta et al. (Eds.): CICBA 2023, CCIS 1955, pp. 301–309, 2024.
https://doi.org/10.1007/978-3-031-48876-4_23

ML algorithms' propensity to predict coronary artery disease, heart failure, stroke, and cardiac arrhythmias served as the main outcome proposed in [4]. In [5] the authors used logistic regression and achieved an accuracy level of 89% to predict coronary disease.

In this work, for the purpose of detecting heart abnormalities, we provide an effective computational model. We focused on various learning models such as SVM, Decision Tree, Naïve Bayes, and KNN, out of which the first three are supervised learning algorithms and the last one is an unsupervised lazy learner algorithm. SVM gave us the highest accuracy for the attributes chosen in our dataset. We use the SVM learning algorithm in our back end for this purpose.

However various research papers have come to the conclusion that deep learning algorithms can achieve even more satisfactory results. Considering our dataset which does not possess a similar scale deep learning algorithms would be difficult to apply. Here we have normalized the dataset using the maximum and minimum values of our attributes. Although our original dataset consisted of 14 attributes which include several attributes which are not readily available, we took the most important attributes to build our model. We also build a user interface to capture real-time user data and predict whether the person gets diagnosed with heart disease or not.

2 Proposed Methodology

2.1 Datasets

We have considered the UCI Machine Learning Heart Disease dataset to predict heart disease. Although the dataset contains 14 attributes and 303 rows (Mentioned in Table 1), we have taken only 5 attributes that are available easily, namely age, sex, trestbps, chol, cp to predict if a person has heart disease or not. We noticed that there were no null values in our data set. We also perceived that the values of our attributes were not properly scaled. So, we needed to normalize our data set so that all our attributes are on the proper scale. We also noticed that our data set is balanced so no more pre-processing was required during training. While testing with the user-given data, we made sure that our data is normalized before being fed to the model. A sample of the dataset used in this paper is given in Fig. 1.

Age: Here the person will enter his or her age. Age is an important factor in determining whether a person will have heart disease or not.

Sex: Here the person will enter his or her gender to be male or female.

trestbps: Here the person enters the resting blood pressure(mm Hg on admission to the hospital). It is an important parameter to predict heart disease.

chol: Here the person enters his or her cholesterol measurement in mg/dl. It is another important factor for the determination of heart disease.

Cp: An inelastic pericardium prevents cardiac filling, which leads to constrictive pericarditis (CP), a kind of diastolic heart failure.

Table 1. Heart Disease Dataset Attributes

Attribute	Description	Range
Age	Age of person in years	29–79
Sex	Gender of person (1-M 0-F)	0,1
Cp	Chest pain type	1,2,3,4
Trestbps	Resting blood pressure in mm Hg	94–200
Chol	Serum cholesterol in mg/dl	126–564
Fbs	Fasting blood sugar in mg/dl	0,1
Restecg	Resting Electrocardiographic results	0,1,2
Thalach	Shows the max heart beat of patient	71–202
Exang	Used to identify if there is an exercise induced angina	0,1
OldPeak	ST depression induced by exercise relative to rest	1–3
Slope	Slope of the Peak Exercise ST segment	1,2,3
Ca	Number of major vessels colored by fluoroscopy	0–3
Thal	3 – Normal, 6 – Fixed Defect, 7 – Reversible Defect	3,6,7
Target	Class Attribute, describes final classes in dataset	0,1

	A	B	C	D	E	F
1	age	sex	trestbps	chol	cp	target
2	63	1	145	233	3	1
3	37	1	130	250	2	1
4	41	0	130	204	1	1
5	56	1	120	236	1	1
6	57	0	120	354	0	1
7	57	1	140	192	0	1
8	56	0	140	294	1	1
9	44	1	120	263	1	1
10	52	1	172	199	2	1
11	70	1	145	174	0	0
12	62	1	120	281	1	0
13	35	1	120	198	0	0
14	59	1	170	288	3	0
15	64	1	125	309	2	0
16	47	1	108	243	2	0
17	57	1	165	289	0	0
18	55	1	160	289	0	0
19	64	1	120	246	0	0

Fig. 1. Snapshot of the Dataset

2.2 Machine Learning Algorithms

We have used four machine Learning Algorithms in this study.

Support Vector Machine (SVM): SVM is a relatively recent promising classifier that can be used to classify linear as well as non-linear instances. It is an extension of a soft maximal margin classifier. SVM is primarily meant for 0–1 classification, but an updated SVM may also classify data into several categories. Using kernels, SVM can enlarge the feature space and modifying the dimensions to achieve non-linear data classification [8].

Naive Bayes: The supervised learning technique known as the Naive Bayes algorithm, which is based on the Bayes theorem, is used to resolve classification issues. It is mostly employed in text categorization with a large training set.

Decision tree: The rule-based learning technique inspired the decision tree classifier. A decision on attribute is identified by a decision node and edges that define variety of decisions. The terminal node represents a class label. Data categorization starts from the root node and grows through a set of condition checks on the feature values.

K-NN Algorithm: The prime aim of KNN classifier is to identify your neighbors, and those neighbors will identify your identity. It is one of the lazy learning algorithms, which adapt all data for training while doing forecasting. KNN is suitable for both classification and regression analysis. According to the algorithm, we assume k value as nearest neighbors ($k < < n$), n is the data size. Therefore, the distances between new validation data and the training data are calculated and store them in sorted order. Finally, the first k numbers of distances are selected and assign specific classes to the unlabeled validation data through majority of voting concept [7].

The proposed methodology is given below (Fig. 2):

3 Results

We have tried to build an end-to-end model of heart disease prediction. We have used python for our backend and used four algorithms namely Support Vector Machine (SVM), Decision Tree, Naïve Byes, and KNN. Among them, the Support Vector Machine gives the highest accuracy that is of 88%. Therefore, we have chosen the SVM algorithm to build the GUI of the Heart Disease Prediction. Figure 3 shows the heatmap visualization of the confusion matrix using different algorithms. The performance of the algorithms are depicted in Fig. 4 and their accuracy scores are presented in the Table 2.

Table 3 shows the comparison of all 4 supervised learning algorithms using precision, recall and f1-score. It can be noted that Support vector machine-based method attained better accuracy, precision, recall and f1-score.

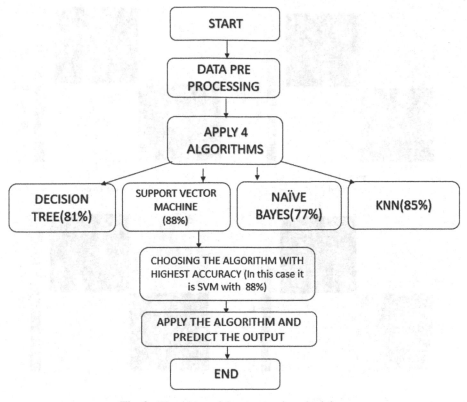

Fig. 2. Flowchart of the proposed methodology

We have used HTML CSS for our front end and integrated both using flask and python programming for the back end. In our user interface, there is a homepage to display details about heart diseases and heart failure. Then going to the next page, we have space to enter details about a person and predict whether he or she is suffering from heart disease or not. The user needs to give input to the five fields: age, gender, blood pressure, cholesterol, and cp in the text boxes and click on Predict button (Fig. 6). If the output is 1 the person suffers from heart disease and must consult any cardiologist and if the output is 0 then the person does not suffer from any heart disease. Figures 5, 6 and 7 give a snapshot of the GUI.

4 Comparison

There are many studies that predicted the heart disease over the years. In this study, we aimed to predict it with easily available features. In Table 4, prediction accuracy of heart disease using same dataset we have used by various authors are mentioned. It can be noted that we have predicted heart disease with 88% accuracy considering only 5 features instead of the 13 features using support vector machine algorithm. We have also developed a GUI-based application to detect the disease easily in this work.

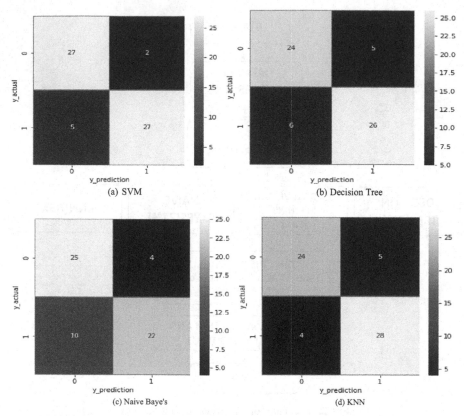

Fig. 3. Heat Map visualization of confusion matrix using different algorithms

Table 2. Accuracy Comparison on Heart Disease Dataset

Algorithm	Accuracy
Naïve Bayes	77%
Support Vector Machine	88%
K-Nearest Neighbor	85%
Decision Tree	81%

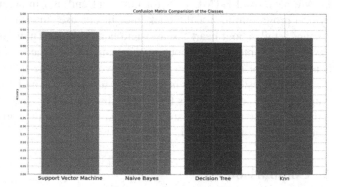

Fig. 4. Accuracy Comparison of Support Vector Machine, Decision Tree, Naïve Byes and KNN

Table 3. Comparison of performance among 4 classifiers on heart disease dataset

Algorithm	Precision	Recall	F1-Score
Naïve Bayes	75.26%	64.25%	69.32%
Support Vector Machine	89.06%	82.25%	85.51%
K-Nearest Neighbor	83.28%	73.42%	78.03%
Decision Tree	79.58%	78.25%	78.90%

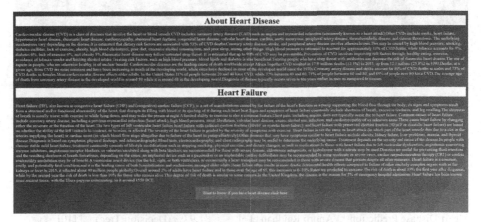

Fig. 5. Home page of our user Interface

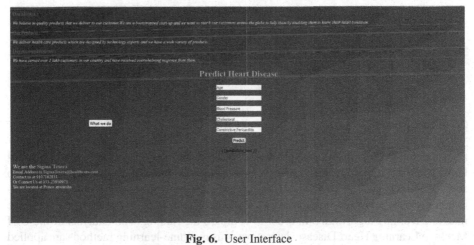

Fig. 6. User Interface

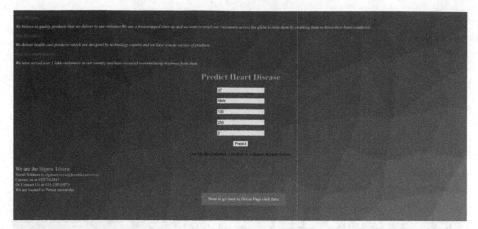

Fig. 7. Prediction output using Support Vector Machine Algorithm in the backend.

Table 4. Comparison Table

Paper	Author	Accuracy	References
Heart Disease Prediction using Machine Learning Techniques	Pooja Anbuselvan	86.89% (Random Forest)	[9]
Heart Disease Prediction using Machine Learning	Apurb Rajdhan et al	81.97% (Decision Tree)	[10]
Heart Disease Prediction Using Machine Learning	Baban.U. Rindhe et al	84.0% (Support Vector Machine)	[11]
Prediction of Cardiovascular Disease using Machine Learning Algorithms	Muktevi Srivenkatesh	71.55% (Support Vector Machine)	[12]

5 Conclusion

An accurate identification of heart disease can reduce the risk of serious health problems, whereas an inaccurate diagnosis can be fatal. The main goal of this research is to suggest a highly accurate machine learning-based cardiovascular disease prediction system, for which the well-known cardiovascular datasets are categorized using cutting-edge machine learning algorithms. In order to compare the findings and analysis of the UCI Machine Learning Heart Disease dataset, various machine-learning methods are applied in this work. However, precise algorithm selection for the particular research area along with interpretation in the appropriate clinical context of the results are also necessary. Therefore, ML algorithms could be connected with electronic health documentation systems and used in clinical performance after being thusly validated, especially in regions with abundant resources. We hope the GUI-based application can help patients to detect the early signs of heart disease.

References

1. Gavhane, A., Kokkula, G., Pandya, I., Devadkar, K.: Prediction of heart disease using machine learning. In: Proceedings of the 2018 Second International Conference on Electronics, Communication and Aerospace Technology (ICECA); 2018; Coimbatore, India
2. Tan, K.C., Teoh, E.J., Yu, Q., Goh, K.C.: A hybrid evolutionary algorithm for attribute selection in data mining. Expert Syst. Appl. **36**(4), 8616–8630 (2009). https://doi.org/10.1016/j.eswa.2008.10.013
3. Rairikar, A., Kulkarni, V., Sabale, V., Kale, H., Lamgunde, A.: Heart disease prediction using data mining techniques. In: Proceedings of the 2017 International Conference on Intelligent Computing and Control (I2C2), Coimbatore, India (2017)
4. Krittanawong, C., et al.: Machine learning prediction in cardiovascular diseases: a meta-analysis. Sci. Rep. **10**(1), 1–11 (2020)
5. Singh, A., Kumar, R.: Heart disease prediction using machine learning algorithms. In: 2020 International Conference on Electrical and Electronics Engineering (ICE3), pp. 452–457. IEEE, February 2020
6. Nahar, J., Imam, T., Tickle, K.S., Chen, Y.-P.P.: Computational intelligence for heart disease diagnosis: a medical knowledge driven approach. Expert Syst. Appl. **40**(1), 96–104 (2013). https://doi.org/10.1016/j.eswa.2012.07.032
7. Dey, L., Chakraborty, S., Biswas, A., Bose, B., Tiwari, S.: Sentiment analysis of review datasets using naive bayes and k-nn classifier. arXiv preprint arXiv:1610.09982 (2016)
8. Chakraborty, S., Kumar, S., Paul, S., Kairi, A.: A study of product trend analysis of review datasets using Naive Bayes, K-NN and SVM classifiers. Int. J. Adv. Eng. Manag. **2**(9), 204–213 (2017)
9. Anbuselvan, P.: Heart disease prediction using machine learning techniques. Int. J. Eng. Res. Technol **9**, 515–518 (2020)
10. Rajdhan, A., Agarwal, A., Sai, M., Ravi, D., Ghuli, P.: Heart disease prediction using machine learning. Int. J. Res. Technol. **9**(04), 659–662 (2020)
11. Rindhe, B.U., Ahire, N., Patil, R., Gagare, S., Darade, M.: . Heart disease prediction using machine learning. Heart Disease **5**(1)
12. Srivenkatesh, M.: Prediction of cardiovascular disease using machine learning algorithms. Int. J. Eng. Adv. Technol **9**(3), 2404–2414 (2020)

Classification of Cricket Shots from Cricket Videos Using Self-attention Infused CNN-RNN (SAICNN-RNN)

Arka Dutta[1,2]([✉]), Abhishek Baral[1,3], Sayan Kundu[1,4], Sayantan Biswas[1,5], Kousik Dasgupta[1], and Hasanujaman[6]

[1] Kalyani Government Engineering College, Kalyani, India
arkadutta.cg@gmail.com
[2] Rochester Institute of Technology, New York, USA
[3] NIT Trichy, Trichy, India
[4] TCS India, Kolkata, India
[5] IIT Bombay, Mumbai, India
[6] Government College of Engineering and Textile Technology, Berhampore, India

Abstract. Millions of people play and enjoy the game of cricket, however, classifying the diverse batting style and postures used frequently by the batsman during a cricket match has always been a difficult proposition. Owing to the immense overlap between postures and various styles of the same shot, it gets extremely harder. Sports experts, trainers, and coaches must learn more about the variety of approaches used by each batsman in both international and local matches in order to guide the team in its entirety and ensure that the training program of cricket players is planned and executed to its fullest potential. The work in this paper thrives on a hybrid deep learning approach that combines convolutional and recurrent neural networks for classifying ten (10) types of cricket shots from match videos. To establish a baseline, a sports CrickShot10 [1] dataset and an open-source cricket video dataset are used. Automatic feature extraction is handled by a hybridized form of convolutional neural network (CNN [11])- recurrent neural network (RNN) combined. Long temporal dependencies are handled by a Gated Recurrent Unit (GRU [12]). It is further improved by adding a Self-attention [20] module that is introduced to the hybrid module to facilitate a semi-supervised approach to extract the key frames from the video. This idea is intended to address the architecture's inconsistent behaviour while processing somewhat long videos, and their inability to give "correct/relevant" frames priority. When results are compared to other modules, they show good accuracy values. Here we focused on 'Accuracy' instead of other evaluation metrics as this is a task of simple classification.

1 Introduction

With the recent rollout of 5G and 6G, video has become widely used for broadcasting on various transmission mediums such as smart television, OTT, and the Internet. Sports broadcasting, with its sizable fan base, is of particular importance. The vast amounts of data, both private and open source, overwhelm data servers daily. This trend has pushed

K. Dasgupta et al. (Eds.): CICBA 2023, CCIS 1955, pp. 310–326, 2024.
https://doi.org/10.1007/978-3-031-48876-4_24

the technical industries to a new level. In each sport, the classification of sports videos is an interesting index. By examining various sports videos obtained from old recordings of live matches, practice matches, and training sessions, one can gain insight into player performance, stamina, abilities, specific tendencies, strengths, and weaknesses.

In this work, we focus on cricket videos due to their widespread appeal in India and the rest of Asia. Data science and scene analysis in cricket enables coaches and trainers to train players and choose tactics to be deployed in the game's broader context through post-game analysis. It also simplifies operations for content handlers and broadcasting firms to run their operations for intelligent context-based searches.

Sustainability has attracted a lot of interest in recent years, and leading research has explored a wide range of techniques to classify visual data and interpret scene context. Deep learning models have been widely used to tackle computer vision and sustainability problems. Cricket shots are mostly analyzed by humans by looking at a sequence of actions, sometimes also taking the game's surroundings into account. In this work, we consider a part of the UCF101 dataset, CrickShot10 [1]. The main objective of this paper is to develop a system that can classify different types of cricket shots based on sequential visual information using visual information in the spatial and time domains.

We propose a hybrid model that combines a convolutional neural network (CNN [11]) and recurrent neural network (RNN [10]) inspired by [19], where the former finds spatial feature extractors by processing information through time using internal memory gates. By combining these two models, we analyze sports video sequences in different combinations and present the experimental results. A gated recurrent unit (GRU [12]) handles long-term temporal dependencies. Additionally, we add a self-attention [20] module to the hybrid model to facilitate the extraction of keyframes in long videos using a semi-supervised approach.

The remainder of the paper is structured as follows: Sect. 2 summarizes related works, Sect. 3 describes the dataset used in this work, Sect. 4 presents the proposed approach's flow diagram and the various models used, Sect. 6 shows the experimental results and comparisons, and Sect. 7 concludes the paper.

2 Related Work

In previous works, several attempts were made to classify different actions in sports [2–5]. And in continuous video classification, people primarily tried four successful architectures:

- Using a time-distributed ConvNet and passing the features to an RNN [10], in one network.
- 3D CNN [11] or deep CNN [11] using the third dimension as a time wrapper.
- Extracting features from each frame with a convolutional network and passing the sequence to a separate RNN [10].
- Hierarchical Vision Transformer using Shifted Window or SWIN Transformers

Most of the methods that have been used in the past take either still images of players posing for different shots from different angles and lighting or short clips (usually 2–5 s long) of players playing the specific shots as their standard dataset.

In [6], eight different cricket shots were classified using deep convolutional neural networks. A 2D and 3D CNN [11] and long short-term memory (LSTM [9, 10]) recurrent neural network (RNN [10]) were used to categorize different cricket shots. Transfer learning from a pre-trained VGG [8] model was also used. The highest accuracy of 90% was achieved using a dataset of 800 cricket shots. For this particular task of cricket video classification, Sen et al. [1] presented a novel approach incorporating a convolutional neural network (CNN [11]) for automatic feature extraction and a gated recurrent unit (GRU [12]) to deal with the long temporal dependencies. This idea worked better than most other existing approaches. So, taking this as a baseline, we will move on to work with its limitations and try to improve the performance metrics. This paper first used two types of architectures - 1) Conventional CNN [11] models built from scratch paired with a recurrent unit, namely the gated recurrent unit (GRU [12]) and 2) dilated CNN [11] models built from scratch and paired with GRU [12]. The authors tried different pre-built models on transfer learning to compare the accuracy metrics with their own models, namely DenseNet169 [14], VGG16 [8], InceptionNetV3 [17], and Xception [18], where all layers were frozen. The model using VGG16 [8] paired with GRU [12] gave the best result in their case.

Contrasting other transfer learning models as found in [3]—InceptionV3 [17], Xception [18], and DenseNet169 [14]—using VGG16 [8], a validation accuracy of 86% could be achieved, which motivated them to further explore VGG16 [8] models. In this case, the authors considered a 180180 px input image and discarded all fully connected layers. Thus, the output from the final layer was (5, 5, 512). Then, two models were derived: Model 1 was designed by making the final 4 layers of VGG16 [8] trainable, and Model 2 by making the final 8 layers of VGG16 trainable. All remaining configurations of the GRU [12] layer, fully connected layers, were kept in a similar fashion.

3 Datasets Description

3.1 UCF101 Subset

UCF101 is an action recognition data set of realistic action videos, collected from YouTube, having 101 action categories. This data set is an extension of the UCF50 dataset, which has 50 action categories. With 13320 videos from 101 action categories, UCF101 gives the largest diversity in terms of actions and with the presence of large variations in camera motion, object appearance and pose, objective scale, viewpoint, cluttered background, illumination conditions, etc., as we show in Fig. 1(a) and 1(b). It is the most challenging data set to date. As most of the available action recognition data sets are not realistic and are staged by actors, UCF101 aims to encourage more research into action recognition by learning and exploring new realistic action categories. As the first step, we worked on a subset of the famous UCF101 large dataset and tried to get details about the best possible models for feature extraction on our data. The UCF101 subset contains five types of similar action Cricket Shot, Punch, Tennis Swing, Playing Cello and Shaving Beard.

The action categories for UCF101 data set are: Apply Eye Makeup, Apply Lipstick, Archery, Baby Crawling, Balance Beam, Band Marching, Baseball Pitch, Basketball

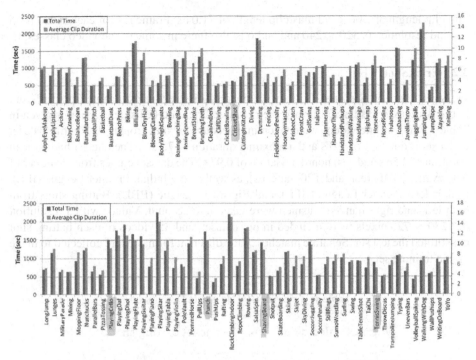

Fig. 1. Video Classes and time distributions of 5 classes in UCF101 Subset

Shooting, Basketball Dunk, Bench Press, Biking, Billiards Shot, Blow Dry Hair, Blowing Candles, Body Weight Squats, Bowling, Boxing Punching Bag, Boxing Speed Bag, Breaststroke, Brushing Teeth, Clean and Jerk, Cliff Diving, Cricket Bowling, Cricket Shot, Cutting In Kitchen, Diving, Drumming, Fencing, Field Hockey Penalty, Floor Gymnastics, Frisbee Catch, Front Crawl, Golf Swing, Haircut, Hammer Throw, Hammering, Handstand Pushups, Handstand Walking, Head Massage, High Jump, Horse Race, Horse Riding, Hula Hoop, Ice Dancing, Javelin Throw, Juggling Balls, Jump Rope, Jumping Jack, Kayaking, Knitting, Long Jump, Lunges, Military Parade, Mixing Batter, Mopping Floor, Nun chucks, Parallel Bars, Pizza Tossing, Playing Guitar, Playing Piano, Playing Tabla, Playing Violin, Playing Cello, Playing Daf, Playing Dhol, Playing Flute, Playing Sitar, Pole Vault, Pommel Horse, Pull Ups, Punch, Push Ups, Rafting, Rock Climbing Indoor, Rope Climbing, Rowing, Salsa Spins, Shaving Beard, Shotput, Skate Boarding, Skiing, Skijet, Sky Diving, Soccer Juggling, Soccer Penalty, Still Rings, Sumo Wrestling, Surfing, Swing, Table Tennis Shot, Tai Chi, Tennis Swing, Throw Discus, Trampoline Jumping, Typing, Uneven Bars, Volleyball Spiking, Walking with a dog, Wall Pushups, Writing On Board, Yo Yo. We have done the train test split on the following database where 70% of the videos of each category were put into the train data and the rest 30% were put into the test data.

We have used CricketShot, PlayingClub, Punch, Saving Beard and TennisSwing video classes from various classes of UCF 101 dataset. There exists 25 groups per action, 4–7 clips per group with a mean clip length of 7.21 s, total duration of 1600 min,

min clip length of 1.06 s and max clip length of 71.04 s. Frame rate of each video is 25 fps and resolution is 320 × 240 and audio is also there in some of the video classes.

3.2 CrickShot10 [1]

In the literature by Sen et al. [1] they obtained 10 different cricket shots from different publicly accessible sources, termed their dataset CricShot10. Its description is given in Table 1. Only offline videos were taken into account for this project. The entire dataset had a short duration of 1.0 s and a maximal duration of 7.72 s. The dataset had a mean duration of 2.56 s and a standard deviation of 0.97 s. The dataset comes from a variety of ICC events (ODI, Test, and T20 matches), as well as the Indian Premier League (IPL), Bangladesh Premier League (BPL), and Big Bash League (BBL). Batting shots from both left- and right-handed batsmen were taken into account. Videos with a resolution of 1280 × 720 pixels were included in our dataset, and 35 videos of each batting shot constituted the test set. Separate matches of the different formats were collected to make up the training set.

Table 1. CrickShot10 [1] Dataset Description

Dataset video quantity for 10 cricket batting shots.

Name	Training Set	Test Set
Cover Drive	153	35
Defensive Shot	157	35
Flick	146	35
Hook	146	35
Late Cut	147	35
Lofted Shot	151	35
Pull	144	35
Square Cut	160	35
Straight Drive	154	35
Sweep	159	35

For Cover-drive, we have used 153 videos for training and 35 videos for the test set. For Defensive Shot, we have used 157 videos for training and 35 videos for test sets. For Flick, we have used 146 videos for training and 35 videos for the test set. For Hook, we have used 146 videos for training and 35 videos for the test set. For Late Cut, we have used 147 videos for training and 35 videos for the test set. For Lofted Shot, we have used 151 videos for training and 35 videos for the test set. For Pull, we have used 144 videos for training and 35 videos for the test set. For Square Cut, we have used 160 videos for training and 35 videos for the test set. For Square Drive, we have used 154 videos for training and 35 videos for the test set. For Sweep, we have used 159 videos for training and 35 videos for the test set.

We have used the same data in the same distribution to get accurate metrics comparison over previous work.

4 Proposed Workflow

In this work inspired from [5], we aim to find the most standardized method of classification of the different cricket shots from player poses based on the simple image preprocessing methods and best accuracy while keeping strict care to minimize the chance for error. We discovered while analyzing existing literature on the theme as mentioned above that, while they work quite well for short video clips, there is still margin and scope for improvement similar to [7]. As well, as mentioned, all these datasets have manually cropped video clips, which cannot simply align with real-time data without introducing manual labour. For this, we have proposed, infuse-based self-attention [20] for semi-supervised detection and summarization of real-time video clips into particular frames with poses and CNN [11] RNN [10] models on them. This idea will not only reduce manual labour but also can prioritize "relevant" frames over less "relevant" ones automatically and can reduce the preprocessing size and underfitting of the RNN [10].

We have begun our work by studying the related works of other researchers and engineers on the topic of working models and preprocessing methods. As the first step, we worked on a subset of the famous UCF101 large dataset and tried to get details about the best possible models for feature extraction in our data. The UCF101 subset containing five type's similar actions I.e Cricket Shot, Punch, Tennis Swing, Playing Cello, and Shaving Beard seemed like quite good groundwork to base on. During the process, we learned the models that were most likely to be suitable, such as different pre-trained Convolutional Neural Network models using transfer learning such as InceptionV3 [17], DenseNet121 [15], ResNet50 [16], NASNetLarge [14], and VGG19 [8]. These models are more likely and standard measures for feature extraction in this particular scenario rather than custom models and other pre-trained models.

1) We start by pre-processing each video and sampling 40 random frames from each of them.
2) Next we pass these frames to the transfer learning CNN [11] models imported from keras backbone pre-trained on imagenet [13]. We use these models as feature extractors for each frame and pass these features to RNN [10] models to work with.
3) Next we use Gated Recurrent Unit architecture, first with 16 layers, followed by another 8 layers and a dropout regularization of 0.4, followed by 8 dense ANN layers with ReLU activation and finally dense layers with softmax activation for output.

4) We now have accuracies for each of the different feature extractors. We compare them and choose the best one to further work with.

5) At this phase we already used all the previously used architectures to deal with this kind of classification and tried to improve on that. Now we are introducing the novelty of our paper. i.e. the self-attention [20] mechanism into the picture.

6) We are introducing a self-attention [20] block in the 2nd set of GRU [12] layers keeping all other requisites and conditions the same as previous.

7) Next we similarly compare the accuracies for models with attention [20] infused with the models without attention [20] infused and go with the best of them.

8) After settling on the best possible model and getting significant improvement over previously used ones we can further improve the accuracies by tuning different hyper-parameters used. Especially the MAX-SEQUENCE LENGTH which is the number of frames to be sampled, the architectures and number of layers of GRU [12] and such (Fig. 2).

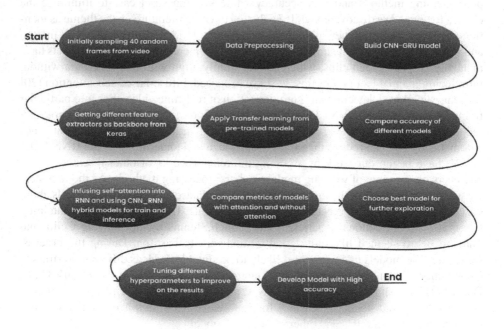

Fig. 2. Proposed Workflow

5   Transfer Learning-Based CNN [11]-RNN [10] Architecture

CNN [11] model's output is fed into a time-distributed wrapper. Weights are updated for all frames if frames from a video are individually passed to their adjacent layer as in [3]. Consequently, differences between video frames are meaningless. Consequently, a time-distributed layer was introduced that provided the option to share layers across video frames. The time-distributed layer's input shape should be in the form of a 5D tensor as in [4]. Succeeding that, the time-distributed flatten operation generated an output shape that could be passed to a recurrent neural network (RNN [10]). To detect actions from a video, the coordinate feature alone is insufficient. It is necessary to know what happened in the previous frame to correctly classify action in a video. Various RNNs [10] were proposed for maintaining this temporal dependency, the input of which is a 3D vector of formats (samples, time steps, units) (Fig. 3).

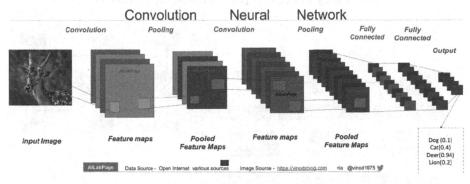

Fig. 3. Basic Block of CNN [11]

Traditional RNNs [10] suffer from the problems of vanishing gradients and exploding gradients. Consequently, the LSTM [9, 10] was proposed. The LSTM [9, 10] algorithm performed admirably in tracking the vanishing gradient and exploding gradient problems, as well as long-term events. Through its various gate concepts, LSTM [9, 10] solves the problem of time dependence. Succeeding that, researchers created GRU [12], a simplified version of LSTM [9, 10]. GRU [12] demonstrated unrivalled success in long-term feature dependability using fewer gates than LSTM [9, 10]. It also reduces the number of trainable parameters by using fewer gates, simplifying the network. The update, reset, and current-memory gates were used in our study. The update gate helps the model determine how much previous knowledge should be passed on to future time steps. Furthermore, the model learns how much of the new state is simply a copy of the old state value, removing the risk of a vanishing gradient. The reset gate aids the model in determining how much previous knowledge it should forget. The current-memory gate calculates the current state value by combining the previous hidden state with the current input (Figs. 4 and 5).

In the past few years, pre-trained models saw high acceptance in computer-vision tasks such as real-time object recognition and image classification as [2]. As a result of learning on a large number of datasets such as ImageNet [13], several pre-trained models are conducive to solving similar problems. High accuracy is not available using shallow learning models because they require a large amount of data. Handling this enormous dataset is almost impossible due to a shortage of available data resources. Since most pre-trained models are generated from a massive dataset containing a few million samples, this typical use of the developed models results in a baseline for further

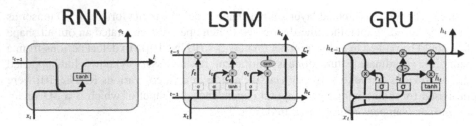

Fig. 4. Basic Block of RNN [10], LSTM [9, 10] and GRU [12]

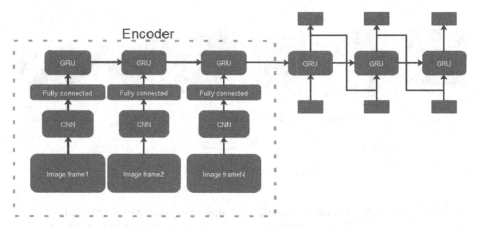

Fig. 5. CNN [11]-RNN [10] (GRU [12]) Combined Architecture

data analysis. Layer freezing is applied to disable the weight updating of the layers of models.

Furthermore, the weights of specific layers can be kept frozen, allowing for weights in the custom dataset to this change. Succeeding the initialization of the pre-trained models, other layers can also be integrated. In our work, we used transfer learning from pre-trained VGG19 [8], InceptionV3 [17], ResNet50 [16], NASNetLarge [14], and DenseNet [15] models. We disallowed weight updates of all pre-trained models by freezing all layers (Figs. 6 and 7).

ImageNet [13] dataset weights were considered for all pre-trained models, and all fully connected layers were discarded. A flattening layer was introduced after loading a pre-trained model, which converted the input shape into a 1D array. The time-distributed wrapper was then initiated to wrap the pre-trained model layers and the flattening layer, which allowed for sharing the layer weights for all sampled video frames. Afterwards, the GRU [12] layer was appended to trace temporal changes across video frames (Fig. 8).

Although LSTM [9, 10]/GRU [12] networks provide much better performance over Vanilla RNNs [10], it still suffers from certain limitations. The recurrent architecture of LSTM [9, 10]/GRU [12] doesn't account for parallel processing making the training procedure slow and cumbersome. Also, random weight initializations can have devastating effects on the performance of the working model. Above all, with more long sequences

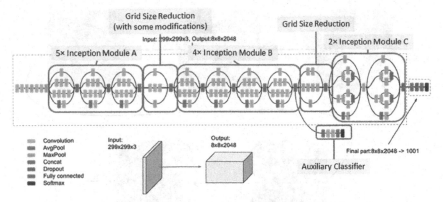

Fig. 6. Inception V3 [17] Model Architecture

```
Model: "feature_extractor"
_____
 Layer (type)                 Output Shape              Param #
=================================================================
 input_4 (InputLayer)         [(None, 224, 224, 3)]     0

 tf.math.truediv_1 (TFOpLamb  (None, 224, 224, 3)       0
 da)

 tf.math.subtract_1 (TFOpLam  (None, 224, 224, 3)       0
 bda)

 inception_v3 (Functional)    (None, 2048)              21802784

=================================================================
Total params: 21,802,784
Trainable params: 21,768,352
Non-trainable params: 34,432
_____
```

Fig. 7. Inception V3 [17] Pre-trained Model Summary

the LSTM [9, 10]/GRU [12] networks become error-prone and give up on long-term dependencies due to memory and hardware constraints. Here comes the Attention [20] mechanism to the rescue.

The attention [20] mechanism allows output to focus attention [20] on input while producing output while the self-attention [20] model allows inputs to interact with each other (i.e. calculate attention [20] of all other inputs with respect to one input).

The scaled dot-product attention [20] first computes a *dot product* for each query, q, with all of the keys, k. It subsequently divides each result by the Square root of the dimension of the k vector and proceeds to apply a softmax function. In doing so, it obtains the weights that are used to *scale* the values, v

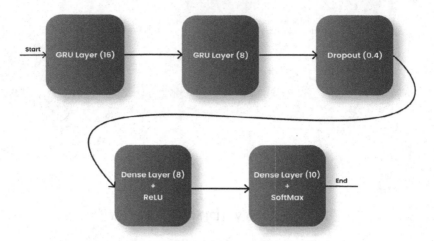

Fig. 8. Sequence Model Architecture (Without Attention [20])

- The first step is multiplying each of the encoder input vectors with three weights matrices (W(Q), W(K), W(V)) that is to be trained during the training process providing three vectors for each of the input vectors: the key vector, the query vector, and the value vector.
- In the next steps we follow the principle formula of self-attention [20] as follows (Fig. 9)

$$Attention(Q, K, V) = softmax\left(\frac{QK^T}{\sqrt{d_k}}\right)V$$

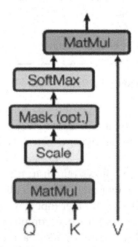

Fig. 9. Self-Attention Mechanism [20]

In this way we calculate self-attention [20] within the GRU [12] encoder decoder block and use it in our combined CNN [11]-RNN [10] model (Fig. 10).

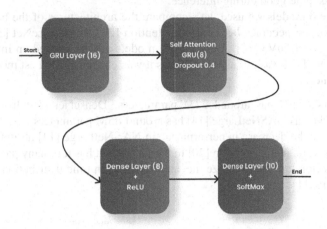

Fig. 10. Sequence Model Architecture (With Attention) [20]

6   Results and Discussions

6.1   Hardware Configuration

We have done this whole work in Google Colaboratory (Free Version) which comes with:

- GPU: 1×Tesla K80, compute 3.7, having 2496 CUDA cores, 12 GB GDDR5 VRAM
- CPU: 1x single core hyper threaded Xeon Processors @2.3 Ghz i.e. (1 core, 2 threads)
- RAM: ~12.6 GB Available
- Disk: ~33 GB Available

6.2   Evaluation

As it's a simple classification task at the end, we initially used classification accuracy as our main metric. We propose to use Precision, Recall and F1 Score next to strengthen our views on results.

6.3   Discussion

We have done training and inference on the UCF101 subset and we have got the following inference:

A. Between the current combination of CNN [11] from 6 transfer learning models i.e. Inception [17], ResNet [16], VGG [8], DenseNet [15] and NASNet [14], in 5 models using Attention block [20] in GRU [12] module out of 6 models outperformed the ones without Attention.

B. With InceptionV3 [17], an accuracy of 65.18% in the case of GRU [12] without attention [20] and & 78.12% in the case of GRU [12] with attention [20] was achieved, which was quite good during inference.
C. Out of the 6 models we used, let's compare the architectures of the best 3 models in terms of test accuracy before using attention [20]. i.e., DenseNet [15], NASNet [14] and InceptionV3 [17]. All of these 3 models are pre-trained on Imagenet [13]. InceptionV3 [17] was discussed before as it was chosen as the best model based on performance.

InceptionV3 [17] has around 22M parameters. DenseNet [15] has around 7M parameters whereas NASNetLarge [14] has around 85M parameters.

We can owe the decrease in performance in NASNetLarge [14] abruptly, unlike all other models while using attention [20] to the fact that it has too many parameters, and the feature vector can't fully utilize the attention [20] in time distribution wrappers of GRU [12] (Fig. 11).

```
Model: "feature_extractor"
_________________________________________________________________
Layer (type)                Output Shape              Param #
-----------------------------------------------------------------
input_6 (InputLayer)        [(None, 224, 224, 3)]     0

tf.math.truediv_2 (TFOpLamb  (None, 224, 224, 3)      0
da)

tf.nn.bias_add (TFOpLambda)  (None, 224, 224, 3)      0

tf.math.truediv_3 (TFOpLamb  (None, 224, 224, 3)      0
da)

densenet121 (Functional)    (None, 1024)              7037504

-----------------------------------------------------------------
Total params: 7,037,504
Trainable params: 6,953,856
Non-trainable params: 83,648
_________________________________________________________________
```

a

```
Model: "feature_extractor"
_________________________________________________________________
Layer (type)                Output Shape              Param #
=================================================================
input_8 (InputLayer)        [(None, 331, 331, 3)]     0

tf.math.truediv_4 (TFOpLamb  (None, 331, 331, 3)      0
da)

tf.math.subtract_2 (TFOpLam  (None, 331, 331, 3)      0
bda)

NASNet (Functional)         (None, 4032)              84916818

=================================================================
Total params: 84,916,818
Trainable params: 84,720,150
Non-trainable params: 196,668
_________________________________________________________________
```

b

Fig. 11. a: DenseNet [15] b: NASNetLarge [14]

Table 2. Comparison of different feature extractor models using accuracy metrics, both using attention [20] and non attention-based models.

Feature Extractor	Test Accuracy Without Attention [20] (After 30 epochs)	Test Accuracy With Attention [20] (After 30 epochs)	Change in Accuracy
DenseNet121 [15]	50.89%	58.48%	+14.91%
NASNetLarge [14]	65.18%	37.05% *	−43.16%
VGG19 [8]	28.12%	55.36%	+96.87%
VGG16 [8]	30.14%	61.21%	+103.08%
ResNet50 [16]	44.2%	44.8%	+1.35%
InceptionV3 [17]	***65.18%***	***78.12%***	***+19.85%***

From Table 2, it can be concluded that there is a bump in the accuracy after using the attention [20] block in GRU [12] in these models, proving the basis of our initial assumption and intuition.

As we said above, we first work on the subset of the UCF101 dataset. After running 30 epochs of the model for training, we inferenced the model on the test data, i.e., videos reserved for the test dataset to get results about accuracy.

We have two accuracy measures for each combination of the model:

1. **CNN [11]-GRU [12] model without self-attention instilled:**

    For the usual RNN [10] module with 16 GRU [12] layers, followed by 8 GRU [12] layers and followed by dense layers with ReLU and finally Softmax, the 6 combinations of transfer learning CNN [11] models, i.e. DenseNet121 [15], NASNetLarge [14], VGG19 [8], VGG16 [8], ResNet50 [16], InceptionV3 [17], we get the accuracy of 50.89%, 65.18%, 28.12%, 30.14%, 44.2% and 65.18% respectively on inferences.

    This result is the average of the best 10 runs of each of these combinations on the Google collaboratory. Here, we can see InceptionV3 [17] and NASNetLarge [14] are consistently providing better results than other models.

2. **CNN [11]-GRU [12], model with self-attention [20] instilled:**

    For the addition of a self-attention [20] module in our 2nd GRU [12] block of 8 layers, preceded by a GRU [12] block of 16 layers and followed by a regular dropout of 0.4 and analogous couples of Dense layers with ReLU and eventually Softmax activation. The 6 combinations of transfer learning CNN [11] models i.e. DenseNet121 [15], NASNetLarge [14], VGG19 [8], VGG16 [8], ResNet50 [16], and InceptionV3 [17], we get the accuracy of 58.48%, 37.05%, 55.36%, 61.21%, 44.8% and 78.12% respectively on inferences.

    This result is the average of the best 10 runs of each of these combinations on the Google collaboratory. This infusion of attention [20] consistently provides a huge bump in accuracy excepting one model (i.e. NASNetLarge [14]). The accuracy bump ranges from 1.35% for ResNet50 [16] to a huge 103.08% for VGG16 [8]. Here again, *InceptionV3 [17] with a huge bump of 19.85% gets an accuracy of 78.12% which is considerably good.*

We performed ablation studies on InceptionV3 [17] using its former versions InceptionV1 [17] and InceptionV2 [17]. These 3 differs in the architecture in following aspects.

In the Inception V2 [17] architecture. The 5×5 convolution of V1 is replaced by the two 3×3 convolutions. This also decreases computational time and thus increases computational speed because a 5×5 convolution is 2.78 more expensive than a 3×3 convolution. So, Using two 3×3 layers instead of 5×5 increases the performance of architecture.

Inception V3 [17] is similar to and contains all the features of Inception V2 [17] with the following changes/additions:

1. Use of RMSprop optimizer.
2. Batch Normalization in the fully connected layer of the Auxiliary classifier.
3. Use of 7×7 factorized Convolution
4. **Label Smoothing Regularization:** It is a method to regularize the classifier by estimating the effect of label-dropout during training. It prevents the classifier to predict

a class too confidently. The addition of label smoothing gives a 0.2% improvement from the error rate.

We have done training and inference on the CricckShot10 subset and we have got the following inference:

A. Between the current combination of CNN [11] from 6 transfer learning models i.e. Inception [17], ResNet [16], VGG [8], DenseNet [15] and NASNet [14], in 5 models using Attention block [20] in GRU [12] module out of 6 models outperformed the ones without Attention.
B. With InceptionV3 [17], an accuracy of 70.14% in the case of GRU [12] without attention [20] and & 87.45% in the case of GRU [12] with attention [20] was achieved, which was quite good during inference.
C. Out of the 6 models we used, let's compare the architectures of the best 3 models in terms of test accuracy before using attention [20]. i.e., DenseNet [15], NASNet [14] and InceptionV3 [17]. All of these 3 models are pre-trained on Imagenet [13]. InceptionV3 [17] was discussed before as it was chosen as the best model based on performance.

InceptionV3 [17] has around 22M parameters. DenseNet [15] has around 7M parameters whereas NASNetLarge [14] has around 85M parameters (Table 3).

Table 3. Comparison of different feature extractor models using accuracy metrics, both using attention [20] and non-attention-based models in CrickShot10.

Feature Extractor	Test Accuracy Without Attention [20] (After 30 epochs)	Test Accuracy With Attention [20] (After 30 epochs)	Change in Accuracy
DenseNet121 [15]	55.63%	67.48%	+21.30%
NASNetLarge [14]	67.16%	65.99% *	−1.74%
VGG19 [8]	30.29%	61.20%	+102.04%
VGG16 [8]	34.42%	71.19%	+106.82%
ResNet50 [16]	47.7%	49.1%	+2.93%
InceptionV3 [17]	*70.14%*	*87.45%*	*+24.67%*

These changes don't provide any significant improvements in accuracy but InceptionV3 [17] surely is much faster and computationally efficient in both UCF101 and CrickShot10 datasets. The MAdds (Multiplication addition), signifying the parametric calculation decrease greatly without compromising the evaluation metrics.

7 Conclusion and Future Works

This paper proposed a hybrid neural network architecture that successfully classified 10 different cricket batting shots from a video, populated by publicly available data sources. We used the UCF101 dataset at first. Experiment results signified that using a pre-trained model is superior when massive data are unavailable. After combining with GRU [12], transfer learning from a pre-trained model outperformed the other models whenever the model was allowed to update its weight according to our dataset. A hybrid CNN [11]–GRU [12] architecture, developed from a pre-trained InceptionV3 [17] model, achieved the highest accuracy of 65.18%. The hybrid architecture paired with our novel addition of Attention [20] to the GRU [12] module produced significantly better results of 78.12% on test data. This idea is a huge improvement. We will infer the model with minor changes and perform hyperparameter tuning on the CrickShot10 [1] dataset.

We hope to achieve an even greater distinction between performances while using Crickshot10 [1] for further exploration. As our theoretical basis suggests, attention [20] should perform significantly better on longer videos. So, the longer the videos, the better the results.

References

1. Sen, A., Deb, K., Dhar, P.K., Koshiba, T.: CricShotClassify: an approach to classifying batting shots from cricket videos using a convolutional neural network and gated recurrent unit. Sensors **21**(8), 2846 (2021)
2. Russo, M.A., Filonenko, A., Jo, K.H.: Sports classification in sequential frames using CNN and RNN. In: Proceedings of the International Conference on Information and Communication Technology Robotics (ICT-ROBOT), Busan, Korea, 6–8 September 2018, pp. 1–3 (2018)
3. Russo, M.A., Kurnianggoro, L., Jo, K.H.: Classification of sports videos with a combination of deep learning models and transfer learning. In: Proceedings of the International Conference on Electrical, Computer and Communication Engineering (ECCE), Cox's Bazar, Bangladesh, 7–9 February 2019, pp. 1–5 (2019)
4. Hanna, J., Patlar, F., Akbulut, A., Mendi, E., Bayrak, C.: HMM based classification of sports videos using color feature. In: Proceedings of the 6th IEEE International Conference Intelligent Systems, Sofia, Bulgaria, 6–8 September 2012, pp. 388–390 (2012)
5. Cricri, F., et al.: Sport type classification of mobile videos. IEEE Trans. Multimed. **16**, 917–932 (2014). https://doi.org/10.1109/TMM.2014.2307552
6. Khan, M.Z., Hassan, M.A., Farooq, A., Khan, M.U.G.: Deep CNN based data-driven recognition of cricket batting shots. In: 2018 International Conference on Applied and Engineering Mathematics (ICAEM), pp. 67–71. IEEE (2018)
7. Semwal, A., Mishra, D., Raj, V., Sharma, J., Mittal, A.: Cricket shot detection from videos. In: 2018 9th International Conference on Computing, Communication and Networking Technologies (ICCCNT), pp. 1–6. IEEE (2018)
8. Simonyan, K., Zisserman, A.: Very deep convolutional networks for large-scale image recognition. arXiv preprint arXiv:1409.1556 (2014)
9. Hochreiter, S., Schmidhuber, J.: LSTM can solve hard long time lag problems. In: Advances in Neural Information Processing Systems, vol. 9 (1996)
10. Sherstinsky, A.: Fundamentals of recurrent neural network (RNN) and long short-term memory (LSTM) network. Phys. D **404**, 132306 (2020)
11. O'Shea, K., Nash, R.: An introduction to convolutional neural networks. arXiv preprint arXiv:1511.08458 (2015)
12. Chung, J., Gulcehre, C., Cho, K., Bengio, Y.: Empirical evaluation of gated recurrent neural networks on sequence modeling. arXiv preprint arXiv:1412.3555 (2014)

13. Deng, J., Dong, W., Socher, R., Li, L.J., Li, K., Fei-Fei, L.: ImageNet [13]: a large-scale hierarchical image database. In: 2009 IEEE Conference on Computer Vision and Pattern Recognition, pp. 248–255. IEEE (2009)

14. Zoph, B., Vasudevan, V., Shlens, J., Le, Q.V.: Learning transferable architectures for scalable image recognition. In: Proceedings of the IEEE Conference on Computer Vision and Pattern Recognition, pp. 8697–8710 (2018)

15. Huang, G., Liu, Z., Van Der Maaten, L., Weinberger, K.Q.: Densely connected convolutional networks. In: Proceedings of the IEEE Conference on Computer Vision and Pattern Recognition, pp. 4700–4708 (2017)

16. He, K., Zhang, X., Ren, S., Sun, J.: Deep residual learning for image recognition. In: Proceedings of the IEEE Conference on Computer Vision and Pattern Recognition, pp. 770–778 (2016)

17. Szegedy, C., et al.: Going deeper with convolutions. In: Proceedings of the IEEE Conference on Computer Vision and Pattern Recognition, pp. 1–9 (2015)

18. Chollet, F.: Xception [18]: deep learning with depthwise separable convolutions. In: Proceedings of the IEEE Conference on Computer Vision and Pattern Recognition (CVPR), Honolulu, HI, USA, 21–26 July 2017, pp. 1251–1258 (2017)

19. Ali, L., Alnajjar, F., Jassmi, H.A., Gocho, M., Khan, W., Serhani, M.A.: Performance evaluation of deep CNN-based crack detection and localization techniques for concrete structures. Sensors 21(5), 1688 (2021)

20. Vaswani, A., et al.: Attention is all you need. In: Advances in Neural Information Processing Systems, vol. 30 (2017)

Attention-Residual Convolutional Neural Network for Image Restoration Due to Bad Weather

Madhuchhanda Dasgupta$^{(\boxtimes)}$ ⓘ, Oishila Bandyopadhyay ⓘ,
and Sanjay Chatterji

Indian Institute of Information Technology Kalyani, Kalyani, India
{madhuchhanda_phd19,oishila,sanjayc}@iiitkalyani.ac.in

Abstract. Image quality degrades due to various reasons. In some circumstances, different weather conditions like fog, mist or rain have an impact on image visibility. Dust and pollution in the air can reduce the clarity of images taken outside. Thus, input images with poor visibility may reduce the effectiveness of computer vision related applications. The automated traffic monitoring systems, computer vision based smart systems used in different vehicles are few examples of such applications. Image restoration is essential of such applications for accurate implementation. In the proposed work, an end-to-end network is designed to restore images affected by rain, fog, dust and pollution. An integrated Convolutional Neural Network (CNN) with channel attention method is proposed for image restoration. In the proposed work a CNN is designed to reduce the loss between input degraded image and clear ground-truth image. Channel attention technique based on Style-based Recalibration Module (SRM) is applied on convolutional feature maps to improve the visibility of the restored image. The model is trained on a synthesized dataset and it is then evaluated on both synthesized and real-world outdoor and traffic images. The experimental results demonstrate that the proposed method is more effective to several state-of-the-art methods both quantitatively and visually.

Keywords: Computer Vision · Image Restoration · Convolutional Neural Network (CNN) · Channel based Attention · Style-based Recalibration Module (SRM)

1 Introduction

Outdoor images loss their clear visibility mainly due to atmospheric phenomena like rain, fog, dust or pollution. In rainy conditions, captured images suffer from haziness due to light scattering along with non-linear distortion by rain streaks. In addition fog, mist, dust and pollution badly decrease the clarity of the captured images.

The degradation of images severely affect the outdoor computer vision applications like traffic surveillance, autonomous navigation and driving etc. Image

K. Dasgupta et al. (Eds.): CICBA 2023, CCIS 1955, pp. 327–338, 2024.
https://doi.org/10.1007/978-3-031-48876-4_25

restoration is an essential preprocessing task before implementation of vision related applications with accuracy. One such implementation is traffic surveillance system [5]. For accurate automated traffic monitoring, clear visibility of image captured by surveillance camera is essential. Hence, image dehazing is prerequisite for any vision related application.

Several research work have been reported on image restoration. Initial approaches are based on traditional image processing methods to perform dehazing [1,6,14]. In past, researchers have proposed different methods [1,4,11] to remove rain streaks from images captured during rain.

Recent days, Convolutional Neural Network (CNN) based methods [3,9,19] have done huge development in image de-raining as well as in image de-hazing. CNN is an integral part of feature learning and exposes many hidden features. In CNN non-linear mapping is done between input degraded image and the expected ground truth image.

In the proposed work, CNN based network with channel attention technique is applied to restore the visibly degraded image due to bad weather. The main contributions of the work are given as follows.

- A CNN is designed to do mapping between degraded and clear images by minimizing the error directly from data.
- Extracted feature maps from CNN are processed on channel attention based Style-based Recalibration Module (SRM) [12] to enhance the network restoration capacity without increasing number of parameters or the network architecture complexity.
- Experiments are conducted on real as well as on synthesized images to examine the efficiency of proposed network in terms of both quantitatively and visually and achieves state-of-the-art results.

The remaining sections of the paper are arranged as follows. Image rain removal and image de-hazing methods are discussed in Sect. 2. The proposed methodology is presented in Sect. 3. In Sect. 4, experimental result analysis are done and conclusion is drawn in Sect. 5.

2   Related Work

2.1   Image Rain Removal

Rain is a natural weather phenomenon that affects the clarity badly. Rain removal is a very challenging task. The rain streaks obstruct, blur the captured image. Along with rain, mist or fog severely reduce the visibility by scattering of light in the line of sight. The occlusion generates not only due to rain but also fog is the reason that comes with rain. The fog degrades the scene transparency heavily as proportional to the object distance increases from camera.

Earlier, rain removal approaches are based on traditional image processing methods [1,4,11,13] and recent days methods are mostly applying convolutional neural network based data-driven manners. Barnum et al. [1] proposed a model for analysis of rain and snow and that is in frequency space and successfully applied that approach for videos with both scene and camera motions. Chen et al. [4] developed a novel low-rank appearance model which removes rain streaks. As rain streaks have similar pattern, the method captures the spatio-temporally correlated rain streaks. kim et al. [11] proposed an adaptive rain streak removal algorithm by first detecting rain streak regions and then perform the non-local means filtering on the detected rain streak regions. Li et al. [13] applied layer priors for rain removal. The method over-smooth the background image where the priors are based on Gaussian mixture models.

It is comparatively recent work and achieve state-of-the-art performance.

Recent days, several deep learning methods are developed for removing weather related artifacts from images. CNN are applied for rain removal and achieved state-of-the-art performance like other computer vision related applications. Fu et al. [7] applied CNN to learn the direct mapping relationship between rainy image and clear image from the training data. Yang et al. [19] jointly detect and remove rain from the degraded images by designing a multi-task network. Hu et al. [10] introduced a deep network that learns the features via a depth-guided attention mechanism to produce a clear image from a rainy input image. Yang et al. [19] proposed a recurrent network for rain detection and removal. Conditional Generative Adversarial Networks (cGANs) is applied in image deraining introduced by Hettiarachchi et al. [9].

2.2   Image Dehazing

Image dehazing is an ill-posed problem. The haze removal model can be formulated as:

$$I(x) = J(x)t(x) + A(1 - t(x)) \tag{1}$$

where I is the captured hazy image, x represents image pixel coordinates, J is the original haze free image, t is known as the medium transmission map and A is the atmospheric light. $t(x)$ can be represented be Eq. 2

$$t(x) = e^{-\beta d(x)} \tag{2}$$

where $d(x)$ is the scene depth and β is the scattering coefficient of the atmosphere. In dehazing problem, the main challenge is unknown transmission map where the key parameter is global atmospheric light. In most of the existing dehazing work, haze free image is restored by estimating transmission map t and atmospheric light A. In literature a number of traditional prior-based methods are introduced based on low-level image statistics.

R Fattal [6] introduces a new method for estimating the optical transmission in hazy images for given single input image. He et al. [8] describe the Dark Channel Prior (DCP), a statistic observation of the transmission map. The method is based on a key observation most local patches that estimates the thickness of the haze which helps to recover a clear haze-free image. The method is one of the most influential single-image dehazing approaches. Previous works are based on patch-based prior methods to solve the single image dehazing problem. Berman et al. [2] first introduced an non-local prior based algorithm for image dehazing. Omer et al. [16] first introduced color-lines in the RGB color space.

Deep networks have a large number of successful implementations in dehazing work also. DehazeNet, introduced by Cai et al. [3] trains a CNN model to map hazy to haze-free patches. Qin et al. [17] presented an feature fusion attention network (FFA-Net) where Channel Attention and Pixel Attention mechanism are combined to restore haze-free image. The Feature Attention (FA) module is used to adaptively learn the feature weights respective of assigning more wight to important features. Yu et al. [20] proposed method has applied transfer learning along with Residual Channel Attention Block for image de-hazing.

The proposed method focuses on restoration of images affected by rain streak, fog, or haze. Due to limited existing dataset, the training is performing with synthesized dataset. The testing is conducted on both real and synthesized outdoor images. Results show the effectiveness of the proposed method in comparison with other standard methods discussed in Result Analysis subsection.

3 Methodology

The proposed end-to-end network takes a poor visibility image (due to haze, rain or fog) as input, processes the image and produces a restored image as output. The proposed model has three main modules i.e., feature extraction, channel attention method on residual module and reconstruction of the image (shown in Fig. 1). In the proposed network, a convolutional neural network is designed for extracting the features from the input image. The channel attention method is applied on the convolution feature maps. Finally, reconstruction is performed to obtain the restored image.

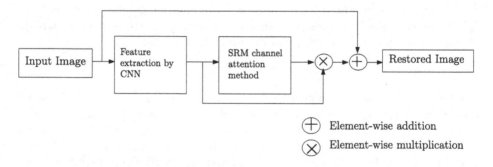

Fig. 1. Overview of the proposed method

3.1 Feature Extraction

The proposed CNN consists of four convolutional layers. The degraded image is passed as input to the designed convolutional network. The network processes the image through its convolutional layers. Each layer is formed by applying convolution operation on the previous layer feature maps. The convolution filters are used with sufficient discriminating attributes to differentiate target object from other things. The input image $I(x)$ has 3 colour channels and convolution operations are performed by 5×5 filter with stride 1. Bilateral Rectified Linear Unit (BReLU) activation function is applied after each convolutional layer.

At first, input degraded image is passed as image vector in the input layer on the CNN. On the first hidden layer, convolution operation is performed on the input image vector to extract the low-level features like contours, edges. On this layer, filters act as edge detectors that align with the direction of rain streaks and object edges. The second layer enhances the features progressively. The third convolutional layer performs the rain streaks removal so the third layer generated feature maps look smoother in comparison with previous layer generated feature maps. Then the fourth convolutional layer performs reconstruction and enhances the smoothed details with respect to image content (Table 1).

Table 1. Convolutional Neural Network Architecture of the proposed model

CNN Architecture
Input(512×512), Number of channels: 3
Conv_layer1: 5×5 Convolution + BReLu + Max Pooling 2×2, Number of filters: 16
Conv_layer2: 5×5 Convolution + BReLu + Max Pooling 2×2, Number of filters: 32
Conv_layer3: 5×5 Convolution + BReLu + Max Pooling 2×2, Number of filters: 64
Conv_layer4: 5×5 Convolution + BReLu + Local Extremum, Number of filters: 64

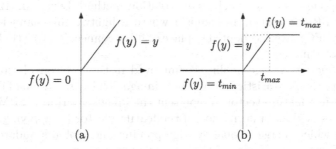

Fig. 2. (a) Rectified Linear Unit (ReLU), (b) Bilateral Rectified Linear Unit (BReLU)

In most CNN design for classification problems ReLU is preferable but it is not suitable for the regression problems like image restoration. Specifically, ReLU returns the value provided as input directly or the value is zero for zero or negative input. In image restoration, the output values of the last layer feature map may be bounded (both lower and upper bound) within a small range which is shown in Fig. 2, [3]. In that case, BReLU is preferred to take care of those instances.

In the proposed CNN architecture, max-pooling operation is applied to reduce the dimension of the feature map for the first three conv layers. In contrast of max-pooling operation, in the last layer of the proposed network local extremum operation is applied to preserves resolution which helps in image restoration.

$$F_4^i(x) = \max_{y \in \Omega(x)} F_3^i(y) \tag{3}$$

where $\Omega(x)$ is an $f_3 \times f_3$ neighbourhood centered at x and the output dimension of the fourth layer $n_4 = n_3$.

The designed CNN is effective at feature extraction and assists to recognize and remove haze effects and rain streaks from the processed image. It is an trainable end-to-end system where the network parameters like filters, biases associated with convolutional layers are learned during training process.

3.2 Channel Attention

Attention mechanism dynamically choose the weight of the features depending upon the importance of the input image. In attention, the input feature maps (generated by CNN) are processed with the attention function that identifies the discriminative region of the image and extracts the necessary information. In the proposed CNN, the fourth layer has 64 filters that generates 64 channels. Among those channels, attention score is provided to those channels which are more important. Accordingly weight is assigned by learning attention magnitude to the channels. Channel attention method deals with what to focus on the image. In CNN, different channel may represent different objects in different channel-wise feature maps. Channel Attention adaptively modify the weights of the channel to pay the attention for selection process. Here, Style-based Recalibration Module (SRM) is applied as a part of channel attention method. Lee et al. [12] proposed lightweight SRM attention mechanism where a lightweight channel-wise fully-connected (CFC) layer is adopted in place of fully-connected layer (FC) to reduce the computational cost.

At first global average pooling is employed in the last convolutional feature maps to express the statistics of the whole image. The aggregation of the features is represent in a feature vector to represent the image descriptor. SRM technique initially collects global information of the feature vector by applying style pooling (SP(.)) which merges global average pooling and global standard deviation pooling. SP store the values of the input features to improve its capability to capture global information.

Let f_c be the output feature map of the fourth convolutional layer of the proposed CNN having c feature maps of size $h \times w$. After applying the global average pooling, the vector size reduces to $1 \times 1 \times c$ from $h \times w \times c$.

$$g_p = \frac{1}{h \times w} \sum_{i=1}^{h} \sum_{j=1}^{w} f_c(i, j) \tag{4}$$

where $f_c(i, j)$ is the feature value at position (i, j) in the feature maps. To generate the attention vector s, a channel-wise fully connected (CFC(.)) layer (i.e., fully connected per channel) followed by batch normalization BN and sigmoid function σ are applied in a sequence.

$$s = F_{srm}(f_c, \theta) = \sigma(BN(CFC(SP(f_c)))) \tag{5}$$

Here, theta is a set of parameters which is learned to produce the attention weights. The attention vector is the collection of all attention weights. Each weight relates to a certain type of noise (rain streaks, haze, or fog). To get the effect of attention, the input feature map of the attention method is multiplied with the attention vector i.e. $Y = F_{srm} f_c$.

3.3   Reconstuction of Image

Finally, the element-wise addition operation is performed in the reconstruction module between the input poor visibility image (I) and the attentional feature map vector (Y) to obtain the restored output image. The process is as shown in Fig. 1.

Loss Function. The loss or error is minimized during the training of the network and L1 loss is used for optimization of the proposed network. The Least Absolute Deviations (LAD) L1 loss function is adopted to calculate the loss as:

$$L1 = \frac{1}{N} \sum_{i=1}^{N} \|y_{predicted} - y_{groundtruth}\| \tag{6}$$

N is a batch of training pairs.

4   Experimental Results

4.1   Implementation

Training. During the training process, the basic learning rate is initially set as 0.0001. It has been reduced by a factor of 0.03 after every $20,000$ iterations. The iteration process continued till $100,000$ iterations. The Stochastic Gradient Descent (SGD) optimization algorithm is used to train the proposed network for best selection of the model parameters to achieve optimum fit of the proposed model.

The proposed network is implemented on a system with Nvidia GeForce RTX 3050Ti GPU and an Intel(R) Core (TM) i7 CPU@2.3GHz.

4.2 Datasets

Training Datasets. RainCityscapes Dataset [10] affected by rain streaks and fog on real outdoor 295 images. It has 262 images for training and 33 images for testing. The proposed network is trained on this dataset. Rain800 [23] is also used for training the model. Among the 800 images of this dataset, 700 images are kept for training and rest 100 images are for testing.

Test Datasets. The network is tested on real-world outdoor hazy and rainy images as well as on degraded traffic images. During testing rainy, hazy images are restored using this model in an end to-end manner. On average, the proposed network takes around 0.1 seconds to process a 512×512 image.

4.3 Result Analysis

Both quantitative and qualitative experiments are conducted for evaluation of the proposed work.

Evaluation Metrics. The Peak Signal to Noise Ratio (PSNR) and Structural Similarity Index Measure (SSIM) are used to quantitatively evaluate the rain and haze removal results of the proposed method in comparison with other state-of-the-art methods as shown in Table 2. A higher PSNR or SSIM value indicates a better result. The proposed model exhibits highest PSNR and SSIM value for both rain streak and haze removal methods.

Comparisons are done with five different state-of-the-art deraining algorithms which are the DID-MDN, GMM, JORDER, DSC, CGANet, DCPDN, ADNet as well as with DCPDN, ADNET dehazing methods. The results of comparisons are shown in Table 2 (Figs. 3 and 4).

Table 2. Comparison with the state-of-the-art methods using the PSNR and SSIM on the test set of RainCityscapes [10]

Type of De-hazing	Model	PSNR	SSIM
Rain removal	DID-MDN [22]	28.43	0.9349
	GMM [13]	28.132	0.9231
	JORDER [19]	15.10	0.7592
	DSC [15]	16.25	0.7746
	CGANet [9]	28.24	0.933
Haze removal	DCPDN [21]	28.52	0.9277
	ADNet [18]	20.40	0.8243
Rain-streaks and haze removal	**proposed method**	**29.12**	**0.9403**

Fig. 3. Qualitative results of the proposed method. Upper row shows degraded images and bottom row shows corresponding derain-dehaze images.

Ablation Study. To examine the best selection between performance and parameter size of the proposed CNN, experiments are conducted on number of filters. On the same dataset, the model is trained and Table 3 shows the PSNR, SSIM values with its corresponding number of filters.

Fig. 4. Qualitative results of the proposed method on real-world traffic images. (a–c) Input image; (d–f)) Restored image

Generally, the performance of the CNN is improving when the network depth is increased. Therefore, with the number of increasing filters, better performance could be achieved for the network. Though for fast performance gain, small network is preferred. It is seen that the larger filter size may grab richer structural information which shows better result but it may lead to over-fitting. In a CNN design, for large number of filters and increasing the layer number of the network may cause exploding gradient problem. For large network, weights grow exponentially and derivatives are large then gradient will increase exponentially. This problem is called exploding gradient. In this situation, the model is not learning much on the training data. The model becomes unstable for effective learning.

Alternatively, for smaller derivative, the gradient will decrease exponentially when propagate through the model and gradient may vanishes which is called vanishing gradient problem. If vanishing gradient occurs, the model will go slow during training phase.

In the proposed CNN design, four layers are taken and last two layers has filter size 64. The proposed architecture design of CNN shows better performance in terms of both speed and accuracy so this model is taken for further experiments.

5   Conclusion

A novel deep learning approach is proposed for single image both de-raining and de-hazing. An end-to-end system is developed where the feature extraction is performed by using convolutional layers and a non-linear BReLU activation function is used for regression. For image restoration, the BReLU is applied rather than the ReLU or Sigmoid activation functions to maintain bilateral constraint and local linearity. In order to improve the output of the model, an attention mechanism known as SRM is applied. This mechanism has a lightweight architecture and is implemented on convolutional feature maps. Comparing the proposed method to the current state-of-the-art methods, the proposed method achieves higher efficiency and outstanding restoration results. In the future, efforts to restore images with more complicated backgrounds such as dense haze or rain steaks will be explored.

Table 3. Evaluation of the proposed network using different number of filters on the same dataset

Method	No. of filters	PSNR	SSIM
Proposed method	16	27.12	0.91893
	32	27.31	0.92217
	64	29.12	0.9403
	128	27.03	0.92103

References

1. Barnum, P.C., Narasimhan, S., Kanade, T.: Analysis of rain and snow in frequency space. Int. J. Comput. Vision **86**(2), 256–274 (2010)
2. Berman, D., Avidan, S., et al.: Non-local image dehazing. In: Proceedings of the IEEE Conference on Computer Vision and Pattern Recognition, pp. 1674–1682 (2016)
3. Cai, B., Xu, X., Jia, K., Qing, C., Tao, D.: Dehazenet: an end-to-end system for single image haze removal. IEEE Trans. Image Process. **25**(11), 5187–5198 (2016)
4. Chen, Y.L., Hsu, C.T.: A generalized low-rank appearance model for spatio-temporally correlated rain streaks. In: Proceedings of the IEEE International Conference on Computer Vision, pp. 1968–1975 (2013)
5. Dasgupta, M., Bandyopadhyay, O., Chatterji, S.: Automated helmet detection for multiple motorcycle riders using CNN. In: 2019 IEEE Conference on Information and Communication Technology, pp. 1–4 (2019). https://doi.org/10.1109/CICT48419.2019.9066191
6. Fattal, R.: Single image dehazing. ACM Trans. Graph. (TOG) **27**(3), 1–9 (2008)
7. Fu, X., Huang, J., Ding, X., Liao, Y., Paisley, J.: Clearing the skies: a deep network architecture for single-image rain removal. IEEE Trans. Image Process. **26**(6), 2944–2956 (2017)
8. He, K., Sun, J., Tang, X.: Single image haze removal using dark channel prior. IEEE Trans. Pattern Anal. Mach. Intell. **33**(12), 2341–2353 (2010)
9. Hettiarachchi, P., Nawaratne, R., Alahakoon, D., De Silva, D., Chilamkurti, N.: Rain streak removal for single images using conditional generative adversarial networks. Appl. Sci. **11**(5), 2214 (2021)
10. Hu, X., Fu, C.W., Zhu, L., Heng, P.A.: Depth-attentional features for single-image rain removal. In: Proceedings of the IEEE/CVF Conference on Computer Vision and Pattern Recognition, pp. 8022–8031 (2019)
11. Kim, J.H., Lee, C., Sim, J.Y., Kim, C.S.: Single-image deraining using an adaptive nonlocal means filter. In: 2013 IEEE International Conference on Image Processing, pp. 914–917. IEEE (2013)
12. Lee, H., Kim, H.E., Nam, H.: SRM: a style-based recalibration module for convolutional neural networks. In: Proceedings of the IEEE/CVF International Conference on Computer Vision, pp. 1854–1862 (2019)
13. Li, Y., Tan, R.T., Guo, X., Lu, J., Brown, M.S.: Rain streak removal using layer priors. In: Proceedings of the IEEE Conference on Computer Vision and Pattern Recognition, pp. 2736–2744 (2016)
14. Huang, D.A., Kang, L.W., Wang, Y.C.F., Lin, C.W.: Self-learning based image decomposition with applications to single image denoising. IEEE Trans. Multimedia **16**(1), 83–93 (2014)
15. Luo, Y., Xu, Y., Ji, H.: Removing rain from a single image via discriminative sparse coding. In: Proceedings of the IEEE International Conference on Computer Vision, pp. 3397–3405 (2015)
16. Omer, I., Werman, M.: Color lines: image specific color representation. In: Proceedings of the 2004 IEEE Computer Society Conference on Computer Vision and Pattern Recognition, CVPR 2004, vol. 2, pp. II–II. IEEE (2004)
17. Qin, X., Wang, Z., Bai, Y., Xie, X., Jia, H.: FFA-net: feature fusion attention network for single image dehazing. In: Proceedings of the AAAI Conference on Artificial Intelligence, vol. 34, pp. 11908–11915 (2020)

18. Tian, C., Xu, Y., Li, Z., Zuo, W., Fei, L., Liu, H.: Attention-guided CNN for image denoising. Neural Netw. **124**, 117–129 (2020)
19. Yang, W., Tan, R.T., Feng, J., Liu, J., Guo, Z., Yan, S.: Deep joint rain detection and removal from a single image. In: Proceedings of the IEEE Conference on Computer Vision and Pattern Recognition, pp. 1357–1366 (2017)
20. Yu, Y., Liu, H., Fu, M., Chen, J., Wang, X., Wang, K.: A two-branch neural network for non-homogeneous dehazing via ensemble learning. In: Proceedings of the IEEE/CVF Conference on Computer Vision and Pattern Recognition, pp. 193–202 (2021)
21. Zhang, H., Patel, V.M.: Densely connected pyramid dehazing network. In: Proceedings of the IEEE Conference on Computer Vision and Pattern Recognition, pp. 3194–3203 (2018)
22. Zhang, H., Patel, V.M.: Density-aware single image de-raining using a multi-stream dense network. In: Proceedings of the IEEE Conference on Computer Vision and Pattern Recognition, pp. 695–704 (2018)
23. Zhang, H., Sindagi, V., Patel, V.M.: Image de-raining using a conditional generative adversarial network. IEEE Trans. Circuits Syst. Video Technol. **30**(11), 3943–3956 (2019)

Deep Learning-Based Intelligent GUI Tool For Skin Disease Diagnosis System

Mithun Karmakar$^{(\boxtimes)}$, Subhash Mondal, and Amitava Nag

Computer Science and Engineering, Central Institute of Technology Kokrajhar, BTR, Kokrajhar, Assam 783370, India

{m.karmakar,ph22cse1001,amitava.nag}@cit.ac.in

Abstract. Skin diseases are generally normal around the globe, as people get skin diseases because of inheritance and natural elements. Dermatologists rely heavily on visual examinations to diagnose skin diseases. However, this method can be inaccurate and time-consuming. The development of the technique in deep learning (DL) and the availability of GPUs can expand and improve the quality of computer-aided disease diagnostics systems. This paper proposes a DL-based smartphone application to aid a dermatologist in diagnosing skin disease in real-time. In the proposed work, we first used fine-tuned DenseNet201 for feature extraction and SVM to accurately classify normal and abnormal skin. A Deep Ensemble CNN (DECNN) framework with DenseNet-201, Resnet50, and MobileNet is further used for skin disease categorization if abnormal skin is detected. The experimental outcome of this study demonstrates that the framework can achieve an 84% accuracy in skin disease classification and outperform existing state-of-the-art works. The simple implementation and acceptable accuracy of the proposed method can be helpful for dermatologists in the diagnosis of skin disease.

Keywords: Deep Learning · Convolutional Neural Network (CNN) · Skin Diseases Diagnosis · Deep Ensemble Convolutional Neural Network (DECNN) · DenseNet

1 Introduction

The human body's most important organ is the skin. It has a two square yard surface area and weighs between 6 and 9 lb. The skin separates the outside world from the inside of the body. It controls body temperature and protects the body from viruses, bacteria, allergens, and fungi. Situations that irritate, change the texture of, or injure the skin can cause swelling, burning, redness, and itching. Acne, alopecia, ringworm, and eczema are just a few examples of skin conditions that can have an impact on a person's appearance [1]. Skin can also deliver a variety of malignant tumours. Image processing methods like segmentation, filtering, and feature extraction are used to find these abnormalities. According to statistics, approximately eight million people in India suffer from skin diseases. [2] Skin disease affects more than just the skin's surface. It can significantly impact a person's daily life, destroying confidence, halting activity, and causing sadness. The worst-case scenario is death. Because it is a serious issue that must be addressed, it is critical to take skin diseases seriously, identify them early, and prevent their spread. Many factors, including the parameters considered, influence disease detection. To begin, capture an image, apply noise-reduction filters, segment the image to extract useful information, perform feature extraction based on input parameters, and finally, classify diseases using appropriate classifiers.

Skin diseases impair the patient's mental health. It can make a patient feel insecure and even depressed. Thus, skin diseases can be fatal. It's a serious issue that needs to be addressed. As a result, detecting skin diseases early on and preventing their spread is critical. Human skin is erratic and all over the place due to the complexity of spikes, injury structures, moles, tone, the presence of thick hairs, and other befuddling highlights. Skin disease early detection can be cost-effective and accessible even in remote areas. Early mindfulness necessitates identifying the infected skin area and the infection. This paper proposes a system that allows users to detect and identify skin diseases.

People nowadays suffer from skin diseases, and more than 900 million people are affected by them [3]. Furthermore, the rate of skin infection is rapidly increasing. It will kill you in the worst-case scenario. It is a serious issue that must be addressed, so taking skin diseases seriously, identifying them early, and preventing their spread is critical. Many factors, including the parameters used, influence disease detection. Using the correct classifiers, diagnose diseases after applying noise-reduction filters, segmenting the image to extract meaningful information, and feature extraction depending on input parameters. Melanoma is the most prevalent skin disease. The prevalence of nevus is high, particularly in rural areas. Skin conditions that are not addressed early enough can harm the body and even spread infection from one person to the next [4]. Skin diseases can be prevented by exploring the infected region at the beginning phase. The characteristics of skin images vary, so it is moving position to devise a productive and powerful calculation for programmed identification of the skin disease and its seriousness. Skin tone and skin color assume a significant part in skin infection discovery. Color and coarseness of skin are outwardly unique. Programmed handling of such pictures for skin investigation requires a quantitative discriminator to separate the disease. The proposed framework is a combo model utilized for counteracting and early identifying skin diseases like Melanoma, Nevus, etc. Skin disease finding relies upon various qualities like color, shape, texture, etc. Different doctors will treat distinctively for the same symptoms. Early detection is critical in skin disease treatment; subsequent treatment is dependent on early detection.

Various deep learning-based strategies for automating the classification of skin diseases have been developed in recent years [5]. However, the vast majority rely solely on dermoscopy images and ignore the patient's clinical history, a key piece of evidence for a clinical diagnosis.

1.1 Objective

The objective of this study can be summarized into the following points:

- To provide a cutting-edge diagnostic system that satisfies the real-time and extensible demands of medical services for the early diagnosis of skin diseases.

- To collect real-time normal skin images.
- Develop a Deep Learning-based intelligent Android app tool that generally can determine the affected areas in the image and then identify the disease in the specified region.

1.2 Contribution

The primary contributions of the planned effort are summarized below:

- We have designed an intelligent mobile application to identify the visual defects of human skin in real-time.
- We have fine-tuned DenseNet201 for feature extraction and used SVM to classify normal and abnormal skin accurately.
- We have introduced a Deep Ensemble CNN (DECNN) framework with DenseNet-20, Resnet50, and MobileNet for skin disease classification, which increased the performance.
- We have created a real-time customized normal and healthy skin image dataset.

The rest of this article is structured as follows: Sect. 2 compiles a list of all related works completed in this field. Section 3 discusses the approach used. The details of the experimental setup are described in Sect. 4. The task is completed in the final segment (Sect. 5).

2 Related Work

J. Lin et al. proposed an SD-198-P dataset in their research [6], which includes additional high-level position information in the SD-198 dataset to guide the generation of better in-depth visual features. This method outperformed the most recent cutting-edge clinical skin disease classification methods. A. Sallam et al. [7] developed an advanced diagnostic system for skin disease detection in 2019 that meets the requirements of real-time and extensibility of medical services. The proposed method offers offline diagnoses for users who do not have access to the Internet, as well as online diagnoses via an on-cloud service. In testing cases, the average obtained accuracy is 83%. N. Hameed et al. [8] proposed a multi-class intelligent skin lesion classification diagnosis scheme. The proposed scheme employs a hybrid approach, which includes a deep convolution neural network and an error-correcting output codes (ECOC) support vector machine (SVM). The overall accuracy achieved with ECOC SVM is 86.21%. Chang et al. used U-net to segment melanoma dermoscopy pictures. Then, for the purpose of classifying skin lesions, the segmented and original dermoscopy images were both fed into a deep network made up of two Inception V3 networks. The segmentation and classification models performed well on the ISIC dataset, according to experimental findings.

In May 2019, Akar et al. [10] published a cloud-based skin lesion diagnosis system based on CNN. The user takes a photo with the Android-based app and uploads it to the cloud. Then, a deep learning-based classifier is hosted on a server to filter and classify uploaded lesion photos. Furthermore, in [11], Hameed et al. introduced an Android App for detection of skin disease and provide accurate and useful dermatological data on four skin diseases. It is a step toward developing mobile applications that can diagnose and treat users without requiring them to visit dermatologists. For melanoma and psoriasis, this method's accuracy is 82.5% and 90.09%, respectively.

Dorin et al. [12] presented a two-step method for classifying skin cancer images that use transfer learning and deep learning. The prediction model for testing data is 75% accurate. Zhe Wu et al. [13] investigated various CNN algorithms based on clinical photos for face skin disease categorization. When the performances were compared, the transfer learning models had higher average precision and recall for almost all structures. The mean recall and precision were 77.0% and 70.8%, respectively.

Deep learning is a sort of machine learning that combines numerous layers of shallow and nonlinear modules to automatically learn hierarchical data features. It converts data into meaningful representations for discrimination. Olga et al. proposed the LeNet network for handwritten digit recognition as early as 1998 [14]. However, due to a lack of computational power, supporting the required amount of power computation required significant work. This method was successfully used until 2012, when it vastly outperformed previous methods of machine learning for visual recognition tasks in an ImageNet large-scale competition called the International Long-Term Visual Recognition Challenge (ILSVRC).

Andre G. C. Pacheco et al. [15] developed a skin cancer diagnostic using pictures and meta-data. The dataset is divided into nine classes. Nonetheless, one of them is an outlier and does not appear on it, resulting in an accuracy of 89%. The findings show that the deep learning-based skin illness picture identification strategy performs better at diagnosing skin diseases than dermatologists and other computer-aided treatment approaches, particularly since the multi-deep learning model fusion method has the best recognition impact.

3 Proposed Framework

This article proposes a deep learning-based framework to identify skin diseases. The proposed framework is divided into three subparts (Fig. 1):

- **Deep Learning based training and testing of the models:** Here, the Skin image dataset is split into training and testing sets. The training set is then augmented and used for training DenseNet201 with SVM architecture for binary classification (Normal and Abnormal). However, the accuracy was too low when the same architecture was applied to multi-class classification. So, we tried training different models individually and then used weighted average ensemble learning to them. Out of all the different combinations of the models, the best accuracy was given by ensembling Densenet201, Resnet-50, and MobileNet models. The above three pre-trained models were considered with the default parameters passed through the existing architecture for the initial model training and testing and finally deployed the ensemble techniques over the models. Now, this ensemble learning model will classify the multiple classes.
- **Skin image capturing module for real-time testing**: after the models are trained, we deployed the model in the backend of the mobile application. Inside this app, the user can capture or take images from the gallery, and the image is sent for processing to the backend

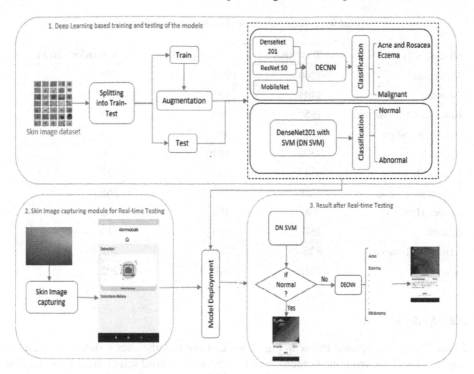

Fig. 1. Proposed framework for skin disease detection

- **Result after Real-time testing:** The image which is sent to the backend will first classify if it is normal or abnormal with the help of DenseNet201 with the SVM model. If the model classifies it as normal, then the app displays the outcome on the result page and exits the program, and if the model classifies the image as abnormal, then for further classification, the image is given to DECNN (Deep Ensemble Convolutional Neural Network) model. Then this model will display which class of skin disease the image belongs to.

3.1 Dataset Description

For the experimental purpose here, various skin disease datasets are used. The datasets are collected from Kaggle [16] and ISIC 2019 [17]. The final dataset is 10415 images belonging to ten classes. We used a 0.80: 0.20 image ratio to train and validate the model. Table 1. Indicates the images belonging to each class of disease types.

Table 1. Target outcome disease data distribution

Disease's Type	Total Image	Training (80%)	Validation (20%)
Malignant	1240	992	248
Benign	1404	1123	281
Basal Cell Carcinoma	195	716	179
Actinic Keratosis	870	696	174
Nevus	1300	1040	260
Dermatofibroma	614	491	122
Melanoma	1329	1063	266
Herpes HPV	508	406	102
Eczema	851	680	310
Acne and Rosacea	826	660	202
Normal	1012	810	202

3.2 Android Tool

In the flowchart depicted below in Fig. 2, we can see that the user should first open the application. Then from the homepage of the app user should select the camera icon to capture or upload an image from the gallery after that image is pre-processed and given to the DenseNet with an SVM model to classify it into Normal and Abnormal classes. If the model classifies it as normal, the app displays the result on the result page and exits the program. And if the model classifies the image as Abnormal, then for further classification, the image is given to DECNN (Deep Ensemble Convolutional Neural Network) model. Then this model will display which class of skin disease the image belongs to.

4 Experimental Results

To train the network, the Python programing language in the Google Colab environment simulation platform with GPU and TPU enable in cloud infrastructure was used in this study. In this test, 8802 images were considered to deploy training model as a input dataset, and 2047 images were used to test the model performance. The four analyses that determine the best architecture are Accuracy (Acc), True Positive Rate (TPR) or sensitivity, True Negative Rate (TNR) or specificity, and precision. To maintain a maximum value of fitness (F), the accuracy, sensitivity, specificity, and precision should be maximized and evaluated using the best architecture principle presented in Eq. 1. The confusion matrix was derived, and the True positive (TP), True negative (TN), False Positive (FP), and False Negative (FN) values were used to obtain the performance metrics like Acc.

$$F = 1/3[Acc + TPR + TNR] \tag{1}$$

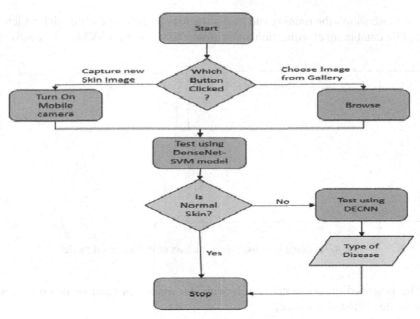

Fig. 2. Flowchart of the Android Application

Accuracy (Acc): It determines the number of correctly classified TP, TN, FP, and FN. Formula 2 can be used to calculate it.

$$Acc = \frac{TP + TN}{TP + TN + FP + FN} \tag{2}$$

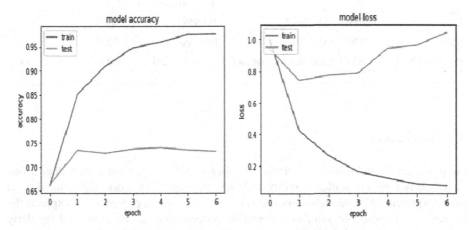

Fig. 3. Accuracy and loss of the proposed model

Figure 3 depicts the variation in training and testing accuracy as well as training and testing loss per epoch. We ran seven epochs and can see the differences in the graph.

Figure 4 also shows the training and validation loss of the proposed model, which was created by combining classification and feature extraction with SVM and DensNet121.

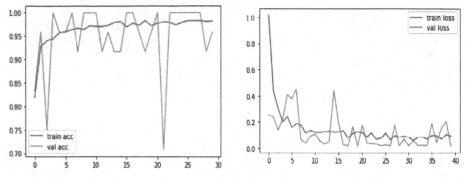

Fig. 4. Training loss and validation loss of the proposed model

The proposed experimental results with the other comparative literature results analysis are tabulated in Table 2.

Table 2. Comparative result analysis with literature

Ref.	Year	Dataset	Backbone	Accuracy (%)	GUI
[18]	2017	ISIC 2016	VGG-16	81.33	No
[19]	2017	ISIC 2016	VGG-16	79.2	No
[20]	2019	ISIC 2017	DenseNet161 and ResNetInception	72.3	No
[21]	2019	ISIC 2017	NASNet	42.0	No
[22]	2020	ISIC 2017	ResNet-50	75.9	No
Proposed Model	**2023**	**Customized Dataset**	**DenseNet201**	**84.0**	**Yes**

5   Conclusion

Deep learning approaches to skin disease offer significant potential advantages, one of which is their unparalleled ability to lessen the repetitive work and clinical asset strain experienced by dermatologists. Precise recognition is a pressure that expands the interest in a dependable automated detection process that can be embraced regularly in the analytic interaction by the master and non-master clinicians. Deep learning is a comprehensive subject that requires a wide range of information in engineering, data, computer science, and medicine. With the nonstop turn of events in the above fields, deep learning is going through a quick turn of events and has drawn into consideration of various nations. Deep learning for identifying skin diseases is a potential technique soon, fuelled by more reasonable arrangements, programming that can rapidly gather and thoughtfully process massive amounts of information, and hardware that can achieve what individuals cannot.

References

1. Skin Diseases: Cleveland Clinic. https://my.clevelandclinic.org/health/diseases/21573-skin-diseases. Accessed 01 Feb 2023
2. Brenaut, E., Misery, L., Taieb, C.: Sensitive skin in the Indian population: an epidemiological approach. Front. Med. (Lausanne) **6** (2019)
3. Recognizing neglected skin diseases: WHO publishes pictorial training guide, 08 June 2018. https://www.who.int/news/item/08-06-2018-recognizing-neglected-skin-diseases-who-pub lishes-pictorial-training-guide. Accessed 30 Apr 2023
4. Seth, D., Cheldize, K., Brown, D., Freeman, E.F.: Global burden of skin disease: inequities and innovations. Curr. Dermatol. Rep. **6**(3), 204–210 (2017)
5. Li, H., Pan, Y., Zhao, J., Zhang, L.: Skin disease diagnosis with deep learning: a review. Neurocomputing **464**, 364–393 (2021)
6. Lin, J., Guo, Z., Li, D., Hu, X.: Automatic classification of clinical skin disease images with additional high-level position information. In: 2019 Chinese Control Conference (CCC), Guangzhou, China (2019)
7. Sallam, A., Ba Alawi, A.E.: Mobile-based intelligent skin diseases diagnosis system. In: 2019 First International Conference of Intelligent Computing and Engineering (ICOICE), Hadhramout, Yemen (2019)
8. Hameed, N., Shabut, A.M., Hossain, M.A.: Multi-class skin diseases classification using deep convolutional neural network and support vector machine. In: 12th International Conference on Software, Knowledge, Information Management & Applications (SKIMA), Phnom Penh, Cambodia (2018)
9. Chang, H.: Skin cancer reorganization and classification with deep neural network. In: Computer Vision and Pattern Recognition (2017)
10. Akar, E., Marques, O., Andrews, W.A., Furht, B.: Cloud-based skin lesion diagnosis system using convolutional neural networks. In: Arai, K., Bhatia, R., Kapoor, S. (eds.) CompCom. AISC, vol. 997, pp. 982–1000. Springer, Cham (2019). https://doi.org/10.1007/978-3-030-22871-2_70
11. Hameed, S.A., Haddad, A., Hadi Habaebi, M., Nirabi, A.: Dermatological diagnosis by mobile application. Bull. Electr. Eng. Inform. **8**(3) (2019)
12. Moldovan, D.: Transfer learning based method for two-step skin cancer images classification. In: E-Health and Bioengineering Conference (EHB), Iasi, Romania (2019)
13. Wu, Z., Zhao, S., Peng, Y., He, X.: Studies on different CNN algorithms for face skin disease classification based on clinical images. Data-Enabl. Intell. Digit. Health IEEE Access **7**, 66505–66511 (2019)
14. Russakovsky, O., Deng, J., Su, H., Krause, J.: ImageNet large scale visual recognition challenge. Int. J. Comput. Vision **115**, 211–252 (2015)
15. Pacheco, A.G., Krohling, R.A.: The impact of patient clinical information on automated skin cancer detection. In: Computers in Biology and Medicine, vol. 116 (2020)
16. L. Skin Lesion Images for Melanoma Classification. https://www.kaggle.com/datasets/and rewmvd/isic-2019
17. ISIC Challenge Datasets (2019). https://challenge.isic-archive.com/data/#2019. Accessed 15 Sept 2022

18. Menegola, A., Fornaciali, M., Pires, R., Bittencourt, F.V.: Knowledge transfer for melanoma screening with deep learning. In: IEEE 14th International Symposium on Biomedical Imaging (ISBI 2017), Melbourne, VIC, Australia (2017)
19. Barata, C., Marques, J.S., Celebi, M.E.: Deep attention model for the hierarchical diagnosis of skin lesions. In: IEEE/CVF Conference on Computer Vision and Pattern Recognition Workshops (CVPRW), Long Beach, CA, USA (2019)
20. Bisla, D., Choromanska, A., Berman, R.S., Stein, J.A.: Towards automated melanoma detection with deep learning: data purification and augmentation. In: IEEE/CVF Conference on Computer Vision and Pattern Recognition Workshops (CVPRW), Long Beach, CA, USA (2019)
21. Tschandl, P., Argenziano, G., Razmara, M., Yap, J.: Diagnostic accuracy of content-based dermatoscopic image retrieval with deep classification features. Br. J. Dermatol. **181**(1), 155–165 (2019)
22. Akar, E., Marques, O., Andrews, W.A., Furht, B.: Cloud-based skin lesion diagnosis system using convolutional neural networks. In: Arai, K., Bhatia, R., Kapoor, S. (eds.) CompCom. AISC, vol. 997, pp. 982–1000. Springer, Cham (2019). https://doi.org/10.1007/978-3-030-22871-2_70

Author Index

K. Dasgupta et al. (Eds.): CICBA 2023, CCIS 1955, pp. 349–351, 2024.
https://doi.org/10.1007/978-3-031-48876-4

Printed in the United States
by Baker & Taylor Publisher Services

Printed in the United States
by Baker & Taylor Publisher Services